CARS
A CELEBRATION

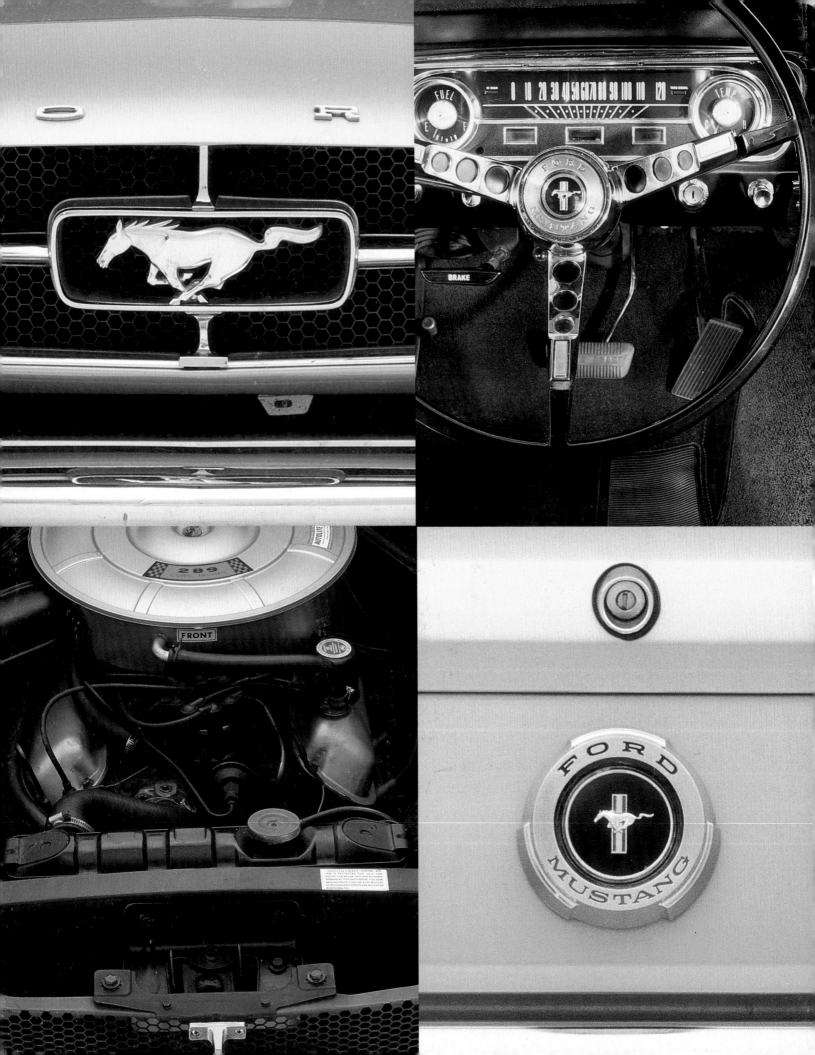

limiters that will automatically reduce and control the pace at which we travel. Cars with large engines will suffer a much greater tax burden, while the company car, that mainstay of our automotive economy, also looks set to be taxed into oblivion. The golden age of the car is coming to an end.

But there is one crumb of comfort. Old cars, or classic cars, the delicious confections you see in the pages of this book, will survive. Our automotive heritage will be left largely unmolested. As long as we have the funds, we can still go out and buy an MGA, Austin-Healey, or Sunbeam Tiger, most of which will have been painstakingly restored to pristine health. The legislators won't bother us, the environmentalists won't see us as a threat, and, if we can find a clear stretch or road with a couple of sweeping bends, we can still recapture the magic of 20th-century driving.

So sit back, scan these pages, and revel in the history of one of industrial society's most captivating and evocative products. Hopefully you'll understand just how much the car has given us, and in many ways how it's always been more sinned against than sinful. In a world gone crazy with creeping political correctness, we must never be afraid to appreciate and celebrate the enormous contribution the car has made to art, literature, pop culture, mobility, and sheer convenience.

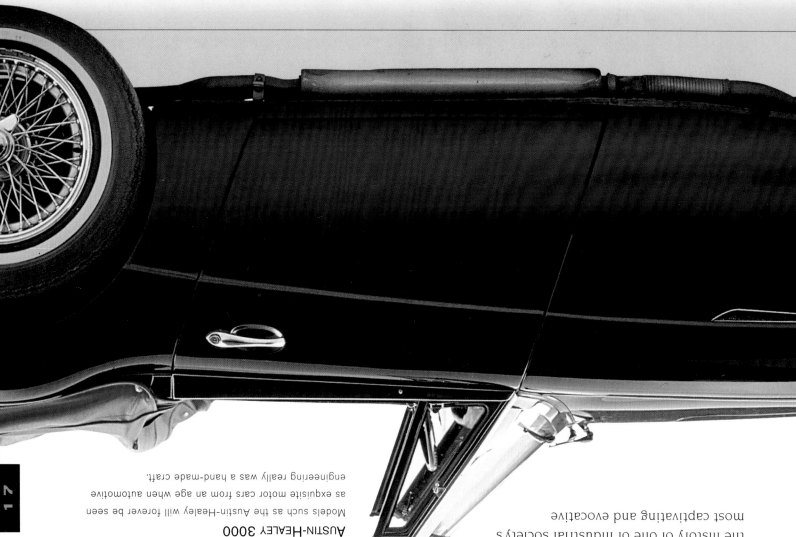

AUSTIN-HEALEY 3000

Models such as the Austin-Healey will forever be seen as exquisite motor cars from an age when automotive engineering really was a hand-made craft.

17

MERCEDES A CLASS

Models such as the Mercedes A Class are setting the trend for a new type of automotive architecture – small and compact on the outside, but with a clever use of space on the inside.

greeted with rapturous applause, and both are selling like the elixir of youth. Even a volume car manufacturer like Britain's Rover deliberately covered its 75 line with heritage styling cues. Liberal use of chrome, an interior copied from the '60s P6 model, and even doors which followed the lines of the '60s P5 sedan and coupe have made Italian automotive journalists vote the 75 1999's most beautiful car.

FUTURE FEDERAL INTERVENTION

But this sudden flowering of stylistic innocence and retrospective design can't last. The force of the future will change the shape of cars forever and the way we perceive them. Small cars like the aluminum-bodied Audi A2 and the Mercedes A Class, with its engine located under the floor, will set the stylistic agenda for decades to come. There will be new materials, new engines, more use of space, and less use of fuel – a combination of engineering and social constraints that will redraw the entire parameters of the automotive order. Instead of buying a car, we may even find ourselves renting a personal mobility solution. For a monthly fee we could have access to a pool of tiny ecomobiles, or be able to lease a 4x4 for the winter, a minivan for vacations, a convertible for the

summer, and a motorcycle for spring. Even the way we buy cars is changing. Within a few years the conventional car dealer and his showroom may be a thing of the past, with consumers buying cars over the internet or by email. Dealers will become service and warranty centers, and manufacturers will deal directly with the general public. As car buyers, we're becoming ever more demanding, even despotic, obsessed with value, service, and quality. Carmakers that can't, or won't, meet the new challenges of the all-powerful consumer simply won't survive.

But one of the biggest threats to cars and our enjoyment of them will come from big brother. Governments all over the world are seizing on the car as a destructive force. With Pavlovian-like reactions, they are reducing speed limits, installing speed cameras, and burdening drivers with so many tax duties that some car owners are now paying more to run their cars every year than they pay in income tax. In the UK, 80 percent of the price of fuel currently goes into the government's coffers, and politicians have actually publicly admitted that they don't want to build more roads because more people will use them. There's grim talk of draconian speeding penalties and satellite-based speed-

miles (402,000 kilometers) isn't unheard of either. Engineering integrity and reliability are no longer a distant pipe dream, they are an everyday reality.

THE ESSENCE OF MOTORING

The problem is, subconsciously we actually don't want zero-defect cars, which partly illustrates how bizarre our love-hate relationship with the horseless carriage has become. Sure, rationally we know that we want our cars to go and stop properly. But emotionally we actually prefer the idiosyncrasies and temperament of older cars. We're amused and captivated by their noises, smells, creaks, and groans. We actually like their whining gearboxes and an engine note that sounds like someone tearing cotton sheets. Just ask a Lexus engineer. When Toyota launched the Lexus LS 400 in 1990, it made it cathedral-quiet, banishing every sensation and tremor of movement, ending up with a luxury car that was as silent as a church mouse in carpet slippers. Several years later, Toyota's customers made it put some of the noises back in, complaining that they felt too insulated and detached from the road. The zero-defect car might appeal to an Asian obsession with order and perfection, but most Western drivers prefer their cars to be like people. They want them to be flawed but interesting.

And carmakers have become keenly aware of this confusing contradiction in the consumer's psyche. They may have spent decades trying to sell their products on technological supremacy and excellence, but they now realize that one of the strongest imperatives in the car buyer's psychology is actually having a car that has personality and character. We don't, emphatically don't, want cars that are like washing machines and clothes driers. The Japanese auto industry of the 1970s and '80s churned out millions upon millions of Toyota Corollas that may have been endlessly reliable, but they all had the desirability of an old shoe.

LEXUS LS 400
Who says we want a flawless car? It's ironic that, as society seems to strive for technological perfection, Lexus had to put the rattles and squeaks back into their over-insulated LS 400.

RETURN TO RETRO

This is why in the past five years we have seen a raft of specialized, separate-looking, and retro-styled cars being produced. The Audi TT, with its bullet-shaped profile, has been a huge success. So too have the Mazda MX-5, Dodge Viper, and Plymouth Prowler. And now Ford has relaunched a modern recreation of the 1955 Thunderbird, and DaimlerChrysler has its wild child Pronto Cruiser, which looks like a '40s hot rod. Both cars have been

McLAREN F1
The McLaren F1 is a prime example of how speed remains king in the world of supercars, hitting 60 mph (96 km/h) in 3.2 seconds, and with a top speed in excess of 370 km/h (230 mph).

of the most sophisticated, complicated, and brilliant creations in the history of human enterprise. The sheer effort, creativity, intelligence, imagination, and tenacity that has gone into the evolution of the car are our finest achievements. If you forget for a moment all the anticar rhetoric and consider just how far the motorized box has advanced in a single century, you can't fail to be slack-jawed in amazement. Compared to houses, clothes, telephones, televisions, and half a hundred other products, the car is completely unparalleled in its technical and engineering brilliance.

RELIABLE ENGINEERING

And it's a brilliance that shines from every panel. From the packaging of the Mini and Fiat 500, through the mass-produced reliability of the VW Beetle and Citroën 2CV, to the epic speeds of the Porsche GTR and McLaren F1, cars have become so slick that they make other consumer durables seem positively neolithic. But not only have cars become hi-tech, they've become incredibly reliable too. And I'm not talking about the gritty hardiness of a Ford Escort, but the tremendous and almost unyielding longevity of a Mercedes 190 or VW Golf. When you think just what a car has to do, the hundreds of thousands of miles it has to cover, and the neglect its many owners make it suffer, it's a wonder it ever works at all. Yet they do, and most of the time perfectly.

The greatest tribute we can pay to the engineers of the auto industry is to say that there really are no bad cars produced by manufacturers anymore. And, broadly speaking, such lavish praise is true. We've reached the age of the zero-defect car, which has a practical working life of over 150,000 miles (241,000 kilometers). In fact, depending on how well it's been looked after, a quarter of a million

**MERCEDES BENZ
300SL Gullwing**

The Gullwing amazed when it was first released because it combined visual beauty with astounding performance.

you've got enough money, you can buy straight off the showroom floor. And we're talking road cars here, not record-breakers, which are available to ordinary, if affluent, members of the general public. And the speed thing, those massive leaps in automotive technological progress, is one of the auto industry's most awesome achievements. From Karl Benz's original bag of parts has grown one

Mercedes per square mile than anywhere else on earth. They can never be driven at their maximum speed, and rarely accelerated under full throttle, but we know such cars aren't bought as mere modes of transportation. They're aphrodisiacs, automotive jewelry, bought and worn for the simple purpose of sexual display and arousal.

Aldous Huxley once said that "Speed is the only truly modern sensation." And by that he meant that the excitement of going fast is the one feeling that nature didn't create. Man created speed or, more properly, the car did. One hundred years of engineering has raised the car's maximum speed from a glacial 5 mph (8 km/h) to an incredible 250 mph (402 km/h), an astonishing velocity which, if

1959 CADILLAC CONVERTIBLE

Cars from the Fifties were true artistic reflections of the era in which they were created. And fins were the ultimate design statement.

automotive press had mentioned a top speed of 174 mph (280 km/h), the car assumed iconic status in less than 24 hours. Pictures and breathlessly excited road-tests were beamed all over the world; but nobody bothered to mention that at low speeds it drove like a truck and that it was as well built as a contemporary Fiat. The Daytona became a god simply because of how fast it could go.

So no one of our strongest emotional bonds with the car comes from its power. A fast car has apparently endless reserves of power, which offer a huge erotic attraction. All car designers try to build in the appearance of that power, and the marketing men sell it shamelessly. It can be mechanical power measured in horsepower, or financial power measured by the amount of money that a car costs. Whatever its form, all the research says that car buyers find it hugely arousing and desirable. Just consider Los Angeles, a city so gridlocked that the average speed is slower than Karl Benz's original boneshaker. Yet LA has more Porsches, Ferraris, and

In '50s and '60s Europe, car design took a much purer and reductive course. Instead of transatlantic excess, there was economy of line and simplicity of form. A Ferrari 250 Lusso is one of the world's most beautiful cars, yet its "art" lies in its smooth tapering shape, tense muscular haunches, and sleek elegance of line. Instead of marveling at fins, Dagmars, and chromium dollar grins, we look in wonder at the Lusso's classic, simple beauty. And the same is true of the AC Ace, with its chaste, simple, and sweeping profile, completely unadorned and unaffected by stylistic conceits. Few cars have the integrity of line of the Ace, and fewer still are so agonizingly pretty. But whether the metal was penned in Detroit or Thames Ditton, the designer's goal was always the same – to create something so visually sensual that an instant emotional connection is made with the onlooker. And for the 20th century onlooker, cars became a new art form.

HOOKED ON SPEED

Yet it was art coupled with tremendous power. Karl Marx wrote that "Nature doesn't build machines. They are the products of human will over nature. They are the power of knowledge writ large." And that power is the car's most important attraction. We may have been impressed by the '50s Mercedes Benz 300SL Gullwing's doors and fuel injection, we may have felt warm regard for its muscular Teutonic styling, but the real charisma, the real attraction came from the fact that it could crack 150 mph (241 km/h), with the racing versions capable of up to 175 mph (282 km/h). In 1954, when the 300SL was launched, 150 mph (241 km/h) was an unbelievable speed for a human being to travel and almost akin to flying. That something as beautiful and technically brilliant as the Gullwing could also propel its private owner at unheard of speeds was why it became an instant legend and one of the most desirable consumer products on the face of the earth. The same thing happened when the Ferrari Daytona was launched in 1968. Once the

designed by a select handful of inspired visionaries, unlike today, when hundreds of company designers, engineers, lawyers, and accountants pore and argue over the shape, style, and size of their products. The Jaguar E-Type was literally shaped by just one man, as was the Porsche 356 and the Ferrari Dino. And that's why we're so emotionally attached to classic cars. The pure creative impulse that created them was rarely diluted by the demands, cynicisms, and prejudices of commercial committees with the artistic sensibilities of vampire bats.

ARTISTIC DESIGN

If we stand back and consider the Jaguar E-Type, surely the world's most beautiful car, we see a silhouette of outstandingly fine balance, proportion, and harmony of line. But more than its tremendous physical presence, it possessed an unprecedented emotional magic, radiating messages of speed, sexuality, power, and beauty. In fact, appreciating the proportions of an elderly Jag is the nearest most of us have ever been to the criticism and consumption of art.

I know I'm pouring this on thickly, but applying the word art to old cars is not misguided. American cars of the '50s and '60s were as artistically audacious as an Andy Warhol screen print. They were gilded land yachts, painted in two-tone pastel hues, glittering with half a ton of chromium symbolism, good enough to eat. Their riots and tantrums of styling flourishes had no real technical justification, but were placed there purely and simply for our aesthetic edification. As GM's design boss Harley Earl put it: "Every time we look at a Cadillac, we take a short emotional vacation."

Throughout the 20th century, car designers overdrew on the bank account of ingenuity. By pushing stylistic boundaries as far as they could, they came up with curved windshields, twin headlights, tilting steering wheels, and electric windows. The relentless pursuit of "good design" actually made cars better, more refined, and more convenient.

smaller and given us freedom, mobility, joy, and wonder. Without the car, our society would have been completely different. If it didn't already exist, we'd have to invent it all over again. If we're really honest with ourselves, we should consider our generation lucky to have been part of the car's greatest years. Car historians of the future will wax lyrical over the accessibility, affordability, and sheer glamour of 20th-century cars. And if you think cars are treated as icons now, wait another 10 years. When the world is charging up its battery packs or refueling its hydrogen tanks, cars like Ford Mustangs, Jaguar E-Types, and Porsche 356s will be seen as works of art. Old cars (perhaps by then they'll be calling them "real cars") will be considered even more iconic, products of a golden age when the consumer had unimaginable levels of choice. And, yes, back then they really could drive flat out.

CREATIVE CLASSICS

And that's really what this book is all about, a simple celebration of the ingenuity, style, technical audacity, and beauty of the car. The past century has given us some utterly incredible machines, which we'll never see made again. Cars were once

NEW POWER

With the realization that conventional oil will really run dry in a few years' time, manufacturers are increasingly turning to alternative fuel sources to power their cars.

would have thought that Mercedes-Benz or DaimlerChrysler would be in financial trouble, that household names like Oldsmobile, Honda, Mitsubishi, Vauxhall, and Ford would be anxiously looking at their balance sheets, wondering how they got it all so horribly wrong? From the scores of manufacturers that proliferated through the Fifties and Sixties, in a few years we're likely to end up with maybe just six international car companies, products of a merger and acquisition survival strategy. Like the cars they make, the motor mandarins are finding life in the 21st century very tough indeed.

But the metamorphosis of the car industry and the car, the "Big Change," is relentlessly and remorselessly taking place. Right now we are able to buy cars that produce zero emissions. Cars like the Toyota Prius, Honda Insight, and GM's EV1 are genuinely environmentally friendly and are a practical alternative to the internal combustion engine. Mercedes' diminutive Smart Car is a cheerful vision of the future. Small and frugal, it consumes space and fuel at half the rate of conventional autos. Hydrogen cells, long-range battery packs, liquified gas propulsion, hybrids, and dual-fuel cars are all just a few years away from serious volume production. The momentum of change is now unstoppable, and the conventional combustion engine simply won't survive for much longer in its present form. White-coated engineers in every car company in the world are working night and day to solve one of the biggest design dilemmas civilization has ever faced – to create a new form of propulsion and fuel source that will protect both the world and our future.

A POSITIVE CONTRIBUTION

Yet against this whirlwind of environmental censure it's easy to forget just how important, beneficial, and plain wonderful the car has been over the past century. Apart from providing millions of people with millions of jobs, it's made the world much

a snail's pace. In fact, it's quicker to walk. In Athens there's so much pollution that the death rate on bad-air days climbs 500 percent. In Brazil congestion is at such levels that the government limits road use by a rotation system that keeps one fifth of all cars off the road every day. In Prague, in the Czech Republic, a regular pall of smog has meant that police have to man roadblocks to prevent all but the most essential traffic from entering the city center. But the most frightening thought is that by 2030 there could be as many as a billion cars on the surface of the earth, a terrifying figure that means that the global auto industry will produce more cars in the next 30 years than it has in the entire last century.

And that's why the last five years have been some of the car's most difficult. Carmakers are making too many, many governments have become rabidly anticar, legislation is becoming draconian, future fuel sources are in doubt, and every single person laying claim to a level head knows that cars are killing us. Which is why car owners all over the world are becoming one of the most heavily taxed and legislated-against groups in society. Road fatalities, excessive speed, global warming, gridlock, congestion, asthma – the charges against the car

stack up to shoulder height. And the jury's unanimous verdict is an emphatic "guilty." If global car use is left unchecked, the world will become one enormous traffic jam. If the car carries on polluting as it has, we'll all choke to death. If China and India suddenly wanted the same level of personal mobility as the West, then the world's oil resources would run out next Thursday. Experts believe that we have used nearly a trillion barrels of oil over the last 100 years and that we have perhaps another 800 billion barrels left in financially feasible reserves. But world oil consumption isn't standing still at around 70 billion barrels a day. It's increasing by as much as four percent each year. In Taiwan oil imports have risen 70 percent in the last four years, and in China the figure is up by a staggering 37 percent.

DECLINE OF THE MANUFACTURERS

The car companies, those trillion-dollar multinationals that were once the world's most powerful consumer force, are now buckling too. One by one they've fallen by the wayside, victims of overproduction, complacency, governmental constraint, global restructuring, and the impossible logistics of worldwide supply and demand. Who

SMART CAR
Mercedes' vision of the future is already here, an eco-friendly package with low fuel costs and easily replaced body parts.

surrender the car's allure, excitement, and power, and willingly accept a much less glamorous and erotic alternative of practical and eco-friendly transportation.

PHENOMENAL GROWTH

You see, the automobile has reached a critical moment in its development. Since 1970, the American vehicle population has grown six times more quickly than the human population, two-and-a-half times faster than the number of households, and double the rate of new drivers. Americans represent only five percent of the world's population but own 36 percent of the world's cars. In a country with 3.8 million miles (6.1 million kilometers) of streets and highways, that's one car for every 40 yards of tarmac. In Britain, 250,000 miles (402,500 kilometers) of roads cater to 20 million vehicles, or 20 yards for every car. And those cars consume half the world's oil and create 15 percent of its greenhouse gas emissions. In London, Tokyo, and New York the daily metropolitan marathon moves at

EASTERN POTENTIAL

Countries such as China and India are still under-developed as far as motorized transport is concerned. It is likely that their bikes will, over the next few decades, be replaced by cars.

And yet the world now says it has had enough of cars. We, as consumers and motorheads, may be as obsessed as ever, but society and nature are buckling under the weight of the horseless carriage. Never in his wildest dreams could Karl Benz have guessed just how many cars like his would eventually be made, and never could he have known the sheer force, impact, and damage they'd cause. In fact it's fair to say that the car is now entering its twilight years. Emotionally we can still forgive it almost anything, but intellectually we all know its days are numbered. Fuel-efficient cars are the only answer to the world's pollution and congestion Armageddon, and for the first time in its history the car industry is actually looking ahead, visualizing not only the end of the oil era but also a global warming crisis that won't easily be solved without changing the way the world drives. We will always need personal mobility, and we will always see the means of individual transportation as one of our inalienable democratic freedoms, but none of it can stay unchanged. All too soon we will have to

THE FIRST CAR
Karl Benz's original car is a far cry from the technology now standard in today's fast, reliable production models.

INTRODUCTION

As I write, the car is celebrating its centennial. One hundred years ago, the first Benz shuddered to life, beginning a journey that would eventually change the world. In those 10 decades, the car has altered beyond all recognition and transformed the lives of everybody across countries and entire continents. No other mechanical invention has ever made such an emotional connection with those who use it, and none offers the same heady mix of freedom, speed, power, sex, and sensuality. Cars are not just functional objects to be used by reasonable people, they're the most compelling and charismatic of all 20th century products. We've become utterly dependent on them both as forms of transportation and symbols of success. Our roads, literature, and culture are thick with the things. Novelist Stephen King once described car ownership as "a parody of the act of love." And he was right. Cars are the ultimate gods of an age that has always worshipped the machine.

City Gridlock
One of the prices paid by mass car ownership is that highways get gridlocked, resulting in the average speed on urban roads being not much more than it was 100 years ago – often less.

FERRARI
Berlinetta Boxer
260–263

FERRARI Daytona
264

FERRARI 400 GT
265

FERRARI
Testarossa
266–269

FIAT 500D
270–273

FORD GT40
274–277

FORD
Thunderbird (1955)
278–281

FORD
Fairlane 500 Skyliner
282–285

FORD Falcon
286–289

FORD
Galaxie 500XL Sunliner
290–293

FORD
Thunderbird (1963)
294–297

FORD Mustang
298–301

FORD
Shelby Mustang GT500
302–305

GORDON KEEBLE GT
306–309

HOLDEN FX
310–311

HUDSON Super Six
312–315

HUDSON Hornet
316–319

JAGUAR XK120
320–323

JAGUAR C-Type
324–327

JAGUAR XK150
328–329

JAGUAR E-Type
330–333

JENSEN Interceptor
334–335

KAISER Darrin
336–339

KAISER
Henry J. Corsair
340–343

LAMBORGHINI Miura
344–347

LAMBORGHINI
Countach
348–351

LANCIA
Aurelia B24 Spider
352–355

LANCIA Stratos
356–359

LANCIA
Delta HF Integrale
360–363

LAND ROVER Series 1
364–367

LINCOLN Capri
368–371

LINCOLN
Continental
372–375

LINCOLN
Continental Mk IV
376–379

LOTUS Elite
380–383

LOTUS Elan Sprint
384–387

MASERATI Ghibli
388–391

MASERATI Kyalami
392–395

MAZDA RX7
396–399

MERCEDES
300SL Gullwing
400–403

MERCEDES 280SL
404–407

MERCURY Monterey
408–411

MERCURY Cougar
412–415

MG TC Midget
416–419

MG A
420

MG B
421

MORGAN Plus Four
422–425

MORRIS
Minor MM Convertible
426–429

LONDON, NEW YORK, DELHI, PARIS
MUNICH, AND JOHANNESBURG

PRODUCED FOR DORLING KINDERSLEY BY
PHIL HUNT (EDITORIAL)
MARK JOHNSON DAVIES (DESIGN)

SENIOR EDITOR
NICKI LAMPON

SENIOR ART EDITOR
KEVIN RYAN

MANAGING EDITOR
SHARON LUCAS

SENIOR MANAGING ART EDITOR
DEREK COOMBES

DTP DESIGNER
SONIA CHARBONNIER

PRODUCTION CONTROLLER
LOUISE DALY

First published in Great Britain in 2001
by Dorling Kindersley Limited,
80 Strand, London WC2R 0RL

2 4 6 8 10 9 7 5 3 1

Library of Congress Cataloging-in-Publication Data
Willson, Quentin.
Cars: a celebration/Quentin Willson.
p. cm
Includes index.
ISBN 0-7894-8155-3 (alk. paper)
1. Automobiles–Pictorial works. 2. Automobiles
–History. I. Title.
TL15 .W514 2001
629.222'09–dc21

Colour reproduction by Colourscan, Singapore
Printed and bound by Mohndruck GmbH, Gutersloh,
Germany

See our complete catalogue at
www.dk.com

Note on Specification Boxes
Every effort has been made to ensure that the
information supplied in the specification boxes is
accurate. Unless otherwise indicated, all figures
pertain to the particular model in the specification
box. Engine capacity for American cars is measured
in cubic inches (cid). A.F.C. is an abbreviation for
average fuel consumption.

CONTENTS

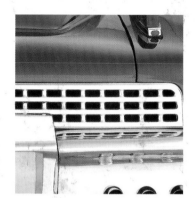

CARS
A CELEBRATION

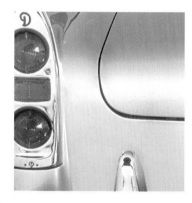

QUENTIN WILLSON

A DORLING KINDERSLEY BOOK

GALLERY OF
CARS

AC | Ace-Bristol

The most handsome British roadster of its day

AGONIZINGLY PRETTY, the AC Ace catapulted the homespun Thames Ditton company into the automotive limelight, instantly earning it a reputation as maker of svelte sports cars for the tweedy English upper classes. Timelessly elegant, swift, poised, and mechanically uncomplicated, the Ace went on to form the platform for the legendary AC Cobra (*see pages* 24–27). Clothed in a light alloy body and powered by a choice of AC's own delicate UMB 2.0 unit, the hardier 2.0 Bristol 100D2 engine, or the lusty 2.6 Ford Zephyr powerplant, the Ace not only drove well but also looked great. Its shape has guaranteed the Ace a place in automotive annals. Chaste, uncluttered, and simple, it makes a Ferrari look top-heavy and clumsy. Purists argue that the Bristol-powered version is the real thoroughbred Ace, closest to its original inspiration, the Bristol-powered Tojeiro prototype of 1953.

KNOWN AS SUPERLEGGERA CONSTRUCTION, A NETWORK OF STEEL TUBES WAS COVERED BY ALUMINUM PANELS, BASED ON THE OUTLINE OF THE 1949 FERRARI 122

"The AC was simplicity itself – a box for the engine, a box for the people, and a box for the luggage."

FOLDING PLEXIGLAS SIDE WINDOWS HELPED TO PREVENT TURBULENCE IN THE COCKPIT AT HIGH SPEED

LATER ACES HAD A REVISED REAR DECK, WITH A BIGGER TRUNK AND SQUARE TAILLIGHTS

MODEL AC Ace-Bristol (1956–61)

PRODUCTION 463

BODY STYLE Two-seater sports roadster.

CONSTRUCTION Space-frame chassis, light alloy body.

ENGINE Six-cylinder push-rod 1971cc.

POWER OUTPUT 105 bhp at 5000 rpm (optional performance tune 125 bhp).

TRANSMISSION Four-speed manual Bristol gearbox (optional overdrive).

SUSPENSION Independent front and rear with transverse leaf spring and lower wishbones.

BRAKES Front and rear drums. Front discs from 1957.

MAXIMUM SPEED 117 mph (188 km/h)

0–60 MPH (0–96 km/h) 9.1 sec

0–100 MPH (0–161 km/h) 27.2 sec

A.F.C. 21.6 mpg (7.6 km/l)

> "Proof of the dictum that less is more, the Ace's gently sweeping profile is a triumph of form over function."

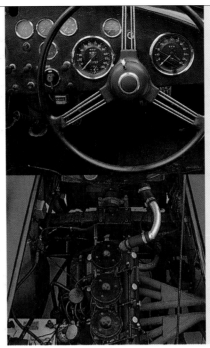

INTERIOR In pure British tradition, the Ace's cockpit was a stark affair, with gauges and switches haphazardly scattered across the dash. The two larger dials were a speedometer reading to 130 mph (209 km/h) – with a clock inset into the dial – and a tachometer maxing at 6000 rpm..

ENGINE Shared by the BMW 328, the hemi-head 125 bhp 2-liter Bristol engine was placed well back in the bay and offered as a performance conversion for the Ace. With triple Solex carbs, push-rod overhead-valve gear, a light alloy head, and a cast-iron crankcase, the Ace was a club racer's dream.

STEERING WHEEL WAS SHARED WITH THE AUSTIN HEALEY (SEE PAGES 54–61) AND THE DAIMLER SP DART (SEE PAGES 204–07)

THE ACE'S WIDE, TOOTHY GRIN FED AIR INTO THE LARGE RADIATOR THAT WAS SHARED BY THE AC TWO-LITER SEDAN

259 GRP

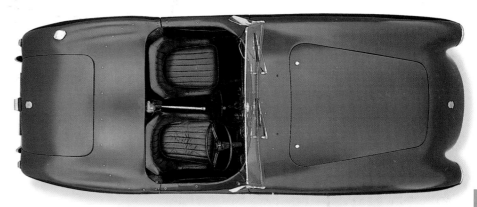

RACING THOROUGHBRED

The 18 percent rearward bias to the Ace-Bristol's weight distribution contributed to its thrilling performance. An Ace-Bristol recorded an average of 97 mph (156 km/h) over 2,350 miles (3,781 kilometers) at the 1957 Le Mans 24 Hours, the fastest ever for a Bristol-engined car.

FOR DIEHARDS WHO ALWAYS DROVE WITH THE TOP DOWN, A TONNEAU COVER COULD BE ATTACHED WHICH KEPT YOUR FEET WARM WHILE YOUR FACE FROZE

259 GRP

GB

AC Cobra 427

A unique fusion of US power and British style

AN UNLIKELY ALLIANCE between AC Cars, a traditional British carmaker, and Carroll Shelby, a charismatic Texas racer, produced the legendary AC Cobra. AC's sports car, the Ace (*see pages* 20–23) was turned into the Cobra by shoehorning in a series of Ford V8s, starting with 4.2 and 4.7 Mustang engines. In 1965, Shelby, always a man to take things to the limit, squeezed in a thunderous 7-liter Ford engine in an attempt to realize his dream of winning Le Mans.

Although the 427 was not fast enough to win, and failed to sell in any quantity, it was soon known as one of the most aggressive and romantic cars ever built. GTM 777F at one time held the record as the world's fastest accelerating production car, and in 1967 was driven by the British journalist John Bolster to record such Olympian figures as an all-out maximum of 165 mph (265 km/h) and a 0–60 (96 km/h) time of an unbelievable 4.2 seconds.

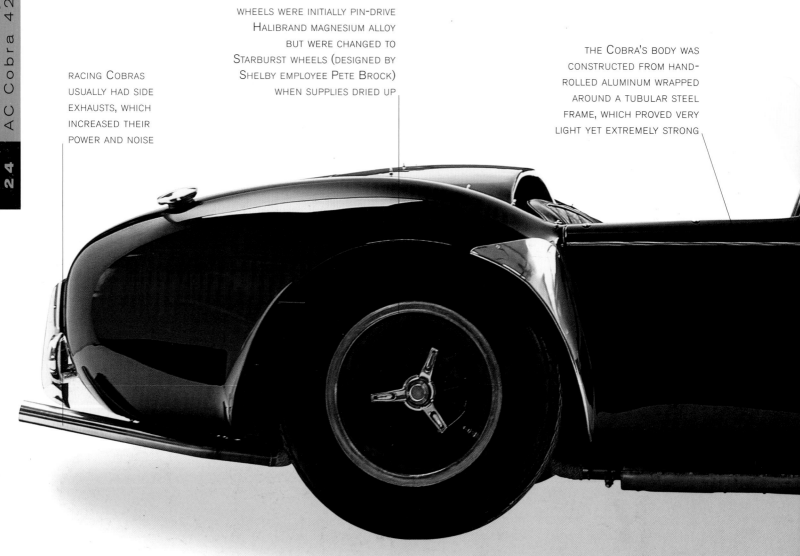

RACING COBRAS USUALLY HAD SIDE EXHAUSTS, WHICH INCREASED THEIR POWER AND NOISE

WHEELS WERE INITIALLY PIN-DRIVE HALIBRAND MAGNESIUM ALLOY BUT WERE CHANGED TO STARBURST WHEELS (DESIGNED BY SHELBY EMPLOYEE PETE BROCK) WHEN SUPPLIES DRIED UP

THE COBRA'S BODY WAS CONSTRUCTED FROM HAND-ROLLED ALUMINUM WRAPPED AROUND A TUBULAR STEEL FRAME, WHICH PROVED VERY LIGHT YET EXTREMELY STRONG

MODEL AC Cobra 427 (1965–68)

PRODUCTION 316

BODY STYLE Light alloy, two-door, two-seater, open sports.

CONSTRUCTION Separate tubular steel chassis with aluminum panels.

ENGINE V8, 6989cc.

POWER OUTPUT 425 bhp at 6000 rpm.

TRANSMISSION Four-speed all-synchromesh.

SUSPENSION All-around independent with coil springs.

BRAKES Four-wheel disc.

MAXIMUM SPEED 165 mph (265 km/h)

0–60 MPH (0–96 km/h) 4.2 sec

0–100 MPH (0–161 km/h) 10.3 sec

A.F.C. 15 mpg (5.3 km/l)

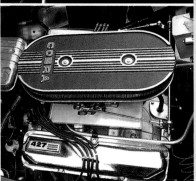

INTERIOR The interior was basic, with traditional 1960s British sports car features of black-on-white gauges, bucket seats, and wood-rim steering wheel. 427 owners did not care about creature comforts, only raw power, great brakes, and good suspension.

ENGINE The mighty 7-liter 427 block had years of NASCAR (National Association for Stock Car Auto Racing) racing success and easily punched out power for hours. The street version output ranged from 300 to 425 bhp.

SPEEDY APPEAL

Even the "baby" 4.7-liter Cobras were good for 138 mph (222 km/h) and could squeal up to 60 mph (96 km/h) in under six seconds. But while street versions could muster at least 300 bhp, competition 427s could exceed 500 bhp.

TOKEN BUMPERS WERE CHROMED TUBES, WITH THE EMPHASIS ON SAVING WEIGHT — RACERS TOOK THEM OFF COMPLETELY

EARLY COBRAS HAD 260CID ENGINES. LATER CARS WERE EQUIPPED WITH MUSTANG 289 V8S

"The 427 looked fast standing still. Gone was the lithe beauty of the original Ace, replaced by bulbous fenders, fat wheels, and rubber wide enough to climb walls."

Raised in Dallas, Carroll Shelby tried chicken farming, trucking, and was even a partner in a hamburger stand before he won a road race in Oklahoma in a borrowed MG TC at the age of 29. He went on to win Le Mans in 1959, and seven years later helped Ford win it too. He developed the best Mustang ever, advised Rootes on the Sunbeam Tiger, and, of course, created the iconic Cobra. Despite heart and kidney transplants, Shelby is still very active, devoting most of his time to charity. He lives with his wife in California.

THE CHASSIS WAS VIRTUALLY ALL NEW AND THREE TIMES STRONGER THAN THE EARLIER COBRA 289'S, WITH COMPUTER-DESIGNED ANTI-DIVE AND ANTI-SQUAT CHARACTERISTICS

GTM 777F

AC 428

Italian design flair hides the beast within

THE AC 428 NEEDS a new word of its very own – "brutiful" perhaps, for while its brute strength derives from its Cobra forebear, the 428 has a sculpted, stately beauty. This refined bruiser was born of a thoroughbred crossbreed of British engineering, American power, and Italian design. The convertible 428 was first seen at the London Motor Show in October 1965; the first fixed-head car – the fastback – was ready in time for the Geneva Motor Show in March 1966. But production was beset by problems from the start; first cars were not offered for sale until 1967, and as late as March 1969, only 50 had been built. Part of the problem was that the 428 was priced between the more expensive Italian Ferraris and Maseratis and the cheaper British Astons and Jensens. Small-scale production continued into the 1970s, but its days were numbered and it was finally done for by the fuel crisis of October 1973; the last 428 was sold in 1974.

THE FIRST CONVERTIBLES HAD A DETACHABLE METAL TONNEAU TO COVER THE TOP WHEN FOLDED, BUT THIS WAS SOON ABANDONED

EARLY CARS HAD ALUMINUM DOORS AND HOOD; LATER MODELS WERE ALL STEEL

THE 18-GALLON (82-LITER) FUEL TANK WAS FILLED THROUGH A FLAP ON THE REAR DECK

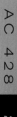

MODEL AC 428 (1966–73)

PRODUCTION 80 (51 convertibles, 29 fastbacks)

BODY STYLES Two-seat convertible or two-seat fastback coupe.

CONSTRUCTION Tubular-steel backbone chassis/separate all-steel body.

ENGINES Ford V8, 6997cc or 7016cc.

POWER OUTPUT 345 bhp at 4600 rpm.

TRANSMISSION Ford four-speed manual or three-speed auto; Salisbury rear axle with limited-slip differential.

SUSPENSION Double wishbones and coil spring/telescopic shock units front and rear.

BRAKES Servo-assisted Girling discs all around.

MAXIMUM SPEED 139.3 mph (224 km/h) (auto)

0–60 MPH (0–96 km/h) 5.9 sec (auto)

0–100 MPH (0–161 km/h) 14.5 sec

A.F.C. 12–15 mpg (4.2–5.3 km/l)

FRONT SUSPENSION
UTILIZED UNEQUAL-
LENGTH WISHBONES
WITH COMBINED
COIL-SPRING
AND SHOCK
ABSORBERS

LIKE THE COBRA, THE
428'S VAST HOOD WAS
HINGED AT THE FRONT.
UNDER-HOOD HEAT
MEANT THAT THE
ENGINE OIL COULD
LITERALLY BOIL

LCD 1

"If you own one of the few 428s still around today, you have got a rare thing – a refined muscle car, a macho GT with manners and breeding."

INTERIOR Switchgear may be scattered around like confetti, but the instruments are grouped clearly in front of the driver. The speedo on the left reads to an optimistic 180 mph (290 km/h), while the tachometer on the right stops at 8000 rpm. The 428 incorporated top-quality leather seats and chrome-plated fixtures.

ENGINE Pre-1967, the car used the same 427 cubic inch (6998cc) V8 as the Cobra so was originally known as the AC 427. In 1967, it gained the Ford Galaxie engine *(see pages 290–93)* and an extra cubic inch. Both four-speed manual and three-speed automatic transmissions were available.

THE 428 FEATURED PARTS FROM OTHER MANUFACTURERS; THE REAR LIGHTS, FOR EXAMPLE, WERE SUPPLIED BY FIAT

THE LETTERS AC DERIVED FROM AUTOCARRIER, THE COMPANY'S NAME UNTIL IT BECAME KNOWN AS AC CARS LTD. IN 1922

LCD 1

ALFA ROMEO Spider

One of Alfa's most romantic confections

DRIVEN BY DUSTIN HOFFMAN to the strains of Simon and Garfunkel in the film *The Graduate*, the Alfa Spider has become one of the most accessible cult Italian cars. This is hardly surprising when you consider the little Alfa's considerable virtues: a wonderfully responsive all-alloy, twin-cam engine; accurate steering; sensitive brakes; a finely balanced chassis; and movie star looks. There's a reason it has been called the poor man's Ferrari. First launched at the Geneva Motor Show in 1966, Alfa held a worldwide competition to find a name for their new baby. After considering 140,000 entries, with suggestions like Lollobrigida, Bardot, and even Stalin, they settled on Duetto, which neatly summed up the car's two's-company-three's-a-crowd image. Despite the same price tag as the much faster and more glamorous Jaguar E-Type (*see pages 330–33*), the Spider sold over 100,000 units during its remarkable 26-year production run.

"The Spider has to be one of Alfa's great postwar cars, not least because of its contemporary design."

THE SPIDER'S BODYWORK CORRODED ALARMINGLY QUICKLY DUE TO ITS POOR-QUALITY STEEL, SCANT RUSTPROOFING, AND INADEQUATE DRAINAGE

THE SPIDER'S TOP WAS BEAUTIFULLY EFFECTIVE — IT COULD BE RAISED WITH ONLY ONE ARM WITHOUT LEAVING THE DRIVER'S SEAT

SPIDERS HAD HUGE TRUNKS BY SPORTS CAR STANDARDS, WITH THE SPARE WHEEL TUCKED NEATLY AWAY UNDER THE TRUNK FLOOR

MODEL Alfa Romeo 1300 Junior Spider (1968–78)

PRODUCTION 7,237

BODY STYLE Two-door, two-seater.

CONSTRUCTION All-steel monocoque body.

ENGINE All-alloy twin-cam 1290cc.

POWER OUTPUT 89 bhp at 6000 rpm.

TRANSMISSION Five-speed.

SUSPENSION *Front:* independent; *Rear:* live axle with coil springs.

BRAKES Four-wheel disc.

MAXIMUM SPEED 106 mph (170 km/h)

0–60 MPH (0–96 km/h) 11.2 sec

0–100 MPH (0–161 km/h) 21.3 sec

A.F.C. 29 mpg (10.3 km/l)

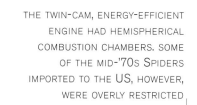

THE TWIN-CAM, ENERGY-EFFICIENT ENGINE HAD HEMISPHERICAL COMBUSTION CHAMBERS. SOME OF THE MID-'70S SPIDERS IMPORTED TO THE US, HOWEVER, WERE OVERLY RESTRICTED

AMC Pacer

The car with a body almost as wide as it was long

THE 1973 FUEL CRISIS hit America's psyche harder than the Russians beating them into space in the Fifties. Cheap and unrestricted personal transportation had been a way of life, and then suddenly Americans faced the horrifying prospect of paying more than 40 cents a gallon. Overnight, stocks in car manufacturers became as popular as Richard Nixon. Detroit's first response was to kill the muscle car. The second was to revive the "compact" and invent the "subcompact." AMC had first entered the subcompact market in 1970 with its immensely popular Gremlin model, but the 1975 Pacer was a different beast. Advertised as "the first wide small car," it had the passenger compartment of a sedan, the nose of a European commuter shuttle, and no back end at all. Ironically, it wasn't even that economical; but America didn't notice because it was on a guilt trip, buying over 70,000 of the things in '75 alone.

"In the mid-Seventies, the Pacer was sold as the last word; 'the face of the car of the 21st century,' bragged the ads."

ORIGINALLY SLATED TO USE URETHANE BUMPERS, PRODUCTION PACERS WERE EQUIPPED WITH STEEL VERSIONS TO SAVE MONEY

THE AERODYNAMIC WINDSHIELD AIDED FUEL ECONOMY AND REDUCED THE AMOUNT OF INTERIOR NOISE

"Though the Pacer received plaudits from some, other pundits of the time called it a 'football on wheels' and a 'big frog.'"

Pacer

MODEL AMC Pacer

PRODUCTION 72,158 (1975)

BODY STYLE Three-door sedan.

CONSTRUCTION Steel unitary body.

ENGINES 2232cid, 258cid sixes.

POWER OUTPUT 90–95 bhp.

TRANSMISSION Three-speed manual with optional overdrive, optional three-speed Torque-Command automatic.

SUSPENSION *Front*: coil springs; *Rear*: semi-elliptic leaf springs.

BRAKES Front discs, rear drums.

MAXIMUM SPEED 105 mph (169 km/h)

0–60 MPH (0–96 km/h) 14 sec

A.F.C. 18–24 mpg (6.4–8.5 km/l)

INTERIOR Inside was stock Detroit, with sporty front bucket seats and a cheesy polyurethane dash. Having the largest glass area of any contemporary American sedan made the $425 All Season air-conditioning option almost obligatory.

REAR ASPECT Unbelievably, the Pacer's rear end inspired the comely rump of the Porsche 928, though there's no doubting the fact that both cars had excellent rearward vision. In 1977, Pacers were stretched by a further 4 in (10 cm) and offered as station wagons.

"*Motor Trend* magazine called the Pacer's styling 'the most innovative of all US small cars.' Credit went to Richard Teague, who also designed the '84 Jeep Cherokee."

ADAPTABILITY EVEN STRETCHED TO THE FRONT OF THE CAR; 26 PERCENT OF ALL PACERS HAD RECLINING FRONT SEATS

"Originally, AMC envisaged the Pacer to be equipped with a rotary engine that GM had been developing. The idea was dropped, and sixes were used instead."

THERE WAS MORE HEADROOM AND LEGROOM THAN THE CONTEMPORARY CHEVELLE OR TORINO, MAKING THE PACER FEEL SPACIOUS

ASTON MARTIN DB4

A British classic with serious attitude

THE DEBUT OF THE DB4 in 1958 heralded the beginning of the Aston Martin glory years, ushering in the breed of classic six-cylinder DB Astons that propelled the company onto the world stage. Earlier postwar Astons were fine enthusiasts' road cars, but with the DB4 Astons acquired a new grace and refinement that was, for many, the ultimate flowering of the grand tourer theme. The DB4 looked superb and went like the wind. The DB5, which followed, will forever be remembered as the James Bond Aston; and the final expression of the theme came with the bigger DB6. The cars were glorious, but the company was in trouble. David Brown, the millionaire industrialist owner of Aston Martin, and the DB of the model name, had a dream. But, in the early Seventies, with losses of $2.4 million a year, he bailed out of the company, leaving a legacy of machines that are still talked about with reverence as the David Brown Astons.

Superleggera

LIGHTWEIGHT

Superleggera refers to a technique where aluminum-alloy body panels are rolled over a framework of steel tubes.

THE RIDE WASN'T QUITE AS IMPRESSIVE AS THE REST OF THE CAR — REAR SUSPENSION WAS THROUGH BASIC LEVER-ARM UNITS

WHILE REAR SEATS IN THE FIXED-HEAD OFFERED LIMITED SPACE, THERE WAS NO DISPUTING THE RICHNESS AND QUALITY OF THE CONNOLLY LEATHER

BUMPER OVERRIDERS WERE FROM THE BRITISH MK2 FORD ZEPHYR AND ZODIAC

MODEL Aston Martin DB4 (1958–63)

PRODUCTION 1,040 (fixed head); 70 (convertible); 95 (fixed-head DB4 GTs)

BODY STYLES Fixed-head coupe or convertible.

CONSTRUCTION Pressed-steel and tubular inner chassis frame, with aluminum-alloy outer panels.

ENGINES Inline six 3670cc/3749cc.

POWER OUTPUT 240 bhp at 5500 rpm.

TRANSMISSION Four-speed manual (with optional overdrive).

SUSPENSION *Front*: independent by wishbones, coil springs, and telescopic shocks; *Rear*: live axle located by trailing arms and Watt linkage with coil springs and lever-arm shocks.

BRAKES Four-wheel disc.

MAXIMUM SPEED 140+ mph (225+ km/h)

0–60 MPH (0–96 km/h) 8 sec

0–100 MPH (0–161 km/h) 20.1 sec

A.F.C. 14–22 mpg (3.6–7.8 km/l)

FRONT SUSPENSION WAS
DOUBLE WISHBONES
WITH COIL SPRINGS AND
TELESCOPIC SHOCKS

INTERIOR The dash is a gloriously unergonomic triumph of form over function; gauges are scattered all over an instrument panel deliberately similar to the car's grinning radiator grille. While rear seats in the fixed-head offer limited space, the richness and quality of the Connolly leather make up for it.

ENGINE It looks very much like the contemporary Jaguar XK twin-cam straight-six, but Tadek Marek's design was both more powerful and vastly more complicated. Triple SU carburetors show this to be a Vantage engine with larger valves, providint the DB4 with an extra 20 bhp.

"The DB4's stance is solid and butch, but not brutish – more British Boxer than lumbering Bulldog, aggressive yet refined."

DIPPING REARVIEW MIRROR WAS ALSO FOUND IN MANY JAGUARS OF THE PERIOD

FRONT INDICATORS AND REAR LIGHTS WERE STRAIGHT OFF THE UTILITARIAN LAND ROVER

1037 TE

MICHAEL CAINE

In *The Italian Job*, Michael Caine could take his pick from a Lamborghini Miura, two Jaguar E-Types, a flock of Mini Coopers, and an Aston Martin DB4. During filming, Caine's favorite car was the silver Aston, a 1962 Volante registered 163 ELT, which was eventually pushed off a cliff by a Mafia bulldozer. In reality it was a mocked-up Lancia that was used in the cliff stunt, the Aston being deemed too valuable. Caine drove the 163 ELT around for awhile in the Seventies, and the car still survives, completely restored and still in its original Silver Birch livery.

Aston Martin DB4

41

COMPLEX CURVES MEANT THE TRUNK LID WAS ONE OF THE MOST DIFFICULT-TO-PRODUCE PANELS ON THE ENTIRE CAR

1037 TE

ASTON MARTIN V8

Staple transportation for aristocrats and James Bond

A NEAR TWO-TON Goliath powered by an outrageous handmade 5.3-liter engine, the DBS V8 was meant to be Aston's moneymakerfor the 1970s. Based on the six-cylinder DBS of 1967, the V8 did not appear until April 1970. With a thundering 160 mph (257 km/h) top speed and incredible sub seven-second 0–60 time, Aston's new bulldog instantly earned a place on every millionaire's shopping list. The trouble was that it drove into a worldwide recession – in 1975 the Newport Pagnell factory produced just 19 cars. Aston's bank managers were worried men, but the company pulled through. The DBS became the Aston Martin V8 in 1972 and continued until 1989, giving birth to the legendary 400 bhp Vantage and gorgeous Volante Convertible. Excessive, expensive, impractical, and impossibly thirsty, the DBS V8 and AM V8 are wonderful relics from a time when environmentalism was just another word in the dictionary.

"DBS was one of the first
Astons with a chassis and departed
from the traditional Superleggera
tubular superstructure of
the DB4, 5, and 6."

THE SMOOTH
TAPERING COCKPIT
LINE IS AN ASTON
HALLMARK ECHOED IN
THE CURRENT DB7

THE DISCREET
REAR SPOILER WAS
PART OF THE
GENTLY SWEEPING
FENDER LINE

THE V8'S ALUMINUM BODY WAS HAND-SMOOTHED AND LOVINGLY FINISHED

ASTON MARTIN

MODEL Aston Martin V8 (1972–89)

PRODUCTION 2,842 (including Volante and Vantage)

BODY STYLE Four-seater coupe.

CONSTRUCTION Aluminum body, steel platform chassis.

ENGINE Twin OHC alloy 5340cc V8.

POWER OUTPUT Never released but approx. 345 bhp (Vantage 400 bhp).

TRANSMISSION Three-speed auto or five-speed manual.

SUSPENSION Independent front, De Dion rear.

BRAKES Four-wheel disc.

MAXIMUM SPEED 161 mph (259 km/h); 173 mph (278 km/h) (Vantage)

0–60 MPH (0–96 km/h) 6.2 sec (Vantage 5.4 sec)

0–100 MPH (0–161 km/h) 14.2 sec (Vantage 13 sec)

A.F.C. 13 mpg (4.6 km/l)

INTERIOR Over the years the DBS was skilfully updated, without losing its traditional ambience. Features included leather and wood surroundings, air-conditioning, electric windows, and radio cassette. Nearly all V8s were ordered with Chrysler TorqueFlite automatic transmission.

ENGINE The alloy V8 was first seen in Lola sports-racing cars. The massive air-filter box covers a quartet of twin-choke Weber carbs, which guzzle one gallon of fuel for every 13 miles (4.6 kilometers), and much less if you put your foot to the floor and decide to really enjoy yourself.

TWIN PIPES

Handmade bumpers covered huge twin exhausts – a gentle reminder of this Aston's epic V8 grunt. A V8 Volante featured in the James Bond film *The Living Daylights*. In 1964 a DB5 was the first Aston to star alongside James Bond in *Goldfinger*.

SHAPELY "CLIFF-HANGER" NOSE WAS ALWAYS A DBS TRADEMARK

MASSIVE HOOD POWER BULGE WAS TO CLEAR FOUR CARBURETORS

CHIN SPOILER AND UNDERTRAY HELPED REDUCE FRONT-END LIFT AT HIGH SPEED

B391 AJD

"Cars with incredible presence, Astons were good enough for James Bond, King Hussein of Jordan, Peter Sellers, and even the Prince of Wales."

PRODIGIOUS REAR OVERHANG MADE THE REAR ASPECT LOOK CLUTTERED

THIN TINTED REAR WINDOW GAVE THE DRIVER LIMITED REARWARD VISION

B391 AJD

AUDI Quattro Sport

A technical trailblazer that set the rallying world alight

THE MOST EXPENSIVE and exclusive Audi ever sold was the $90,000, 155 mph (250 km/h) Quattro Sport. With a short wheelbase, all-alloy 304 bhp engine, and a body made of aluminum-reinforced fiberglass and Kevlar, it has all the charisma, and nearly all the performance, of a Ferrari GTO. The Quattro changed the way we think about four-wheel drive. Before 1980, four-wheel drive systems had floundered through high cost, weight, and lousy road behavior.

Everybody thought that if you bolted a four-wheel drive system onto a performance coupe it would have ugly handling, transmission whine, and an insatiable appetite for fuel. Audi's engineers proved that the accepted wisdom was wrong, and by 1982, the Quattro was a World Rally Champion. Gone, but not forgotten, the Quattro Sport is now a much admired collectors' item, valued at considerably more than its original price.

BAUR BADGING
Some body parts were made by the German coachbuilder Baur, who also made the early BMW 3-Series Convertible. The body shells were welded by a team of 22 craftsmen.

THOUGH THE RIDE WAS HARDER THAN ON NORMAL QUATTROS, STEERING WAS QUICKER

INTERAXLE DIFFERENTIAL ON THE QUATTRO WAS BORROWED FROM THE VW POLO

BOX WHEELARCHES ARE A QUATTRO HALLMARK, AND ESSENTIAL TO COVER THE FAT 9Jx15 WHEELS

"From any angle, the Sport is testosterone on wheels, with a butch and aggressive four-square stance."

MODEL Audi Quattro Sport (1983–87)

PRODUCTION 220 (all LHD)

BODY STYLE Two-seater, two-door coupe.

CONSTRUCTION Monocoque body from Kevlar, aluminum, fiberglass, and steel.

ENGINE 2133cc five-cylinder turbocharged.

POWER OUTPUT 304 bhp at 6500 rpm.

TRANSMISSION Five-speed manual, four-wheel drive.

SUSPENSION All-around independent.

BRAKES Four-wheel vented discs with switchable ABS.

MAXIMUM SPEED 155 mph (250 km/h)

0–60 MPH (0–96 km/h) 4.8 sec

0–100 MPH (0–161 km/h) 13.9 sec

A.F.C. 17 mpg (6 km/l)

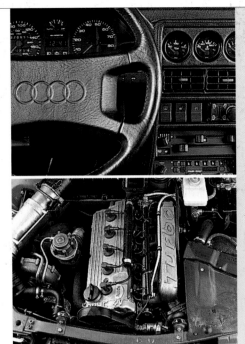

INTERIOR While the dashboard layout is nothing special, everything in front of the driver is typically Germanic – clear, neat, and easy to use. The only touch of luxury in the Quattro is half-leather trim. It looked like it could seat four people but was in practice a two-seater only.

ENGINE The five-cylinder 2133cc alloy engine is 50 lb (22.7 kg) lighter than the stock item, with twin overhead cams, four valves per cylinder, a giant turbocharger, and Bosch LH-Jetronic injection. Center Torsen differential gives a 50/50 front-to-rear split. Rear differential lock disengaged at 15 mph (24 km/h).

CINDER-BLOCK STYLING MEANT THAT THE QUATTRO'S AERODYNAMICS WERE POOR AT 0.43CD

AUSTIN Mini Cooper

A souped-up version of the original small car

THE MINI COOPER was one of Britain's great sports car legends, an inspired confection that became the definitive rally car of the Sixties. Because of its size, maneuverability, and front-wheel drive, the Cooper could dance around bigger, more unwieldy cars and scuttle off to victory. Even driven to the absolute limit, it would still cling limpetlike around corners long after rear-wheel drive cars were sliding sideways. The hot Mini was a perfect blend of pin-sharp steering, terrific handling balance, and a feeling that you could get away with almost anything. Originally the brainchild of race car builder John Cooper, the Mini's designer, Alec Issigonis, thought it should be a "people's car" rather than a performance machine and did not like the idea of a souped-up Mini. Fortunately BMC (British Motor Corporation) did and agreed to a trial run of just 1,000 cars. One of its better decisions.

"The Cooper S, built between 1963 and 1967, came in a choice of 970 or 1071cc engines and had wider wheels and different badging than the stock Cooper."

WITH A LOW CENTER OF GRAVITY AND A WHEEL AT EACH EXTREME CORNER, THE MINI HAD THE PERFECT CREDENTIALS FOR SOLID HANDLING

THERE WAS A BIG PRICE DIFFERENCE BETWEEN THE COOPER AND THE COOPER S – $1595 FOR THE STANDARD CAR AND $1950 FOR THE S

ON RACING COOPERS THE WINDSHIELD WAS GLASS, BUT ALL OTHER WINDOWS WERE MADE OUT OF PLEXIGLAS TO SAVE WEIGHT

MODEL Austin Mini Cooper (1963–69)

PRODUCTION 145,000 (all models)

BODY STYLE Sedan.

CONSTRUCTION All-steel two-door monocoque mounted on front and rear subframes.

ENGINES Four-cylinder 970cc/997cc/998cc/1071cc/1275cc.

POWER OUTPUT 65 bhp at 6500 rpm to 76 bhp at 5800 rpm.

TRANSMISSION Four-speed, no synchromesh on first.

SUSPENSION Independent front and rear suspension with rubber cones and wishbones (Hydrolastic from late 1964).

BRAKES Lockheed front discs with rear drums.

MAXIMUM SPEED 100 mph (161 km/h)

0–60 MPH (0–96 km/h) 12.9 sec

0–100 MPH (0–161 km/h) 20 sec

A.F.C. 30 mpg (10.6 km/l)

INTERIOR The Cooper has typical rally-car features: wood-rim Moto-Lita wheel, fire extinguisher, Halda trip meter, tachometer, stopwatches, and maplight. The only features that would have been standard equipment are the center speedo, heater, and switches.

ENGINE The 1071cc A-series engine would rev to 7200 rpm, and was able to produce 72 bhp. Crankshaft, con-rods, valves, and rockers were all toughened, and the Cooper also had a bigger oil pump and beefed-up gearbox.

"The Cooper's rally success in the 1960s is testament to the work of the British Motor Corporation's proactive Competitions Department."

FOR NIGHT RALLY STAGES, COOPERS NEEDED MAXIMUM ILLUMINATION. STRAPS HELD ON THE HEADLIGHT STONE-PROTECTORS

FRONT GRILLE WAS QUICK-RELEASE TO ALLOW ACCESS FOR EMERGENCY REPAIRS TO DISTRIBUTOR, OIL COOLER, STARTER MOTOR, AND ALTERNATOR

24PK

JOHN COOPER

Born in Surrey, England, in 1923, John Cooper inherited his love of cars from his father, who ran a local garage. In 1946 John built a motorcycle-engined special known as the Cooper-Jap Mark 1. A meeting with Alec Issigonis saw Cooper asking if he could tune up the then-new Mini, and from then the Mini Cooper became a rallying legend.

COMPETITIONS DEPARTMENTS OFTEN SWAPPED LICENSE PLATES, BODYSHELLS, AND CHASSIS NUMBERS, MAKING IT HARD TO IDENTIFY GENUINE CUSTOM COOPERS

ROOF-MOUNTED SPOTLIGHT COULD BE ROTATED FROM INSIDE THE CAR

GB 24PK

AUSTIN-HEALEY Sprite Mk1

A sports classic in the true British tradition

SOME AUTOMOTIVE ACADEMICS believe that all the best car designs have a recognizable face. If that is indeed the case, few cars have a cuter one than this insolent little fellow, with that ear-to-ear grinning grille and those wide-open, slightly astonished eyes. Of course, it is those trademark bulging peepers that prompted the nickname "Frogeye," by which everyone now recognizes this engaging character. In fact, many of the Frogeye's features were born out of necessity.

The Donald Healey Motor Company and Austin had already teamed up by producing the Austin-Healey 100. In 1958, its little brother, the Sprite, was born, a spartan sports car designed at a reduced price and based on the engine and running gear of the Austin A35 sedan, with a bit of Morris Minor thrown in for good measure. Yet the Frogeye really was a sports car and had a sweet raspberry exhaust note to prove it.

IT IS NOT SO MUCH A TRUNK, BECAUSE IT DOES NOT OPEN; MORE A LUGGAGE LOCKER WITH ACCESS BEHIND THE REAR SEATS

PLEXIGLAS REAR WINDOW OFFERED ONLY LIMITED REAR VISION

"The Frogeye's design has a classic simplicity, free of needless chrome decoration."

MODEL Austin-Healey Sprite Mk1 (1958–61)

PRODUCTION 38,999

BODY STYLE Two-seater roadster.

CONSTRUCTION Unitary body/chassis.

ENGINE BMC A-Series 948cc, four-cylinder, overhead valve.

POWER OUTPUT 43 bhp at 5200 rpm.

TRANSMISSION Four-speed manual, synchromesh on top three ratios.

SUSPENSION *Front:* independent, coil springs and wishbones; *Rear:* quarter-elliptic leaf springs, rigid axle.

BRAKES Hydraulic, drums all around.

MAXIMUM SPEED 84 mph (135 km/h)

0–60 MPH (0–96 km/h) 20.5 sec

A.F.C. 35–45 mpg (12.5–16 km/l)

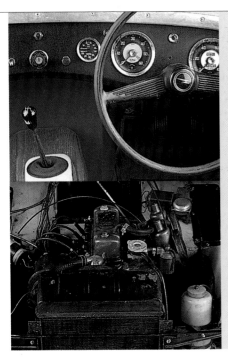

INTERIOR The Frogeye fits like a glove. Side curtains rather than roll-down windows gave some extra elbow room, and everything is within reach of the driver – speedo on the right, tachometer on the left, and a well-placed stubby gear stick.

ENGINE The Austin-Morris A-series engine was a little gem. It first appeared in the Austin A35 sedan and went on to power several generations of Mini. In the Frogeye it was modified internally with extra strong valve springs and equipped with twin SU carbs.

THE FROGEYE'S LOW STANCE AIDED FLAT CORNERING. GROUND CLEARANCE WAS BETTER THAN IT LOOKED: JUST UNDER 5 IN (12.7 CM)

DONALD HEALEY'S ORIGINAL DESIGN INCORPORATED RETRACTING HEADLIGHTS LIKE THE LATER LOTUS ELAN (SEE PAGES 384–87), BUT EXTRA COST RULED THESE OUT

"The Frogeye's pert looks were only part of the car's cult appeal; for with its firm, even harsh, ride it had a traditional British sports car feel."

Outright winner of the '31 Monte Carlo Rally, Donald Healey could easily have become a motorsport legend. But he preferred building cars to racing them and, after WWII, designed Healey sports cars with Alvis and Riley engines. His greatest moment came with the massively successful Austin-Healey of 1952, a collaboration with Leonard Lord of Austin. Donald Healey probably did more for the prestige of British sports cars than any other man.

AUSTIN-HEALEY 3000

A surefooted thoroughbred sports car

THE HEALEY HUNDRED was a sensation at the 1952 Earl's Court Motor Show in London. Austin's Leonard Lord had already contracted to supply the engines, but when he noticed the sports car's impact, he decided he wanted to build it too – it was transformed overnight into the Austin-Healey 100. Donald Healey had spotted a gap in the American sports car market between the Jaguar XK120 (*see pages* 320–23) and the cheap MG T series (*see pages* 416–19). His hunch was right, for about 80 percent of all production went Stateside. Over the years this rugged bruiser became more civilized. In 1956, it received a six-cylinder engine in place of the four; but in 1959 the 3000 was born. It became increasingly refined, with front disc brakes and then roll-up windows, and was ever faster. Our featured car is the last of the line, a 3000 Mk3. Although verging on grand-tourer territory, it is also the fastest of all Big Healeys and still a true sports car.

"The two major influences on the Healey's changing faces were the needs of the American market and the impositions of Austin."

WIRE WHEELS WITH KNOCK-OFF HUBS WERE OPTIONS ON SOME MODELS, STANDARD ON OTHERS; WHITEWALLS USUALLY SIGNIFY AN AMERICAN CAR

IN 1962, THE 3000 ACQUIRED A WRAPAROUND WINDSHIELD AND ROLL-UP WINDOWS, AS THE ONCE RAW SPORTS CAR ADOPTED TRAPPINGS OF SOPHISTICATION

Austin Healey
3000 Mk III

MODEL Austin-Healey 3000 (1959–68)

PRODUCTION 42,926 (all 3000 models)

BODY STYLES Two-seater roadster, 2+2 roadster, 2+2 convertible.

CONSTRUCTION Separate chassis/body.

ENGINE 2912cc overhead-valve, straight-six.

POWER OUTPUT 3000 Mk1: 124 bhp at 4600 rpm. 3000 Mk2: 132 bhp at 4750 rpm. 3000 Mk3: 150 bhp at 5250 rpm.

TRANSMISSION Four-speed manual with overdrive.

SUSPENSION *Front*: independent coil springs and wishbones, antiroll bar; *Rear*: semi-elliptic leaf springs. Lever-arm shock absorbers all around.

BRAKES Front discs; rear drums.

MAXIMUM SPEED 110–120 mph (177–193 km/h)

0–60 MPH (0–96 km/h) 9.5–10.8 sec

A.F.C. 17–34 mpg (6–12 km/l)

INTERIOR Once spartan, the interior of the Austin-Healey became increasingly luxurious, with a polished veneer dash and even a lockable glove compartment to complement the fine leather and rich carpet. One thing remained traditional – engine heat meant the cabin was always a hot place to be.

ENGINE The Healey 3000's straight-six block had been bored out from 2639cc in 1959 and was the butchest of the big bangers, pumping out a hefty 150 bhp. The longer engine meant that the radiator had to be pushed forward, with the hood scoop clearing the underhood protrusion to aid airflow.

"From the start, the styling was always a major asset; and the 3000 Mk3 is the eventual culmination of the combined American and British styling forces."

FROM THE TRADITIONAL HEALEY DIAMOND GRILLE, THE MOUTH OF THE AUSTIN-HEALEY DEVELOPED INTO A WIDE GRIN

AS THE HEALEY 3000 BECAME BEEFIER THROUGH THE SIXTIES, MODERN RADIAL TIRES HELPED KEEP IT ON COURSE

YMO 37F

PERIOD ADVERTISEMENT

Contemporary advertising portrayed the 3000 as a thoroughbred sports car for the well-heeled. The Austin-Healey put on weight over the years, and became gradually more refined in the process, but stayed true to its original sports car spirit.

THE FIRST PROTOTYPE REAR-END TREATMENTS FEATURED FADDISH FINS THAT WERE REPLACED BY A CLASSIC ROUND RUMP

UPDATED WEATHER EQUIPMENT WAS AN IMPROVEMENT ON EARLIER EFFORTS, WHICH TOOK TWO JUGGLERS 10 MINUTES TO ERECT

YMO 37F

BENTLEY R-Type Continental

One of the world's all-time great cars

IN ITS DAY the Bentley Continental, launched in 1952, was the fastest production four-seater in the world and acclaimed as "a modern magic carpet which annihilates distance"; 43 years later, it is rightly considered one of the greatest cars of all time. Designed for the English country gentleman, it was understated but had a lithe, sinewy beauty rarely seen in other cars of its era. Rolls-Royce's brief was to create a fast touring car for plutocrat customers, and to do that they had to reduce both size and weight. Aluminum construction helped the weight, while wind tunnel testing created that slippery shape. Those emergent fins at the back were not for decoration – they actually aided the car's directional stability. But such avant-garde development did not come cheap. In 1952, the R-Type Continental was the most expensive production car in the world at £7,608 – today's equivalent of almost $750,000.

> "Today, this exemplar of breeding and privilege stands as a resplendent memorial to the affluence and optimism of Fifties' Britain."

THE CONTINENTAL HAD AN EXCEPTIONAL RIDE – IT WAS A CAR THAT BEGGED YOU TO PRESS ITS ACCELERATOR TO THE FLOOR AND REASSURED YOU WITH ITS POWERFUL BRAKES

THE CONTINENTAL BEARS AN UNCANNY RESEMBLANCE TO A PININFARINA R-TYPE PROTOTYPE SHOWN AT THE 1948 PARIS SALON

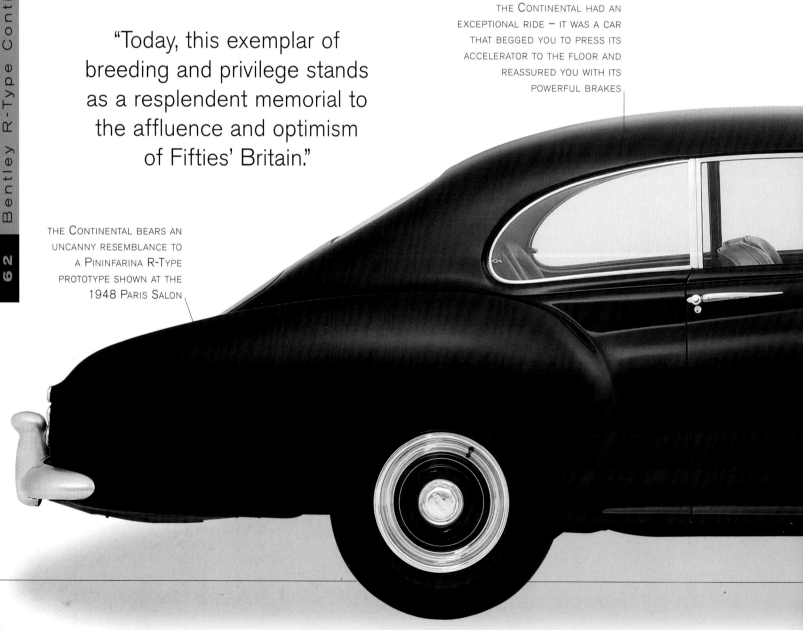

"The Continental spent much time in a wind tunnel to establish air drag during forward motion."

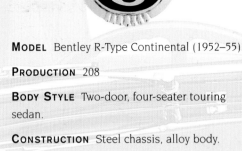

MODEL Bentley R-Type Continental (1952–55)

PRODUCTION 208

BODY STYLE Two-door, four-seater touring sedan.

CONSTRUCTION Steel chassis, alloy body.

ENGINES 4566cc or 4887cc straight-sixes.

POWER OUTPUT Never declared, described as "sufficient."

TRANSMISSION Four-speed synchromesh manual or auto option.

SUSPENSION Independent front with wishbones and coil springs, rear live axle with leaf springs.

BRAKES Front discs, rear drums.

MAXIMUM SPEED 115 mph (185 km/h)

0–60 MPH (0–96 km/h) 13.5 sec

0–100 MPH (0–161km/h) 36.2 sec

A.F.C. 19.4 mpg (6.9 km/l)

INTERIOR The beautifully detailed dashboard mirrored the Continental's exterior elegance. The first R-Types had manual gearboxes with a right-hand floor-mounted stick, thus reflecting the car's sporty character. Later models were offered with automatic boxes as an option and were equipped on 46 of the 208 cars.

ENGINE Continentals used a 4-liter straight-six engine of 4566cc, which was increased to 4887cc in May 1954 and was known as the big bore engine. Carburation was by two SU HD8 units. It allowed the car to reach 50 mph (80 km/h) in first gear and almost 120 mph (193 km/h) in top.

"Such was the lure, and indeed the cost, of the Continental that it was first introduced on an export-only basis."

FRONT FOG LIGHTS USED TO BE KNOWN AS "PASS LIGHTS" FOR PASSING

CLASSIC GOTHIC RADIATOR SHELL WAS CONSIDERED FAR MORE SPORTY THAN ROLLS-ROYCE'S DORIC EXAMPLE

UKL 109

In 1920 W.O., as he was called, built the first chassis and engine for a three-liter Bentley car in London. But after selling 3,000 cars, and a series of Le Mans wins, the 1931 stock-market crash saw Bentley Motors in financial trouble, and they were bought out by Henry Royce. W.O. resigned in 1935 to become technical director of Lagonda.

PILLAR BOX REAR
WINDOW WAS A
THROWBACK TO
PREWAR CARS

GB

UKL 109

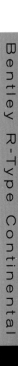

BENTLEY Flying Spur

Custom-built refinements with Rolls engineering

ARGUABLY THE MOST beautiful postwar Bentley, the Flying Spur was the first four-door Continental. Initially, Rolls-Royce would not allow builder H.J. Mulliner to use the name Continental, insisting it should only apply to two-door cars. After months of pressure from Mulliner, R.R. relented and allowed it to be known as a proper Continental. More than worthy of the hallowed name, the Flying Spur was launched in 1957, using the standard S1 chassis. In 1959 it inherited R.R.'s 220 bhp, oversquare, light-alloy V8, and by July 1962 the bodyshell was given the double headight treatment and upgraded into what some consider to be the best of the breed – the S3 Flying Spur. Subtle, understated, and elegant, Flying Spurs are rare and in their day were among the most admired and refined machines in the world. Although sharing much with the Standard Steel Bentley, they cost some $7,000 more than the stock item.

V8 HAD ALUMINUM CYLINDER HEADS, BLOCK, AND PISTONS

FPG 74B

MODEL S3 Bentley Continental H.J. Mulliner Flying Spur (1962–66)

PRODUCTION 291

BODY STYLE Four-door, five-seater.

CONSTRUCTION Aluminum body, separate steel cross-braced box section chassis.

ENGINE V8, 6230cc.

POWER OUTPUT Never officially declared.

TRANSMISSION Four-speed automatic.

SUSPENSION *Front*: independent coil springs and wishbones; *Rear*: semi-elliptic leaf springs.

BRAKES Four-wheel Girling drums.

MAXIMUM SPEED 115 mph (185 km/h)

0–60 MPH (0–96 km/h) 10.8 sec

0–100 MPH (0–161 km/h) 34.2 sec

A.F.C. 13.8 mpg (4.9 km/l)

"Although customers had to wait months for their cars, the finished product was considered the zenith of good taste and refinement."

INTERIOR INCLUDED CAREFULLY DETAILED SWITCHGEAR, THE FINEST LEATHER AND WALNUT, AND WEST OF ENGLAND CLOTH

BMW Isetta

Outstanding economy from the original bubble car

YOU'VE GOT TO ADMIT that BMW has come a long way since its Isetta "bubble car." One of the best-selling vehicles in Fifties Germany, the weird little economy runabout was just one of a range of frugal microcars designed to offer cheap mobility to war-wracked Europe. Originally built by ISO of Italy, BMW signed an agreement to produce the Isetta using its own 295cc motorcycle engine. The Isetta's claim to fame is that it was the first practical, usable, and successful variant of the "bubble car" breed. Sprightly, ferociously economical, and very fashionable, BMW Isettas were driven by Fifties well-heeled types and race-car drivers with a sense of humor. Despite costing as much as a full-size Morris Minor (*see pages* 426–29), they sold surprisingly well. Today, survivors are fiercely prized, and a mint example will actually sell for more than a restored MGB GT.

EASY ACCESS
When the front door was opened, the steering wheel swung clear for easier access. Dash and instruments moved too.

"The Isetta offered drivers fantastic economy at a time when fuel was like liquid gold."

ISETTA

MODEL BMW Isetta "Plus" (1959)

PRODUCTION 200,000 (total)

BODY STYLE Three-seater bubble.

CONSTRUCTION Steel body and chassis.

ENGINE BMW 295cc single cylinder.

POWER OUTPUT 13 bhp.

TRANSMISSION Four-speed manual.

SUSPENSION *Front*: independent; *Rear*: leaf springs.

BRAKES Girling hydraulic.

MAXIMUM SPEED 55 mph (89 km/h)

0–60 MPH (0–96 km/h) N/A

A.F.C. 80 mpg (28 km/l)

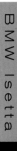

INTERIOR The interior was pretty austere, with just a single central speedometer and controls for the electric starter and indicators. Heater was an optional extra but standard on "Plus" models, which also boasted a map pocket attached to the inside of the front door.

ENGINE The four-stroke, air-cooled engine was well tried and gave a decent performance of 55 mph (89 km/h). Motorcycle heritage meant that reliability was strong too, with no major problems. The gearbox had four forward speeds, but a reverse gear cost extra.

ADVERTISING
Billed as the "perfect family second car," Isettas may have been cheap to run but cost $2,250 – more than a Ford Popular.

UNBELIEVABLY, A FACTORY-PREPARED ISETTA ACTUALLY COMPLETED THE GRUELING 1,000-MILE (1610-KM) MILLE MIGLIA RACE AT AN AVERAGE SPEED OF 49.6 MPH (79.8 KM/H)

CHROME EYEBROWS ON FRONT LIGHTS WERE A PERIOD ACCESSORY AND MADE THE BMW ISETTA'S FRONTAL ASPECT LOOK EVEN MORE LIKE A LITTLE FACE

SKINNY TIRES WERE LONG-LIFE DUNLOP TUBELESS AND THE SAME DIAMETER AS A BRITISH MINI'S

URBAN HEAVEN

The Isetta could be parked in the tightest of spaces, with occupants able to step straight out of the door and onto the sidewalk.

"Handling was surprisingly nimble, despite all that weight at the back and only three wheels."

THE MOTORCYCLE ENGINE GULPED AIR THROUGH A CRUDELY CUT VENT IN FRONT OF THE REAR WHEEL

THIS RARE "PLUS" EXAMPLE IS FINISHED IN THE CORRECT SHADE OF RIVIERA BLUE AND WAS REGISTERED IN MARCH 1959

6911 PO

BMW 507

A German beauty that almost broke the company

WHO WOULD HAVE thought that in the mid-Fifties BMW would have unveiled something as voluptuously beautiful as the 507. The company had a fine pre-World War II heritage that culminated in the crisp 328, but it did not resume car manufacturing until 1952, with the curvy, but slightly plump, six-cylinder 501 sedan. Then, at the Frankfurt show of late 1955, they hit us with the 507, designed by Count Albrecht Goertz. The 507 was a fantasy made real; not flashy, but dramatic and with poise and presence. BMW hoped the 507 would straighten out its precarious finances, winning sales in the lucrative American market. But the BMW's exotic looks and performance were more than matched by an orbital price. Production ended in March 1959 after just 252 – some say 253 – had been built. In fact, the 507 took BMW to the brink of financial oblivion; yet if that had been the last BMW it would have been a beautiful way to die.

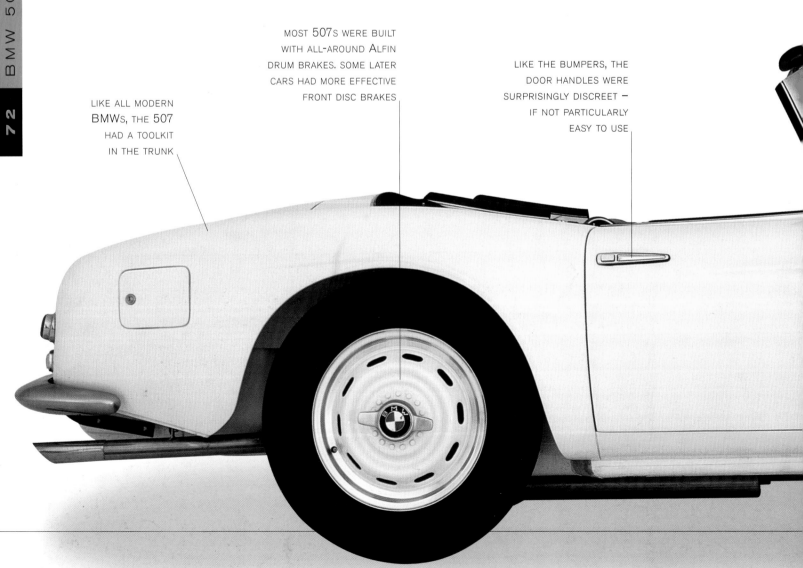

MOST 507S WERE BUILT WITH ALL-AROUND ALFIN DRUM BRAKES. SOME LATER CARS HAD MORE EFFECTIVE FRONT DISC BRAKES

LIKE THE BUMPERS, THE DOOR HANDLES WERE SURPRISINGLY DISCREET – IF NOT PARTICULARLY EASY TO USE

LIKE ALL MODERN BMWS, THE 507 HAD A TOOLKIT IN THE TRUNK

"You rarely see a 507 with its top raised, but it is simple to erect and remarkably handsome."

MODEL BMW 507 (1956–59)

PRODUCTION 252/3, most LHD

BODY STYLE Two-seater roadster.

CONSTRUCTION Box section and tubular steel chassis; aluminum body.

ENGINE All-aluminum 3168cc V8, two valves per cylinder.

POWER OUTPUT 150 bhp at 5000 rpm; some later cars 160 bhp at 5600 rpm.

TRANSMISSION Four-speed manual.

SUSPENSION *Front:* unequal-length wishbones, torsion-bar springs, and telescopic shock absorbers; *Rear:* live axle, torsion-bar springs.

BRAKES Drums front and rear; front discs and rear drums on later cars.

MAXIMUM SPEED 125 mph (201 km/h); 135–140 mph (217–225 km/h) with optional 3.42:1 final drive.

0–60 MPH (0–96 km/h) 9 sec

A.F.C. 18 mpg (6.4 km/l)

"Designer Albrecht Goertz's aluminum body is reminiscent of the contemporary – and slightly cheaper – Mercedes-Benz 300SL roadster."

INTERIOR The 507, unlike the contemporary 503, has a floor-mounted stick to operate the four-speed gearbox. On the dash, a clock is flanked by a speedo and tacho. There are gimmicky horn-pulls behind the steering wheel, but other features predicted later innovations; some cars had internally adjustable door mirrors.

ENGINE The 3.2-liter all-aluminum engine was light and powerful and pushed out 150 bhp in standard form. When linked to an optional 3:42 to 1 final drive ratio, souped-up 160 bhp versions were good for 140 mph (225 km/h). Twin Zenith carbs are the same as those of the contemporary Porsches.

EIGHT BMW STYLIZED PROPELLER ROUNDELS GRACED THE 507, NINE IF YOU INCLUDED THE BADGE IN THE CENTER OF THE STEERING WHEEL

THE 507'S BODY WAS AN ALL-ALUMINUM AFFAIR ATOP A SIMPLE TUBULAR CHASSIS

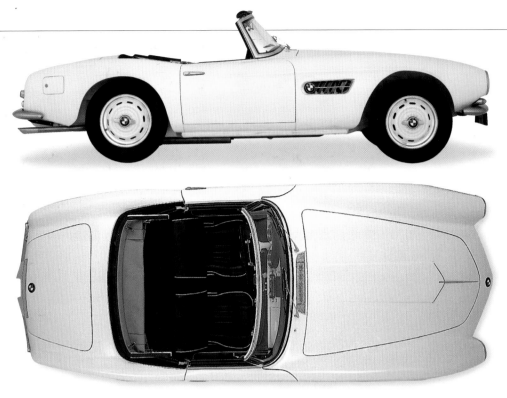

"As a drive, the 507 tended toward marked understeer; so instant was its throttle response that the tail easily spun out."

THE BMW HAD A BRISK, WHOLESOME BARK AND THE UNMISTAKABLE CREAMY WUFFLE OF A V8 CAME THROUGH THE EXHAUST

BMW 3.0CSL

Elegant tourer with a successful racing career

ONE LITTLE LETTER can make so much difference. In this case it is the L at the end of the name tag that makes the BMW 3.0CSL so special. The BMW CS pillarless coupes of the late Sixties and early Seventies were elegant and good-looking tourers. But add that L and you have a legend. The letter actually stands for "Leichtmetall," and when tacked to the rump of the BMW it amounts to warpaint. The original CSL of 1974 had a 2985cc engine developing 180 bhp, no front bumper, and a mixture of aluminum and thin steel body panels. In August 1972, a cylinder-bore increase took the CSL's capacity to 3003cc and allowed it into Group 2 for competition purposes. But it is the funky-fendered, so-called "Batmobile" homologation special that really boils the blood of boy racers. An ultimate road car, great racer, rare, short-lived, and high-priced, this charismatic, pared-down Beemer has got copy book classic credentials.

AIR VENTS BEHIND THE BMW REAR-PILLAR BADGE HELPED TO COOL THINGS DOWN IN THE CABIN

STANDARD TIRES WERE 195/70 14 MICHELIN XWXS. 7 IN (18 CM) LIGHT-ALLOY ALPINA WHEELS WERE COVERED BY CHROME-PLATED ARCH EXTENSIONS

MODEL BMW 3.0CSL (1971–74)

PRODUCTION 1,208 (all versions)

BODY STYLE Four-seater coupe.

CONSTRUCTION Steel monocoque, steel and aluminum body.

ENGINES 2985cc, 3003cc, or 3153cc inline six.

POWER OUTPUT 200 bhp at 5500 rpm (3003cc).

TRANSMISSION Four-speed manual.

SUSPENSION *Front*: MacPherson struts and antiroll bar; *Rear*: semitrailing swinging arms, coil springs, and antiroll bar.

BRAKES Servo-assisted ventilated discs front and rear.

MAXIMUM SPEED 135 mph (217 km/h) (3003cc)

0–60 MPH (0–96 km/h) 7.3 sec (3003cc)

0–100 MPH (0–161 km/h) 21 sec (3003cc)

A.F.C. 22–25 mpg (7.8–8.8 km/l)

INTERIOR British-spec CSLs, like this car, retained Scheel lightweight bucket seats but had carpets, electric windows (front and rear), power steering, and a sliver of wood. The steering wheel came straight out of the CS/CSi. The cabin was light and airy despite the black interior, though all that glass made it a hot ride.

ENGINE In genuine racing trim the Batmobile's 3.2-liter straight-six engine gave nearly 400 bhp and, for 1976, nearly 500 bhp with turbocharging. But road cars like this British-spec 3003cc 3.0CSL – increased from 2985cc for homologation purposes – gave around 200 bhp on fuel injection.

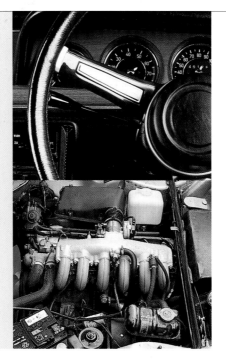

"For homologation purposes, at least 500 road cars had to be equipped with a massive rear spoiler – it was considered so outrageous that most were supplied for owners to attach at their discretion."

"LEICHTMETALL" MEANT THAT BODY PANELS ON THE CSL WERE MADE OF ALUMINUM AND THINNER-THAN-STANDARD STEEL

GERMAN-MARKET CSLS HAD NO FRONT BUMPER AND A FIBERGLASS REAR BUMPER; THIS CAR'S METAL ITEMS SHOW IT TO BE A BRITISH-SPEC MODEL

BMW M1

Acclaimed as one of the original supercars

THE M1 – A SIMPLE NAME, a simple concept. M stood for Motorsport GmbH, BMW's competition division; and the number one? Well, this was going to be a first; for this time BMW was not just going to develop capable racers from competent sedans and coupes. They were going to build a high-profile, win-all racer, with road-worthy versions basking in the reflected glory of on-track success. A prototype first ran in 1977, with the M1 entering production in 1978. By the end of manufacture in 1980, a mere 457 M1s had been built, making it one of the rarest and most desirable of modern BMWs. Though its racing career was only briefly distinguished, it is as one of the all-time ultimate road cars that the M1 stands out, for it is not just a 162 mph (261 km/h) "autobahnstormer." It is one of the least demanding supercars to drive, a testament to its fine engineering, and is in many ways as remarkable as the gorgeous 328 of the 1930s.

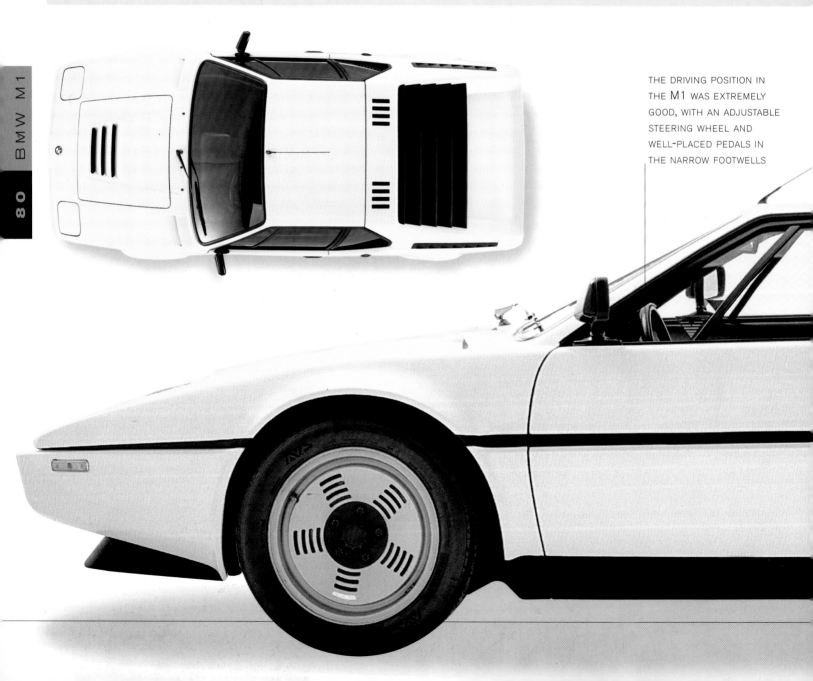

THE DRIVING POSITION IN THE M1 WAS EXTREMELY GOOD, WITH AN ADJUSTABLE STEERING WHEEL AND WELL-PLACED PEDALS IN THE NARROW FOOTWELLS

//M1

MODEL BMW M1 (1978–80)

PRODUCTION 457, all LHD

BODY STYLE Two-seater mid-engined sports.

CONSTRUCTION Tubular steel space-frame with fiberglass body.

ENGINE Inline six, four valves per cylinder, dohc 3453cc.

POWER OUTPUT 277 bhp at 6500 rpm.

TRANSMISSION Combined ZF five-speed gearbox and limited slip differential.

SUSPENSION Coil springs, wishbones, and Bilstein gas-pressure telescopic shock absorbers front and rear.

BRAKES Servo-assisted ventilated discs all around.

MAXIMUM SPEED 162 mph (261 km/h)

0–60 MPH (0–96 km/h) 5.4 sec

A.F.C. 24–30 mpg (8.5–10.6 km/l)

BUICK Roadmaster (1949)

A voluptuous model with bold styling motifs

THE '49 ROADMASTER took the market's breath away. With a low silhouette, straight hood, and fastback styling, it was a poem in steel. The first Buick with a truly new postwar look, the '49 was designed by Ned Nickles using GM's new C-body. It also boasted two bold new styling motifs: Ventiports and an aggressive 25-tooth "Dollar Grin" grille. Harley Earl's aesthetic of aeronautical entertainment worked well, and Buick notched up nearly 400,000 sales that year. Never mind that the windshield was still two-piece, that there was no power steering, and that the engine was a straight-eight – it looked gorgeous and came with the new Dynaflow automatic transmission. The Roadmaster, like the '49 Cadillac (*see pages* 102–05), was a seminal car that gave Buick a distinction never seen before. It was also the first flowering of the most flamboyant decade of car design ever seen.

GUN-SIGHT HOOD ORNAMENT, BUCKTOOTH GRILLE, AND VENTIPORTS WERE FLASHY STYLING METAPHORS THAT WOULD BECOME FAMOUS BUICK TRADEMARKS

OPEN VENTIPORTS WERE SEALED MIDYEAR BECAUSE A HIGH-SCHOOL PRINCIPAL COMPLAINED THAT MALE STUDENTS USED THOSE ON HIS ROADMASTER TO RELIEVE THEMSELVES

Roadmaster

BUICK

"For years GM's copywriters crowed that 'when better cars are built, Buick will build them.'"

MODEL 1949 Buick Roadmaster Series 70 Sedanette

PRODUCTION 18,415 (1949)

BODY STYLE Two-door fastback coupe.

CONSTRUCTION Steel body and chassis.

ENGINE 320cid straight-eight.

POWER OUTPUT 150 bhp.

TRANSMISSION Two-speed Dynaflow automatic.

SUSPENSION Front and rear coil springs.

BRAKES Front and rear drums.

MAXIMUM SPEED 100 mph (161 km/h)

0-60 MPH (0–96 km/h) 17 sec

A.F.C. 20 mpg (7 km/l)

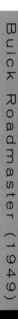

INTERIOR The instrument panel was new for '49 and described as "pilot centered" because the speedo was positioned straight ahead of the driver through the steering wheel. The design was taken from Harley Earl's Buick Y-Job. The driver looked through a split windshield with curved glass.

ENGINE The Roadie had a Fireball straight-eight cast-iron 320cid engine that always started with a roar because the starter switch was connected to the accelerator and engaged by depressing the pedal all the way to the floor. The Fireball pushed out 150 horses and breathed through Stromberg or Carter carbs.

CHEAPER BUICKS HAD ONLY THREE VENTIPORTS; THE LAVISH ROADMASTER HAD FOUR

THE CLASSIC VERTICAL GRILLE BARS WERE REPLACED FOR THE 1955 MODEL YEAR

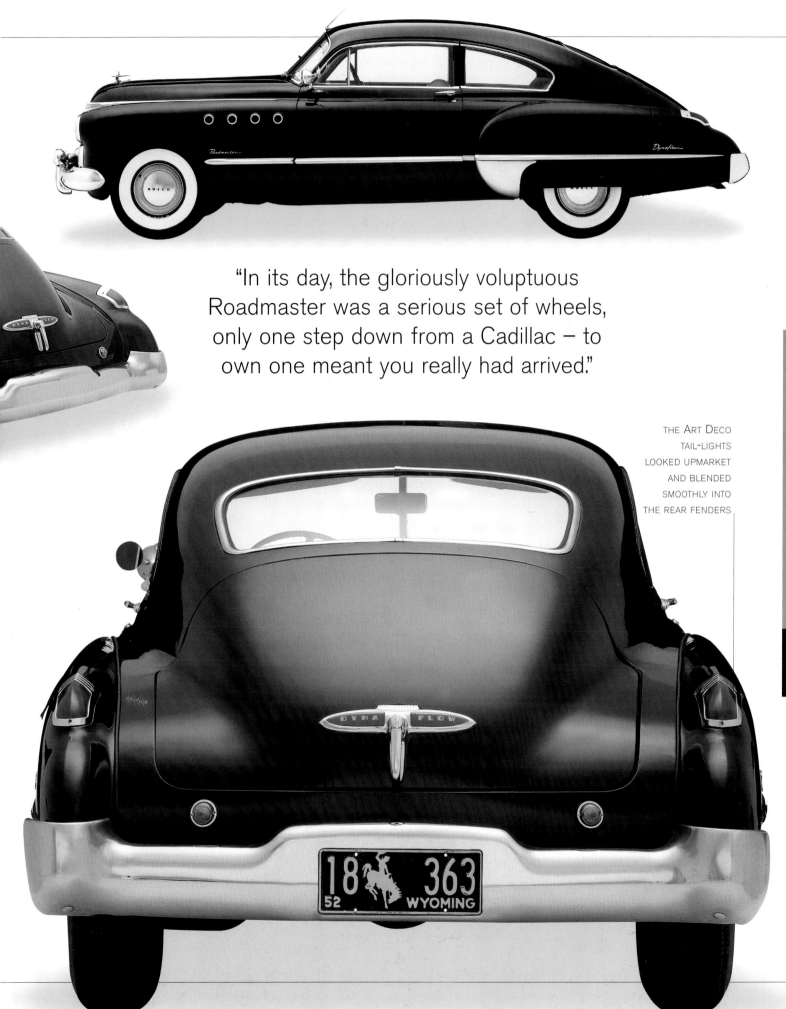

"In its day, the gloriously voluptuous Roadmaster was a serious set of wheels, only one step down from a Cadillac – to own one meant you really had arrived."

THE ART DECO
TAIL-LIGHTS
LOOKED UPMARKET
AND BLENDED
SMOOTHLY INTO
THE REAR FENDERS

BUICK Roadmaster (1957)

Individuality sacrificed for trendy jet-age styling

IN 1957, AMERICA was gearing up for the Sixties. Little Richard screamed his way to the top with "Lucille," and Elvis had nine hits in a row. Jack Kerouac penned his immortal novel On the Road, inspiring carloads of Americans to seek the adman's "Promised Land" along Ike's new interstates. Fins and chrome were applied with a trowel, and General Motors spent several hundred million dollars refashioning its Buick model line. The Roadmaster of 1957 was low and mighty, a massive 17 ft 11 in (5.46 m) long and 6 ft (1.83 m) wide. Power was up to 300 bhp, along with trendy dorsal fins, sweepspear body moldings, and a trio of chrome chevrons on the rear quarters. Four Ventiports, a Buick trademark harking back to the original 1949 Roadmaster, still graced the sweeping front fenders. But America did not take to Buick's new look, particularly some of the Roadmaster's fashionable jet-age design motifs.

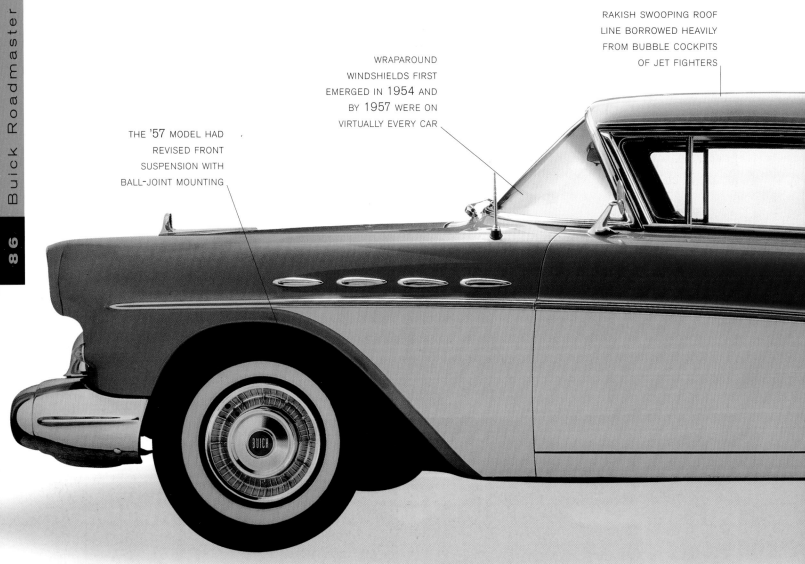

RAKISH SWOOPING ROOF LINE BORROWED HEAVILY FROM BUBBLE COCKPITS OF JET FIGHTERS

WRAPAROUND WINDSHIELDS FIRST EMERGED IN 1954 AND BY 1957 WERE ON VIRTUALLY EVERY CAR

THE '57 MODEL HAD REVISED FRONT SUSPENSION WITH BALL-JOINT MOUNTING

MODEL Buick Roadmaster (1957)

PRODUCTION 36,638 (1957)

BODY STYLE Two-door, five-seater hardtop coupe.

CONSTRUCTION X-braced chassis with steel body.

ENGINE V8, 364cid.

POWER OUTPUT 250 bhp at 4400 rpm (standard tune).

TRANSMISSION Dynaflow two-speed automatic.

SUSPENSION Independent coil springs.

BRAKES Hydraulic servo drums all around.

MAXIMUM SPEED 112 mph (180 km/h)

0–60 MPH (0–96 km/h) 10.0 sec

0–100 MPH (0–161 km/h) 21.2 sec

A.F.C. 12 mpg (4.2 km/l)

INTERIOR Roadmaster standard special equipment included a Red Liner speedometer, a glove compartment lamp, a trip mileage indicator, and a color-coordinated dash panel. From 1955 Roadmasters could be ordered with a choice of 10 types of interior trim.

ENGINE The hot Buick's 5.9-liter V8 pushed out 300 bhp; it was capable of 112 mph (180 km/h) and could hit 60 mph (96 km/h) in 10 seconds. Dynaflow transmission had variable pitch blades that changed their angle like those of an airplane propeller. The V8 had a compression ratio of 10:1.

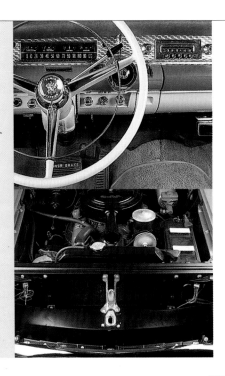

"Aircraft design exerted a big influence on automotive styling in the Fifties, and the '57 Roadmaster was no exception."

GIANT CHROME PROTUBERANCES SUGGESTED JET-TURBINE POWER

POWER-ASSISTED STEERING AND DYNAFLOW AUTOMATIC TRANSMISSION BECAME STANDARD ON ALL ROADMASTERS FROM 1953

1957 SAW THE RETURN OF THE CLASSIC VERTICAL BARS, WHICH HAD BEEN DROPPED IN 1955

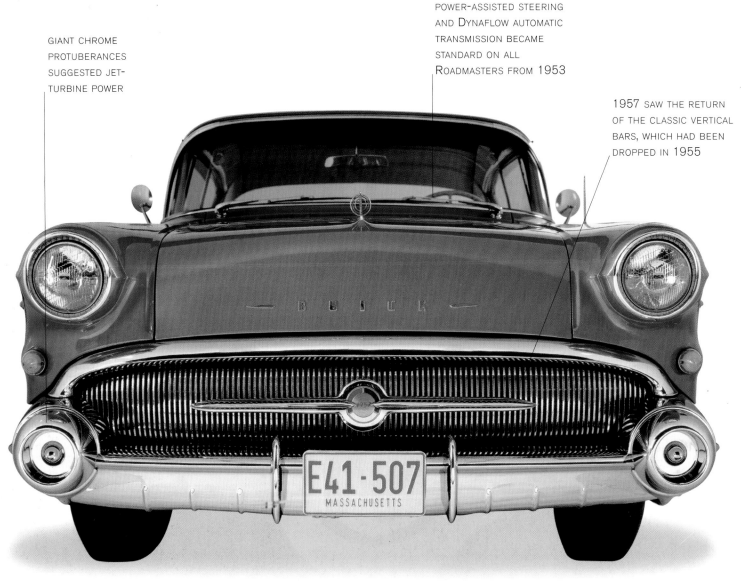

E41-507
MASSACHUSETTS

FIN FASHION
The Roadmaster showed that tailfin fashion was rising to ridiculous heights. Unfortunately, by '57 that chaste individuality had gone, and the Roadmaster looked very much like every other American car.

"The Roadmaster was one of Buick's most luxurious models and wore its hood ornament with pride."

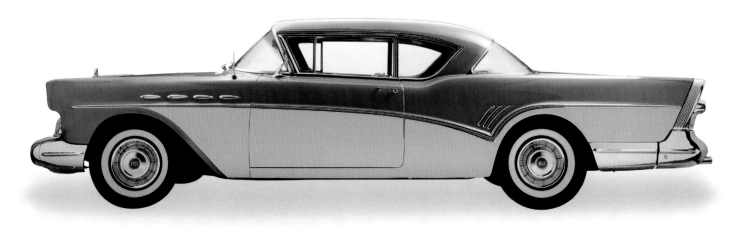

THE CAVERNOUS TRUNK COULD ACCOMMODATE ALMOST ANYTHING YOU COULD BUY AT THE DEPARTMENT STORE IN THE CONSUMER-DRIVEN FIFTIES

SMALL TINTED REAR WINDOW DIDN'T OFFER MUCH ASSISTANCE TO THE DRIVER WHEN REVERSING

ROADMASTER

E41-507
MASSACHUSETTS

BUICK Limited Riviera

The glitziest of the company's models to date

WHEN YOUR FORTUNES are flagging, you pour on the chrome. As blubbery barges go, the '58 Limited has to be one of the gaudiest. With a length of 19 ft (5.78 m) and tipping the scales at two tons, the Limited is empirical proof that 1958 was really not Buick's happiest year. Despite all that twinkling kitsch and the reincarnated Limited badge last seen in 1942, the bulbous Buick bombed. For a start, GM's Dynaflow automatic transmission was not up to Hydra-Matic standards, the Limited's brakes were reluctant to work, and its air suspension system turned out to be unreliable. Furthermore, in what was a recession year for the industry, the Limited had been priced into Cadillac territory – $33 more than the Series 62. Total production for the Limited in 1958 was a very limited 7,436 units. By the late Fifties, Detroit had lost its way, and the '58 Limited was on the road to nowhere.

> "Buick's answer to an aircraft carrier was a riot of ornamentation. At rest, the Limited looked like it needed a fifth wheel to support that weighty rear overhang."

AS WELL AS THIS FOUR-DOOR RIVIERA, THE 700 SERIES ALSO INCLUDED A TWO-DOOR VERSION AND A CONVERTIBLE

AIR-POISE SUSPENSION WAS AN OPTION THAT USED PRESSURIZED AIR BLADDERS FOR A SUPPOSEDLY SMOOTH HYDRAULIC RIDE. THE SYSTEM OFTEN FAILED, HOWEVER, AND LITERALLY LET ITSELF DOWN

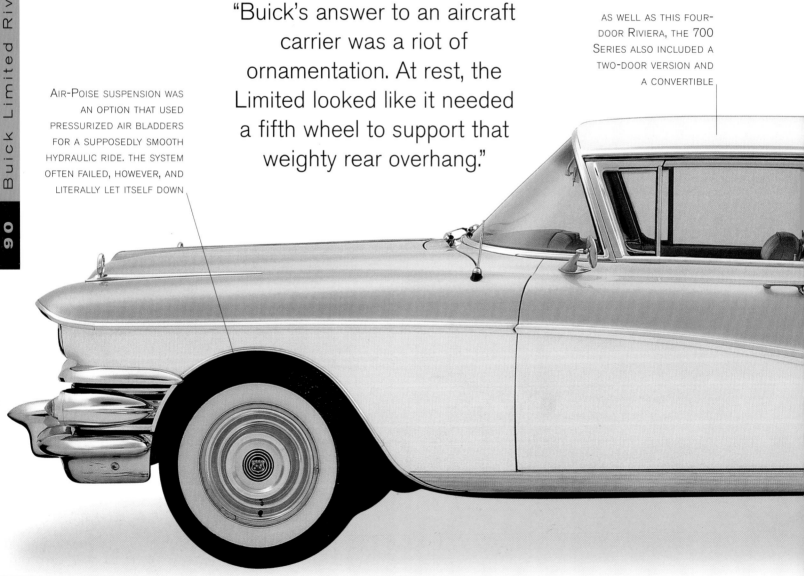

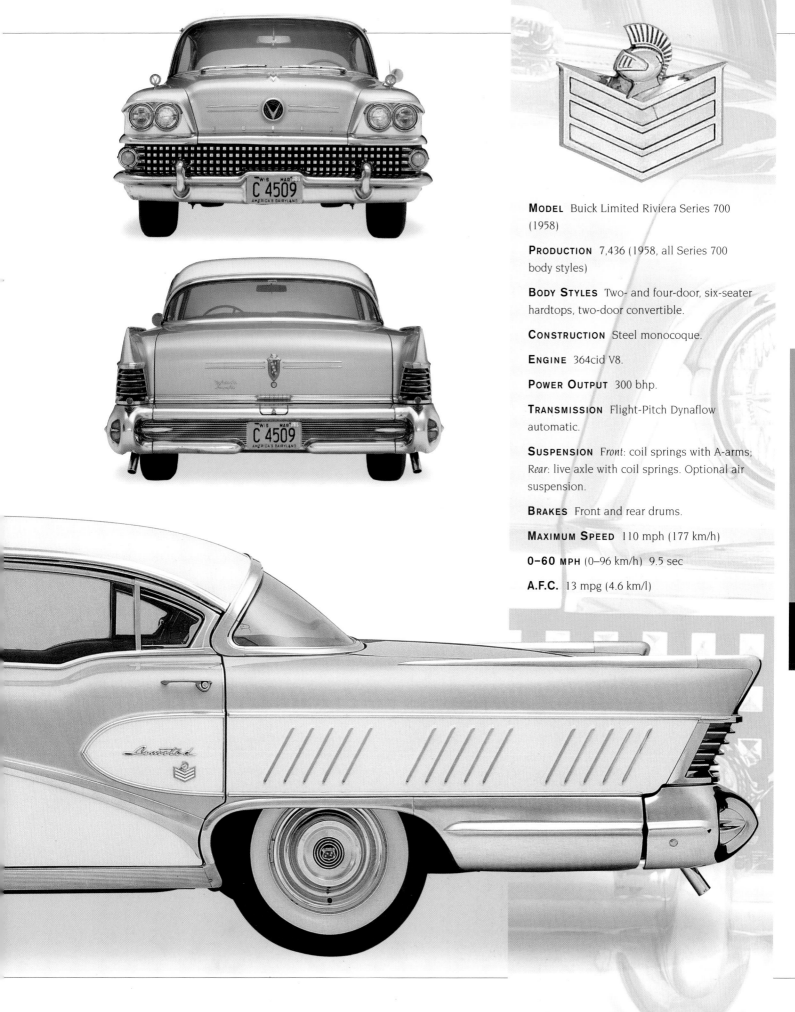

MODEL Buick Limited Riviera Series 700 (1958)

PRODUCTION 7,436 (1958, all Series 700 body styles)

BODY STYLES Two- and four-door, six-seater hardtops, two-door convertible.

CONSTRUCTION Steel monocoque.

ENGINE 364cid V8.

POWER OUTPUT 300 bhp.

TRANSMISSION Flight-Pitch Dynaflow automatic.

SUSPENSION *Front*: coil springs with A-arms; *Rear*: live axle with coil springs. Optional air suspension.

BRAKES Front and rear drums.

MAXIMUM SPEED 110 mph (177 km/h)

0–60 MPH (0–96 km/h) 9.5 sec

A.F.C. 13 mpg (4.6 km/l)

INTERIOR Power steering and brakes were essential and came as standard on the Limited Riviera. Other standard equipment included an electric clock, cigarette lighters, and electric windows. Interiors were trimmed in gray cloth and vinyl or Cordaveen. Seat cushions had Double-Depth foam rubber.

ENGINE The valve-in-head B12000 engine kicked out 300 horses, with a 364 cubic inch displacement. These specifications were respectable enough on paper, but on the road the Limited was too heavy to be anything other than sluggish. Which wasn't a bad thing considering that the brakes weren't too good.

FENDER ORNAMENTS MAY LOOK ABSURD BUT WERE USEFUL IN PARKING THE BUICK'S HUGE GIRTH

THE "FASHION-AIRE DYNASTAR" GRILLE CONSISTED OF NO FEWER THAN 160 CHROME SQUARES, EACH WITH FOUR POLISHED FACETS

WIS MAR 58
C 4509
AMERICA'S DAIRYLAND

"Unique to the Limited were 15 utterly pointless chrome slashes down both rear fenders."

THE TRUNK WAS BIG ENOUGH TO HOUSE A FOOTBALL TEAM

THE BUICK'S BUTT WAS A CONFUSED JUMBLE OF BOSOMY CURVES, SLANTING FINS, AND HORIZONTAL FLASHINGS

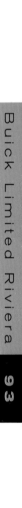

BUICK Riviera (1964)

America's answer to the Bentley Continental

In '58, so the story goes, GM's design supremo Bill Mitchell was entranced by a Rolls-Royce he saw hissing past a London hotel. "What we want," said Mitchell, "is a cross between a Ferrari and a Rolls." By August 1960, he'd turned his vision into a full-size clay mock-up. One of the world's most handsome cars, the original '63 Riviera locked horns with Ford's T-Bird and was GM's attempt at a "Great New American Classic Car." And it worked. Separate and elegant, the Riv was a clever amalgam of razor edges and chaste curves, embellished by just the right amount of chrome. Beneath the exquisite lines were a cross-member frame, a 425cid V8, power brakes, and a two-speed Turbine Drive tranny. In the interests of exclusivity, Buick agreed that only 40,000 would be made each year. With ravishing looks, prodigious performance, and the classiest image in town, the Riv ranks as one of Detroit's finest confections.

"The Riv pandered to Ivy League America's obsession with aristocratic European thoroughbreds like Aston Martin, Maserati, and Jaguar."

RELATIVELY COMPACT, THE RIVIERA WAS CONSIDERABLY SHORTER AND LIGHTER THAN OTHER BIG BUICKS

OPTIONAL WHITEWALLS AND FORMULA FIVE CHROME-LOOK STEEL WHEELS MADE A CUTE CAR EVEN CUTER

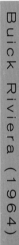

MODEL Buick Riviera (1964)

PRODUCTION 37,958 (1964)

BODY STYLE Two-door hardtop coupe.

CONSTRUCTION Steel body and chassis.

ENGINE 425cid V8.

POWER OUTPUT 340–360 bhp.

TRANSMISSION Two- or three-speed automatic.

SUSPENSION Front and rear coil springs.

BRAKES Front and rear drums.

MAXIMUM SPEED 120–125 mph (193–201 km/h)

0–60 MPH (0–96 km/h) 7.7 sec

A.F.C. 12–16 mpg (4.2–5.7 km/l)

Buick Riviera (1964)

95

INTERIOR The sumptuous Riv was a full four-seater, with the rear seat divided to look like buckets. The dominant V-shaped center console mushroomed from between the front seats to blend into the dashboard. The car's interior has a European ambience that was quite uncharacteristic for the period. In addition, the substantial trunk could take two sets of golf clubs with ease.

ENGINE '64s had a 425cid Wildcat V8 that could be tickled up to 360 horses, courtesy of dual four-barrels. *Car Life* magazine tested a '64 Riv with the Wildcat unit and stomped to 60 mph (96 km/h) in a scintillating 7.7 seconds. Buick sold the tooling for the old 401 to Rover, which used it to great success in its Range Rover. The Gran Sport option had limited slip diff, and "Giro-Poise" roll control.

CONWAY TWITTY, THE CROONER OF SUCH TUNES AS *IT'S ONLY MAKE BELIEVE*, OWNED THE '64 RIV ON THESE PAGES, ADDING HIS OWN LICENSE PLATE

'63 AND '64 RIVS HAVE CLASSIC EXPOSED DOUBLE HEADLIGHTS. '65 MODELS HAD HEADLIGHTS THAT WERE HIDDEN BEHIND ELECTRICALLY OPERATED, CLAMSHELL DOORS

AMERICA'S DAIRYLAND
TWITTY
JAN WISCONSIN

"Superbly understated, razor-edged styling made for a clean, crisp-looking machine. The rear view was a study in simplicity."

Vice-President of GM's styling department, and the man behind the Buick Riviera, Oldsmobile Tornado, and Mako Shark Corvette, Bill Mitchell learned all about cars from his Buick dealer father. Creator of the 1938 Cadillac Sixty Special, Mitchell was a close protegé of Harley Earl and is widely credited for giving American cars of the Sixties their wide, low stance. However, his tenure at GM through the Seventies meant he was blamed for the era's bland design. He hated the fashion for downsizing and retired in 1977, setting up a consultancy working for Goodyear and Yamaha.

ONE OPTIONAL EXTRA WAS A REMOTE-CONTROLLED TRUNK LID, WHICH WAS PRETTY NEAT FOR '64

BUICK

AMERICA'S DAIRYLAND
TWITTY
JAN WISCONSIN 85

BUICK Riviera (1971)

Controversial styling on a classic coupe

THE '63 RIVIERA had been one of Buick's best-sellers, but by the late Sixties it was lagging far behind Ford's now-luxurious Thunderbird. However, the Riviera easily outsold its stablemate, the radical front-wheel drive Toronado; but for '71 Buick upped the stakes by unveiling a new Riviera that was a little bit special. The new model had become almost a caricature of itself, now bigger and more brash than it ever was before. Handsome and dramatic, the "boat-tail," as it was nicknamed, had its stylistic roots in the split rear-window Sting Ray of '63. It was as elegant as Jackie Onassis and as hard-hitting as Muhammad Ali. Its base price was $5,251, undercutting the archrival T-Bird by a wide margin. Designer Bill Mitchell nominated it as his favorite car of all time and, while sales hardly went crazy, at last Buick had a flagship model that was the envy of the industry. It was the coupe in which to make a truly stunning entrance.

SOFT-RAY TINTED GLASS HELPED KEEP THINGS COOL, WHILE SEATING COULD BE ALL-VINYL BENCH SEATS WITH CUSTOM TRIM OR FRONT BUCKETS

"The Riviera's styling may have been excessive, but it still made a capacious five-seater, despite the fastback roof line and massive rear window."

THE 455CID BLOCK COULD PUMP OUT 315 BHP AND REACH 60 MPH (96 KM/H) IN 8.4 SECONDS

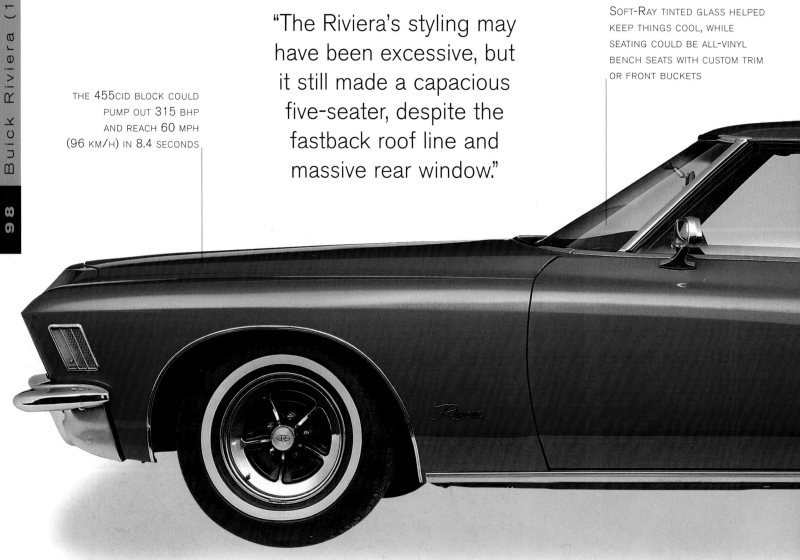

MODEL Buick Riviera (1971)

PRODUCTION 33,810 (1971)

BODY STYLE Two-door coupe.

CONSTRUCTION Steel body and box-section chassis.

ENGINE 455cid V8.

POWER OUTPUT 315–330 bhp.

TRANSMISSION Three-speed Turbo Hydra-Matic automatic.

SUSPENSION *Front:* independent coil springs; *Rear:* self-leveling pneumatic bellows over shocks.

BRAKES Front discs, rear drums.

MAXIMUM SPEED 125 mph (201 km/h)

0–60 MPH (0–96 km/h) 8.4 sec

A.F.C. 12–15 mpg (4.2–5.3 km/l)

INTERIOR Although the Seventies cabin was plush and hedonistic, it was more than a little plasticky. After 1972, the rear seat could be split 60/40 – pretty neat for a coupe. The options list was infinite and you could swell the car's sticker price by a small fortune. Tilt steering wheel came as standard.

ENGINE The Riviera came with GM's biggest mill, the mighty 455. The even hotter Gran Sport option made the massive V8 even smoother and quieter and offered big-buck buyers an impressive 330 bhp. One reviewer said of the GS-engined car, "there's nothing better made on these shores."

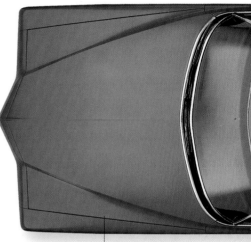

DARING LINES SUCH AS THESE HAD NEVER BEFORE BEEN SEEN ON A PRODUCTION CAR AND WERE CARRIED THROUGH TO THE THRUSTING, POINTED GRILLE

THE 122 IN (3.1 M) WHEELBASE MADE THE '71 BOAT-TAIL LONGER THAN PREVIOUS RIVIERAS

LAND OF ENCHANTMENT
AMY 589
72 NEW MEXICO USA

"The rear was a Bill Mitchell classic that had his trademark stamped all over it, the GM supremo having also designed the '63 Sting Ray coupe's rear."

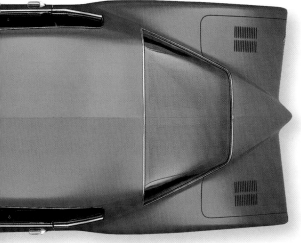

DARING REAR

The muscular rear flanks flow into the boat-tail rear. Despite this, critics were not unanimous in their praise for the design, and even Bill Mitchell found himself having to defend the '71 Riv's rear styling.

ELECTRIC TRUNK RELEASES ARE NOT A MODERN PHENOMENON — THEY WERE ON THE '71 RIVIERA'S OPTIONS LIST

ONE-PIECE REAR WINDSHIELD CURVED DOWNWARD, BUT THE VIEW FROM THE REAR-VIEW MIRROR WAS SLIGHTLY RESTRICTED

LAND OF ENCHANTMENT
AMY ☼ 589
72 NEW MEXICO USA

CADILLAC Series 62

One of America's outstanding postwar cars

WE OWE A LOT TO the '49 Cadillac. It brought us tailfins and a high-compression V8. Harley Earl came up with those trendsetting rear rudders, and John F. Gordon the performance engine. Between them they created the basic grammar of the postwar American car. In 1949, the one millionth Caddy rolled off the production line, and the stunning Series 62 Fastback or Sedanette was born. Handsome and quick, with Hydra-Matic transmission and a curved windshield, it was a complete revelation. Everybody, even the haughty British and Italians, nodded sagely in admiration, and at a whisker under $3,000, it stopped the competition dead in their tracks. As Cadillac ads boasted: "The new Cadillac is not only the world's most beautiful and distinguished car, but its performance is a challenge to the imagination." The American Dream and the finest era in American cars began with the '49 Cadillac.

THE FAMOUS STREAMLINED ART DECO GODDESS HOOD ORNAMENT FIRST APPEARED AFTER THE WAR AND CONTINUED UNCHANGED UNTIL 1956

TRENDSETTING NEW OHV 331 CID V8 DEVELOPED 162 BHP AND WEIGHED 188 LB (85 KG) LESS THAN THE RELIABLE BUT BULKY L-HEAD DESIGN

FRONT WINDOWS AND SEATS WERE HYDRAULICALLY OPERATED

"Bill Mitchell admitted that the P-38 Lockheed Lightning 'handed us a trademark nobody else had'."

MODEL Cadillac Series 62 (1949)

PRODUCTION 92,554 (1949, all body styles)

BODY STYLE Two-door, five-seater fastback.

CONSTRUCTION Steel body and chassis.

ENGINE 331cid V8.

POWER OUTPUT 162 bhp.

TRANSMISSION Four-speed Hydra-Matic automatic.

SUSPENSION *Front:* coil springs; *Rear:* leaf springs.

BRAKES Front and rear drums.

MAXIMUM SPEED 100 mph (161 km/h)

0–60 MPH (0–96 km/h) 13.4 sec

A.F.C. 17 mpg (6 km/l)

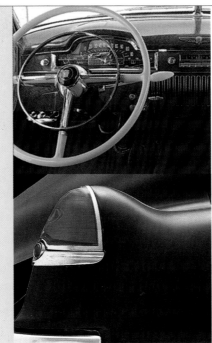

INTERIOR The '49 Cadillac's cabin was heavily chromed and oozed quality. Interior colors were either gray-blue or brown with wool carpets to match and a choice of leather or cloth seats. Steering was Saginaw, with standard four-speed Hydra-Matic automatic transmission.

FIN DETAIL The rear fins were inspired by the Lockheed P-38 airplane. They became a Caddy trademark and would reach a titanic height on '59 models. The gas cap was hidden under the taillight, a Cadillac trait since 1941. Other plane-inspired details included chrome slashes on the wheelarches.

"Cadillac advertisements trumpeted that the '49 was 'the world's most beautiful car,' and the elegant styling caught the public's imagination."

THE "V" EMBLEM BELOW THE CREST DENOTED V8 POWER; THE BASIC BADGE DESIGN REMAINED UNALTERED UNTIL 1952

PROTOTYPE ENGINE WAS FOUND TO BE PERFECT AFTER 541 HOURS' TESTING

THE GRILLE WAS HEAVIER ON THE '49 THAN ON THE '48

LG·136
NY EMPIRE STATE 57

The high priest of American car design, Harley Earl may have started his career styling cars for the stars in Hollywood, but it was his move to GM, Detroit, which made him synonymous with the excess, show, and glamour of Fifties USA. Earl gave the American car its attitude and confidence, turning cars into objects of desire.

AMONG MINOR DESIGN CHANGES FROM 1948 WAS THE MORE SQUARED-OFF REAR

LG·136
NY EMPIRE STATE 57

Cadillac Series 62

105

CADILLAC Eldorado (1953)

The first-of-kind and possibly the best

FOR 1950s AMERICA, cars did not come much more glamorous than the 1953 Eldorado. "A car apart – even from other Cadillacs," assured the advertising copy. The first Caddy to bear the Eldo badge, it was seen as the ultimate and most desirable American luxury car, good enough even for Marilyn Monroe and Dwight Eisenhower. Conceived as a limited edition, the '53 brought avant-garde styling cues from Harley Earl's Motorama Exhibitions. Earl was Cadillac's inspired chief designer, while Motorama were yearly futuristic car shows where his whims of steel took on form. At a hefty $7,750, nearly twice as much as the regular Cadillac Convertible and five times as much as an ordinary Chevrolet, the '53 was special. In 1954, Cadillac cut the price by half and soon Eldorados were leaving showrooms like heat-seeking missiles. Today collectors regard the '53 as the one that started it all – the first and most fabulous of the Eldorados.

"As Cadillac's finest flagship, the Eldorado had image by the bucketful. The 331 cubic inch V8 was the most powerful yet, and the body line was ultrasleek."

AT THE TIME THE '53 WAS AMERICA'S MOST POWERFUL CAR, WITH A CAST-IRON V8, FOUR-BARREL CARBURETOR, AND WEDGE CYLINDER HEAD

MODEL Cadillac Eldorado Convertible (1953)

PRODUCTION 532 (1953)

BODY STYLE Five-seater convertible.

CONSTRUCTION Steel bodywork.

ENGINE 5424cc V8.

POWER OUTPUT 210 bhp at 4150 rpm.

TRANSMISSION Three-speed Hydra-Matic Dual-Range automatic.

SUSPENSION *Front:* independent MacPherson strut; *Rear:* live axle with leaf springs.

BRAKES Front and rear drums.

MAXIMUM SPEED 116 mph (187 km/h)

0-60 MPH (0–96 km/h) 12.8 sec

0-100 MPH (0–161 km/h) 20 sec

A.F.C. 14–20 mpg (5–7 km/l)

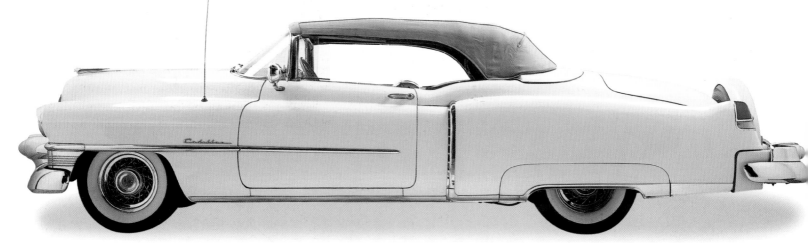

"With the standard convertible weighing 300 lb (136 kg) less, the Eldorado was actually the slowest of the Cadillacs."

SLICK DESIGN

The Orlon acrylic top disappeared neatly below a steel tonneau panel, giving the Eldorado a much cleaner uninterrupted line than other convertibles. In another neat design touch, the '53's body line made a dip near the door handle that imitated the cut-down doors of British sports cars.

THE HEAVILY CHROMED, HAND-OPERATED SWIVELING SPOTLIGHT DOUBLED AS A DOOR MIRROR

AIR-CONDITIONING BOOSTED THE CAR'S WEIGHT TO 4,800 LB (2,177 KG), BUT TOP SPEED WAS STILL A BRISK 116 MPH (187 KM/H)

CALIFORNIA
DRM CARS

"The twin exhausts emerge from the rear bumper – the beginnings of "jet-age" styling themes which would culminate in the riotous 1959 Cadillac."

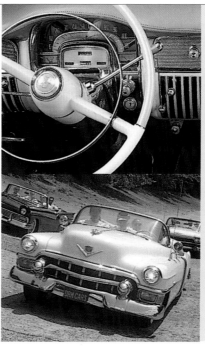

INTERIOR Standard equipment on the Eldo Convertible was hydraulic window lifts, leather and cloth upholstery, tinted glass, vanity and side mirrors, plus a self-tuning radio. Three-speed Hydra-Matic Dual-Range automatic transmission came as standard.

CADILLAC NAME Cadillac registered their famous shield motif in 1906, the coat of arms of Le Sieur Antoine de la Mothe Cadillac, a French knight born in 1658. The gold V in their badge is in honor of Cadillac's golden anniversary in 1952.

THE STANDARD CADILLAC WRAPAROUND WINDSHIELD WAS FIRST SEEN ON THE '53

THE TRUNK-MOUNTED SPARE WHEEL WAS AN AFTERMARKET CONTINENTAL TOURING KIT

COLORS AVAILABLE WERE ALPINE WHITE, AZTEC RED, AZURE BLUE, AND ARTISAN OCHRE

MISSILE-SHAPED PROTUBERANCES WERE KNOWN AS DAGMARS AFTER A LUSHLY UPHOLSTERED STARLET OF THE DAY

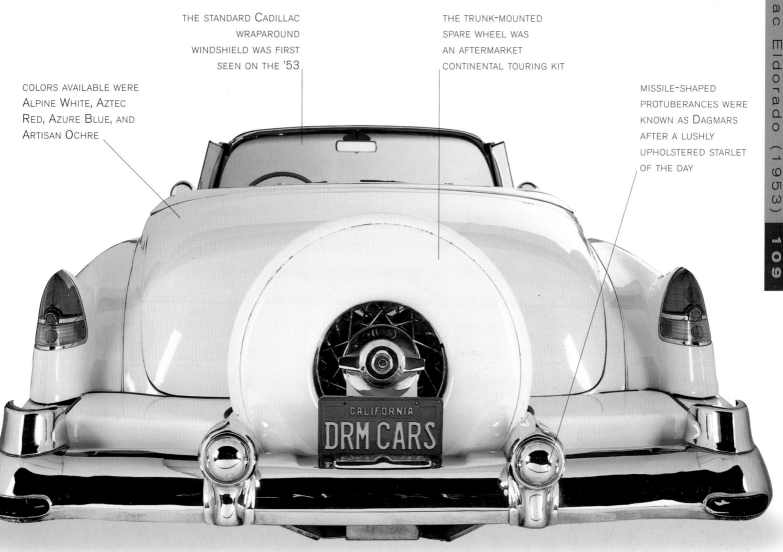

CADILLAC Convertible

A styling icon that personified the era

No CAR BETTER SUMS UP America at its peak than the 1959 Cadillac – a rocket-styled starship for orbiting the galaxy of new freeways in the richest and most powerful country on earth. With 42-inch (107-cm) fins, the '59 Cad marks the zenith of American car design. Two tons in weight, 20 ft (6.1 m) long, and 6 ft (1.83 m) wide, it oozed money, self-confidence, and power. Under a hood almost the size of Texas nestled an engine almost as big as California. But while it might have looked like it was jet-powered, the '59 handled like the *Exxon Valdez*. No matter. The '59 Cad will always be remembered as a glorious monument to the final years of shameless American optimism. And for a brief, hysterical moment the '59 was the preeminent American car, the ultimate in crazed consumerism. Not a car, but an exemplar of its time that says more about Fifties America than a trunk of history books. The '59 *was* the American Dream.

"With a hood the size of an aircraft carrier, the '59 Cad was perfect for a society where a car's importance was defined by the length of its nose."

THE PRICE TO PAY FOR THE EXCESSIVE HOOD WAS THAT THE FRONT END WAS NOTORIOUS FOR VIBRATION

WITH ITS TOP FURLED, THE CADILLAC HAD AN UNINTERRUPTED, DART-LIKE PROFILE

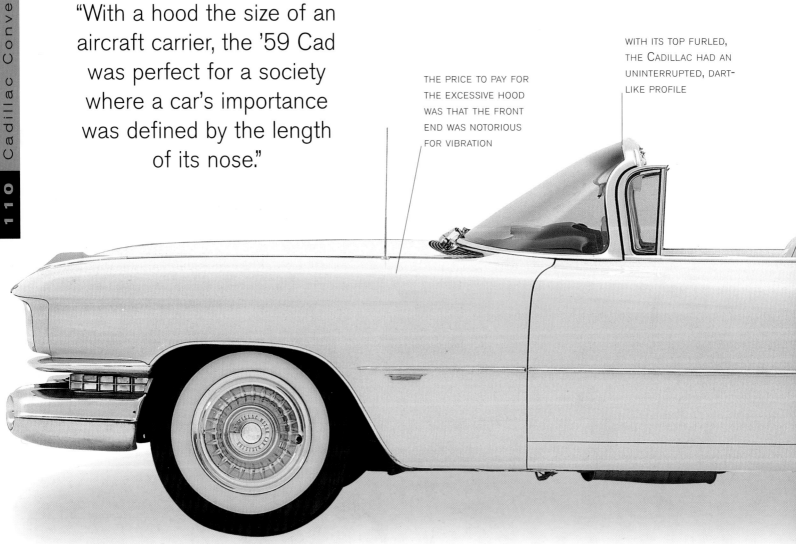

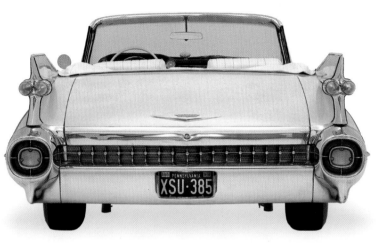

MODEL Cadillac Eldorado Convertible (1959)

PRODUCTION 11,130 (1959)

BODY STYLE Two-door, six-seater
convertible.

CONSTRUCTION X-frame chassis, steel body.

ENGINE 6.3-liter (390cid) V8.

POWER OUTPUT 325/345 bhp at 4800 rpm.

TRANSMISSION GM three-speed Hydra-Matic
automatic.

SUSPENSION All-around coil springs with
optional Freon-12 gas suspension.

BRAKES Four-wheel hydraulic power-assisted
drums.

MAXIMUM SPEED 112 mph (180 km/h)

0–60 MPH (0–96 km/h) 10.3 sec

0–100 MPH (0–161 km/h) 23.1 sec

A.F.C. 8 mpg (2.8 km/l)

CHROME WAISTLINE STRIP
GAVE BODY PANELS
PROTECTION AGAINST
JEALOUS CHEVROLETS

INTERIOR Detailing within the Caddy can only be described as baroque, with large helpings of chrome all around. As well as power brakes and steering, auto transmission, central locking, and tinted glass, you could also specify the automatic headlight dimming option.

ENGINE The monster 6.3-liter V8 engine had a cast-iron block, five main bearings, and hydraulic valve lifters, pushing out a not inconsiderable 325 bhp at 4800 rpm. The featherlight power steering required only three-and-a-half turns lock-to-lock, but you needed a 24-ft (7.3-m) turning circle.

"For one hysterical model year the Eldorado was the preeminent American automobile."

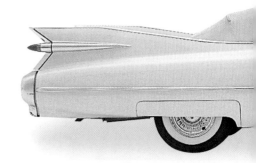

DOUBLE HEADLIGHTS WERE A STYLING ESSENTIAL ON ALL AMERICAN CARS OF THE PERIOD

STEEP, WRAPAROUND WINDSHIELD COULD HAVE COME OUT OF A FIGHTER PLANE

THE '59 HAD A BIG THIRST, WITH A 21-GALLON (95.5-LITER) GAS TANK, 2.9-GALLON (13-LITER) TRANSMISSION, AND 1.25-GALLON (5.7-LITER) RADIATOR CAPACITY

TOP FINNAGE

The '59's outrageous fins, which are the highest of any car in the world, are accentuated by its very low profile – 3 in (8 cm) lower than the '58 model's already modest elevation. The fins were calculated to lend lifeless steel the allure of speed and escape.

SEATS SAT 4 IN (10 CM) LOWER THAN THE '57 MODEL, ACCENTUATING THE '59'S CRAZY FINS

THE TRUNK WAS CAVERNOUS AND COULD HOLD FIVE WHEELS AND TIRES

THE CONTROVERSIAL FINS WERE KNOWN AS "ZAPS" AND WERE LATER RIDICULED

EXTRAVAGANT MOUNDS OF CHROME MIGHT LOOK LIKE TURBINES BUT CONCEALED BACKING LIGHTS

AUG PENNSYLVANIA 18 59
XSU·385

CADILLAC Eldorado (1976)

The last of the convertible leviathans

By 1976, CADILLACS had become so swollen that they plowed through corners, averaged 13 mpg (4.6 km/l), and were as quick off the line as an M24 tank. Despite a massive 500cid V8, output of the '76 Eldo was a lowly 190 horsepower, with a top speed of just 109 mph (175 km/h). Something had to change, and Cadillac's response had been the '75 Seville. But the '76 Eldo marked the end of an era for another reason – it was the last American convertible.

Cadillac was the final automobile manufacturer to delete the ragtop from their model lineup, and when it made the announcement that the convertible was to be phased out at the end of '76, the market fought to buy up the last 200. People even tried to cut in line by claiming they were distantly related to Cadillac's founder. One 72-year-old man in Nebraska bought six of them. A grand American institution had quietly passed away.

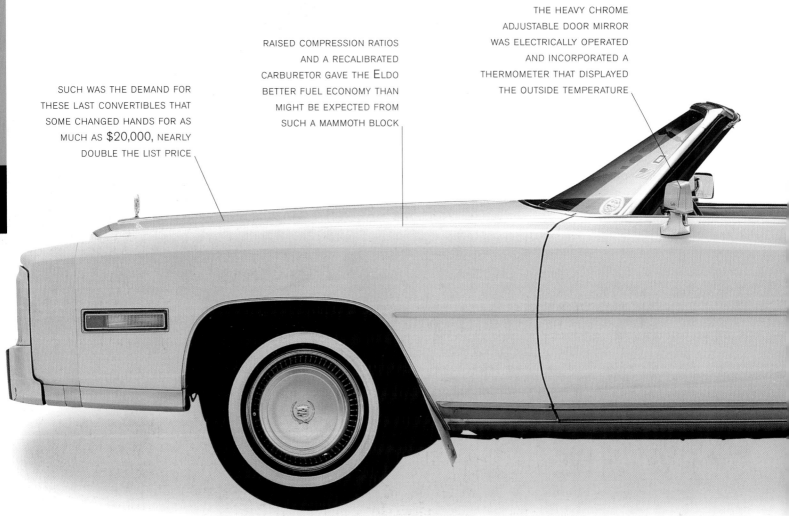

THE HEAVY CHROME ADJUSTABLE DOOR MIRROR WAS ELECTRICALLY OPERATED AND INCORPORATED A THERMOMETER THAT DISPLAYED THE OUTSIDE TEMPERATURE

RAISED COMPRESSION RATIOS AND A RECALIBRATED CARBURETOR GAVE THE ELDO BETTER FUEL ECONOMY THAN MIGHT BE EXPECTED FROM SUCH A MAMMOTH BLOCK

SUCH WAS THE DEMAND FOR THESE LAST CONVERTIBLES THAT SOME CHANGED HANDS FOR AS MUCH AS $20,000, NEARLY DOUBLE THE LIST PRICE

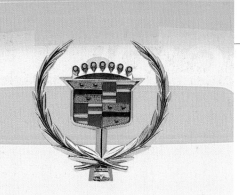

MODEL Cadillac Eldorado Convertible (1976)

PRODUCTION 14,000 (1976)

BODY STYLE Two-door, six-seater convertible.

CONSTRUCTION Steel body and chassis.

ENGINE 500cid V8.

POWER OUTPUT 190 bhp.

TRANSMISSION Three-speed Turbo Hydra-Matic automatic.

SUSPENSION Front and rear independent coil springs with automatic level control.

BRAKES Four-wheel discs.

MAXIMUM SPEED 109 mph (175 km/h)

0–60 MPH (0–96 km/h) 15.1 sec

A.F.C. 13 mpg (4.6 km/l)

INTERIORS COULD BE SPECIFIED
IN MERLIN PLAID, LUSH VELOUR,
MANSION KNIT, OR 11 TYPES OF
SIERRA GRAIN LEATHER

INTERIOR Technically advanced options were always Cadillac's forte. The Eldo was available with an airbag, Dual Comfort front seats with fold-down armrests, and a six-way power seat. In addition, the Twilight Sentinel headlights option operated the headlights according to outside conditions.

ENGINE Already strangled by emission pipes, the need to maximize every gallon meant that the Eldorado's massive 500cid V8 was embarrassingly lethargic when it came to speed. Even lower ratio rear axles were used to boost mileage. All Eldorados incorporated a catalytic convertor.

"The Cadillac shield harks back to 1650 and the original French Cadillac family. French model names were used in 1966 with the Calais and DeVille lines."

THE '76 CONVERTIBLE HAD BIG VITAL STATISTICS, MEASURING 225 IN (5.7 M) LONG AND 80 IN (2 M) WIDE

ELDOS COULD BE ORDERED IN 21 DIFFERENT BODY COLORS, WITH SIX CONVERTIBLE-TOP HUES

CADILLAC Seville

A downsizing success from the kings of excess

BY THE EARLY SEVENTIES, the corpulent Cadillac could average only 12 mpg (4 km/l). The energy crisis of '74 made the now-obese line a soft target, and suddenly high-profile establishment figures were hastily trading in their gas guzzlers for a BMW or Mercedes. A celebrated cartoon of the day showed a Caddy owner, hand over his eyes, pointing a revolver at his doomed Eldorado. Enter the Seville, which debuted in 1975 and was deliberately European in size, ride, handling, and economy. There was little ornamentation, and it was half a hood shorter than other Cadillacs. The press called it "the best Caddy for 26 years," even if it did have to suffer indignities like a diesel engine option and fuel-economy computer. A compromise car it may have been, but the downsized Caddy sold strongly from day one and helped Cadillac weather the worst recession since 1958. For a small car, the Seville was a portent of big things to come.

"Launch price of the Seville was $13,700, $6,000 less than a comparable Mercedes, and sales of the new car rightly worried the German manufacturer."

STANDARD EQUIPMENT INCLUDED TILT STEERING WHEEL, A FUEL-MONITORING SYSTEM, POWER SEATS, AND CONTROLLED-CYCLE WIPERS

OTHER NAMES CONSIDERED INCLUDED SIERRA, MEDICI, MINUET, COUNCILLOR, AND RENAISSANCE

MODEL Cadillac Seville (1978)

PRODUCTION 56,985 (1978)

BODY STYLE Four-door sedan.

CONSTRUCTION Steel unitary body.

ENGINE 350cid V8.

POWER OUTPUT 170 bhp.

TRANSMISSION Three-speed Turbo Hydra-Matic automatic.

SUSPENSION *Front:* coil springs; *Rear:* leaf springs with self-leveling ride.

BRAKES Front vented discs, rear drums.

MAXIMUM SPEED 115 mph (185 km/h)

0–60 MPH (0–96 km/h) 11.5 sec

A.F.C. 15.5 mpg (5.5 km/l)

Cadillac Seville **119**

INTERIOR Interior trim on the Seville was standard Dover cloth in seven colors, or optional Sierra Grain leather in 10 shades. A novel trip-computer option offered 11 digital displays indicating fuel load, inside and outside temperature, engine speed, and even estimated arrival time.

ENGINE The '75 Seville's standard 350cid Oldsmobile-sourced V8 engine had electronic fuel injection and was mounted on a steel subframe secured to the body with Isoflex damping cushions to reduce harshness and noise vibration. In 1978 came the addition of a 350cid diesel V8, Cadillac's first oil burner.

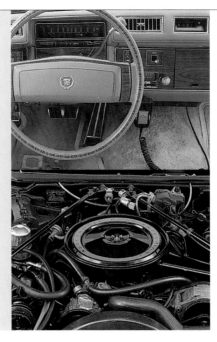

THE SEVILLE'S FRONT END WAS UNMISTAKABLY CADILLAC, WITH CROSS-HATCH GRILLE AND CLASSIC HOOD CREST ORNAMENT

THE SEVILLE HAD A DELCO "FREEDOM" BATTERY THAT NEVER NEEDED FILLING UP

"*Fortune* magazine named the Seville as one of the US's best-designed products."

THE GENTLY TAPERING REAR DECK, SIMPLE REAR LIGHT AND BUMPER TREATMENT, AND HIDDEN EXHAUSTS WERE A FAR CRY FROM THE EXCESS OF FULL-SIZED CADILLACS

BODIES USED ZINCROMETAL TO RESIST RUST AND WERE FINISHED WITH A GENEROUS SEVEN COATS OF PAINT

CHEVROLET Corvette

A fantasy show car turned into gorgeous reality

A CARICATURE OF A European roadster, the first Corvette of 1953 was more show than go. With typical arrogance, Harley Earl was more interested in the way it looked than the way it went. But he did identify that car consumers were growing restless and saw a huge market for a new type of auto opium. With everybody's dreams looking exactly the same, the plastic 'Vette brought a badly needed shot of designed-in diversity. Early models may have been cramped and slow, but they looked like they'd been lifted straight off a Motorama turntable, which they had. Building them was a nightmare though, and for a while GM lost money on each one. Still, nobody cared because Chevrolet now had a new image – as the company that came up with the first American sports car. And it was also proof positive that not everybody wanted to pilot slushy barges that stretched to half-a-block long.

SMALL BUMPERS MEANT THAT IMPACT PROTECTION MAY HAVE BEEN VESTIGIAL, BUT THE FIBERGLASS BODY TOOK KNOCKS WELL

THE ENGINE WAS MOUNTED WELL BACK WITHIN THE FRAME TO IMPROVE HANDLING

THE CLEVERLY PACKAGED FIBERGLASS BODY WAS RATHER TRICKY TO MAKE, WITH NO LESS THAN 46 DIFFERENT SECTIONS

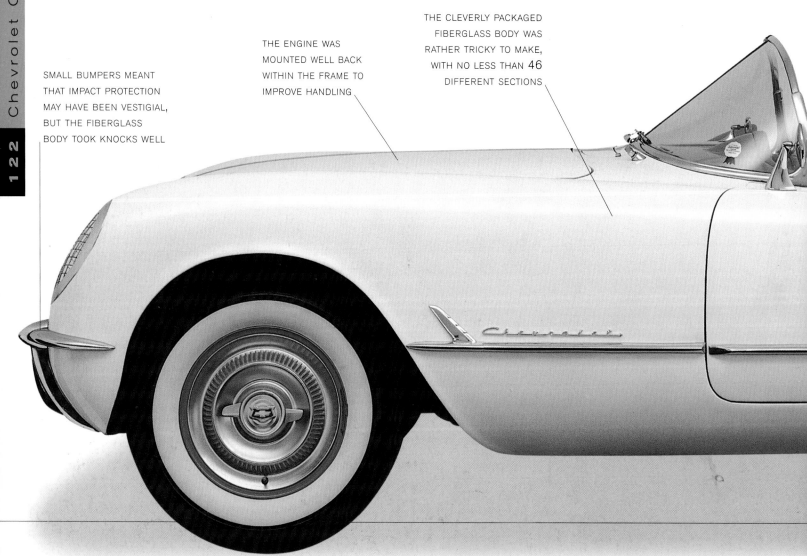

"Sales of the the first 'Vette were so poor that it nearly didn't make it past its first year."

MODEL Chevrolet Corvette (1954)

PRODUCTION 3,640 (1954)

BODY STYLE Two-door, two-seater sports.

CONSTRUCTION Fiberglass body, steel chassis.

ENGINE 235.5cid straight-six.

POWER OUTPUT 150 bhp.

TRANSMISSION Two-speed Powerglide automatic.

SUSPENSION *Front:* coil springs; *Rear:* leaf springs with live axle.

BRAKES Front and rear drums.

MAXIMUM SPEED 107 mph (172 km/h)

0-60 MPH (0–96 km/h) 8–12 sec

A.F.C. 20 mpg (7 km/l)

INTERIOR An aeronautical fantasy, the Corvette's dashboard had a futuristic, space-age feel. Not until 1958 was the row of dials repositioned to a more practical, front of the driver, location. Like the British sports cars it copied, the '54 'Vette's door handles lived on the inside of the car.

ENGINE The souped-up Blue Flame Six block may have had triple carburetors, higher compression, and a high-lift cam, but it was still old and wheezy – top speed was a very modest 107 mph (172 km/h). 'Vettes had to wait until 1955 for the V8 they deserved, when a base 265cid block was introduced.

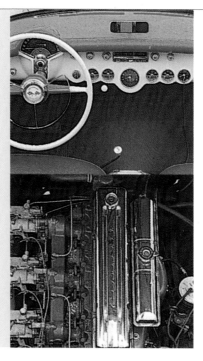

"The 'Vette's shape was based on the 1952 EX-122 show car, and was one of the few Motorama dream cars to go into production virtually unchanged."

HARLEY EARL ADMITTED THAT THE SHARK-TOOTH GRILLE WAS COPIED FROM CONTEMPORARY FERRARIS

STONE-GUARDS ON LIGHTS WERE CULLED FROM EUROPEAN RACING CARS, BUT WERE CRITICIZED FOR BEING TOO FEMININE

MN·1744
NY EMPIRE STATE 57

EARLY CARS HAD
LICENSE PLATES IN A
PLASTIC NICHE THAT
MISTED UP. CHEVROLET
INSERTED TWO BAGS
OF DESICCANT
MATERIAL TO ABSORB
THE MOISTURE

OUTBOARD-MOUNTED
REAR LEAF SPRINGS
HELPED CORNERING
STABILITY

MN·1744
NY EMPIRE STATE 57

CHEVROLET Bel Air

A stylish Fifties' icon dripping with nostalgia

CHEVROLET CALLED THEIR '57 line "sweet, smooth, and sassy," and the Bel Air was exactly what America wanted – a junior Cadillac. Finny, trim, and handsome, and with Ed Cole's Super Turbo-Fire V8, it boasted one of the first production engines to pump out one horsepower per cubic inch. Chevy copywriters screamed "the Hot One's even hotter," and Bel Airs became kings of the street. Production that year broke the 1½ million barrier and gave Ford the fright of its life. The trouble was that the "Hot One" was forced to cool it when the Automobile Manufacturers' Association urged carmakers to put an end to their performance hysteria. Today, the Bel Air is one of the most widely coveted US collector's cars and the perfect embodiment of young mid-Fifties America. In the words of the Billie Jo Spears song, "Wish we still had her today; the good love we're living, we owe it to that '57 Chevrolet."

"Immediately after it was introduced, the elegant and perfectly proportioned '57 Bel Air was rightly hailed as a design classic."

IF BUICK COULD ADD VENTIPORTS, SO COULD CHEVROLET, THOUGH THE BEL AIR'S ONLY LASTED A COUPLE OF YEARS

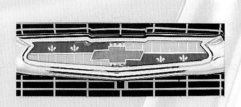

MODEL Chevrolet Bel Air Convertible (1957)

PRODUCTION 47,562 (1957)

BODY STYLE Two-door convertible.

CONSTRUCTION Steel body and box-section chassis.

ENGINES 265cid, 283cid V8s.

POWER OUTPUT 162–283 bhp (283cid V8 fuel injected).

TRANSMISSION Three-speed manual with optional overdrive, optional two-speed Powerglide automatic, and Turboglide.

SUSPENSION *Front:* independent coil springs; *Rear:* leaf springs with live axle.

BRAKES Front and rear drums.

MAXIMUM SPEED 90–120 mph (145–193 km/h)

0–60 MPH (0–96 km/h) 8–12 sec

A.F.C. 14 mpg (5 km/l)

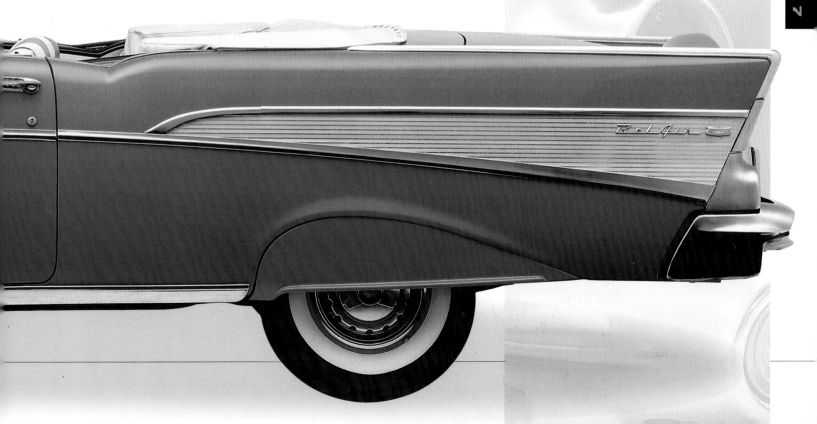

INTERIOR The distinctive two-tone interiors were a delight. Buyers were spoiled with choices and could opt for a custom color interior, power convertible top, tinted glass, vanity mirror, ventilated seat pads, power windows, and even a tissue dispenser.

FUEL CAP In common with Lincoln and Cadillac, Chevrolet incorporated the gas caps on their models into the chrome molding at the rear edge of the left tail fin. And averaging just 14 mpg (5 km/l), the car's flap was opened many times to fill the tank.

AERONAUTICAL COMPARISONS
Chevrolet, like everybody else, was eager to cash in on the jet age, but in reality this '55 Bel Air looks positively dumpy next to the fighter plane.

THE BEL AIR
CONVERTIBLE COULD
BE EQUIPPED WITH
AN OPTIONAL POWER-
OPERATED TOP

WHEN EQUIPPED WITH
THE SOLID-LIFTER
FUEL-INJECTED V8,
THE BEL AIR WAS A
DEVASTATINGLY
QUICK CAR

"The '57 Bel Air sums up America's most prosperous decade better than any other car of the time. Along with hula hoops, drive-in movies, and rock 'n' roll, it has become a Fifties icon."

CONTINENTAL SPARE WHEEL CARRIER WAS A DE LUXE OPTION AND MADE THE CONVERTIBLE A DREAM COME TRUE

CHEVROLET Bel Air Nomad

A revival of the original Town and Country theme

IF YOU THOUGHT BMW and Mercedes were first with the sporty uptown carryall, think again. Chevrolet kicked off the genre as far back as 1955. The Bel Air Nomad was a development of Harley Earl's dream-car wagon based on the Chevrolet Corvette, which he fielded at the four-city Motorama of 1954. Although it looked like other '55 Bel Airs, the V8 Nomad was the most expensive Chevy ever at $2,571, a whole $265 more than the to-die-for Bel Air ragtop. But despite the fact that *Motor Trend* described the '57 Nomad as "one of the year's most beautiful cars," with only two doors its appeal was limited. Its large glass area made the cabin too hot, and the tailgate let in water. No surprise then that it was one of Chevy's least popular models. Sales never broke the magic 10,000 barrier, and by 1958, the world's first sports wagon, and now a milestone car, had been dropped from the lineup.

"Unveiled in January 1954, the Motorama Nomad was such a hit that a production version made it into the '55 brochures."

DRUM BRAKES PROVIDED THE STOPPING POWER ON ALL FOUR WHEELS

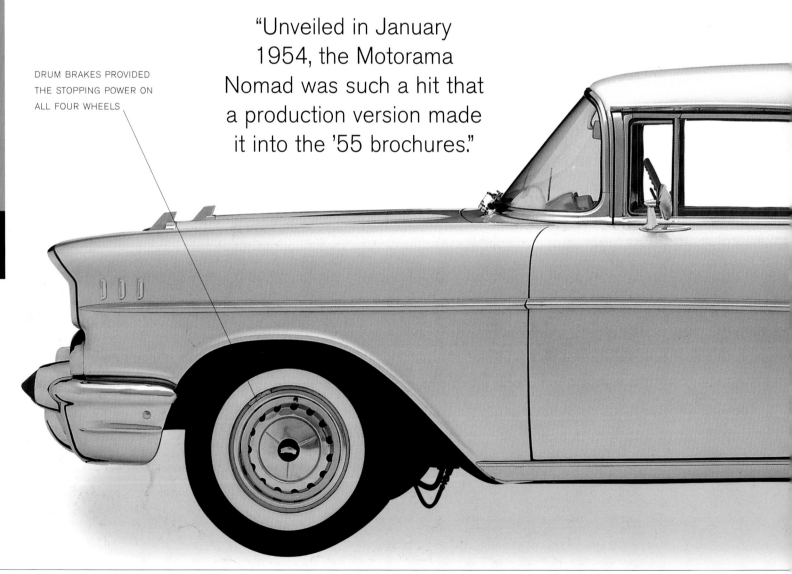

"The Nomad was a reaction against the utilitarian functionalism of the boxy wooden station wagons that had become ubiquitous in suburban America."

MODEL Chevrolet Bel Air Nomad (1957)

PRODUCTION 6,103 (1957)

BODY STYLE Two-door station wagon.

CONSTRUCTION Steel body and chassis.

ENGINES 235cid six, 265cid V8.

POWER OUTPUT 123–283 bhp.

TRANSMISSION Three-speed manual with overdrive, two-speed Powerglide automatic, and optional Turboglide.

SUSPENSION *Front*: coil springs; *Rear*: leaf springs.

BRAKES Front and rear drums.

MAXIMUM SPEED 90–120 mph (145–193 km/h)

0–60 MPH (0–96 km/h) 8–11 sec

A.F.C. 15–19 mpg (5.3–6.7 km/l)

INTERIOR The Nomad's embellished tailgate lifted to reveal a massive cargo area, with the floor covered in linoleum. Comfort extras available for the driver and passengers included power seat and, for the first time, seat belts and shoulder harnesses.

ENGINE The base unit was a 235cid six, but many Nomads were equipped with the Bel Air's grunty 265cid V8, which had a choice of Carter or Rochester two-barrel carburetor. For an extra $484 you could even specify a fuel-injected block, which boosted power output.

MOTORAMA 'VETTE ROOF LINE WAS ADAPTED FOR PRODUCTION NOMADS IN JUST TWO DAYS

TINTED GLASS WAS AN OPTIONAL EXTRA, AS WAS TWO-TONE TRIM

CHEVY TRIED TO LOWER THE NOMAD'S HIGH PRICE BY USING EXTERIOR TRIM THAT WAS IDENTICAL TO THE OTHER BEL AIR MODELS

NOV VANCOUVER B.C. 19-57
YSU 702
MAGGIE'S 57 CHEVY

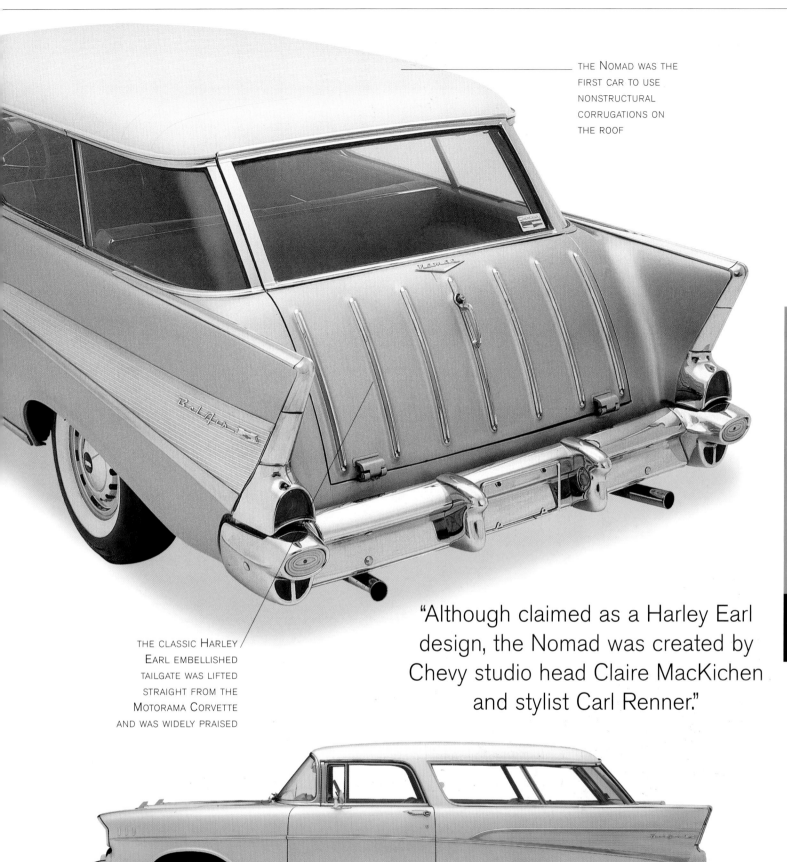

THE NOMAD WAS THE FIRST CAR TO USE NONSTRUCTURAL CORRUGATIONS ON THE ROOF

THE CLASSIC HARLEY EARL EMBELLISHED TAILGATE WAS LIFTED STRAIGHT FROM THE MOTORAMA CORVETTE AND WAS WIDELY PRAISED

"Although claimed as a Harley Earl design, the Nomad was created by Chevy studio head Claire MacKichen and stylist Carl Renner."

CHEVROLET 3100 Stepside

Functional transportation with added style

CHEVY WAS ON A high in the mid-Fifties. With the 'Vette, the Bel Air, and its new V8, it was America's undisputed top car manufacturer. A boundless optimism percolated through all divisions, even touching such prosaic offerings as trucks. And the definitive Chevy pickup has to be the '57 pickup. It not only had that four-stroke overhead-valve V8 mill, but also various De Luxe options and a smart new restyle that offered a leaner look over the rather dumpy previous models. No wonder it was nicknamed "a Cadillac in drag." Among the most enduring of all American design statements, the '57 had clean, well-proportioned lines, a minimum of chrome, and integrated fenders. Chevrolet had turned the pickup from a beast of burden into a personalized workhorse complete with all the accessories of gracious living usually seen in a boulevard cruiser.

THE SMALL-BLOCK V8 PRODUCED 150 BHP AND COULD CRUISE AT 70 MPH (113 KM/H). FROM '55, ALL CHEVYS USED OPEN-DRIVE INSTEAD OF AN ENCLOSED TORQUE-TUBE DRIVELINE

THE STEPSIDE WAS AS STYLIZED INSIDE AS OUT, WITH A GLOVE COMPARTMENT, HEAVY CHROME SWITCHES, AND A V-SHAPED SPEEDO. DE LUXE MODELS HAD A LARGER, WRAPAROUND WINDSHIELD

"The neat rear step on the outside of the body allowed access to the load area and gave the Stepside its name."

Chevrolet 3100

MODEL Chevrolet 3100 Stepside (1957)

PRODUCTION Not available

BODY STYLE Two-seater, short-bed pickup.

CONSTRUCTION Steel body and chassis.

ENGINES 235cid six, 265cid V8.

POWER OUTPUT 130–150 bhp.

TRANSMISSION Three-speed manual with optional overdrive, optional three-speed automatic.

SUSPENSION *Front*: coil springs; *Rear*: leaf springs.

BRAKES Front and rear drums.

MAXIMUM SPEED 80 mph (129 km/h)

0–60 MPH (0–96 km/h) 17.3 sec

A.F.C. 17 mpg (6 km/l)

CHEVROLET Impala

The first year of a Sixties' American institution

In the Sixties, unbridled consumerism began to wane. America turned away from the politics of prosperity and, in deference, Chevrolet toned down its finny Impala. The '59's gothic cantilevered batwings went, replaced by a much blunter rear deck. But while Fifties excess just wasn't cool anymore, the '60 Impala was no shrinking violet. Tired of gorging on gratuitous ornamentation, US drivers were offered a new theology – performance. Freeways were one long concrete loop, premium gas was cheap, and safety and environmentalism were nightmares still to come. For $333 extra, the Sports Coupe could boast a 348cid, 335 bhp Special Super Turbo-Thrust V8. The '59 Impala was riotous, and the '60 stylistically muddled, but within a year the unruliness would disappear altogether. These crossover Chevrolets are landmark cars – they ushered in a new decade that would change America and Americans forever.

CHEVY'S TRUMP CARD WAS AN OPTION LIST NORMALLY FOUND ON LUXURY AUTOS, LIKE AIR-CONDITIONING, POWER STEERING AND WINDOWS, AND SIX-WAY POWER SEAT

IMPALAS COULD BE WARMED UP CONSIDERABLY WITH SOME VERY SPECIAL ENGINES

AT $15 A SET, WHEEL DISCS WERE A CHEAP ACCESSORY. SLICK WHITEWALLS WERE YOURS FOR JUST $36

MODEL Chevrolet Impala Sports Coupe (1960)

PRODUCTION Not available

BODY STYLE Two-door coupe.

CONSTRUCTION Steel body, separate chassis.

ENGINES 235cid straight-six, 283cid, 348cid V8s.

POWER OUTPUT 135–335 bhp (348cid turbo V8).

TRANSMISSION Three-speed manual, optional four-speed manual, two-speed Powerglide automatic, or Turboglide automatic.

SUSPENSION *Front*: upper and lower A-arms, coil springs; *Rear*: coil springs with live axle.

BRAKES Four-wheel disc.

MAXIMUM SPEED 90–135 mph (145–217 km/h)

0–60 MPH (0–96 km/h) 9–18 sec

A.F.C. 12–16 mpg (4.2–5.7 km/l)

INTERIOR Inside, the Impala was loaded with performance metaphor: central speedo, four gauges, and a mock sports steering wheel with crossed flags. The sporty steering wheel was inspired by another model in the Chevy range, the Corvette. This car also incorporates power windows and dual Polaroid sun visors.

ENGINE Two V8 engine options offered consumers seven heady levels of power, from 170 to 335 horses. Cheapskates could still specify the ancient Blue Flame Six, which wheezed out a miserly 135 bhp. Seen here is the 185 bhp, 283cid V8. Positraction, heavy-duty springs, and power brakes were optional.

"The Impala debuted in '58 as a limited edition model, but went on to become the most popular car in '60s America."

THE IMPALA'S COIL SPRING SUSPENSION WAS SUPERIOR TO THE LEAF-SPRING REAR SYSTEM FOUND ON RIVAL CARS

THE FRONT OF THE IMPALA WAS MEANT TO BE QUIET AND CALM AND A MILLION MILES FROM THE DERANGED DENTISTRY OF MID-FIFTIES GRILLE TREATMENTS

19 KENTUCKY '69
101-740
BOYD

"The '60's toned-down fins were an answer to charges that the '59's uproarious rear end was downright dangerous."

THE '60 IMPALA SPORTED MUCH TAMER SPREAD WING FINS THAT SUGGESTED A SEAGULL IN FLIGHT

CHEVROLET Corvette Sting Ray

The 'Vette's most attractive incarnation

THE CHEVROLET CORVETTE is America's native sports car. The "plastic fantastic," born in 1953, is still plastic and still fantastic nearly 50 years later. Along the way, in 1992, it notched up a million sales, and it is still hanging in there. Admittedly it has mutated over the years, but it has stayed true to its roots in one very important aspect. Other American sports car contenders, like the Ford Thunderbird (*see pages* 278–81), soon abandoned any sports car pretensions, adding weight and middle-aged girth, but not the Corvette. All Corvette fans have their favorite eras: for some it is the purity of the very first generation from 1953; others favor the glamorous 1956–62 models; but for many the Corvette came of age in 1963 with the birth of the Sting Ray. With roots going back to the Sting Ray Special Racer and experimental XP720, the luscious 1963–67 Sting Rays are the most collectable of all.

"The Sting Ray was a bold design breakthrough, giving concrete expression to many of the ideas of new GM styling chief, Bill Mitchell."

IN 1965 THE STING RAY GOT FOUR-WHEELED DISC BRAKES IN PLACE OF ALL-AROUND DRUMS

CONVERTIBLES WERE OFFERED WITH A BEAUTIFUL, SNUG-FITTING DETACHABLE HARDTOP FROM 1964, RATHER THAN THE SOFT TOP AS HERE

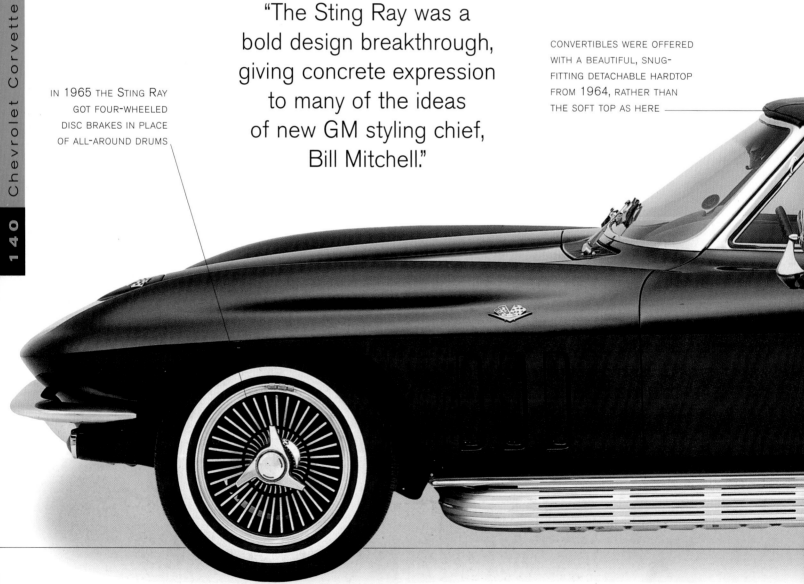

MODEL Chevrolet Corvette Sting Ray (1963–67)

PRODUCTION 118,964

BODY STYLES Two-door sports convertible or fastback coupe.

CONSTRUCTION Fiberglass body; X-braced pressed-steel box-section chassis.

ENGINES OHV V8, 5359cc (327cid), 6495cc (396cid), 7008cc (427cid).

POWER OUTPUT 250–375 bhp (5359cc), 390–560 bhp (7008cc).

TRANSMISSION Three-speed manual, optional four-speed manual, or Powerglide auto.

SUSPENSION Independent all around. *Front*: unequal-length wishbones with coil springs; *Rear*: transverse leaf springs.

BRAKES Drums to 1965, then discs all around.

MAXIMUM SPEED 152 mph (245 km/h, 7008cc)

0–60 MPH (0–96 km/h) 5.4 sec (7008cc)

0–100 MPH (0–161 km/h) 13.1 sec (7008cc)

A.F.C. 9–16 mpg (3–5.7 km/l)

INTERIOR The Batmobile-style interior, with twin-hooped dash, is carried over from earlier Corvettes but updated in the Sting Ray. The deep-dished, wood-effect wheel comes close to the chest, and power steering was an option. Tachometer, seat belts, and electric clock came as standard.

ENGINE Sting Rays came in three engine sizes – naturally all V8s – with a wide range of power options from 250 bhp to more than twice that. This featured car is a 1966 Sting Ray with "small block" 5359cc V8 and Holley four-barrel carb. Three-speed manual transmission was standard.

"Until 1963, all Corvettes were open roadsters, but with the arrival of the Sting Ray, a fixed-head coupe was now also available."

TWIN, POP-UP HEADLIGHTS WERE HIDDEN BEHIND ELECTRICALLY OPERATED COVERS; MORE THAN A GIMMICK, THEY AIDED AERODYNAMIC EFFICIENCY

YOU CAN TELL THIS IS A "SMALL BLOCK" ENGINE – THE HOOD POWER BULGE WAS WIDENED TO ACCOMMODATE THE "BIG BLOCK" UNIT

19 MICHIGAN 71
RMG·319
GREAT LAKE STATE

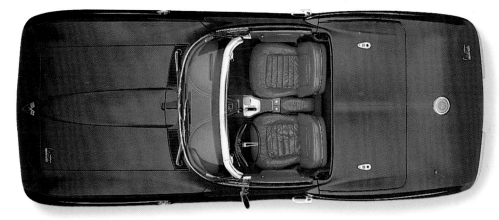

1963 SPLIT-SCREEN COUPE

The distinctive two-piece rear window was used for 1963 only. Bill Mitchell, GM's head of styling, loved it, but humorless critics and the motoring press decided it was "dumb and blocked rear vision." This "design failing" is now the most sought after of fixed-head Sting Rays.

POSITIVE TRACTION
REAR AXLE COULD BE
SPECIFIED FOR AN
EXTRA $42

19 MICHIGAN 71
RMG·319
GREAT LAKE
STATE

CHEVROLET Corvair Monza

Early success hit by stiff competition and a critic

BY 1960, SALES OF DINOSAURS were down, small-car imports were up, and Detroit finally listened to a market screaming for economy compacts. Then along came Chevrolet's adventurous answer to the Volkswagen Beetle (*see pages* 546–49), the pretty, rear-engined Corvair, which sold for half the price of a Ford Thunderbird (*see pages* 294–97). But problems soon arose. GM's draconian cost-cutting measures meant that a crucial $15 suspension stabilizing bar

was omitted from production and, as a result, early Corvairs handled like dogs. The suspension was redesigned in '65, but by this time it was too late. Bad news also came in the form of Ralph Nader's book *Unsafe at Any Speed*, which lambasted the Corvair. The new Ford Mustang (*see pages* 298–301), which had become the hot compact, didn't help either. By 1969, it was all over for the Corvair. GM's stab at downsizing had been a disaster.

DESPITE THE PUBLIC'S INTEREST IN ECONOMY, 53 PERCENT OF ALL CORVAIRS HAD AUTOMATIC TRANSMISSION

SHATTER-RESISTANT SIDE MIRROR CAME AS STANDARD

WIRE WHEEL COVERS WERE A PRICEY $59 OPTIONAL EXTRA. WHITEWALLS COULD BE ORDERED FOR AN EXTRA $29

Corvair

MODEL Chevrolet Corvair Monza (1966)

PRODUCTION 60,447 (1966, Monza only)

BODY STYLES Two- and four-door, four-seater coupe and convertible.

CONSTRUCTION Steel unitary body.

ENGINES 164cid flat sixes.

POWER OUTPUT 95–140 bhp.

TRANSMISSION Three-speed manual, optional four-speed manual, or two-speed Powerglide automatic.

SUSPENSION Front and rear coil springs.

BRAKES Front and rear drums.

MAXIMUM SPEED 105–120 mph (169–193 km/h)

0–60 MPH (0–96 km/h) 11–15.2 sec

A.F.C. 20 mpg (7 km/l)

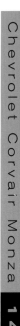

INTERIOR The all-vinyl interior was very European, with bucket seats and telescopic steering column. The restrained steering wheel and deep-set instruments could have come straight out of a BMW. The dials were recessed to reduce glare.

ENGINE Corvair buyers had a choice of alloy, air-cooled, horizontal sixes. The base unit was a 164cid block with four Rochester carburetors developing 140 bhp. The hot turbocharged motors were able to push out a more respectable 180 bhp.

"After very few design changes for the first five years, the new body design for '65 had a heavy Italian design influence and smooth-flowing lines."

OPTIONS ON OFFER INCLUDED A HAND-RUBBED WALNUT STEERING WHEEL AND A WINDSHIELD-MOUNTED AUTOMATIC COMPASS

THE CORVAIR'S REAR-ENGINED FORMAT MEANT THAT STORAGE SPACE UNDER THE HOOD WAS MASSIVE

BUYERS COULD CHOOSE FROM 15 EXTERIOR COLORS, A NUMBER OF WHICH WERE ONLY AVAILABLE ON THE CORVAIR MONZA

PENNSYLVANIA
N62·804

"The new Corvair initially sold well but floundered from 1966 in the face of the rival Ford Mustang and Nader's damning book."

Consumer advocate Ralph Nader published his scathing indictment on American auto safety, *Unsafe at Any Speed*, in 1965. The lead chapter tore into Chevrolet's Corvair, which Nadar claimed was dangerously unstable and responsible for hundreds of rollover accidents. A furious GM hired private detectives to discredit Nader, but their clumsy efforts backfired, and he was awarded $425,000 in compensation.

PENNSYLVANIA
N62·804

CHEVROLET Camaro RS

Pure muscle to compete with the original pony car

RUMORS THAT GENERAL MOTORS had at last come up with something to steal sales from Ford's enormously successful Mustang (*see pages* 298–301) swept through the American auto industry in the spring of 1966. Codenamed Panther, the Camaro touched down in showrooms on September 21. The Pony Car building-block philosophy was simple: sell a basic machine and allow the customer to add their own extras. The trouble was that the Camaro had an options list as arcane and complicated as a lawyer's library. From Strato-Ease headrests to Comfort-Tilt steering wheel, the Camaro buyer was faced with an *embarras de richesse*. But it worked. Buyers ordered the Rally Sport equipment package for their stock Camaros and suddenly they were kings of the street. Go-faster, twin-lined body striping, hidden headlights, and matte black taillight bezels were all calculated to enhance the illusion of performance pedigree.

"Chevy's Camaro was the chosen pace car for both the 1967 and '69 Indy 500s, and some of the production replicas were convertibles."

THE DESIGNERS HAD CREATED A SLEEK CONVERTIBLE – WHEN THE CAMARO RAISED ITS ROOF, THE PURITY OF LINE WAS NOT DISTURBED

LENGTHENING THE WHEELBASE CREATED A LARGE FRONTAL OVERHANG OF 36⅝ IN (93 CM)

Chevrolet Camaro

MODEL Chevrolet Camaro RS Convertible (first generation, 1967–70)

PRODUCTION 10,675 (1967, RS), 195,765 (1967, coupe), and 25,141 (1967, convertible)

BODY STYLE Two-door, four-seater convertible.

CONSTRUCTION Steel monocoque.

ENGINE 327cid small block V8.

POWER OUTPUT 210 bhp at 4800 rpm.

TRANSMISSION Three- or four-speed manual or two- or three-speed auto.

SUSPENSION *Front:* independent; *Rear:* leaf springs.

BRAKES Drums with optional power-assisted front discs.

MAXIMUM SPEED 110 mph (177 km/h)

0–60 MPH (0–96 km/h) 8.3 sec

0–100 MPH (0–161 km/h) 25.1 sec

A.F.C. 18 mpg (6.4 km/l)

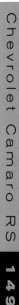

"The market accepted the Camaro as a solid response to the Ford Mustang. Its styling was cleaner, more European, and less boxy."

STICK-ON RS PINSTRIPING HELPED FLATTER THE CAMARO'S CURVES

GM LIKED TO THINK THAT THREE PASSENGERS COULD BE SEATED IN THE REAR WHEN IN REALITY ONLY TWO COULD BE SEATED COMFORTABLY

BY 1968 THE CIRCULAR SIDE MIRRORS HAD BEEN REPLACED BY RECTANGULAR VERSIONS

CHEVROLET
SRR 35F
67 CAMARO

INTERIOR The dashboard had the usual period fare, with acres of plastic and mock wood-grain veneer. Color-keyed all-vinyl trim and Strato bucket seats were a standard Camaro feature. This model is equipped with the optional four-speed manual gearbox.

ENGINE The basic V8 powerplant for Camaros was the trusty small block cast-iron 327cid lump, which, with a bit of tweaking, evolved into the 350cid unit of the desirable SS models. Compression ratio was 8.8:1, and it produced 210 bhp at 4800 rpm.

CENTER-MOUNTED
GAS CAP HAD THE
RS EMBLEM
INSCRIBED ON IT

ALL-RED TAILLIGHT
LENSES WITH BLACK
BEZELS WERE AN
RS FEATURE

CHEVROLET
SRR 35F
67 CAMARO

CHEVROLET Corvette Stingray

The fastest, most powerful sports car on the market

THE AUTOMOTIVE PRESS really lashed into the '69 Shark, calling it a piece of junk, a low point in Corvette history, and the beginning of a new trend toward the image-and-gadget car. Instead of testing the 'Vette, *Car and Driver* magazine simply recited a litany of glitches and pronounced it "too dire to drive," sending ripples of rage through GM. To be frank, the '69 was not the best 'Vette ever. Styling was boisterous, trunk space vestigial, the seats had you sliding all over the place,

and the general build was shoddy. Two great engines saved the day, the 327cid and three incarnations of the big-block 427. With the hottest L88 version peaking at 160 mph (257 km/h), these were cars that were race-ready from the showroom floor. Despite the vitriol, the public liked their image, gadgets, and grunt, buying 38,762 of them, a production record unbroken for the next six years – empirical proof that, occasionally, car journalists are full of hot air.

"GM chief Bill Mitchell said that sharks were exciting to look at and wanted to design a car with similar lines."

TIRES WERE F70x15s AND COULD BE SPECIFIED IN A NUMBER OF DIFFERENT STYLES, INCLUDING WITH WHITE LETTERING AS HERE

HALF OF '69 PRODUCTION WERE COUPES WITH TWIN LIFT-OFF ROOF PANELS AND A REMOVABLE WINDOW – MAKING THIS STINGRAY ALMOST A CONVERTIBLE

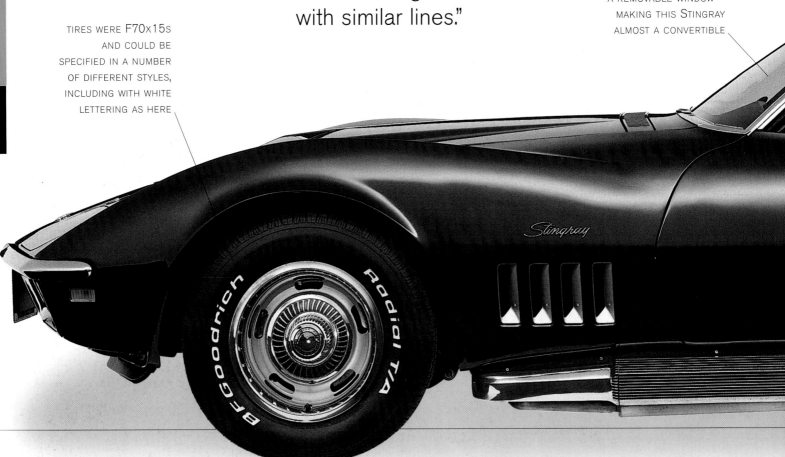

MODEL Chevrolet Corvette Stingray (1969)

PRODUCTION 38,762 (1969)

BODY STYLES Two-seater sports and convertible.

CONSTRUCTION Fiberglass, separate chassis.

ENGINES 327cid, 427cid V8s.

POWER OUTPUT 300–500 bhp.

TRANSMISSION Three-speed manual, optional four-speed manual, or three-speed Turbo Hydra-Matic automatic.

SUSPENSION *Front:* upper and lower A-arms, coil springs; *Rear:* independent with transverse strut and leaf springs.

BRAKES Front and rear discs.

MAXIMUM SPEED 117–170 mph (188–274 km/h)

0–60 MPH (0–96 km/h) 5.7–7.7 sec

A.F.C. 10 mpg (3.5 km/l)

INTERIOR A major drawback of the '69 model was its sharply raked seats, which prevented the traditional Corvette arm-out-of-the-window pose. While the telescopic tilt column and leather trim were optional extras, the glove compartment was standard from 1968.

ENGINE If the stock 427 block was not enough, there was always the 500 bhp ZL1, a 170 mph (274 km/h) racing option package. To discourage amateur racers, no heater was installed in the ZL1; only two were ever sold to retail customers.

SHARK-BASED DESIGN

Bill Mitchell's love of sharks meant that in 1960 a prototype car was made called the Mako Shark. The end result was the 1963 Sting Ray, reputedly Mitchell's favorite piece of work. A further prototype in 1966 ended up as this 1968–72 generation Stingray.

REAR RACK HELPED WHEN THERE WAS LUGGAGE TO BE TRANSPORTED SINCE THERE WASN'T MUCH ROOM IN THE TRUNK

WHEEL-RIM WIDTH INCREASED TO 8 IN (20 CM) IN 1969, WIDE ENOUGH TO CLIMB A WALL

CORVETTE

SEAT BELTS FASTENED?
Y 1980
. 73 OHIO .

A high-performance challenger to the T-Bird

NOW THE WORLD'S LARGEST producer of motor vehicles, Chevrolet kicked off the Seventies with its Ford Thunderbird (*see pages* 294–97) chaser, the 1970 Monte Carlo. Hailed as "action and elegance in a sporty personal luxury package," it was only available as a coupe and came with power front discs, Elm-Burl dash panel inlays, and a choice of engines that ranged from the standard 350cid V8 to the Herculean SS 454. Chevy ads promised that "good taste speaks for itself," and, at $3,123 in base form, it was cheap compared to the $5,000 needed to buy a Thunderbird. But the T-Bird had become as urbane as Dean Martin, and the Monte couldn't match the Ford's élan. Even so, despite a six-week strike that lost Chevrolet 100,000 sales, over 145,000 Monte Carlos found buyers, which, compared to a mere 40,000 T-Birds, made Chevy's new personal luxury confection a monster hit.

"Stylistically, the long hood and short trunk promised performance and power."

THE SMOOTH-CENTERED WHEEL TRIMS WERE NOT POPULAR WITH BUYERS AND, IN '71, CHROMED MOCK-WIRE WHEELS WERE OFFERED

THE MONTE CARLO'S SLIPPERY AERODYNAMICS AND NEAR PERFECT POWER-TO-WEIGHT DISTRIBUTION TURNED IT INTO A FINE HIGH-PERFORMANCE MACHINE

THE RADIO ANTENNA WAS HIDDEN IN THE WINDSHIELD

Monte Carlo

MODEL Chevrolet Monte Carlo (1970)

PRODUCTION 145,975 (1970)

BODY STYLE Two-door, five-seater coupe.

CONSTRUCTION Steel body and chassis.

ENGINES 350cid, 400cid, 454cid V8s.

POWER OUTPUT 250–360 bhp.

TRANSMISSION Three-speed manual, optional two-speed Powerglide automatic, or three-speed Turbo Hydra-Matic automatic.

SUSPENSION *Front*: coil springs; *Rear*: leaf springs.

BRAKES Front and rear drums.

MAXIMUM SPEED 115–132 mph (185–211 km/h)

0–60 MPH (0–96 km/h) 8–14 sec

A.F.C. 15–20 mpg (5.3–7 km/l)

INTERIOR The Monte Carlo's cabin was Chevrolet's most luxurious for the year but was criticized for having limited front and rear legroom. Center console and bucket seats were an option, as was the special instrumentation package of tach, ammeter, and temperature gauge at $68.

ENGINE The potent SS 454 option was a modest $147, and its 360 bhp output meant it was able to catapult the Monte Carlo to 60 mph (96 km/h) in less than eight seconds. It made the Monte Carlo the car of choice for many short-track stock-car racers.

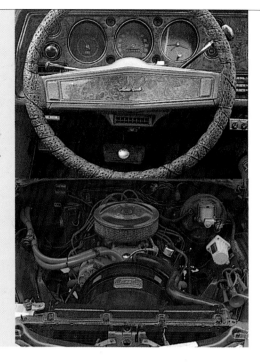

"The Monte Carlo used the same platform as the redesigned 1969 Pontiac Grand Prix."

BLACK VINYL TOP WAS A $120 OPTION. BUYERS COULD ALSO CHOOSE BLUE, DARK GOLD, GREEN, OR WHITE

IN '72, VERTICAL PARKING LIGHTS WERE PLACED INBOARD OF THE HEADLIGHTS

THE SINGLE HEADLIGHTS WERE MOUNTED IN SQUARE-SHAPED HOUSINGS, AND THE GRID-TEXTURED GRILLE WAS SIMPLE AND CLEAN

VIA-537
ARCADIA

"The sporty checkered flag motif didn't really reflect the Monte's marketplace – owners were respectable, middle-aged types."

ANOTHER OPTION AVAILABLE, AND EQUIPPED ON THIS CAR, WAS REAR ANTISWAY BARS

CHEVROLET Nova SS

Pocket dynamo packing a real punch

THE NOVA NAME first appeared in 1962 as the top-of-the-line model of Chevrolet's new Falcon-buster compact, the Chevy II. Evolving into a line of its own, by '71 the Nova's Super Sport (SS) package was one of the smallest muscle cars ever fielded by Detroit. In an era when performance was on the wane, the diminutive banshee found plenty of friends among the budget drag-racing set. That strong 350cid V8 just happened to be a small-block Chevy, perfect for all those tuneable manifolds, carbs, headers, and distributors courtesy of a huge customization industry. Some pundits even went so far as hailing the Nova SS as the Seventies equivalent of the '57 Chevy. Frisky, tough, and impudent, the SS was a Nova to die for. Quick and rare, only 7,016 '71 Novas sported the magic SS badge. Performance iron died a death in '72, making these last-of-the-line '71s perfect candidates for the "Chevy Muscle Hall of Fame."

THE NOVA'S SHELL WOULD LAST FOR 11 YEARS AND WAS SHARED WITH BUICK, OLDSMOBILE, AND PONTIAC

THE HANDSOME SPORTMAG FIVE-SPOKE ALLOYS WERE AN $85 OPTION

SIDE MARKER LIGHTS WERE FORCED ON THE NOVA AFTER FEDERAL SAFETY LEGISLATION WAS PASSED

"Playing on the pony car slogan, Nova ads in the Seventies ran the copy line 'Long Hood, Short Price.'"

MODEL Chevrolet Nova SS (1971)

PRODUCTION 7,016 (1971)

BODY STYLE Two-door, five-seater coupe.

CONSTRUCTION Steel unitary body.

ENGINE 350cid V8.

POWER OUTPUT 245–270 bhp.

TRANSMISSION Three-speed manual, optional four-speed manual, or three-speed automatic.

SUSPENSION *Front:* coil springs; *Rear:* leaf springs.

BRAKES Front discs, rear drums.

MAXIMUM SPEED 120 mph (193 km/h)

0–60 MPH (0–96 km/h) 6.2 sec

A.F.C. 20 mpg (7 km/l)

INTERIOR Nova features included front armrests, antitheft steering wheel-column lock, and ignition key alarm system. The SS package bought a sports steering wheel and special gauges, but air-conditioning and a center console were options.

ENGINE The two- or four-barrel 350cid V8 ran on regular fuel and pushed out 245 and 270 ponies respectively. At one point, Chevrolet planned to squeeze the massive 454cid V8 from the Chevelle into the Nova SS, but regrettably they dropped the idea.

DUAL-CIRCUIT BRAKES AS WELL AS IMPACT-ABSORBING STEERING WERE OBLIGATORY REQUIREMENTS

IN '71, THE OPTION OF A FOUR-CYLINDER BLOCK WAS WITHDRAWN ON THE NOVA; LESS THAN ONE PERCENT OF '70 NOVA BUYERS CHOSE A FOUR

WIDE-PROFILE, BIAS BELTED, WHITE-LETTERED E70x14 TIRES WERE STANDARD SS FARE

"Advertised as the 'Not Too Small Car,' the Nova looked like a scaled-down version of the Chevelle and debuted in 1968 to rave reviews."

FEDERAL LEGISLATION IN 1968 MEANT THAT THE NOVA WAS FORCED TO INCORPORATE A REAR WINDOW DEFOGGER

CHEVROLET Camaro SS396

A sports package with individuality and style

AFTER A SUCCESSFUL DEBUT in '67, the Camaro hit a slump in '72. Sluggish sales and a 174-day strike at the Lordstown, Ohio, plant meant Camaros were in short supply and only 68,656 were produced that year. Worse still, 1,100 half-finished cars sitting on the assembly lines couldn't meet the impending '73 bumper impact laws, so GM was forced to junk them all. There were some dark mutterings in GM boardrooms. Should the Camaro be canned? 1972 also saw the end of the Super Sport (SS) package. *Road & Track* magazine mourned its passing, hailing the .S396 as "the best car built in America in 1971." But the early Seventies were a bad trip for the automobile, and the Camaro would rise again; five years later it had risen from the ashes and was selling over a quarter of a million units – and with a design that survived 11 years without any serious alteration. This is one American icon that refuses to die.

THE CAMARO WAS DESIGNED USING COMPUTER TECHNOLOGY; THE SMOOTH, HORIZONTAL SURFACES BLENDED TOGETHER IN AN AERODYNAMICALLY FUNCTIONAL SHAPE

"The Camaro lured eyes and dollars away from the traditional European performance machines and became one of the most recognized American GTs of the Seventies."

THE LEGENDARY 454CID V8, WITH A MIND-BLOWING 425 BHP, WAS DEFINITELY NOT FOR THE FAINTHEARTED

MODEL Chevrolet Camaro SS396 (1972)

PRODUCTION 6,562 (SS, 1972)

BODY STYLE Two-door coupe.

CONSTRUCTION Steel body and chassis.

ENGINES 350cid, 396cid, 402cid, 454cid V8s.

POWER OUTPUT 240–425 bhp.

TRANSMISSION Three-speed manual, optional four-speed manual, or automatic.

SUSPENSION *Front:* coil springs; *Rear:* leaf springs.

BRAKES Front power discs and rear drums.

MAXIMUM SPEED 125 mph (201 km/h)

0–60 MPH (0–96 km/h) 7.5 sec

A.F.C. 15 mpg (5.3 km/l)

"Chevy spent big bucks on becoming performance heavyweights, and the Camaro was a successful racing model in the early '70s."

COMFORT-TILT WHEEL, SPECIAL INSTRUMENTATION, AND CENTER CONSOLE WERE CONVENIENCE OPTIONS

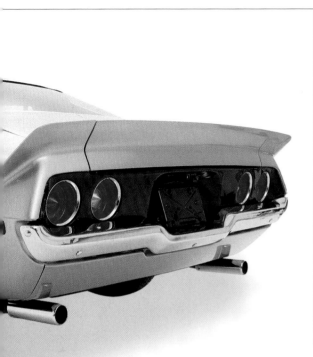

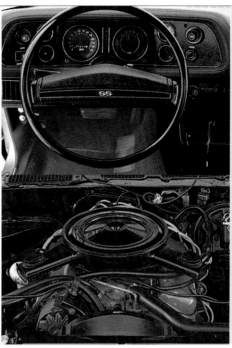

INTERIOR Interiors were generally quite basic. Revisions for '72 were limited and mostly confined to the door panels – these now included map bins and coin holders under the door handles. The high-back seats are a clue that this is a post-'70 model.

ENGINE Camaros came with a range of engines to suit all pockets and for all types of drivers. The entry-level V8 was just $96 more than the plodding straight-six. The block featured here is the lively 396cid V8, one of three engine options for the SS package.

THE BLACK REAR PANEL WAS UNIQUE TO THE SS396

YOU COULD BUY SPRAY-ON LIQUID TIRE CHAIN TO IMPROVE TRACTION

1776 · Bicentennial · 1976
GNL 158
77 · SOUTH CAROLINA ·

CHRYSLER Imperial

Top-of-the-line sedan with limited appeal

IN 1950 CHRYSLER was celebrating its silver jubilee, an anniversary year with a sting in its tail. The Office of Price Stabilization had frozen car prices, there was a four-month strike, and serious coal and steel shortages were affecting the industry. The '50 Imperial was a Chrysler New Yorker with a special roof and interior trim from the Derham Body Company. The jewels in Chrysler's crown, the Imperials were meant to lock horns with the best of Cadillac, Packard, and Lincoln. With Ausco-Lambert disc brakes, Prestomatic transmission, and a MoPar compass, they used the finest technology Chrysler could muster. The trouble was, only 10,650 Imperials drove off the lot in 1950, the hemi-head V8 wouldn't arrive until the next year, buyers were calling it a Chrysler rather than an Imperial, and that frumpy styling looked exactly like what it was – yesterday's dinner warmed up again.

THE FRONT WINDOW WAS STILL OLD-FASHIONED TWO-PIECE FLAT GLASS, WHICH MADE THE IMPERIAL LOOK ANTIQUATED

THE SEMIAUTOMATIC GEARBOX ALLOWED THE DRIVER TO USE A CLUTCH TO PULL AWAY, WITH THE AUTOMATIC TAKING OVER AS THE CAR ACCELERATED

THE INDUSTRY'S FIRST DISC BRAKES CAME AS STANDARD ON CHRYSLER CROWN IMPERIALS

"One claim to fame was that MGM Studios used an Imperial-based mobile camera car in many of its film productions."

MODEL Chrysler Imperial (1950)

PRODUCTION 10,650 (1950)

BODY STYLE Four-door sedan.

CONSTRUCTION Steel body and chassis.

ENGINE 323cid straight-eight.

POWER OUTPUT 135 bhp.

TRANSMISSION Prestomatic semiautomatic.

SUSPENSION *Front:* coil springs; *Rear:* live axle.

BRAKES Front and rear drums, optional front discs.

MAXIMUM SPEED 100 mph (161 km/h)

0–60 MPH (0–96 km/h) 13 sec

A.F.C. 16 mpg (5.7 km/l)

INTERIOR Chrysler's interiors were as restrained and conservative as the people who drove them. Turn-key ignition replaced push-button in 1950, which was also the first year of electric windows. The Safety-Level ride ensured that the comfort factor for passengers was high.

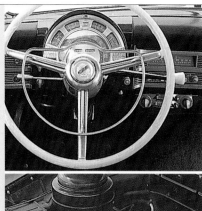

ENGINE The inline L-head eight developed 135 bhp and had a cast-iron block with five main bearings. The carburetor was a Carter single-barrel, and Prestomatic automatic transmission with fluid drive came as standard. Cycle-Bonded brake linings and a waterproof ignition system were also standard features.

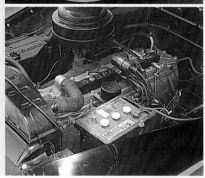

"The celebrated designer Virgil Exner joined Chrysler in 1949 but arrived too late to improve the looks of the moribund Imperial."

WHEELBASE MEASURED 131½ IN (334 CM), WHICH WAS 14 IN (36 CM) SHORTER THAN THE CROWN IMPERIAL

WINDSHIELD WASHERS WERE AVAILABLE AS AN OPTIONAL EXTRA

FIFTIES CHRYSLERS

Bulky, rounded Chryslers were some of the biggest cars on the road in 1950. The Imperials had Cadillac-style grilles, and the Crown Imperial was a long limousine to rival Cadillac's 75.

THE IMPERIAL WEIGHED
JUST UNDER 1,000 LB
(454 KG) LESS THAN
THE CROWN IMPERIAL

NEW "CLEARBAC"
REAR WINDOW
USED THREE
PIECES OF GLASS
THAT WERE DIVIDED
BY CHROME STRIPS

CHRYSLER New Yorker

Award-winning design with a simplicity of line

WHY CAN'T THEY MAKE cars that look this good anymore? The '57 New Yorker was the first and finest example of Chrysler's "Forward Look" policy. With the average American production worker earning $82.32 a week, the $4,259 four-door hardtop was both good-looking and expensive. The car's glorious lines seriously alarmed Chrysler's competitors, especially since the styling was awarded two gold medals, the suspension was by newfangled torsion bar, and muscle was courtesy of one of the most respected engines in the world – the hemi-head Fire Power. Yet "the most glamorous cars of a generation" cost Chrysler a whopping $300 million and sales were disappointing. One problem was a propensity for rust, along with shabby fit and finish; another was low productivity – only a measly 10,948 four-door hardtop models were produced. Even so, the New Yorker was certainly one of the most beautiful cars Chrysler ever made.

CONSIDERING THE EXCESSES OF THE ERA, THE NEW YORKER'S HUGE EXPANSE OF GLASS, LOW BELT LINE, AND SLINKY PROFILE WERE COMMENDABLY SUBTLE

TORQUEFLITE AUTOMATIC TRANSMISSION WAS FIRST SEEN THIS YEAR

TORSION-AIRE RIDE PROVIDED THE NEW YORKER WITH EXCEPTIONAL HANDLING

MODEL Chrysler New Yorker (1957)

PRODUCTION 34,620 (all body styles, 1957)

BODY STYLE Four-door, six-seater hardtop.

CONSTRUCTION Monocoque.

ENGINE 392cid V8.

POWER OUTPUT 325 bhp.

TRANSMISSION Three-speed TorqueFlite automatic.

SUSPENSION *Front*: A-arms and longitudinal torsion bar; *Rear*: semi-elliptic leaf springs.

BRAKES Front and rear drums.

MAXIMUM SPEED 115 mph (185 km/h)

0–60 MPH (0–96 km/h) 12.3 sec

A.F.C. 13 mpg (4.6 km/l)

INTERIOR The impressive array of equipment on the New Yorker included power windows, a six-way power seat, Hi-Way Hi-Fi phonograph, Electro-Touch radio, rear seat speaker, Instant Air heater, handbrake warning system, Air-Temp air-conditioning, and tinted glass.

ENGINE The top-of-the-line model had a top-of-the-line engine. The hemi-head was the largest production unit available in 1957. Bore and stroke were increased and displacement raised by nearly 10 percent. It was efficient, ran on low-octane gas, and could be highly souped up.

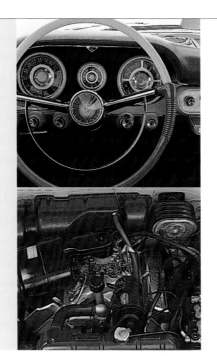

"The New Yorker's shape was awarded two Grand Prix D'Honneur and two gold medals by the Industrial Designers Institute."

CAPTIVE-AIRE TIRES WERE AVAILABLE, WITH PROMISES THAT THEY WOULDN'T LET THEMSELVES DOWN

"The New Yorker's unified design was created by the mind of one man – Virgil Exner – rather than by a committee, and it shows."

RATHER THAN LOOKING OVERSTYLED, THE REAR END AND DECK WERE ACTUALLY QUITE RESTRAINED

Mid-point in a series of performance sedans

"RED HOT AND RAMBUNCTIOUS" is how Chrysler sold the 300F. It may be one of the strangest slogans of any American carmaker, but the 300F really was red hot and a serious flying machine that could top 140 mph (225 km/h). The rambunctious refers to the ram-air induction on the bad-boy 413cid wedge-head V8. Ram tuning had long been a way of raising torque and horsepower for drag racing, and it gave the 300F a wicked performance persona. One of Virgil Exner's

happier designs, the 300F of 1960 had unibody construction, a French Pont-A-Mousson four-speed gearbox, and front seats that swiveled toward you when you opened the doors. It also boasted Chrysler's best styling effort since 1957. But at $5,411, it was no surprise that only 964 coupes found buyers. Nevertheless, it bolstered Chrysler's image, and taught it plenty of tuning tricks for the muscle-car wars that were revving up just around the corner.

"The 300 Series started life in 1955 when Chrysler came up with the first production sedan to kick out 300 bhp."

NEW FOR 1960 WAS A QUIRKY SYSTEM WHEREBY WHEN EITHER DOOR WAS OPENED, SELF-ACTIVATED SWIVELING SEATS WERE AUTOMATICALLY PIVOTED OUTWARD

THE MAGNIFICENT BLOCK SECURED THE FIRST SIX PLACES FOR 300FS IN THE 1960 FLYING MILE COMPETITION AT DAYTONA, WITH A TOP SPEED OF 145 MPH (233 KM/H)

FRONT TORSION BAR SUSPENSION AND EXTRA-STRENGTH LEAF SPRINGS MEANT THE 300F HANDLED WELL

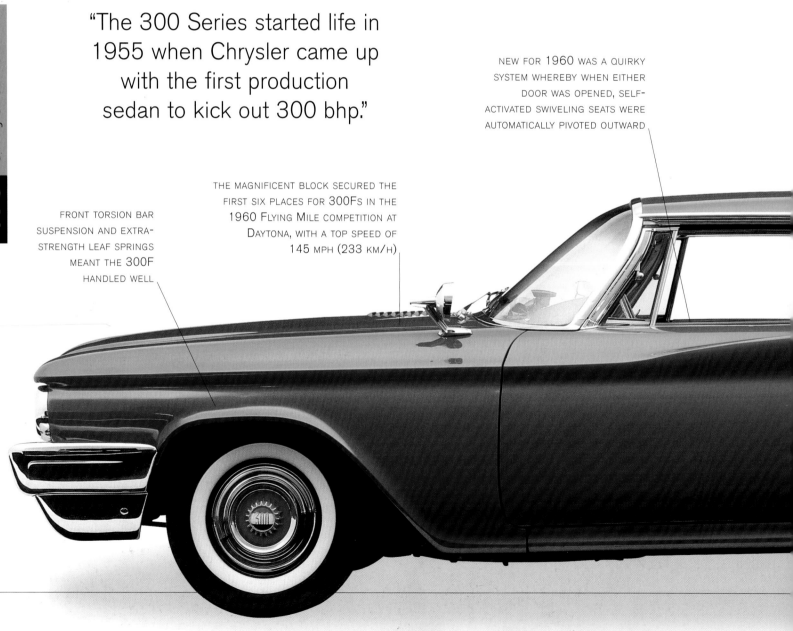

Chrysler

MODEL Chrysler 300F (1960)

PRODUCTION 1,212 (1960, both body styles)

BODY STYLES Two-door coupe
and convertible.

CONSTRUCTION Steel unitary body.

ENGINE 413cid V8.

POWER OUTPUT 375–400 bhp.

TRANSMISSION Three-speed push-button
automatic, optional four-speed manual.

SUSPENSION *Front*: torsion bars;
Rear: leaf springs.

BRAKES Front and rear drums.

MAXIMUM SPEED 140 mph (225 km/h)

0–60 MPH (0–96 km/h) 7.1 sec

A.F.C. 12 mpg (4.2 km/l)

Chrysler 300F **177**

PROMOTIONAL MATERIAL

Advertising for the 300F called it "the sixth of a famous family" and "leader of the clan." The phrase "brutiful brutes" was coined to describe the 300 Series, intimating the marriage of power and style that was carried through in the cars. The only 300 without a letter was the '63, which would have read as a confusing 300I.

SOLEX TINTED GLASS WAS A $43 OPTIONAL EXTRA

"The 300F was one of America's most powerful cars – a souped up version recorded a one-way run of an amazing 189 mph (304 km/h) on the Bonneville salt flats."

INTERIOR The 300F's "Astra-Dome" instrumentation was illuminated at night by electroluminescent light, giving a soft, eerie glow through the translucent markings on the gauges. It was technically daring and boasted six different laminations of plastic, vitreous, and phosphor.

ENGINE The 375 bhp 413cid V8 breathed through two Carter four-barrels with 30-inch rams and was a real gem of an engine. Chrysler carefully calculated optimum inlet manifold length and placed carburetors on the end of the tubes rather than the traditional inline, to give a steady build-up of power along the torque curve.

THE 300F'S RAZOR-SHARP REAR FINS WERE CRITICIZED BY RALPH NADER IN HIS BOOK *UNSAFE AT ANY SPEED* AS "POTENTIALLY LETHAL"

QUESTIONABLE REAR DECK TREATMENT WAS KNOWN AS "FLIGHT-SWEEP" AND AVAILABLE ON OTHER CHRYSLERS

POWER ANTENNA WAS A $43 OPTION; THIS CAR ALSO HAS THE GOLDEN TONE RADIO ($124)

LSU CENTENNIAL 83 138 13 LOUISIANA 60

Chrysler

CHRYSLER 300L

Last and least-loved of a respected series

BACK IN '55, Chrysler debuted their mighty 300 "Letter Car." The most powerful automobile of the year, the 300C kicked off a new genre of Gentleman's Hot-Rod that was to last for more than a decade. Chrysler cleverly marked annual model changes with letters, running from the 300B in 1956 all the way through – the letter I excepted – to this 300L in 1965. And '65 was the swan song year for the Letter Series. The 300L sat on high-performance rubber and suspension and was powered by a high-output 413cid 360 bhp mill. By the mid-Sixties, though, the game had changed, and Chrysler was pumping its money into muscle-car iron like the Charger and GTX, an area of the market where business was brisk. The 300L was the last survivor of an era when the Madison Avenue advertising men were still trying to persuade us that an automobile as long as a freight train could also be a sports car.

BELT LINES WERE LOWER AND ROOF LINES HIGHER THIS YEAR, WHICH INCREASED THE GLASS AREA AND MADE THE INTERIOR FEEL EVEN MORE CAVERNOUS

300Ls HAD UNIBODY CONSTRUCTION, WITH THE FRONT SUBFRAME BOLTED RATHER THAN WELDED ONTO THE MAIN STRUCTURE

TORSION-BAR FRONT SUSPENSION GAVE THE 300L POISE AND ACCURACY

MODEL Chrysler 300L (1965)

PRODUCTION 2,845 (1965)

BODY STYLES Two-door hardtop and convertible.

CONSTRUCTION Steel unitary body.

ENGINE 413cid V8.

POWER OUTPUT 360 bhp.

TRANSMISSION Three-speed automatic, optional four-speed manual.

SUSPENSION *Front:* torsion bar; *Rear:* leaf springs.

BRAKES Front and rear drums.

MAXIMUM SPEED 110 mph (177 km/h)

0–60 MPH (0–96 km/h) 8.8 sec

A.F.C. 12–14 mpg (4.2–5 km/l)

INTERIOR Front bucket seats plus a center console were standard on the L, as was the new-for-'65 column instead of push-button automatic gear shift. The rear seat was molded to look like buckets but could actually accommodate three people.

ENGINE The non-Hemi V8 was tough and reliable and gave the 300L very respectable performance figures. The L was quick, agile, and one of the smoothest-riding Letter Series cars made, with 45 bhp more than the standard 300's unit.

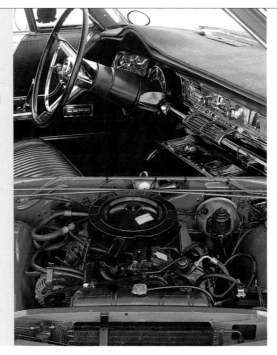

"By the time the famous 300 nameplate had reached its final year, the spark had gone. The 300L is the least special of Chrysler's limited editions."

RED OR BLACK LEATHER COULD BE SPECIFIED FOR THE LAST WORD IN LUXURY

THE BADGE IN THE MIDDLE OF THE GRILLE LIT UP WITH THE HEADLIGHTS

ALASKA 66
98506
1867 NORTH TO THE FUTURE 1967

"Competition was particularly stiff in '65, and the 300L had to fight hard against the Oldsmobile Starfire, the pretty Buick Riviera, and Ford's flashy Thunderbird."

OWNERS HAD PLENTY
OF SPACE TO STORE
LUGGAGE IN THE
MASSIVE TRUNK

REAR AXLES COULD
BE EQUIPPED WITH
POSITIVE TRACTION
AT EXTRA COST

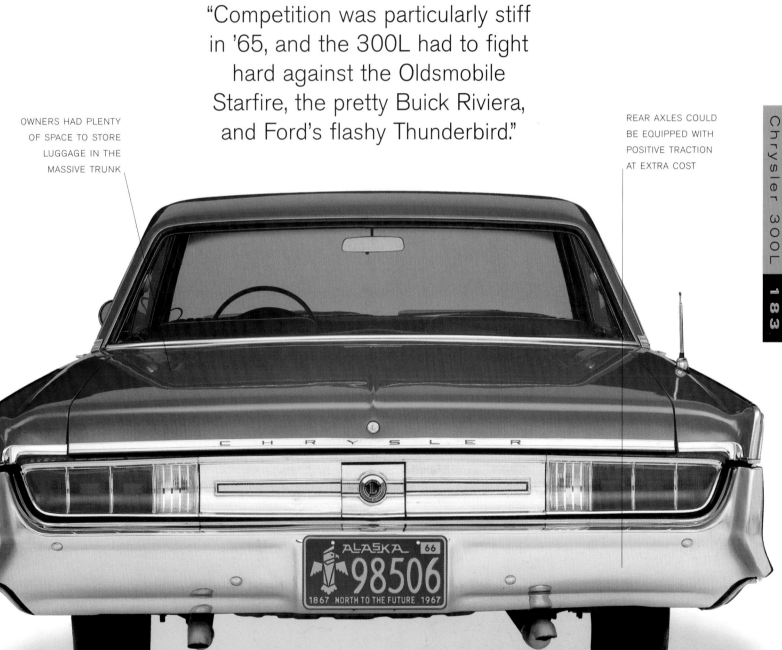

CITROËN Traction Avant

Queen of the road for over two decades

LOVED BY POLITICIANS, poets, and painters alike, the Traction Avant marked a watershed for both Citroën and the world's auto industry. A design prodigy, it was the first mass-produced car to incorporate a monocoque bodyshell with front-wheel drive and torsion-bar springing, and it began Citroën's love affair with the unconventional. Conceived in just 18 months, the Traction Avant cost the French company dearly. By 1934, they had emptied the company coffers, laid off 8,000 workers, and, on the insistence of the French government, were taken over by Michelin, which gave the Traction Avant the backing it deserved. It ran for over 23 years, with over three quarters of a million sedans, fixed-head coupes, and convertibles sold. Citroën's audacious sedan was the most significant and successful production car of its time, eclipsed only by the passage of 20 years and another *voiture revolutionnaire*, the Citroën DS (*see pages* 192–95).

ALL-INDEPENDENT SUSPENSION WITH TORSION-BAR SPRINGING, UPPER WISHBONES, RADIUS ARMS, FRICTION SHOCKS, AND WORM-AND-ROLLER STEERING (LATER RACK-AND-PINION) GAVE CRISP HANDLING

THE HOOD OPENED UP FROM THE SIDE AND WAS A PREWAR FEATURE

THOUGH THE AVANT HAD A 1911CC ENGINE, IT ONLY PUSHED OUT 46 BHP

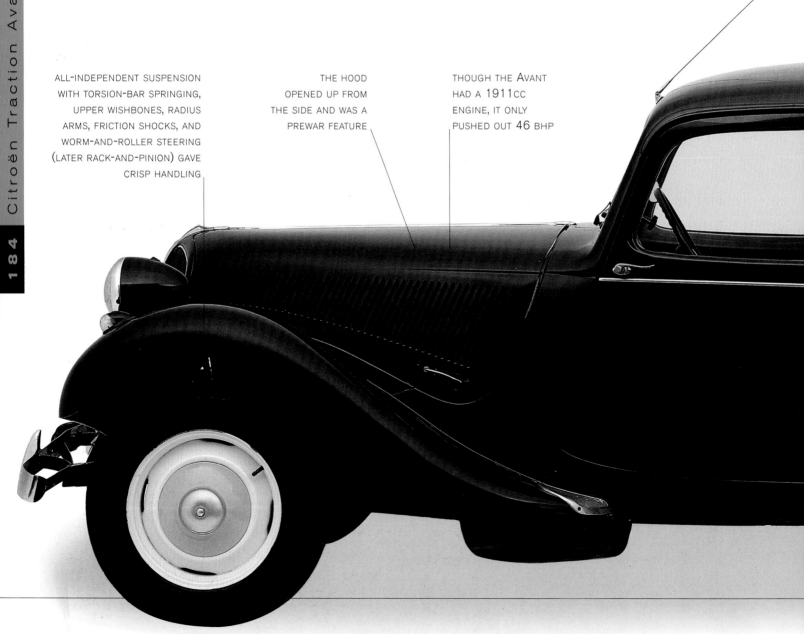

"In 1954, the six-cylinder Traction Avant was known as 'Queen of the Road' because of its hydropneumatic suspension."

MODEL Citroën Traction Avant (1934–55)

PRODUCTION 758,858 (including six-cylinder)

BODY STYLE Five-seater, four-door sedan.

CONSTRUCTION Steel front-wheel drive monocoque.

ENGINE 1911cc inline four-cylinder.

POWER OUTPUT 46 bhp at 3200 rpm.

TRANSMISSION Three-speed manual.

SUSPENSION Independent front and rear.

BRAKES Hydraulic drums front and rear.

MAXIMUM SPEED 70 mph (113 km/h)

0–60 MPH (0–96 km/h) 25 sec

A.F.C. 23 mpg (8.1 km/l)

INTERIOR Three-speed gearbox was mounted ahead of the engine, with synchromesh on second and third. Drive reached the road by Cardin driveshafts and constant velocity joints at the axles. The dash-mounted gearshift lived on in the DS of 1955 *(see pages 192–95).*

ENGINE The Traction's Maurice Sainturat-designed engine was new. "Floating Power" came from a short-stroke four-cylinder unit, with a three-bearing crankshaft and push-rod overhead valves. It all equated to seven French horsepower.

"With aerodynamic styling, unitary steel body, and sweeping fenders without running boards, the Traction Avant was a technical and aesthetic *tour de force*."

ENGINE, GEARBOX, RADIATOR, AND FRONT SUSPENSION WERE MOUNTED ON A DETACHABLE CRADLE FOR EASY MAINTENANCE

307 ET 77

MICHELIN PRODUCED THESE PILOTE WHEELS AND TIRES SPECIALLY FOR THE TRACTION AVANT

IN 1952, CITROËN DISPENSED WITH THE EARLIER "BOBTAIL" REAR END AND GAVE THE TRACTION A "BIG TRUNK"

THE TRACTION LOOKS AND FEELS HUGE AND WAS A REAL HANDFUL IN TIGHT SPACES

307 ET 77

CITROËN 2CV

Over five million buyers of this cute French classic

RARELY HAS A CAR BEEN so ridiculed as the Citroën 2CV. At its launch during the 1948 Paris Salon, journalists lashed into this defenseless runabout with vicious zeal, and everyone who was near Paris at the time claimed to be the originator of the quip, "Do you get a can opener with it?" They all missed the point, for this minimal car was not meant to be measured against other cars; its true rival was the horse and cart, which Citroën boss Pierre Boulanger hoped to replace with his *toute petite voiture* – or very small car. He conceived that it would weigh no more than 661 lb (300 kg), and carry four people at 37 mph (60 km/h), while consuming no more than 56 mpg. As the Deux Chevaux it putt-putted into the history books, selling more than five million by the time of its eventual demise in 1990. As devotees of the 2CV say, "You either love them or you don't understand them."

ALL THE BODY PANELS SIMPLY UNBOLT, AND EVEN THE BODY SHELL IS ONLY HELD IN PLACE BY 16 BOLTS

ALTHOUGH DESIGNERS FLIRTED WITH NOTIONS OF A CHASSISLESS CAR, COST DICTATED A MORE CONVENTIONAL SHEET-STEEL PLATFORM CHASSIS

PREWAR PRODUCTION PROTOTYPES HAD ONLY ONE HEADLIGHT

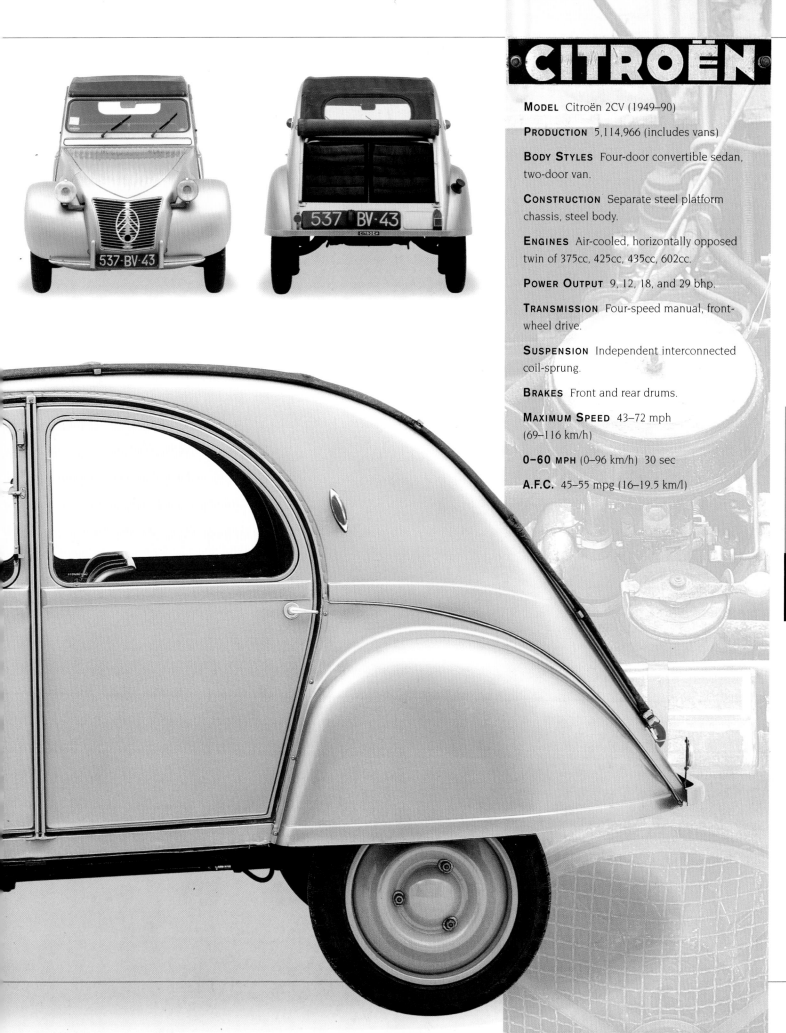

CITROËN

MODEL Citroën 2CV (1949–90)

PRODUCTION 5,114,966 (includes vans)

BODY STYLES Four-door convertible sedan, two-door van.

CONSTRUCTION Separate steel platform chassis, steel body.

ENGINES Air-cooled, horizontally opposed twin of 375cc, 425cc, 435cc, 602cc.

POWER OUTPUT 9, 12, 18, and 29 bhp.

TRANSMISSION Four-speed manual, front-wheel drive.

SUSPENSION Independent interconnected coil-sprung.

BRAKES Front and rear drums.

MAXIMUM SPEED 43–72 mph (69–116 km/h)

0–60 MPH (0–96 km/h) 30 sec

A.F.C. 45–55 mpg (16–19.5 km/l)

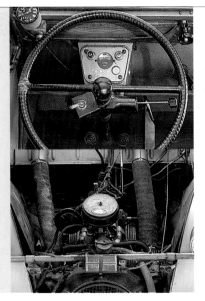

INTERIOR These days they call it driver feedback, but in a classic 2CV you can tell you are moving because the scenery changes – albeit slowly. A speedo and ammeter were the only concessions to modernity. The original fuel gauge was just a calibrated stick.

ENGINE The original 375cc air-cooled twin, as seen here, eventually grew to all of 602cc; but all versions are genuinely happy to rev flat out all day. In fact, most spend all their time being driven at maximum speed and seem to thrive on full revs. All engines are long-lasting.

"Nothing drives like a Citroën 2CV – the handling looks lurid as it leans over wildly. The ride, though, is exceptional."

FRESH AIR WAS OBTAINED BY OPENING THE VENT ON THE SCUTTLE; A MESH STRAINED OUT THE INSECTS AND LEAVES

THE SOPHISTICATED INDEPENDENT SUSPENSION SYSTEM GAVE A SOFT RIDE

GRAY WAS THE ONLY COLOR UNTIL LATE 1959, THEN THE CHOICE DOUBLED TO INCLUDE GLACIER BLUE, WITH GREEN AND YELLOW ADDED IN 1960

537-BV-43

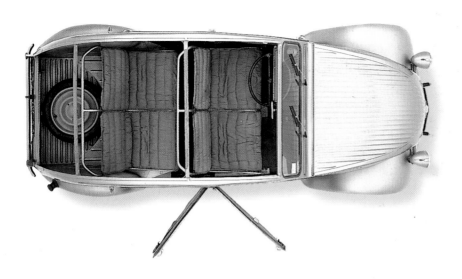

In 1905 André Citroën patented his revolutionary helical gears, which he sold for use in large liners, including the *Titanic*. After WWI he realized the future lay in cars, but by 1934 his once successful company was brought to its knees by the the huge costs of developing the Traction Avant. Michelin, Citroën's greatest creditor, then took control of the company.

ROLL-UP CANVAS TRUNK LID OF THE ORIGINAL SAVED BOTH WEIGHT AND COST; A METAL LID TOOK OVER IN '57 ON FRENCH CARS

537 BV·43

CITROËN

CITROËN DS Decapotable

Bertone-designed lines create a cult design icon

IN 1955, WHEN CITROËN first drove prototypes of their mold-breaking DS through Paris, they were pursued by crowds shouting "La DS, la DS, voila la DS!" Few other cars before or since were so technically and stylistically daring, and, at its launch, the DS created as much press coverage as the death of Stalin. Cushioned on a bed of hydraulic fluid, with a semi-automatic gearbox and self-leveling suspension, it rendered half the world's cars out of date at once.

Parisian carmaker Henri Chapron produced 1,365 convertible DSs using the chassis from the Safari wagon model. Initially Citroën refused to cooperate with Chapron but they eventually sold Decapotable models through its dealer network. At the time, the hip four-seater convertible was considered by many to be one of the most charismatic cars on the market, and today genuine Chapron cars command three to four times the price of their sedan counterparts.

NOVEL SUSPENSION

The DS's fully independent gas suspension gave a magic-carpet ride. The suspension system could also be manually raised to clear rough terrain or navigate flooded roads.

ON ALL DSs THE REAR TRACK WAS NARROWER THAN THE FRONT

BODY PANELS WERE DETACHABLE FOR EASY REPAIR AND MAINTENANCE. REAR FENDERS COULD BE REMOVED FOR WHEEL CHANGING IN MINUTES, USING JUST THE CAR'S JACK

"The slippery, streamlined body cleaved the air with extreme aerodynamic efficiency."

MODEL Citroën DS 21 Decapotable (1960–71)

PRODUCTION 1,365

BODY STYLE Five-seater convertible.

CONSTRUCTION All-steel body with detachable panels, steel platform chassis with welded box section side members.

ENGINE Four-cylinder 2175cc.

POWER OUTPUT 109 bhp at 5550 rpm.

TRANSMISSION Four-speed clutchless semi-automatic.

SUSPENSION Independent all around with hydropneumatic struts.

BRAKES Front discs, rear drums.

MAXIMUM SPEED 116 mph (187 km/h)

0–60 MPH (0–96 km/h) 11.2 sec

0–100 MPH (0–161 km/h) 40.2 sec

A.F.C. 24 mpg (8.5 km/l)

INTERIOR Bertone's asymmetrical dashboard makes the interior look as futuristic as the rest of the car. The single-spoke steering wheel was a Citroën hallmark. The dash-mounted gear lever operated the clutchless semiautomatic box.

ENGINE The DS 21's rather sluggish 2175cc engine developed 109 bhp and was never highly praised, having its origins in the prewar Traction Avant *(see pages 184–87)*. Despite this, front-wheel drive gave unerring high-speed control and maneuverability.

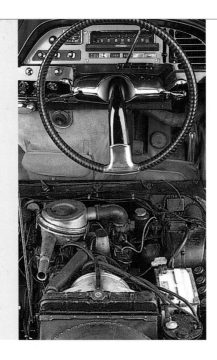

UNDER THE HOOD
Gear shifting and clutch action were aided by hydraulic servos and the DS's pin-sharp rack-and-pinion steering was assisted by hydraulic power.

A MAJOR CHANGE CAME IN 1967 WHEN THE HEADLIGHTS AND OPTIONAL POD SPOT LIGHTS WERE FAIRED IN BEHIND GLASS COVERS

CURVED GLASS AND COPIOUS LAYERS OF FOAM RUBBER INSIDE THE CAR WERE TWO OTHER INNOVATIONS ON THE DS

2724 Y 33

"The French philosopher Roland Barthes was captivated by the DS's design and compared its technical preeminence to the Gothic flourish of medieval cathedrals."

On August 22, 1962, President of France General Charles de Gaulle was traveling in a black DS19. On the outskirts of Paris, 12 terrorist gunmen opened fire on the presidential car. The first shots missed the president, but hit two of the Citroën's tires. The chauffeur floored the throttle, swerved violently to avoid two of the terrorists' cars, and escaped to safety. Investigators later claimed that had the driver tried that maneuver in another car, it would have overturned and killed the president.

ONE OF THE DECAPOTABLE'S TRADEMARKS WAS ANGLED CHROME-PLATED INDICATORS PERCHED ON THE REAR FENDERS

CITROËN SM

Technically advanced with a streamlined profile

THE CITROËN SM MAKES about as much sense as the Concorde, but since when have great cars had anything to do with common sense? It is certainly a flight of fantasy, an extravagant, technical *tour de force* that, as a 16-ft (4.9-m) long streamliner, offered little more than 2+2 seating. The SM's striking, low-drag body was designed by ex-GM stylist Henri de Segur Lauve, and it bristled with innovations – many of them established Citroën hallmarks – like swiveling headlights and self-leveling hydropneumatic suspension. It was a complex car – too complex in fact, with self-centering power steering and brakes that were both powered by (and virtually inoperable without) a high-compression engine-driven pump. And of course there was that capricious Maserati V6 engine. Yet once again Citroën had created an enduringly futuristic car where other "tomorrow cars of today" were soon exposed as voguish fads.

THE TINTED REAR WINDOW, WITH COMPOUND CURVES AND HEATING ELEMENTS, MUST HAVE COST A FORTUNE TO PRODUCE

ONLY THE SM'S OVER-ELABORATE CHROMED REAR "FINS" BETRAY THE GENERAL MOTORS STYLING INFLUENCE

CITROËN SM

MODEL Citroën SM, SM EFI, and SM Auto (1970–75)

PRODUCTION 12,920 (all types, all LHD)

BODY STYLE Two-door, 2+2 coupe.

CONSTRUCTION All-steel unitary, with steel body and aluminum hood.

ENGINES All-aluminum 90-degree V6 of 2670cc (2974cc for SM Auto).

POWER OUTPUT SM: 170 bhp at 5500 rpm; 2974cc: 180 bhp at 5750 rpm.

TRANSMISSION Citroën five-speed manual or Borg-Warner three-speed automatic; front-wheel-drive.

SUSPENSION Hydropneumatic springing; independent transverse arms front, independent trailing arms rear.

BRAKES Discs all around.

MAXIMUM SPEED 137 mph (220 km/h) (SM EFI)

0–60 MPH (0–96 km/h) 8.3 sec (SM EFI)

0–100 MPH (0–161 km/h) 26–30 sec

A.F.C. 15–17 mpg (5.3–6.1 km/l)

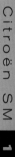

ROLLING ALONG

Despite its size and weight, the SM could be thrown around like a sports car. It rolled, as in this image, like a trawler in a heavy sea and, like all front-wheel drives, understeered strongly, but resolutely refused to let go. Its tapered body was aerodynamically very efficient.

INTERIOR The SM's controls owe more to style than ergonomics. The oval speedo and tachometer are visible through the single-spoke steering wheel, and the perennially confusing cluster of warning lights are positioned to the right.

ENGINE SM stands for Serié Maserati, and the exquisite Maserati all-aluminum V6 engine weighed just 309 lb (140 kg), was only 12 in (31 cm) long, but produced at least 170 bhp. Capacity was initially kept below 2.8 liters to escape France's punitive taxation system.

SLIM WINDSHIELD PILLARS SHOULD HAVE MEANT EXCELLENT VISIBILITY, BUT IN PRACTICE, THE LEFT-HAND DRIVE SM WAS SOMETIMES DIFFICULT TO POSITION ON THE ROAD

THE SM HAD AN ARRAY OF SIX HEADLIGHTS, WITH THE INNER LIGHT ON EACH SIDE SWIVELING AS THE STEERING WAS TURNED

THE SM'S ENGINE WAS MOUNTED BEHIND THE TRANSMISISON AND THUS WELL BEHIND THE FRONT AXLE

"The sleek nose and deep undertray, together with the noticeably tapered rear end, endow the SM with a drag coefficient of 0.27, still respectable today."

LIKE THAT OF MOST FRONT-WHEEL DRIVE CARS, THE SM'S REAR SUSPENSION DID LITTLE MORE THAN HOLD THE BODY OFF THE GROUND

THE BULGE IN THE TAILGATE ABOVE THE REAR LICENSE PLATE WAS FOR PURELY FUNCTIONAL, AERODYNAMIC REASONS

CITROËN'S PUBLICITY MATERIAL TRIED TO HIDE THE FACT, BUT REAR-SEAT LEGROOM AND HEADROOM WERE BARELY SUFFICIENT FOR TWO LARGE CHILDREN

INJECTION ELECTRONIQUE

CITROEN

CONTINENTAL MkII

The epitomy of Fifties' personal luxury

THE IDEA THAT THE Fifties auto industry couldn't make a beautiful car is robustly disproved by the '56 Continental. As pretty as anything from Italy, the Mark II was intended to be a work of art and a symbol of affluence. William Ford was fanatical about his personal project, fighting for a chrome, rather than plastic, hood ornament costing $150, or the price of an entire Ford grille. Even the Continental's prototype clay mockup cost $1 million. But it was that tenacious attention to detail that killed the car. Even with the Mark II's huge $10,000 price tag, the Continental division still hemorrhaged money. Poor sales, internal company struggles, and the fact that it was only a two-door meant that by '58 the Continental was no more. Ironically, one of the most beautiful cars Ford ever made was sacrificed to save one of the ugliest in the upcoming E-Car project – the Edsel (*see pages* 236–43).

"COW BELLY" FRAME WAS SPECIFICALLY DESIGNED TO ALLOW HIGH SEATING WITH A LOW ROOF LINE

"At the rear of the car, trim fins, elegant bumpers, and neat inset taillights meant that the Continental was admired on both sides of the Atlantic."

LIKE ALL US CRUISERS OF THE ERA, THE CONTINENTAL WAS A THIRSTY BEAST, WITH A FIGURE OF 16 MPG (5.7 KM/L)

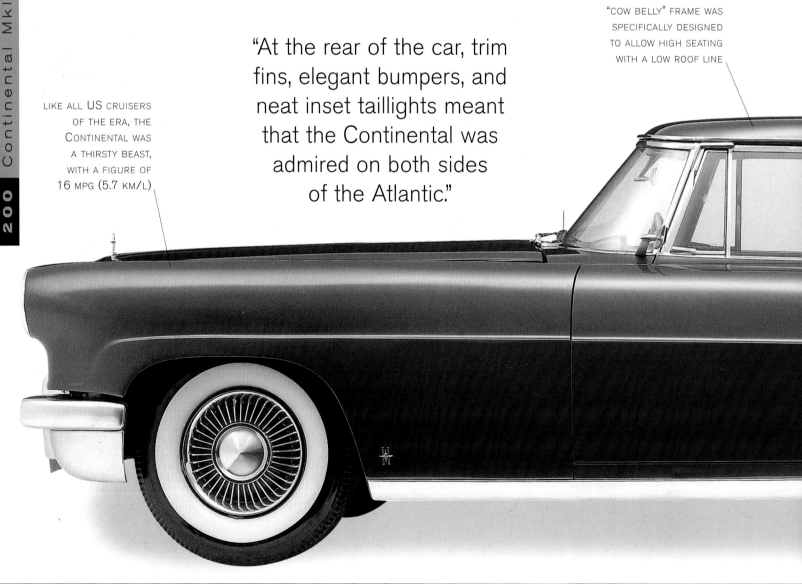

MODEL Continental Mark II (1956)

PRODUCTION 2,550 (1956)

BODY STYLE Two-door, four-seater sedan.

CONSTRUCTION Steel body and chassis.

ENGINE 368cid V8.

POWER OUTPUT 300 bhp.

TRANSMISSION Turbo-Drive three-speed automatic.

SUSPENSION *Front*: independent coil springs; *Rear*: leaf springs.

BRAKES Front and rear drums.

MAXIMUM SPEED 115 mph (185 km/h)

0–60 MPH (0–96 km/h) 12.1 sec

A.F.C. 16 mpg (5.7 km/l)

INTERIOR The classically simple cockpit could have come straight out of a British car. The interior boasted richly grained leathers and lavish fabrics. Self-tuning radio, four-way power seat, dual heater, and map lights were among an impressive array of standard features on the Continental.

ENGINE Powerplants were Lincoln 368cid V8s, specially picked from the assembly line, stripped down, and hand-balanced for extra smoothness and refinement. With the exception of Packard's 374cid unit, this was the largest engine available in a 1956 production car.

"Elvis tried a Continental instead of his usual Cadillacs, and Jayne Mansfield owned one with mink trim."

THE ONLY CONCESSION TO CONTEMPORARY DETROIT ORNAMENTATION WAS HOW THE DIRECTION INDICATORS WERE FAIRED INTO THE FRONT BUMPER

THE HIGH-QUALITY ALL-LEATHER TRIM WAS SPECIALLY IMPORTED FROM BRIDGE OF WEIR IN SCOTLAND

CALIFORNIA 1962 56
VYD 341

DAIMLER SP250 Dart

American styling percolates through to Britain

AN ECCENTRIC HYBRID, the SP250 was the car that sunk Daimler. By the late Fifties, the traditionalist Coventry-based company was in dire financial straits. Hoping to woo the car-crazy Americans, Daimler launched the Dart, with its odd pastiche of British and American styling themes, at the 1959 New York show. Daimler had been making buses out of fiberglass, and the Dart emerged with a quirky, rust-free, glass-reinforced-plastic body. The girder chassis was an unashamed copy of the Triumph TR2 (*see pages 534–37*), and to keep the base price down, necessities like heater, windshield wipers, and bumpers were made optional extras. Hardly a great car, the SP250 was a commercial failure and projected sales of 7,500 units in the first three years dissolved into just 2,644, with only 1,200 going to the US. Jaguar took over Daimler in 1960, and, by 1964, Sir William Lyons had axed the sportiest car Daimler had ever made.

"The guppy-style front could never be called handsome but, when drivers caught it in their rearview mirrors, they knew to move over."

EARLY CARS HAD TO HAVE A STEEL HOOP AROUND THE BULKHEAD TO STOP SCUTTLE SHAKE

FLUTED FENDERS LOOKED STYLISH AND GAVE THE BODY EXTRA RIGIDITY

THE FIBERGLASS HOOD HAD A NASTY HABIT OF SPRINGING OPEN AT HIGH SPEED

MODEL Daimler SP250 Dart (1959–64)

PRODUCTION 2,644 (1,415 LHD, 1,229 RHD)

BODY STYLE Two-door, two-seater sports convertible.

CONSTRUCTION Fiberglass body, steel girder chassis.

ENGINE Iron-block 2548cc V8.

POWER OUTPUT 140 bhp at 5800 rpm.

TRANSMISSION Four-speed manual or three-speed Borg-Warner Model 8.

SUSPENSION Independent front with wishbones and coil springs; rear live axle with leaf springs.

BRAKES Four-wheel Girling discs.

MAXIMUM SPEED 125 mph (201 km/h)

0–60 MPH (0–96 km/h) 8.5 sec

0–100 MPH (0–161 km/h) 19.1 sec

A.F.C. 25 mpg (8.8 km/l)

INTERIOR The cockpit was pure British tradition, with center gauges mounted on an aluminum plate, leather seats and dash, an occasional rear seat, fly-off handbrake, roll-up windows, and thick-pile carpets. The vestigial rear seat could just about accommodate one child or a very tolerant adult.

ENGINE The turbine-smooth, Edward Turner-designed V8 was the Dart's *tour de force*. If you were brave enough, it could reach 125 mph (201 km/h). With alloy heads and hemispherical combustion chambers, it was a gem of a unit that survived until 1969 in the Daimler 250 sedan.

"The Dart stands as a memorial to both the haphazard Sixties British auto industry and its self-destructive love affair with all things American."

BEAUTIFULLY FINISHED CHROME-SURROUNDED GLASS KEPT COCKPIT BUFFETING TO A MINIMUM

THE DART HAD MANY PERIOD DETAILS, LIKE THE TINY CHEVRON-SHAPED SIDELIGHTS ON BOTH FENDERS

4068 WK

RACING DAIMLER

Quick enough in a straight line, corners were the Dart's Achilles' heel and the model never achieved any significant racing success. This period shot shows a Dart pirouetting around Brands Hatch in 1962.

AT HIGH SPEED, THE STEERING WAS VERY HEAVY, THE CHASSIS FLEXED, AND DOORS OPENED ON BENDS IN THE ROAD

THE TOP FURLED AWAY NEATLY BEHIND THE BACKSEAT, COVERED WITH A FABRIC TOP BAG

4068 WK

DATSUN Fairlady

A quaint offering with a hint of European styling

THE SIMILARITY BETWEEN the Datsun Fairlady and the MGB (*see page* 421) is astonishing. The Datsun actually appeared first, at the 1961 Tokyo Motor Show, followed a year later by the MGB. Though its early 1500cc guise lacked both mid-range heave and top-end power, the Fairlady improved dramatically over the years – a foretaste of the Japanese car industry's culture of constant improvement. The later two-liter, twin-carb, five-speed variants of 1967 could reach 125 mph (200 km/h) and even raised eyebrows at American sports car club races. Though never listed in Britain, the Fairlady was aimed at a worldwide market – particularly the United States, where it was known as the Datsun 1500 – but sold only 40,000 in nine years. However, it provided Datsun with invaluable experience and paved the way for the legendary 240Z (*see pages* 212–15), which became one of the world's best-selling sports cars.

"Compared to some of the awkward Asian offerings of the time, the Fairlady was catwalk material."

FRONT SHOCK ABSORPTION WAS INDEPENDENT, COURTESY OF TELESCOPIC SHOCK ABSORBERS, WISHBONES, AND COIL SPRINGS

THE FRONT FENDERS WERE BOLTED ON FOR EASY REPAIR AND REPLACEMENT

"Over nine years Datsun refined the Fairlady until, by the late 1960s, it had evolved into quite a reasonable machine."

Fairlady

MODEL Datsun Fairlady 1600 (1965–70)

PRODUCTION Approx 40,000

BODY STYLE Two-seater sports convertible.

CONSTRUCTION Steel body mounted on box-section chassis.

ENGINE 1595cc four-cylinder.

POWER OUTPUT 90 bhp at 6000 rpm.

TRANSMISSION Four-speed all-synchro.

SUSPENSION *Front*: independent; *Rear*: leaf springs.

BRAKES Front wheel discs, rear drums.

MAXIMUM SPEED 105 mph (169 km/h)

0–60 MPH (0–96 km/h) 13.3 sec

0–100 MPH (0–161 km/h) 25 sec

A.F.C. 25 mpg (8.8 km/l)

INTERIOR The cockpit was typical of the period, with acres of black plastic. The steering wheel would not look out of place in a pickup truck. Interestingly, no attempt was made to make the interior harmonize with the Fairlady's traditional exterior lines.

ENGINE The 1595cc 90 bhp unit was the mainstay of the Fairlady line until 1970. The simple four-cylinder engine had a cast-iron cylinder block and alloy head, breathing through twin Hitachi carbs made under license from SU in England.

"Low and rakish, with classically perfect proportions, the Fairlady has a certain period charm and is one of the best-looking pre-1965 Datsuns."

HANDLING WAS POISED AND SURE-FOOTED, ENDEARING THE FAIRLADY TO AMATEUR RACERS

LATER 2000 MODELS OF THE FAIRLADY PUSHED OUT 145 BHP AND BOASTED A FIVE-SPEED GEARBOX

THOUGH COMPARISONS
WERE MADE WITH THE
MGB, THE FAIRLADY
WAS HIGHER AND
NARROWER THAN THE
BRITISH CAR

EARLY FAIRLADIES
HAD A THIRD
SEAT SET ACROSS
THE CAR BEHIND
THE FRONT
BUCKET SEATS

Fairlady

MUF
625F

DATSUN 240Z

Japan's first world-class sports car

THROUGHOUT THE 1960S, Japanese carmakers were teetering on the brink of a sports car breakthrough. Toyota's 2000GT (*see page* 533) was a beauty, but with only 337 made, it was an exclusive novelty. Honda was giving a try too, with the dainty S600 and S800. As for Datsun, the MGB-lookalike Fairladies were relatively popular in Japan and the United States but virtually unknown elsewhere. The revolution came with the Datsun 240Z, which in one stroke established Japan on the world sports car stage at a time when there was a gaping hole in that sector, particularly in the US. It was even launched in the States in October 1969, a month before its official Japanese release; and on a rising tide of Japanese exports to the US it scored a massive hit. It had the looks, performance, handling, and equipment levels to satisfy sports enthusiasts. A great value sports package that outsold all rivals.

TRUNK-LID AEROFOIL WAS NOT STANDARD 240Z EQUIPMENT IN ALL MARKETS

RHX 156L

RHX 156L

240Z   *Datsun*

DATSUN

MODEL Datsun 240Z (1969–73)

PRODUCTION 156,076

BODY STYLE Three-door, two-seater sports hatchback.

CONSTRUCTION Steel monocoque.

ENGINE Inline single overhead-camshaft six, 2393cc.

POWER OUTPUT 151 bhp at 5600 rpm.

TRANSMISSION All-synchromesh four- or five-speed manual gearbox, or auto.

SUSPENSION *Front*: independent by MacPherson struts, low links, coil springs, telescopic shocks; *Rear*: independent by MacPherson struts, lower wishbones, coil springs, telescopic shocks.

BRAKES Front discs, rear drums.

MAXIMUM SPEED 125 mph (210 km/h)

0–60 MPH (0–96 km/h) 8.0 sec

A.F.C. 20–25 mpg (7–9 km/l)

INTERIOR Cockpit layout was tailored to American tastes of the time, with hooded instruments and beefy controls. The vinyl-covered bucket seats offered generous rear luggage space, but the low seating position – which could accommodate two 6 ft 3 in (1.9 m) adults – marred otherwise excellent visibility.

ENGINE The six-cylinder twin-carb 2.4-liter engine, developed from the four-cylinder unit of the Bluebird saloon range, provided smooth, reliable power. Japanese buyers had the option of a 2-liter version, and there were also 420 cars built for the home market with a more powerful 24-valve twin-cam 2-liter unit.

"As with so many long-lived sports cars, the first-of-a-kind 240Z is seen as the best sports package – lighter and nimbler than its successors."

THIN, RUST-PRONE BODY PANELS WERE ONE OF THE FEW THINGS THAT LET THE 240Z DOWN

THE NAME DATSUN – LITERALLY SON OF DAT – FIRST APPEARED ON A SMALL DAT IN 1932

RHX 156L

"The lines of the 240Z were based on earlier styling exercises by Albrecht Goertz, master stylist of the BMW 507."

AS WITH THE RECESSED LIGHTS AT THE FRONT, THERE IS AN ECHO OF THE E-TYPE JAGUAR FIXED-HEAD COUPE (SEE PAGES 330–33) AT THE REAR

240Z

Datsun

RHX 156L

DELOREAN DMC 12

One of the great modern automotive failures

"THE LONG-AWAITED transport revolution has begun" bellowed the glossy brochures for John Zachary DeLorean's mold-breaking DMC 12. With a unique brushed stainless-steel body, gullwing doors, and an all-electric interior, the DMC was intended as a glimpse of the future. Today its claim to fame is as one of the car industry's greatest failures, on par with the disastrous Edsel (*see pages* 236–43). Despite $143m worth of government aid to establish a factory in

Northern Ireland, DeLorean shut its doors in 1982 with debts of $40m. As for those who bought the cars, they were faced with a litany of quality control problems, from doors that would not open to windows that fell out. Even exposure in the film *Back to the Future* did not help. Success depended on American sales, and the company's forecasts were wildly optimistic. After the initial novelty wore off, word spread that DeLoreans were dogs and sales completely evaporated.

"The DeLorean was targeted at 'the bachelor who's made it,' and part of the design brief was that there had to be room behind the front seats for a full set of golf clubs."

WITH TINY WINDOWS AND CLIMATE CONTROL THAT REGULARLY FAILED, CABIN TEMPERATURES GOT VERY HOT INDEED

CUSTOM-MADE SPOKED ALLOYS WERE SMALLER IN THE FRONT THAN IN THE BACK

MODEL DeLorean DMC 12 (1979–82)

PRODUCTION 6,500

BODY STYLE Two-seater rear-engined sports coupe.

CONSTRUCTION Y-shaped chassis with stainless-steel body.

ENGINE 2850cc OHC V6.

POWER OUTPUT 145 bhp at 5500 rpm.

TRANSMISSION Five-speed manual, optional three-speed auto.

SUSPENSION Independent with unequal length parallel arms and rear trailing arms.

BRAKES Four-wheel discs.

MAXIMUM SPEED 125 mph (201 km/h)

0–60 MPH (0–96 km/h) 9.6 sec

0–100 MPH (0–161 km/h) 23.2 sec

A.F.C. 22 mpg (7.8 km/l)

INTERIOR The leather-clad interior looked imposing, with electric windows, tilting telescopic steering column, double weather seals, air-conditioning, and a seven-position climate control function.

ENGINE The overhead-cam, Volvo-sourced 2.8-liter V6 engine used Bosch K-Jetronic fuel injection. Five-speed manual was standard on the DeLorean, with three-speed automatic transmission optional.

"The gullwing doors and stainless-steel body were cynical marketing ploys that, as everybody involved in the prototype agreed, were more trouble than they were worth."

OVERLOADED DOORS WERE CRAMMED WITH LOCKS, GLASS, ELECTRIC MOTORS, MIRRORS, STEREO SPEAKERS, AND VENTILATION PIPES

HELD BY A PUNY SINGLE GAS STRUT, IT WAS AN ACT OF THE PUREST OPTIMISM TO EXPECT THE DOORS TO WORK CORRECTLY

BRUSHED STAINLESS-STEEL WAS DISLIKED BY COLIN CHAPMAN BUT INSISTED UPON BY DELOREAN HIMSELF. SOON OWNERS FOUND THAT IT WAS IMPOSSIBLE TO CLEAN

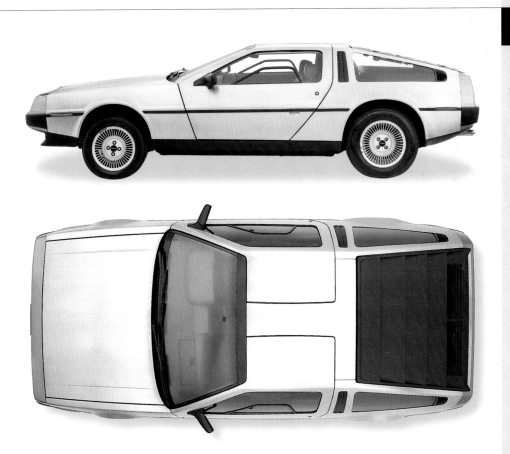

John Zachary DeLorean created a business empire out of other people's money, and then threw it all away. Head of one of General Motors' most profitable divisions, he fought with management, was fired, and went on to create his dream car – the DeLorean DMC 12. He brought hope to strife-torn Belfast, Northern Ireland, with the DeLorean factory, but watched his dream car and company fail, losing millions of American investors' and British taxpayers' money. He was acquitted of a multimillion dollar cocaine deal in the Eighties, and still talks of building another "ethical sports car."

DESOTO Custom

Mid-range convertible with elegant profile

THE DESOTO OF 1950 had a glittery glamor that cheered up postwar America. Hailed as "cars built for owner satisfaction," they were practical, boxy, and tough. DeSoto was a longtime taxi builder that, in the steel-starved years of 1946–48, managed to turn out 11,600 cabs, most of which plied the streets of New York City. Despite more chrome than any other Chrysler product, DeSotos still labored on with an L-head six-pot 250cid mill until the legendary Firedome V8 in 1952. But body

shapes for 1950 were the prettiest ever, and the American public reacted with delight, buying up 133,854 units that year, ranking DeSoto 14th in the industry. Top-line Custom Convertibles had a very reasonable sticker price of $2,578 and came with Tip-Toe hydraulic shift with Gyrol fluid drive as standard. The austere postwar years were a sales Disneyland for the makers of these sparkling cars, but DeSoto's roll couldn't last. By 1961 they'd disappeared forever.

> "DeSoto's volume sellers were its sedans and coupes, which listed at under $2,000 in De Luxe form."

THE TOP MAY HAVE BEEN SLEEK AND CHIC BUT IT HAD TO BE RAISED BY HAND

CONVERTIBLES CAME WITH WHITEWALLS AND WHEEL COVERS AS STANDARD

CHRYSLER SOLD DESOTOS ON SOLIDITY AND VALUE

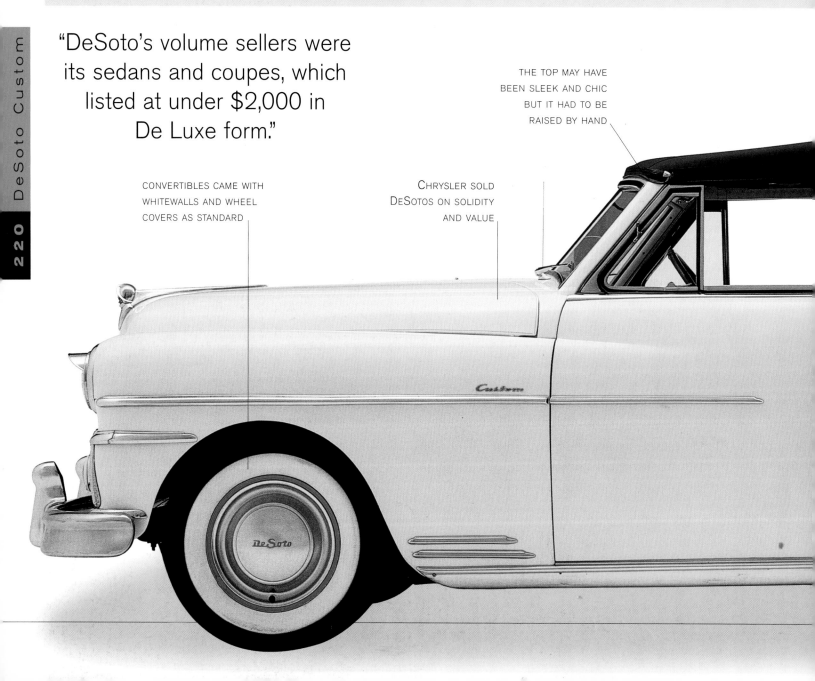

MODEL DeSoto Custom Convertible (1950)

PRODUCTION 2,900 (1950)

BODY STYLE Two-door convertible.

CONSTRUCTION Steel body and box-section chassis.

ENGINE 236.7cid straight-six.

POWER OUTPUT 112 bhp.

TRANSMISSION Fluid drive semiautomatic.

SUSPENSION *Front:* independent coil springs; *Rear:* leaf springs with live axle.

BRAKES Front and rear drums.

MAXIMUM SPEED 90 mph (145 km/h)

0–60 MPH (0–96 km/h) 22.1 sec

A.F.C. 18 mpg (6.4 km/l)

INTERIOR '50 DeSotos came in two trim levels: De Luxe, the poverty package, was outsold three to one by the more plush Custom, at $200 more. Direction indicators and backup lights were offered as standard on the Custom, while options included heater, electric clock, and two-tone paint.

ENGINE The side-valve straight-six was stodgy, putting out a modest 112 bhp through the fluid drive gearbox. This was an innovative semiautomatic preselector with conventional manual operation or semiautomatic kick-down. The DeSoto's top speed of just 90 mph (145 km/h) was not very impressive.

"1950 models are easily spotted by their body-color vertical grille divider, which was unique to this year."

THE MAMMOTH-TOOTH GRILLE DOMINATED THE FRONT ASPECT OF THE DeSoto BUT WOULD BE SCALED DOWN FOR 1951

FLAT GLASS SPLIT WINDSHIELD WAS PARTED WITH A CHROMED CENTER ROD ON WHICH THE REARVIEW MIRROR WAS POSITIONED

1951 WYOMING
18 263

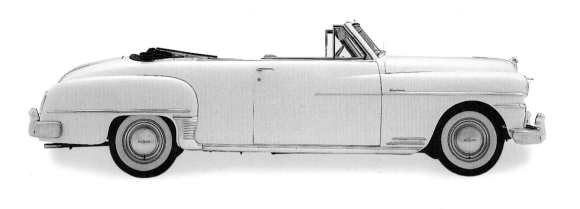

DeSoto Ornament

The optional hood ornament was one Hernando DeSoto, a 17th-century Spanish conquistador. The ornament glowed in the dark.

"DeSoto's role at Chrysler was much like Mercury's at Ford and Oldsmobile's at GM – to plug the gap between budget models and uptown swankmobiles."

THE DeSoto's RUMP WAS LARGE, ROUND, AND UNADORNED, AND TRUNK SPACE WAS CAVERNOUS

THE DeSoto BODY SHAPE STILL CARRIED HINTS OF THE SEPARATE FENDERS OF PREWAR CARS

1951 WYOMING 18 263

DE TOMASO Pantera GT5

An Italian name with real supercar credentials

A SIMPLE SUPERCAR, the Pantera was a charming amalgam of Detroit grunt and Italian glam. Launched in 1971 and sold in North America by Ford's Lincoln-Mercury dealers, it was engineered by Giampaolo Dallara, also responsible for the Lamborghini Miura (*see pages* 344–47). It was powered by a mid-mounted Ford 5.7-liter V8 that could muster 159 mph (256 km/h) and belt to 60 mph (96 km/h) in under six seconds. The formidable 350 bhp GT5 was built after Ford pulled out in 1974 and De Tomaso merged with Maserati. With a propensity for the front end lifting at high speed, hopeless rear visibility, no headroom, awkward seats, and impossibly placed pedals, the Pantera is incredibly flawed, yet remarkably easy to drive. Handling is poised and accurate, with a wall of power that catapults the car to 30 mph (48 km/h) in less time than it takes to pronounce its name.

LIFT-UP REAR PANEL GAVE TOTAL ENGINE ACCESSIBILITY FOR MAINTENANCE

"Fat arches, aggressive GT5 graphics, wide wheels, and ground clearance you could not slide an envelope under make the Pantera look evil."

WITH THE ENGINE SO CLOSE TO THE INTERIOR, THE CABIN TEMPERATURE COULD GET VERY HOT

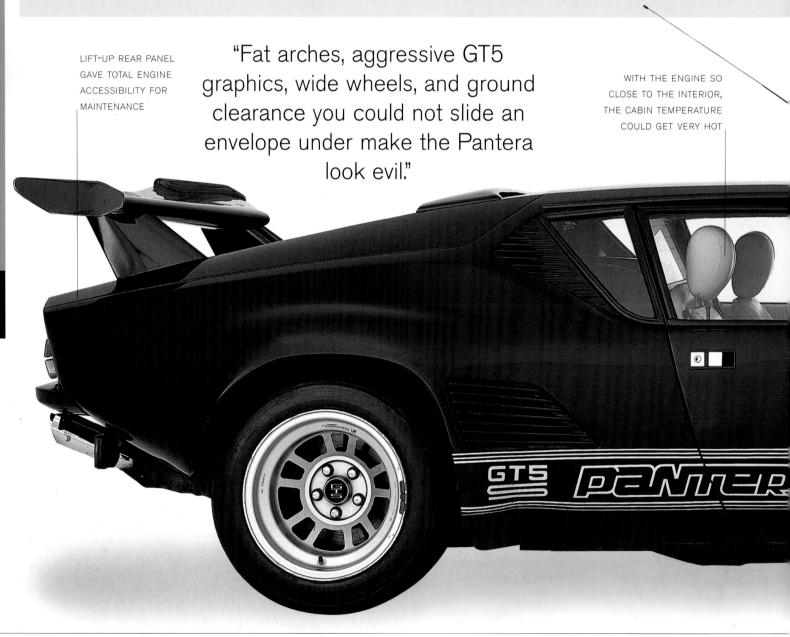

GT5 PANTER

MODEL De Tomaso Pantera GT5 (1974–93)

PRODUCTION Not available

BODY STYLE Mid-engined two-seater coupe.

CONSTRUCTION Pressed-steel chassis body unit.

ENGINE 5763cc V8.

POWER OUTPUT 350 bhp at 6000 rpm.

TRANSMISSION Five-speed manual ZF Transaxle.

SUSPENSION All-around independent.

BRAKES All-around ventilated discs.

MAXIMUM SPEED 159 mph (256 km/h)

0–60 MPH (0–96 km/h) 5.5 sec

0–100 MPH (0–161 km/h) 13.5 sec

A.F.C. 15 mpg (5.3 km/l)

FOUR EXHAUSTS WERE
NECESSARY TO PROVIDE
AN EFFICIENT OUTLET
FOR ALL THAT POWER

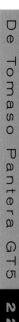

INTERIOR The Pantera requires a typical Italian driving position – long arms and short legs. Switches and dials are scattered all over the place, but some compensation is that the positioning of the powerplant means the glorious engine tone is right next to your ears.

ENGINE The Pantera is really just a big power plant with a body attached. The monster V8 lives in the middle, coupled with a beautifully built aluminum-cased ZF transaxle, which was also used in the Ford GT40 *(see pages 274–77)* and cost more to make than the engine.

THE PANTERA AT SPEED
The huge wing helps downforce, but slows the Pantera down. At the GM Millbrook proving ground in England, a GT5 with the wing in place hit 148 mph (238 km/h); without the wing it reached 151.7 mph (244 km/h).

GIANT PIRELLI RUBBER BELONGED ON THE TRACK AND GAVE ASTONISHING ROAD TRACTION

DESPITE A FRONT SPOILER, THE LIGHT WEIGHT UPFRONT MEANT THAT THE NOSE WOULD LIFT AND THE STEERING WOULD LIGHTEN UP ALARMINGLY AT SPEED

EARLY PANTERAS WOULD OVERHEAT, AND OWNERS WOULD OFTEN SEE THE TEMPERATURE GAUGE CREEP PAST 230°F (110°C)

DO NOT BUY A PANTERA IF YOU ARE OVER 5 FT 10 IN (178 CM) TALL – THERE IS NO HEADROOM

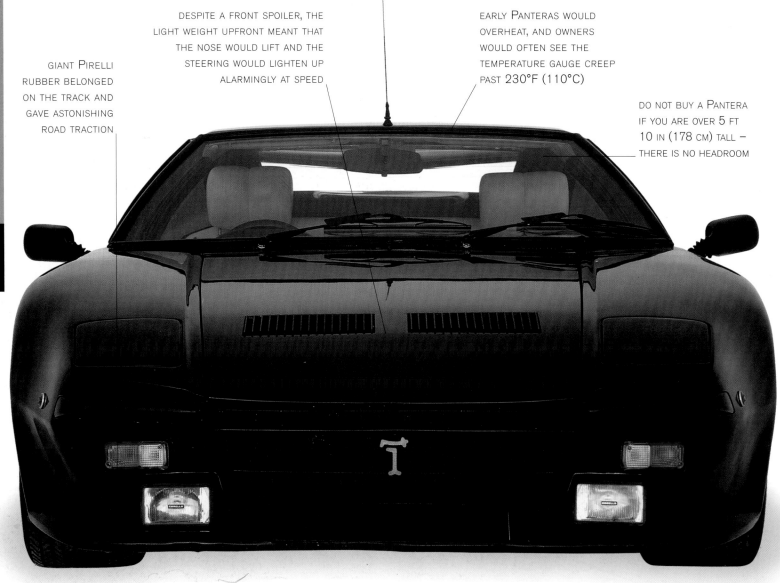

One of Elvis Presley's many cars was a yellow 1970 De Tomaso Pantera that he gave to his wife Priscilla as a birthday present. During their stormy marriage, one particular argument saw "The King" march out to his garage and pump three shots into the Pantera's dash. The very low mileage, Tjaarda-designed supercar still survives as an exhibit of the Petersen Museum in Los Angeles. The three historic bullet holes are still there too.

DODGE Custom Royal Lancer

Fifties' fins and an awesome powerplant

LICKING ITS WOUNDS from the '58 recession, Detroit came up with more metal, muscle, and magnificence than ever before. As always, Chrysler's offerings were the gaudiest, and their '59 Custom Royal had fins and finery to spare. And boy, could it go. Engine options went all the way up to a 383cid D500 motor that heaved out a whopping 345 bhp. "Level Flight" Torsion-Aire suspension was a $127 extra that "lets you corner without side sway, stop without brake

dive." There was no doubt that the copywriters were having a ball. With a "Forward Look" profile, chromed eyebrows, four enormous taillights set in yet more chrome, and topped by towering duotone fins, the Custom Royal was a stylistic shambles. The brochure has a mailman beaming approvingly at the riotous '59 Custom with a catchline that runs, "reflects your taste for finer things." Complete garbage maybe, but that's the way they sold cars in '59.

"In 1957 Chrysler introduced a new type of styling to its whole range – cars should be longer, sleeker, and have exuberant tail fins."

THE RATIO OF GLASS TO SHEET METAL WAS NEARLY ONE-TO-ONE AND GAVE THE COCKPIT AN AIRY FEEL

LESS THAN ONE PERCENT OF ROYALS WERE EQUIPPED WITH THE OPTIONAL AND UNPOPULAR NEWFANGLED AIR SUSPENSION

Custom Royal

MODEL Dodge Custom Royal Lancer (1959)

PRODUCTION 11,297 (1959)

BODY STYLES Two- or four-door, six-seater hardtop.

CONSTRUCTION Steel body and chassis.

ENGINES 230cid six, 326cid, 361cid, 383cid V8s.

POWER OUTPUT 138–345 bhp.

TRANSMISSION Three-speed manual with overdrive, optional three-speed TorqueFlite automatic.

SUSPENSION *Front:* torsion bars; *Rear:* leaf springs.

BRAKES Front and rear drums.

MAXIMUM SPEED 90–120 mph (145–193 km/h)

0–60 MPH (0–96 km/h) 8–14 sec

A.F.C. 12–17 mpg (4.2–6 km/l)

INTERIOR The Custom Royal Lancer's cabin had plenty of toys, including an "Indi-Color" speedometer that changed color as the car's speed increased, variable-speed windshield wipers, padded dash, automatic headlight dimming, and swiveling seats in Jaquard fabric and vinyl.

ENGINE The 361cid Super Ramfire V8 in this Custom Royal pushed out 305 bhp but paled beside the D500 performance option. Its heavy-duty shocks, revised coil springs, and torsion bars gave what *Motor Trend* magazine called "close liaison with the road." D500s were at the top of their class for performance and handling.

LANCER BADGE

The Lancer name actually referred to an upmarket trim level that was standard on all hardtops and convertibles. The Custom Royal was the top offering in Dodge's range.

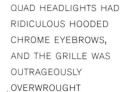

QUAD HEADLIGHTS HAD RIDICULOUS HOODED CHROME EYEBROWS, AND THE GRILLE WAS OUTRAGEOUSLY OVERWROUGHT

R·2885
NY EMPIRE STATE 60

"Despite the raucous rear end, the Custom Royal's rear fins were less exaggerated than most – the '59 Cadillac and Chevy Impala had much wilder rear-fin styling."

DODGE Charger R/T

A star of the screen made of pure muscle

COLLECTORS RANK THE 1968 Dodge Charger as one of the fastest and best-styled muscle cars of its era. This, the second generation of Charger, marked the pinnacle of the horsepower race between American car manufacturers in the late 1960s. At that time, gasoline was 10 cents a gallon, Americans had more disposable income than ever before, and engine capacity was everything to the aspiring car buyer. With its hugely powerful 7.2-liter engine, the Charger 440 was, in reality, a thinly veiled street racer. The Rapid Transit (R/T) version was a high-performance factory option, which included heavy-duty suspension and brakes, dual exhausts, and wider tires. At idle, the engine produced such massive torque that it rocked the car body from side to side. Buyers took the second generation Charger to their hearts in a big way, with sales outstripping the earlier lackluster model by a factor of six.

"The Charger was the creation of Dodge's chief of design, Bill Brownlie, and its clean, voluptuous lines gave this car one of the most handsome shapes of the day."

CHARGERS WERE ALSO FOR THOSE "WHO LIKE IT SOFT INSIDE." ALL HAD STANDARD CLOCK, HEATER, AND CIGARETTE LIGHTER

ENORMOUS 1 IN (25 MM) DIAMETER ANTIROLL BARS ENSURED THAT THE CHARGER HANDLED WELL, DESPITE ITS BULK

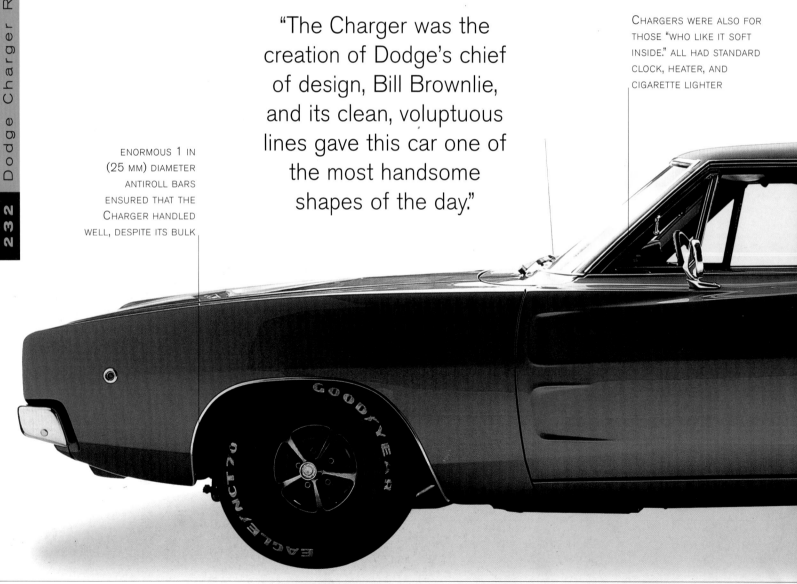

MODEL Dodge Charger (1967–70)

PRODUCTION 96,100

BODY STYLE Two-door, four-seater.

CONSTRUCTION Steel monocoque body.

ENGINE 7.2-liter V8.

POWER OUTPUT 375 bhp at 3200 rpm.

TRANSMISSION Three-speed TorqueFlite auto, or Hurst four-speed manual.

SUSPENSION *Front*: heavy duty independent; *Rear*: leaf springs.

BRAKES Heavy duty, 11 in (280 mm) drums, with optional front discs.

MAXIMUM SPEED 150 mph (241 km/h)

0–60 MPH (0–96 km/h) 6 sec

0–100 MPH (0–161 km/h) 13.3 sec

A.F.C. 10 mpg (3.5 km/l)

Dodge Charger R/T

233

INTERIOR The standard R/T cockpit is functional to the point of being stark. No distractions here – just a matte black dashboard with six gauges that included a 150 mph (241 km/h) speedometer. Factory options included cruise control and a wood-grained steering wheel.

ENGINE The wall-to-wall engine found in the R/T Charger is Dodge's immensely powerful 440 Magnum – a 7.2-liter V8. This stump-pulling powerplant produced maximum torque at a lazy 3200 rpm – making it obscenely quick, yet as docile as a kitten in city traffic. Potent 426cid Hemis put out a staggering 425 bhp.

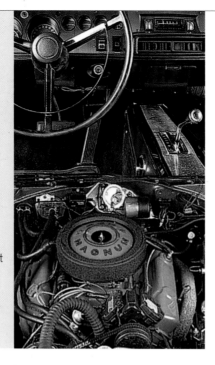

"Charger was an aggressive, warlike name for the ultimate machomobile."

MEAN GRILLE
The concealed front lights disappeared under hinged covers to give the Charger a mean-looking frontal aspect.

COLOR CHOICES ORIGINALLY INCLUDED PLUM CRAZY, GO MANGO, AND TOP BANANA

HAZARD WARNING LIGHTS AND REMOTE-CONTROLLED MIRRORS WERE GROOVY FEATURES FOR 1967

NEAT STYLING FEATURES INCLUDED INDICATOR REPEATERS BUILT INTO THE HOOD SCOOP

NEVADA
OCT481

"A car with star quality, the Charger featured in the classic nine-minute chase sequence in the film *Bullitt*."

CELLULOID STAR

In the 1968 film *Bullitt*, Steve McQueen tears around the Mission district of San Francisco in a dark green Mustang Fastback, chased by villains in a deadly black big-block '68 Charger R/T. Nine minutes of apocalyptic thunder and tire squealing make this the best pursuit ever filmed, period. To take the battering from San Francisco's roller-coaster streets, the Charger's suspension was modified.

"BUTTRESS-BACKED" STYLING WAS AMERICA'S VERSION OF A EUROPEAN 2+2 SPORTS COUPE

NEVADA
OCT481

EDSEL Bermuda

A station wagon with questionable styling

THE BERMUDA'S NAME was chosen from 6,000 possibilities, including Mongoose, Turcotinga, and Utopian Turtletop; and without that infamous grille it wouldn't have been a bad old barge. The rest looked pretty safe and suburban, and even those faddish taillights weren't that offensive. At $3,155 it was the top Edsel wagon, wooing the WASPs with more mock wood than Disneyland. But Ford had oversold the Edsel big time, and every model suffered guilt by association. Initial sales in 1957 were nothing like the predicted 200,000, but weren't disastrous either. The Bermudas, though, found just 2,235 buyers and were discontinued after only one year. By '58, people no longer believed the hype, and Edsel sales evaporated; the company ceased production in November 1959. Everybody knew that the '58 recession killed the Edsel, but at Ford, major players in the project were cruelly demoted or fired.

236 Edsel Bermuda

"Looking back, one wonders how one of the most powerful corporations in the world could possibly have signed off on such a stylistic debacle."

PUSH-BUTTON RADIO WITH MANUAL ANTENNA WAS AN EXPENSIVE $95 OPTION

EDSEL WAGONS WERE BASED ON THE 116 IN (295 CM) FORD STATION WAGON PLATFORM

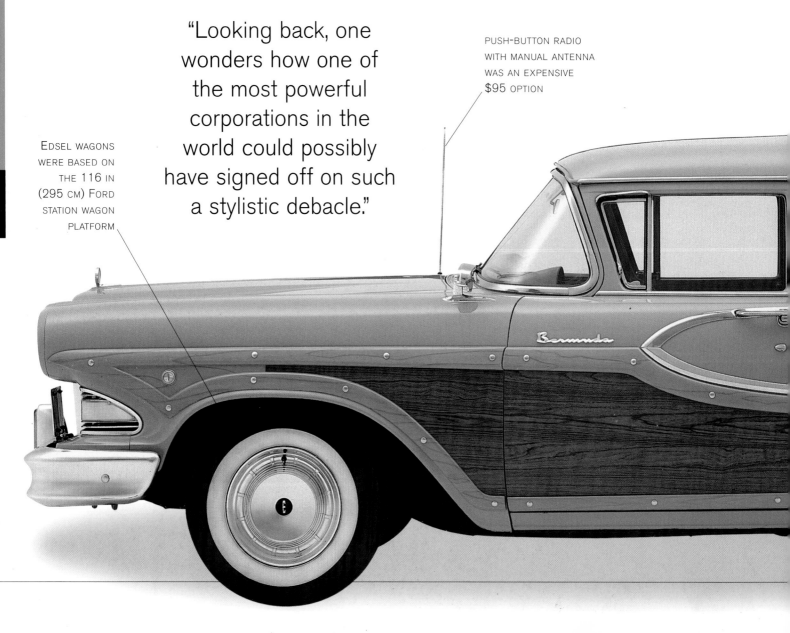

MODEL Edsel Bermuda (1958)

PRODUCTION 1,456 (1958, six-seater Bermudas)

BODY STYLE Four-door, six-seater station wagon.

CONSTRUCTION Steel body and chassis.

ENGINE 361cid V8.

POWER OUTPUT 303 bhp.

TRANSMISSION Three-speed manual with optional overdrive, optional three-speed automatic with or without Teletouch control.

SUSPENSION *Front*: independent coil springs; *Rear*: leaf springs with live axle.

BRAKES Front and rear drums.

MAXIMUM SPEED 108 mph (174 km/h)

0–60 MPH (0–96 km/h) 10.2 sec

A.F.C. 15 mpg (5.3 km/l)

INTERIOR Never one of Edsel's strongest selling points, the Teletouch gear selector was operated by push buttons in the center of the steering wheel. It was gimmicky and unreliable. All wagons had four armrests, two coathooks, dome lights, and vinyl, white headlining.

ENGINE "They're the industry's newest – and the best," cried the advertising. Edsel engines were strong 361 or 410cid V8s, with the station wagons usually powered by the smaller unit. The E400 on the valve covers indicates the unit's amount of torque.

"Despite later criticism of the models' design, advance publicity ensured that 4,000 Edsels were sold when launched on 'Edsel Day,' September 4, 1957."

ZANY BOOMERANG REAR LIGHT CLUSTERS CONTAINED TURN SIGNAL, STOP, AND BACKING LIGHTS

THIS BERMUDA IS PAINTED IN SPRING GREEN, BUT BUYERS HAD A CHOICE OF 161 DIFFERENT COLOR COMBINATIONS

EDSEL Corsair

A well-planned competition-killer that died

BY 1959 AMERICA had lost her confidence; the economy nosedived, Russia was first in space, there were race riots in Little Rock, Arkansas, and Ford was counting the cost of its disastrous Edsel project – close to 400 million dollars. "The Edsel look is here to stay" brayed the ads, but the bold new vertical grille had become a countrywide joke. Sales didn't just die, they never took off, and those who had been rash enough to buy hid their chromium follies in suburban garages. Eisenhower's mantra of materialism was over, and buyers wanted to know more about economical compacts like the Nash Rambler, Studebaker Lark, and the novel VW Beetle. Throw in a confusing 18-model lineup, poor-quality build, and disenchanted dealers, and "The Newest Thing on Wheels" never stood a chance. Now famous as a powerful symbol of failure, the Edsel stands as a telling memorial to the foolishness of consumer culture in Fifties America.

"By the time the Edsel appeared, it was a ridiculous leviathan, hopelessly out of kilter with its time."

THE HOODED CHROME DOOR MIRROR WAS REMOTE-CONTROLLED, AN EXTREMELY RARE AFTERMARKET OPTION

77 PERCENT OF ALL 1959 EDSELS WERE POWERED BY V8S, WITH THE ECONOMY SIX MAKING UP THE NUMBERS

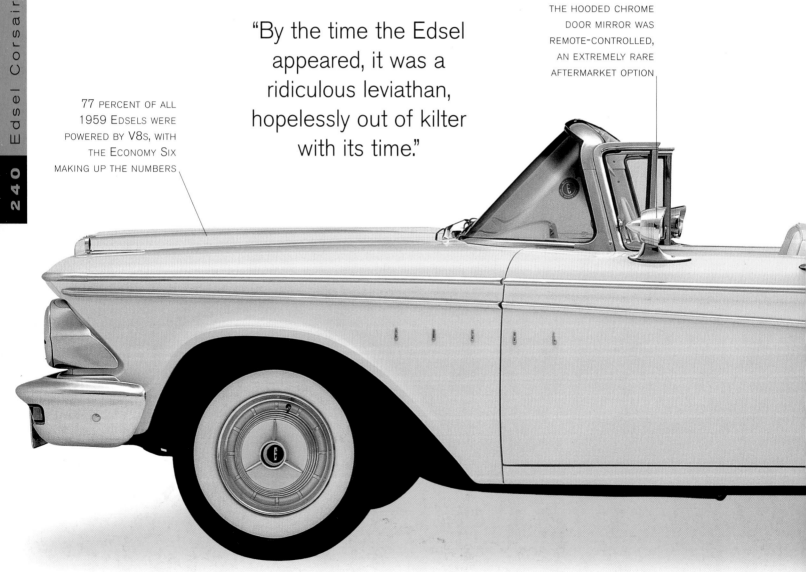

MODEL Edsel Corsair Convertible (1959)

PRODUCTION 1,343 (1959)

BODY STYLE Four-seater coupe.

CONSTRUCTION Steel body and chassis.

ENGINES 332cid, 361cid V8s.

POWER OUTPUT 225–303 bhp.

TRANSMISSION Three-speed manual with optional overdrive, optional two- or three-speed Mile-O-Matic automatic.

SUSPENSION *Front:* independent with coil springs; *Rear:* leaf springs with live axle.

BRAKES Front and rear drums.

MAXIMUM SPEED 95–105 mph (153–169 km/h)

0–60 MPH (0–96 km/h) 11–16 sec

A.F.C. 15 mpg (5.3 km/l)

INTERIOR The dashboard was cleaned up for 1959 and the unreliable Teletouch transmission deleted in favor of a Mile-O-Matic two-speed with column shift. The eight-tube push-button radio was available at $64.95.

IN-CAR VINYL This charming Philips record player is an aftermarket accessory installed in the early 1960s. In combination with the push-button radio, there was no shortage of music choice in the Edsel's cabin.

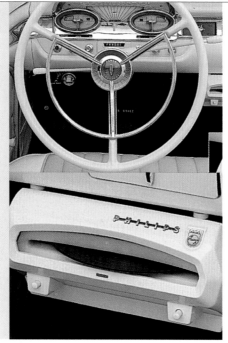

CHASSIS

The substantial steel girder chassis incorporated full-length side rails and five cross-members. Front suspension had ball joints.

WEIGHING IN AT A CONSIDERABLE 3,790 LB (1,719 KG) THE CONVERTIBLE WAS HEAVIER THAN THE SEDAN

CORSAIR CONVERTIBLES ARE THE RAREST '59 EDSELS, WITH ONLY 1,343 LEAVING THE LOUISVILLE PLANT

PUNDITS LAID INTO THE CORSAIR'S GRILLE, COMPARING IT TO A HORSE COLLAR, A MAN SUCKING A LEMON, OR EVEN A TOILET SEAT

19 NEBRASKA 60
35-110
THE BEEF STATE

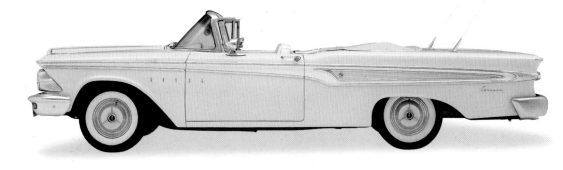

"Ford was desperate and tried to sell the Edsel as 'A new kind of car that makes sense.' Despite this, model year sales were a miserly 45,000."

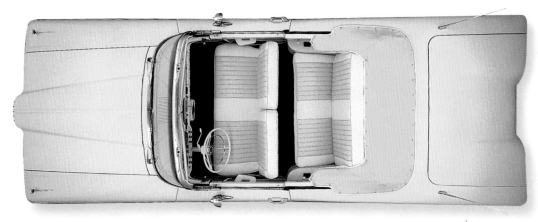

FACEL Vega II

A unique amalgam of styling motifs

WHEN SOMEONE LIKE Pablo Picasso chooses a car, it is going to look good. In its day, the Facel II was a poem in steel and easily as beautiful as anything turned out by the Italian styling houses. It's no wonder then that Facels were synonymous with the Sixties' jet set. Driven by Ringo Starr, Ava Gardner, Danny Kaye, Tony Curtis, François Truffaut, and Joan Fontaine, Facels were one of the most charismatic cars of the day. Even death gave them glamour; the novelist Albert Camus

died while a passenger in his publisher's FVS in January 1960. In 1961, the HK 500 was reskinned, given cleaner lines and an extra 6 in (15 cm) in length, and dubbed the Facel II. At 1.5 tons, the II was lighter than the 500 and could storm to 149 mph (240 km/h). Costing more than the contemporary Aston Martin DB4 (*see pages* 38–41) and Maserati 3500, the Facel II was as immortal as a Duesenberg, Hispano Suiza, or Delahaye. We will never see its like again.

"In terms of finish, image, and quality, Facel Vegas were one of the most successful hand-made supercars."

THE LEATHER BACK SEAT FOLDED DOWN TO MAKE A LUGGAGE PLATFORM

BRAKE LIGHTS WERE CUT OUT OF THE REAR FENDERS AND HELPED TO ENHANCE THE FACEL'S SEAMLESS LINES

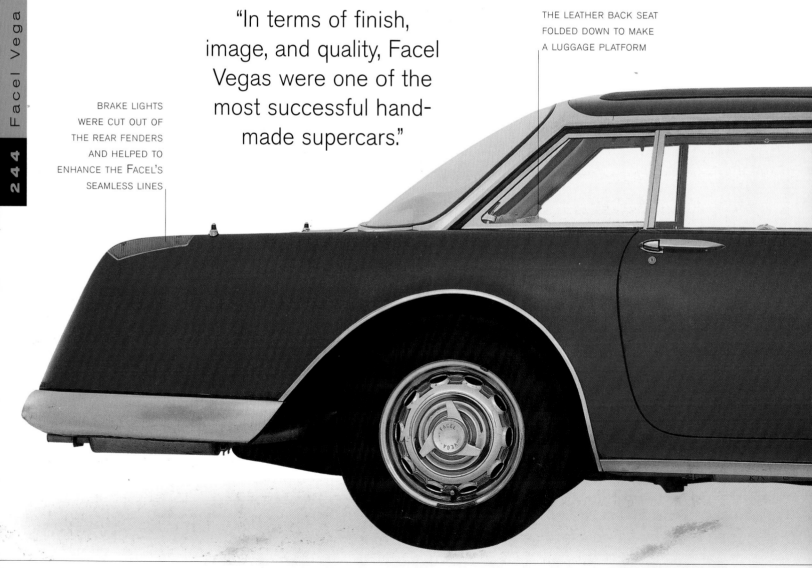

FACEL
FACEL
VEGA
PARIS

MODEL Facel Vega Facel II (1962–64)

PRODUCTION 184

BODY STYLE Two-door, four-seater Grand Tourer.

CONSTRUCTION Steel chassis, steel/light alloy body.

ENGINE 6286cc cast-iron V8.

POWER OUTPUT 390 bhp at 5400 rpm (manual), 355 bhp at 4800 rpm (auto).

TRANSMISSION Three-speed TorqueFlite auto or four-speed Pont-a-Mousson manual.

SUSPENSION *Front*: independent coil springs; *Rear*: leaf springs with live axle.

BRAKES Four-wheel Dunlop discs.

MAXIMUM SPEED 149 mph (240 km/h)

0–60 MPH (0–96 km/h) 8.3 sec

0–100 MPH (0–161 km/h) 17.0 sec

A.F.C. 15 mpg (5.4 km/l)

INTERIOR The steering wheel points straight to the driver's heart and was made of real wood. The dashboard, however, may have looked like wood but it was actually painted metal. Note the unmistakable aircraft-type panel layout with center gauges and the heater controls like hand throttles.

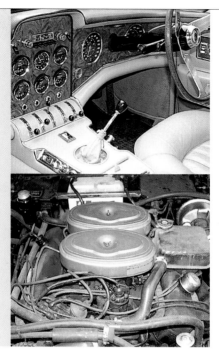

ENGINE The Facel II was powered by a 6286cc cast-iron Chrysler V8 that, when coupled with the rare and bulky four-speed gearbox, pushed out 390 bhp. A prodigious hood bulge was needed to clear the vast oil-drumlike air cleaners, which were positioned over double carburetors.

"The Facel II represents Facel creator Jean Danino's last and greatest achievement."

THE INTIMIDATING FRONTAGE WAS ALL GRILLE BECAUSE THE HOT-RUNNING V8 ENGINE NEEDED ALL THE COOLING AIR IT COULD GET

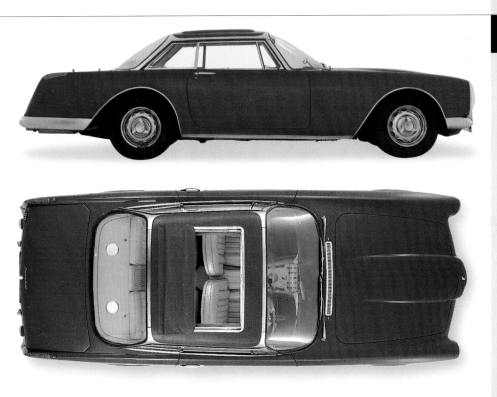

The French Nobel Prize-winning novelist Albert Camus was killed in a Facel Vega on May 4, 1960. The FVS model, driven by his publisher, went out of control and hit a tree broadside at 112 mph (180 km/h) near Villeneuve-la-Guyard. Camus, who was sitting in the passenger seat, was killed instantly. French police had to hide the wreck before souvenir hunters picked the shell clean.

FERRARI 250 GT SWB

An Italian supermodel with racing pedigree

In an era when Ferrari was turning out some lackluster road cars, the 250 GT SWB became a yardstick, the car against which all other GTs were judged and one of the finest Ferraris ever. Of the 167 made between 1959 and 1962, 74 were competition cars – their simplicity made them one of the most competitive sports racers of the Fifties. Built around a tubular chassis, the V12 3.0 engine lives at the front, along with a four-speed gearbox with Porsche internals. But it is that delectable Pininfarina-sculpted shape that is so special. Tense, urgent, but friendly, those smooth lines have none of the intimidating presence of a Testarossa or Daytona. The SWB stands alone as a perfect blend of form and function – one of the world's prettiest cars, and on the track one of the most successful – which is what Enzo Ferrari wanted. "They are cars," he said, "which the sporting client can use on the road during the week and race on Sundays." Happy days.

> "Soft, compact, and rounded, Pininfarina executed the design, while Scaglietti took care of the sheet metal. The result was one of the most charismatic cars ever produced."

INSTEAD OF AIR FILTERS, COMPETITION CARS USED FILTERLESS AIR TRUMPETS

GENTLY TAPERING NOSE WAS A MASTERPIECE OF THE SCULPTOR'S ART

MODEL Ferrari 250 GT SWB (1959–62)

PRODUCTION 167 (10 RHD)

BODY STYLE Two-seater GT coupe.

CONSTRUCTION Tubular chassis with all-alloy or alloy/steel body.

ENGINE 2953cc V12.

POWER OUTPUT 280 bhp at 7000 rpm.

TRANSMISSION Four-speed manual.

SUSPENSION *Front*: independent front coil and wishbones; *Rear*: leaf springs with live rear axle.

BRAKES Four-wheel discs.

MAXIMUM SPEED 147 mph (237 km/h)

0–60 MPH (0–96 km/h) 6.6 sec

0–100 MPH (0–161 km/h) 16.2 sec

A.F.C. 12 mpg (4.2 km/l)

INTERIOR Despite the movie star exterior, the interior is strictly a place of work. Functional dash is basic crackle black with no frills. Sun visors were notably absent. The cockpit was snug and airy but noisy when the key was turned. The bucket seats may have looked supportive but were thinly padded.

ENGINE The V12 power unit had a seven-bearing crankshaft turned from a solid billet of steel, single plug per cylinder, and three twin-choke Weber DCL3 or DCL6 carburetors. Progressively more power was extracted from the engine, with output rising from 240 to 295 bhp.

"The 250 GT had a lightness and fluidity found in only a handful of the world's most precocious sports cars."

SWEEPING BODY PANELS ARE NEAR PRICELESS – EACH WAS HANDMADE WITH SCANT REGARD FOR REPAIR OR REPLACEMENT

ENZO FERRARI

Enzo Ferrari variously tried careers as a journalist and then opera singer but loved cars from his early racing days. His genius flowered in 1946, when he collaborated with Gioacchino Columbo to create the legendary aluminum Ferrari V12. Never a happy man, Ferrari's view on life was constantly colored by disillusionment with his marriage and the pain of his greatest loss, the death of his son Dino.

RUDIMENTARY REAR WINDOW VENT WAS FOR COOLING THE COCKPIT

FERRARI 275 GTB/4

An arresting amalgam of beauty and brawn

THE GTB/4 WAS A hybrid made for two short years from 1966 to 1968. With just 350 built, a mere 27 in righthand drive, it was not one of Ferrari's cash cows. So named for its four camshafts, the GTB still ranks as the finest road car Ferrari produced before Fiat took control of the company. With fully independent suspension, a five-speed gearbox, and a wonderfully fetching Pininfarina-designed and Scaglietti-built body, it was the last of the real Berlinettas. The forerunner of the Daytona (*see page* 264), the GTB was built more for hard running than posing. This was Ferrari's first production four-cam V12 engine, and it allowed the car to hit 160 mph (257 km/h). It was also the first roadworthy prancing horse with an independent rear end. Nimble and compact, with neutral handling and stunning design, this is probably one of the most desirable Ferraris ever made.

THE COCKPIT IS CRAMPED, IMPRACTICAL, AND MAINLY TRIMMED IN DISTINCTLY UNLUXURIOUS VINYL

THE GTB/4'S CHASSIS WAS MADE UP OF A LADDER FRAME BUILT AROUND TWO OVAL-TUBE MEMBERS

"The GTB's type 226 engine was related to the 330 P2 prototypes of the 1965 racing season."

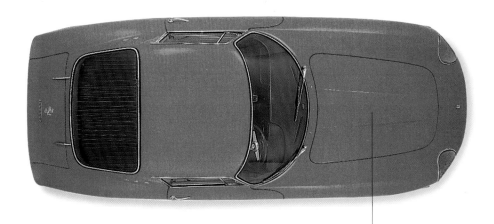

A GENTLE HOOD BULGE WAS NEEDED TO CLEAR THE HUGE AIR CLEANER ATOP SIX WEBER CARBURETORS

MODEL Ferrari 275 GTB/4 (1966–68)

PRODUCTION 350

BODY STYLE Two-seater front-engined coupe.

CONSTRUCTION Steel chassis, aluminum body.

ENGINE 3.3-liter twin overhead-cam dry sump V12.

POWER OUTPUT 300 bhp at 8000 rpm.

TRANSMISSION Five-speed all-synchromesh.

SUSPENSION All-around independent.

BRAKES Four-wheel servo discs.

MAXIMUM SPEED 160 mph (257 km/h)

0–60 MPH (0–96 km/h) 5.5 sec

0–100 MPH (0–161 km/h) 13 sec

A.F.C. 12 mpg (4.2 km/l)

FERRARI 308 GTB

Italian star of the small screen

ONE OF THE BEST-SELLING Ferraris ever, the 308 GTB started life with a fiberglass body designed by Pininfarina and built by Scaglietti. Power was courtesy of the V8 3.0 engine and five-speed gearbox inherited from the 308 GT4. With uptown America as the GTB's target market, federal emission regulations made the GTB clean up its act, evolving into a refined and civilized machine with such hi-tech features as four valves per cylinder and Bosch K-Jetronic fuel-injection. Practical and tractable in traffic, it became the 1980s entry-level Ferrari, supplanting the Porsche 911 (*see pages* 494–95) as the standard issue yuppie-mobile. In the television series *Magnum P.I.*, Tom Selleck gave the 308 prime-time publicity and turned it into an aspirational icon. Prices went crazy, but values have now softened and a good low-mileage 308 is one of the least traumatic and most cost-effective entrées into the prancing horse club.

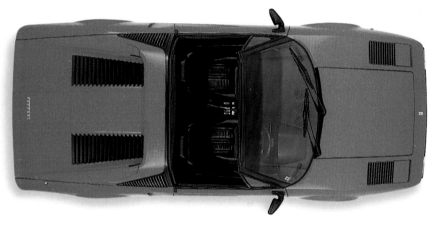

> "The handsome styling is a blend of Dino 246 and 365 GT4. The Dino provided concave rear windows, while the 365 brought double bodyshell appearance."

THE 2926CC V8 HAD DOUBLE OVERHEAD CAMS PER BANK AND FOUR 40 DCNF WEBER CARBURETORS

VENTILATED DISC BRAKES ON ALL FOUR WHEELS WERE NEEDED TO COUNTER THE GTB'S POWER

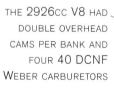

308
GTB

MODEL Ferrari 308 GTB (1975–85)

PRODUCTION 712 (308 GTB fiberglass); 2,185 (308 GTB steel); 3,219 (GTS).

BODY STYLE Two-door, two-seater sports coupe.

CONSTRUCTION Fiberglass/steel.

ENGINE Mid-mounted transverse dohc 2926cc V8.

POWER OUTPUT 255 bhp at 7600 rpm.

TRANSMISSION Five-speed manual.

SUSPENSION Independent double wishbones/coil springs all around.

BRAKES Ventilated discs all around.

MAXIMUM SPEED 154 mph (248 km/h)

0–60 MPH (0–96 km/h) 7.3 sec

0–100 MPH (0–161 km/h) 19.8 sec

A.F.C. 16 mpg (5.7 km/l)

THE GTB ALWAYS HAD A
TIN-TOP ROOF; THE CHIC
GTS HAD A REMOVABLE
TARGA TOP PANEL

FERRARI Dino 246 GT

Yet more sensual lines on the car from the heart

PRETTY ENOUGH TO STOP a speeding train, the Dino came not from Enzo Ferrari's head, but from his heart. The Dino was a tribute to Enzo's son, Alfredino, who died of a kidney disease. Aimed at the Porsche 911 buyer (*see pages* 494–95), the 246 Dino engine came with only half the number of cylinders usually found in a Ferrari. Instead of a V12 configuration, it boasted a 2.4-liter V6 engine yet was nonetheless capable of a very Ferrari-like 148 mph (238 km/h). With sparkling performance, small girth, and mid-engined layout, it handled like a go-kart and could be hustled around with enormous aplomb. Beautifully sculpted by Pininfarina, the 246 won worldwide acclaim as the high point of 1970s automotive styling. In its day, it was among the most fashionable cars money could buy. The rarest Dino is the GTS, with Targa detachable roof panel. The Dino's finest hour was when it was driven by Tony Curtis in the Seventies' British television series *The Persuaders*.

"Early Dinos were constructed from alloy, later ones from steel, with the bodies built by Italian designer Scaglietti."

THE SLEEK AERODYNAMIC SHAPE OF THE ROOF LINE HELPED TO GIVE THE CAR ITS IMPRESSIVELY HIGH TOP SPEED

FOUR EXHAUSTS MEANT THE DINO COULD SOUND ALMOST AS MUSICAL AS A V12

MODEL Ferrari Dino 246 GT (1969–74)

PRODUCTION 2,487

BODY STYLE Two-door, two seater.

CONSTRUCTION Steel body, tubular frame.

ENGINE Transverse 2.4 liter V6.

POWER OUTPUT 195 bhp at 5000 rpm.

TRANSMISSION Five-speed, all synchromesh.

SUSPENSION Independent front and rear.

BRAKES Ventilated discs all around.

MAXIMUM SPEED 148 mph (238 km/h)

0–60 MPH (0–96 km/h) 7.1 sec

0–100 MPH (0–161 km/h) 17.6 sec

A.F.C. 22 mpg (7.8 km/l)

INTERIOR The dashboard is suede and strewn with switches, while the cramped-looking interior is actually an ergonomic triumph. Though the cockpit is hot and noisy, that has not detracted from the car's popularity. Slotting the gearbox though its chrome gate is much like stirring honey.

ENGINE The transversely mounted 2418cc V6 has four overhead-cams, a four-bearing crankshaft, and breathes through three twin-choke Weber 40 DCF carburetors. The unit's power output is 195 bhp at 5000 rpm. This particular engine's distinctive throaty roar is a true Ferrari legend.

"The thin original paint job means that most surviving Dinos will have had at least one body rebuild by now."

WINDSHIELDS DO NOT COME MUCH MORE STEEPLY RAKED THAN THIS ONE

SPARE WHEEL AND BATTERY WERE LOCATED UNDER THE HOOD, LEAVING VERY LITTLE ROOM TO CARRY EXTRAS SUCH AS LUGGAGE

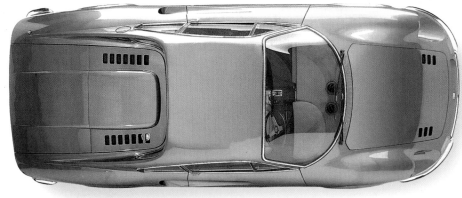

The Persuaders was a Seventies TV series starring Tony Curtis and Roger Moore as two wealthy playboys who solved crimes. At the time it was the most expensive TV series ever made in the UK. Tony Curtis drove a red Ferrari Dino 246, which was featured racing Roger Moore's Aston Martin DBS in the opening credits. The delicate Dino couldn't cope with the arduous demands of filming and often broke down or was damaged. The car's current whereabouts are unknown.

THE SENSUOUS CURVES
ARE UNMISTAKABLY
SUPPLIED BY FERRARI;
THE FERRARI BADGE
AND PRANCING HORSE
WERE ADDED BY A
LATER OWNER

FERRARI Berlinetta Boxer

Rare 12-cylinder Italian beauty with serious cachet

THE BERLINETTA BOXER was meant to be the jewel in Ferrari's crown – one of the fastest GT cars ever. Replacing the legendary V12 Ferrari Daytona (*see page 264*), the 365 BB was powered by a flat-12 "Boxer" engine, so named for the image of the horizontally located pistons punching at their opposite numbers. Mid-engined, with a tubular chassis frame, and clothed in a peerless Pininfarina-designed body, the 365 was assembled by Scaglietti in Modena. First unveiled in 1971 at the Turin Motor Show, the formidable 4.4-liter 380 bhp Boxer was so complex that deliveries to buyers did not start until 1973. The trouble was that Ferrari had suggested that the Boxer could top 185 mph (298 km/h), when it could actually only manage around 172 mph (277 km/h), slightly slower than the outgoing Daytona. In 1976 Ferrari replaced the 365 with the five-liter Boxer 512, yet the 365 is the faster and rarer model, with only 387 built.

"The 365 Boxer was the first mid-engined 12-cylinder production car to carry the Ferrari name."

THE BOXER ENGINE LAYOUT WAS FAVORED BECAUSE IT ALLOWED THE WHOLE CAR TO SIT THAT MUCH LOWER, GIVING BETTER AERODYNAMICS AND A LOWER CENTER OF GRAVITY

THE LOWER BODYWORK WAS FIBERGLASS, ALONG WITH THE WHEELARCH LINERS AND BUMPERS

MODEL Ferrari 365 GT4 Berlinetta Boxer (1973–76)

PRODUCTION 387 (58 RHD models)

BODY STYLE Two-seater sports.

CONSTRUCTION Tubular space-frame chassis.

ENGINE 4.4-liter flat-12.

POWER OUTPUT 380 bhp at 7700 rpm.

TRANSMISSION Five-speed all synchromesh rear-mounted gearbox.

SUSPENSION Independent front and rear.

BRAKES Ventilated front and rear discs.

MAXIMUM SPEED 172 mph (277 km/h)

0–60 MPH (0–96 km/h) 6.5 sec

0–100 MPH (0–161 km/h) 15 sec

A.F.C. 14 mpg (4.2 km/l)

WHEELS WERE THE
SAME AS ON THE
DAYTONA – CAST LIGHT
ALLOY WITH RUDGE
KNOCK-OFF HUBS

Ferrari Berlinetta Boxer **261**

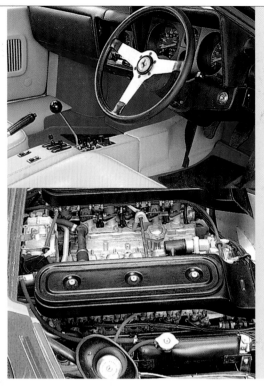

INTERIOR An amalgam of racer and grand tourer, the Boxer's cabin was functional yet luxurious, with electric windows and air-conditioning. Switches for these were positioned on the console beneath the gear lever. The rear-mounted gearbox meant that only a small transmission tunnel was needed.

ENGINE A magnificent piece of foundry art, the flat-12 has a crankshaft machined from a solid billet of chrome-molybdenum steel. Cylinder heads were light alloy, holding two camshafts each. Instead of timing chains, the 365 used toothed composite belts, an innovation in 1973.

HEART OF THE BEAST
The Boxer 4.4-liter engine could produce a jaw-dropping 380 bhp at 7600 rpm. Note the twin air filters, one for each bank of six cylinders.

THE BOXER'S CHASSIS WAS DERIVED FROM THE DINO, WITH A FRAME OF STEEL TUBES AND DOORS, OIL PAN, AND NOSE IN ALUMINUM

SLATTED HOOD COOLING VENT HELPED KEEP INTERIOR CABIN TEMPERATURES DOWN

TESTING THE STALLION
A handful of prototype Boxers – which looked very similar to the final model – were subjected to extensive testing. This one is recognizable by the roof-mounted antenna – factory cars had antennas enclosed in the windshield.

"In the classic car boom of the mid-Eighties, 512 Boxers tripled in value before the crash, with the 365 doubling its price."

FERRARI Daytona

One of the fastest production cars in the world

PREVIOUSLY KNOWN TO every schoolboy as the world's fastest car, the classically sculptured and outrageously quick Daytona was a supercar with a split personality. Under 120 mph (193 km/h), it felt like a truck, with heavy inert controls and crashing suspension. But once the needle was heading for 140 mph (225 km/h), things started to sparkle. With a romantic flat-out maximum of 170 mph (280 km/h), it was the last of the great front-engined V12 warhorses. Launched at the 1968 Paris Salon as the 365 GTB/4, the press immediately named it "Daytona" in honor of Ferrari's success at the 1967 American 24-hour race. Faster than the contemporary Lamborghini Miura (*see pages 344–47*), De Tomaso Pantera (*see pages 224–27*), and Jaguar E-Type (*see pages 330–33*), the chisel-nosed Ferrari won laurels on the racetrack as well as the hearts and pockets of wealthy enthusiasts all over the world.

WITH HAMMOCK-STYLE RACING SEATS, A CORNUCOPIA OF BLACK-ON-WHITE INSTRUMENTS, AND A PROVOCATIVELY ANGLED, EXTRA-LONG GEAR SHIFT, THE CABIN PROMISED SOME SERIOUS EXCITEMENT

AMERICAN SAFETY REGULATIONS DICTATED THAT THE DOUBLE RETRACTABLE HEADLIGHTS COULD BE RAISED IN THREE SECONDS

RBY 8IK

FERRARI 400 GT

An executive offering with discreet lines

THE FIRST FERRARI offered with automatic transmission, the 400 was aimed at the American market and was meant to take the prancing horse into the boardrooms of Europe and the US. But the 400's automatic box was a most un-Ferrarilike device, a lazy three-speed GM Turbo-Hydramatic also used in Cadillac, Rolls-Royce, and Jaguar. It may have been the best self-shifter in the world, but it was a radical departure for Maranello and met with only modest success. The 400 was possibly the most discreet and refined Ferrari ever made. It looked awful in Racing Red – the color of 70 percent of Ferraris – so most were finished in dark metallics. Its massive glass area and thin pillars gave the 400 the best visibility of any Ferrari. The 400 became the 400i GT in 1973 and the 412 in 1985. It became a fashionable alternative for the Eighties executive bored with Daimler Double-Sixes and BMW 750s.

APART FROM THE DELICATE CHIN SPOILER AND BOLT-ON ALLOYS, THE SHAPE WAS PURE 365 GT4 2+2, WITH AMPLE ACCOMMODATION FOR FOUR

MASSIVE GLASS AREA AND THIN PILLARS GAVE THE 400 THE BEST VISIBILITY OF ANY FERRARI

AN-48-TA

FERRARI Testarossa

The epitomy of a truly excessive decade

THE TESTAROSSA WAS NEVER one of Modena's best efforts. Though Ferrari bestowed on its new creation one of the grandest names from its racing past – the 250 Testa Rossa, of which only 19 were built for retail customers – its enormous girth and overstuffed appearance perfectly summed up the Eighties credo of excess. As soon as it appeared on the world's television screens in *Miami Vice*, the Testarossa, or Redhead, became a symbol of everything that was wrong with a decade of rampant materialism and greed. The Testarossa fell from grace rather suddenly. Dilettante speculators bought them new at $100,000 and ballyhooed their values up to a quarter of a million. By 1988, secondhand values were slipping badly, and many an investor saw their car shed three-quarters of its value overnight. Today, a decent used Testarossa struggles to command much more than $60,000. *Sic transit gloria mundi.*

"The cockpit was restrained and spartan, with a hand-stitched leather dashboard and little distracting ornamentation."

STRIKING RADIATOR COOLING DUCTS OBVIATED THE NEED TO SEND WATER FROM THE FRONT RADIATOR TO THE MID-MOUNTED ENGINE, FREEING THE FRONT LUGGAGE COMPARTMENT

testarossa

MODEL Ferrari Testarossa (1988)

PRODUCTION 1,074

BODY STYLE Mid-engined, two-seater sports coupe.

CONSTRUCTION Steel frame with aluminum and fiberglass panels.

ENGINE Flat-12, 4942cc with dry sump lubrication.

POWER OUTPUT 390 bhp at 6300 rpm.

TRANSMISSION Five-speed manual.

SUSPENSION Independent front and rear.

BRAKES Front discs, rear drums.

MAXIMUM SPEED 181 mph (291 km/h)

0–60 MPH (0–96 km/h) 5.3 sec

0–100 MPH (0–161 km/h) 12.2 sec

A.F.C. 12 mpg (4.2 km/l)

INTERIOR The Testarossa's large body meant plenty of cabin space, with more room for both occupants and luggage. But even though electrically adjustable leather seats and air-conditioning came as standard, interior trim was flimsy and looked tired after 70,000 miles (112,000 kilometers).

ENGINE The flat-12 mid-mounted engine had a 4942cc capacity and produced 390 bhp at 6300 rpm. With four valves per cylinder, coil ignition, and fuel injection, it was one of the very last flat-12 GTs. The cooling ducts were for the twin radiators, located forward of the rear wheels to keep heat away from the cockpit.

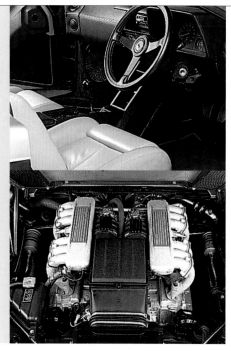

1958 FERRARI TESTA ROSSA

From 1956–62, only 70 Ferrari 250 Testa Rossas were built in total. They won the World Championship in 1958, 1960, and 1961, beaten in 1959 by Stirling Moss' Aston Martin. The distinctive bodywork, with its sloping nose separated from the cutaway front wheelarches, was known as "pontoon-fendered."

THE TESTAROSSA MEASURED A PORTLY 6 FT (1.83 M) ACROSS. WHILE THIS MEANT A BIGGER COCKPIT, THE ULTRAWIDE DOOR SILLS COLLECTED MUD IN WET WEATHER

PROMINENT DOOR MIRRORS ON BOTH SIDES GAVE THE TESTAROSSA AN EXTRA 8 IN (20 CM) IN WIDTH

FRONT SPOILER KEPT THE NOSE FIRMLY ATTACHED TO THE ROAD AND CHANNELED COOLING AIR TO THE FRONT BRAKES

UAE 576

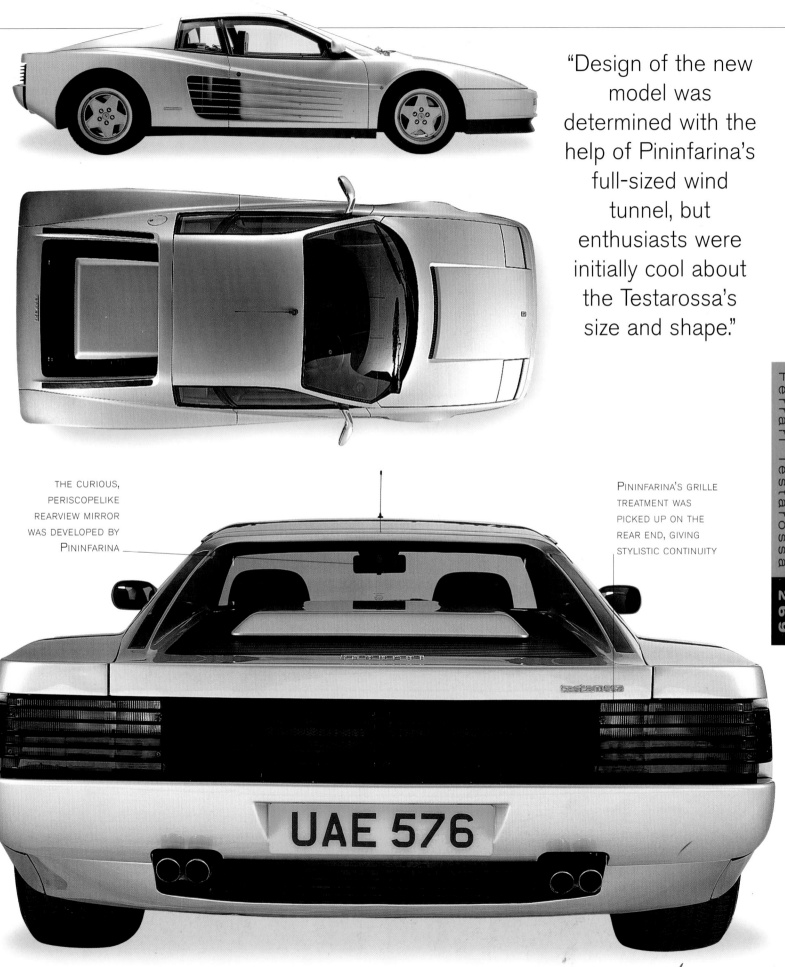

"Design of the new model was determined with the help of Pininfarina's full-sized wind tunnel, but enthusiasts were initially cool about the Testarossa's size and shape."

THE CURIOUS, PERISCOPELIKE REARVIEW MIRROR WAS DEVELOPED BY PININFARINA

PININFARINA'S GRILLE TREATMENT WAS PICKED UP ON THE REAR END, GIVING STYLISTIC CONTINUITY

UAE 576

FIAT 500D

Possibly the cutest car ever made

WHEN THE FIAT 500 Nuova appeared in 1957, longtime Fiat designer Dante Giacosa defended it by saying, "However small it might be, an automobile will always be more comfortable than a motor scooter." Today though, the diminutive runabout needs no defense, for time has justified Giacosa's faith – over four million 500s and derivatives were produced up to the demise of the Giardiniera wagon in 1977. In some senses the Fiat was a mini before the British Mini (*see pages* 50–53), for the baby Fiat not only appeared two years ahead of its British counterpart, but was also 3 in (7.6 cm) shorter. With its 479cc engine, the original 500 Nuova was rather frantic. 1960 saw it grow to maturity with the launch of the 800D, which was pushed along by its enlarged 499.5cc engine. Now at last the baby Fiat could almost touch 60 mph (96 km/h) without being pushed over the edge of a cliff.

"This pert little package is big on charm. From any angle the baby Fiat seems to present a happy, smiling disposition."

REAR-ENGINED LAYOUT SAVED SPACE BY REMOVING THE NEED FOR A TRANSMISSION TUNNEL

MODEL Fiat 500 (1957–77)

PRODUCTION 4 million plus (all models)

BODY STYLES Sedan, convertible. Giardiniera wagon.

CONSTRUCTION Unitary body/chassis.

ENGINES Two-cylinder air-cooled 479cc or 499.5cc.

POWER OUTPUT 17.5 bhp at 4400 rpm (499.5cc).

TRANSMISSION Four-speed nonsynchromesh.

SUSPENSION *Front*: independent, transverse leaf, wishbones; *Rear*: independent semitrailing arms, coil springs.

BRAKES Hydraulic drums.

MAXIMUM SPEED 59 mph (95 km/h)

0–60 MPH (0–96 km/h) 32 sec

A.F.C. 53 mpg (19 km/l)

THE HOOD HOUSED THE GAS TANK, BATTERY, AND SPARE WHEEL, WITH A LITTLE SPACE LEFT FOR A MODEST AMOUNT OF LUGGAGE

INTERIOR The Fiat 500's interior is minimal but functional. There is no fuel gauge, just a light that illuminates when three-quarters of a gallon remains – enough for another 40 miles (64 km). Two average-sized adults can fit in the front, with two children or a grocery bag in the back.

ENGINE The use of an air-cooled engine and only two cylinders in the 500 was a completely new direction for Fiat. The 500 started with a 479cc engine; the 500D adopted the larger 499cc unit of the 500 Sport, which it replaced. All engines, though, were feisty little devils.

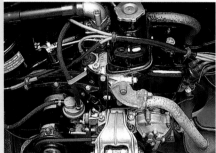

"The baby Fiat was a fine little driver's car that earned press plaudits for its assured and nimble handling."

SOME REAR-ENGINED CARS COPIED FRONT-ENGINED COUSINS WITH FAKE GRILLES AND AIR INTAKES, BUT NOT THE UNPRETENTIOUS FIAT

PRE-1965 MODELS HAD REAR-HINGED, SO-CALLED "SUICIDE" DOORS. AFTER THAT DATE, THE HINGES MOVED TO THE FRONT

DANTE GIACOSA

At the tender age of 26, Dante Giacosa designed the revolutionary Fiat 500A of 1936. His brief came from Fiat's boss, Senator Agnelli, who asked him, "Can you design a small car?" Giacosa nodded, and his Topolino, as the 500 was nicknamed, went on to spawn a whole generation of tiny cars.

SOME 500S HAD SMALL FOLD-BACK SUNROOFS. ON CONVERTIBLES, THE FABRIC ROOF WITH PLASTIC REAR WINDOW ROLLED RIGHT BACK

nuova 500

IH 65-34

FORD GT40

An international project with outstanding success

TO APPLY THE TERM "supercar" to the fabled Ford GT40 is to demean it; in the modern idiom, Jaguar XJ220s, McLaren F1s, and Bugatti EB110s are all the acme of supercar superlatives, but when did any one of them win Le Mans outright? The Ford GT40, though, was not only the ultimate road car but also the ultimate endurance racer of its era. It was so good that arguments are still going on over its nationality. Let us call it a joint design project between the American manufacturer and independent British talent, with a little Italian and German input as well. What matters is that it achieved what it was designed for, claiming the classic Le Mans 24-hour race four times in a row. And there is more to the GT40 than its Le Mans legend. You could, if you could afford it, drive around quite legally on public roads in this 200 mph (322 km/h) projectile. Ultimate supercar? No, it is better than that. Ultimate car? Maybe.

"The graceful and muscular shape was penned in Ford's Dearborn design studios. Requirements included a mid-engined layout and aerodynamic efficiency."

THE COCKPIT MIGHT BE CRAMPED, BUT THE GT40'S IMPRACTICALITY WAS ALL PART OF ITS EXTREME EXTRAVAGANCE

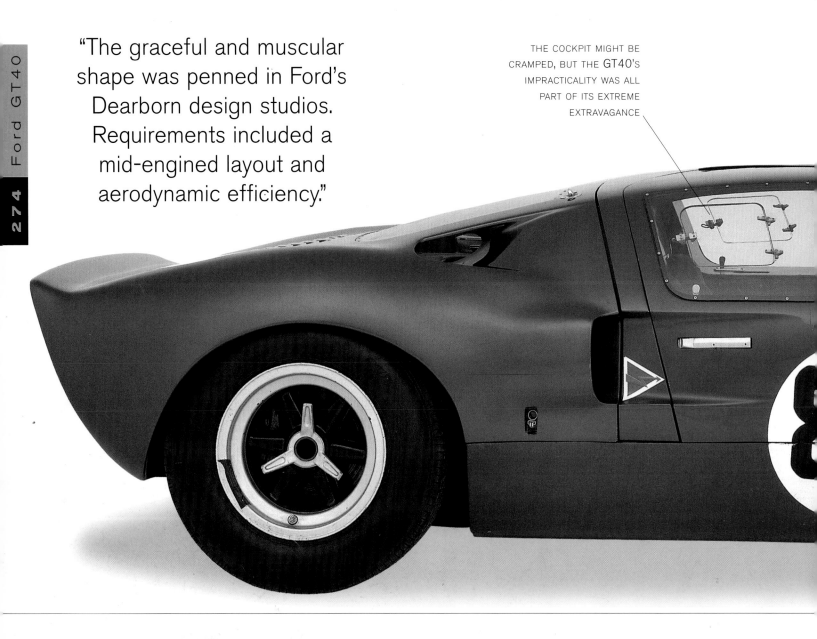

MODEL Ford GT40 MkI, II, III, & IV (1964–68)

PRODUCTION 107

BODY STYLE Two-door, two-seater coupe.

CONSTRUCTION Sheet-steel monocoque (honeycomb MkIV), fiberglass body.

ENGINES Ford V8, 4195cc (MkI), 4727cc (MksI & III), 6997cc (MksII & IV).

POWER OUTPUT From 350 bhp at 7200 rpm (Mk1 4195cc) to 500 bhp at 5000 rpm (MkIV).

TRANSMISSION Transaxle and four- or five-speed ZF gearbox.

SUSPENSION Independent by coil springs and wishbones all around.

BRAKES Ventilated discs all around.

MAXIMUM SPEED 155–200 mph (249–322 km/h, depending on gearing)

0–60 MPH (0–96 km/h) 4.5 sec

0–100 MPH (0–161 km/h) 8.5 sec

A.F.C. 12–16 mpg (4.2–5.7 km/l)

INTERIOR As befits a custom-built racer, the cockpit was designed for business rather than pleasure. Switches and instruments were pure racer, and the low roof line meant that tall drivers literally could not fit in, with the gullwing doors hitting the driver's head.

ENGINE Design of the GT40 was based on an earlier British Lola, including race-car features such as mid-engined layout with gearbox/transaxle at the rear. In Ford's favor were the powerful V8, plenty of bucks, and Henry Ford II's determination to win Le Mans.

"One of the seven MkIII cars produced for the road was actually equipped with a TV."

FUZZY SLIT ABOVE ENGINE COVER GAVE JUST ENOUGH REAR VISION TO WATCH A FERRARI FADE AWAY

FORD Thunderbird (1955)

A brilliantly successful blend of luxury and prestige

CHEVY'S 1954 CORVETTE may have been a peach, but anything GM could do, Ford could do better. The '55 T-Bird had none of the 'Vette's fiberglass nonsense but a steel body and grunty V8 engine. Plus, it was drop-dead gorgeous and offered scores of options, with the luxury of roll-up windows. Nobody was surprised when it outsold the creaky Corvette 24-to-one. But Ford wanted volume, and two-seaters weren't everybody's cup of tea, which is why by 1958 the Little Bird became the Big Bird, swollen by four fat armchairs. Nevertheless, as the first of America's top-selling two-seaters, the Thunderbird fired the public's imagination. For the next decade American buyers looking for lively power in a stylish package would greedily devour every Thunderbird going. The two-seater of 1955–57 has become a design icon, a romantic piece of Fifties ephemera that features in the lyrics of half a dozen cult songs and as many films.

THE RAKISH LONG HOOD AND SHORT REAR DECK RECALLED THE 1940S LINCOLN CONTINENTAL

"The Thunderbird name was chosen after a southwest Native American god who brought rain and prosperity."

MODEL Ford Thunderbird (1955)

PRODUCTION 16,155 (1955)

BODY STYLE Two-door, two-seater convertible.

CONSTRUCTION Steel body and chassis.

ENGINE 292cid V8.

POWER OUTPUT 193 bhp.

TRANSMISSION Three-speed manual with optional overdrive, optional three-speed Ford-O-Matic automatic.

SUSPENSION *Front*: independent coil springs; *Rear*: leaf springs with live axle.

BRAKES Front and rear drums.

MAXIMUM SPEED 105–125 mph (169–201 km/h)

0–60 MPH (0–96 km/h) 7–11 sec

A.F.C. 17 mpg (6 km/l)

INTERIOR Luxury options made the Thunderbird an easy-going companion. On the list were power steering, windows, and brakes; automatic transmission; and even electric seats and a power-assisted top. At $100, the push-button radio was more expensive than power steering.

ENGINE The T-Bird's engine was the new cast-iron OHV 292cid V8 with dual exhausts and four-barrel Holley carb. Compared to the 'Vette's ancient six, the T-Bird's mill offered serious shove. Depending on the state of tune, a very hot T-Bird could hit 60 mph (96 km/h) in just seven seconds.

THE HOOD NEEDED A BULGE TO CLEAR THE LARGE AIR FILTERS. IT WAS STYLISH TOO

In 1956 Marilyn Monroe walked into an LA Ford dealership and bought a Sunset Coral T-Bird with brown and white interior. Monroe was celebrating winning a contract battle with her studio and had been impressed with her then lover, Arthur Miller's, black '55 T-Bird. Monroe owned her T-Bird for two years, after which it disappeared. A Californian collector found it in the '70s and had it completely restored.

APART FROM THE RATHER TOO PROMINENT EXHAUSTS, THE REAR END WAS REMARKABLY UNCLUTTERED

WITH THE TOP UP, HEAT FROM THE TRANSMISSION MADE FOR A HOT COCKPIT. AS A RESULT, VENTILATION FLAPS WERE INTRODUCED ON '56 AND '57 MODELS

CALIFORNIA 19**62** 56
VYD 341

FORD Fairlane 500 Skyliner

A complicated roof system that actually worked

FORD RAISED THE ROOF in '57 with this one – and eyebrows too, for a Ford Fairlane Skyliner pulling up at the curb was an engaging spectacle. The world's only mass-produced retractable hardtop debuted at the New York Show of '56, and the first production version was presented to a bemused President Eisenhower in '57. The Skyliner's balletic routine was the most talked-about gadget for years and filled Ford showrooms with thousands of gawking customers. Surprisingly reliable and actuated by a single switch, the Retrac's roof had 610 ft (185 m) of wiring, three drive motors, and a feast of electrical hardware. But showmanship apart, the Skyliner was pricey and had precious little trunk space or leg room. By '59 the novelty had worn off, and division chief Robert McNamara's desire to end expensive "gimmick engineering" led to the wackiest car ever to come out of Dearborn being axed in 1960.

"Ford spent $18 million testing the Skyliner's roof and, in mechanical efficiency terms, the investment paid off."

A SWITCH ON THE STEERING COLUMN STARTED THREE MOTORS THAT OPENED THE REAR DECK. ANOTHER MOTOR UNLOCKED THE TOP, WHILE A FURTHER MOTOR HOISTED THE ROOF AND SENT IT BACK TO THE OPEN TRUNK SPACE

THE SKYLINER COULD BE SPECIFIED WITH FOUR DIFFERENT V8S RANGING FROM 272 TO 352CID

"Today the Skyliner's clever roof would not get past the concept stage."

MODEL Ford Fairlane 500 Galaxie Skyliner Retractable (1959)

PRODUCTION 12,915 (1959)

BODY STYLE Two-door hardtop with retractable roof.

CONSTRUCTION Steel body and chassis.

ENGINES 272cid, 292cid, 312cid, 352cid V8s.

POWER OUTPUT 190–300 bhp.

TRANSMISSION Three-speed manual, optional three-speed Cruise-O-Matic automatic.

SUSPENSION *Front:* coil springs; *Rear:* leaf springs.

BRAKES Front and rear drums.

MAXIMUM SPEED 105 mph (169 km/h)

0–60 MPH (0–96 km/h) 10.6 sec

A.F.C. 15.3 mpg (5.4 km/l)

INTERIOR As the top-of-the-line Fairlane, the glamorous Skyliner was luxuriously appointed, with color-coordinated seats and dash, and power-assisted steering and brakes. The $19 Lifeguard safety package included a sun visor and a padded instrument panel. This car has Cruise-O-Matic automatic transmission.

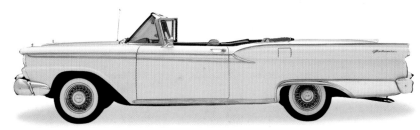

"At two tons and $3,138, the Skyliner was the heaviest, priciest, and least practical Ford in the line. Ironically, the Retrac's biggest fault wasn't electrical problems, but body rust."

RAISING THE ROOF

The whole process of raising the roof took just one minute, but had to be done with the gear-shift in "park" and the engine running. If the electrics failed, there was a manual procedure for getting the roof down, but it was rarely needed.

THOUGH A PARTICULARLY HEAVY CAR, REAR SUSPENSION WAS BY STANDARD LEAF SPRINGS

TINTED GLASS WAS AN OPTIONAL EXTRA, BUT ILL-FITTING WINDOW SEALS WERE AN ALL-SEASON ANNOYANCE

FINS WERE DOWN FOR '59, BUT MISSILE-SHAPED PRESSINGS ON THE HIGHER REAR FENDERS WERE A NEAT TOUCH TO HIDE ALL THAT MOVING METALWORK

FORD Falcon

Simple styling with mass appeal

FORD CHIEF EXECUTIVE Robert McNamara had a soft spot for the Volkswagen Beetle and wanted Dearborn to turn out a small compact of its own. Obsessed with gas mileage and economy, McNamara wanted a four-cylinder, since it was $13.50 cheaper to make, but was persuaded that a six-pot would sell better. On March 19, 1958, Ford approved its small-car program, and the Falcon, the first of the American compacts, was launched in 1960. The press was unimpressed, calling it a modern version of the Tin Lizzy. One car writer said of McNamara: "He wears granny glasses and has put out a granny car." But cash-strapped consumers liked the new Ford, and the Falcon won over 435,000 sales in its first year. The ultimate throwaway car, the Falcon may have been mechanically uninteresting and conventional in looks, but it was roomy, smooth-riding, and delivered a creditable 30 mpg (10.6 km/l).

"The Falcon just about made it to the end of the decade, superseded in 1970 by the compact Maverick."

HALF-A-HOOD SHORTER THAN FULL-SIZE FORDS, THE SLAB-SIDED TWO- OR FOUR-DOOR FALCON COULD COMFORTABLY SEAT SIX

THE FALCON'S STANDARD MILL WAS A 144CID SIX, WHICH THE ADS BOASTED AS HAVING "BIG-CAR PERFORMANCE AND SAFETY"

Falcon

MODEL Ford Falcon (1962)

PRODUCTION 396,129 (1962)

BODY STYLES Two- or four-door hardtops, station wagons, and convertibles.

CONSTRUCTION All-steel unitary construction.

ENGINES 144cid, 170cid sixes, 260cid V8.

POWER OUTPUT 85–174 bhp.

TRANSMISSION Three-speed column-shift synchro manual, optional two-speed Ford-O-Matic automatic.

SUSPENSION *Front*: coil springs; *Rear*: leaf springs.

BRAKES Front and rear drums.

MAXIMUM SPEED 90–110 mph (145–177 km/h)

0-60 MPH (0–96 km/h) 12–18 sec

A.F.C. 25–30 mpg (8.8–10.6 km/l)

Ford Falcon **287**

INTERIOR The austere interior could be upgraded with an $87 Deluxe trim package, which became the Deluxe model in its own right in 1962. A padded dash and visors cost an extra $16, and front safety belts $21. Three-speed manual or four-speed automatic transmission were available.

TAIL LIGHT With its simple, ultra-conservative styling, as on the circular taillights, the Falcon was dubbed by Ford "the easiest car in the world to own." The company also stated that the Falcon offered "plenty of room for six and their luggage" and the hype in this case really was true.

The new International Class Car

Ford Falcon

GROWING SERIES

Base Falcons stickered at just $1,974 in 1960, but the Falcon range gradually expanded to include station wagons, a neat-looking pickup, the Falcon sedan delivery, the Econoline van range, and the sporty Futura Coupe. The Futura Sprint, convertible or hardtop, came with a zesty 260cid V8.

THE ALUMINUM-STAMPED RADIATOR GRILLE CHANGED EVERY YEAR

MID-'62 TWO- AND FOUR-DOOR FALCONS HAD A T-BIRD-STYLE ROOF LINE

FORD

OCT MISSISSIPPI 62
SPB 499
STONE

"The Falcon's styling was as simple as its engineering, with roly-poly rounded edges, creased body sides, and big, circular taillights."

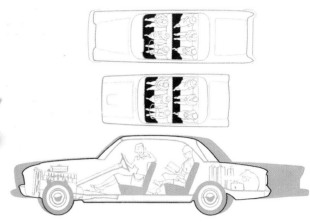

ROOMY INTERIOR

Ford's marketing men boasted that the Falcon offered "honest-to-goodness six-passenger comfort." This was partly as a result of Henry Ford himself, who deemed the Falcon prototype too narrow and insisted that the model should be considerably widened.

REAR WINDOW WAS MASSIVE AND GAVE THE DRIVER EXCELLENT REARWARD VISION

FORD Galaxie 500XL Sunliner

Designed to appeal to a young market

IN '62, FORD WAS SELLING its line as "America's liveliest, most carefree cars." And leading the lively look was the bright new Galaxie. This was General Manager Lee Iacocca's third year at the helm, and he was pitching for the young-guy market with speed and muscle. Clean-cut, sleek, and low, the Galaxie line was just what the boys wanted, and it drove Ford into a new era. The new-for-'62 500XL was a real piece, with XL standing for "extra lively" and making the 500 one of the first cars to kick off Ford's new Total Performance sales campaign. The 500XL Sunliner Convertible was billed as a sporty ragtop and cost an eminently reasonable $3,350. Engines were mighty, rising from 292 through 390 to 406cid V8s, with a Borg-Warner stick-shift four-speed option. Ford learned an important lesson from this car. Those big, in-yer-face engines clothed in large, luxurious bodies would become seriously hip.

"The Galaxie had an especially quiet ride because it was soundproofed at various points."

STOCK GALAXIES LUMBERED AROUND WITH A 223CID SIX OR 292CID V8. THE 500XL OWNER COULD CHOOSE FROM A LINE OF THUNDERBIRD V8S THAT INCLUDED THE 390CID SPECIAL, AS HERE, AND A 405 BHP 406CID V8

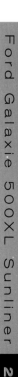

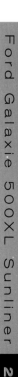

MODEL Ford Galaxie 500XL Sunliner
Convertible (1962)

PRODUCTION 13,183 (1962)

BODY STYLE Two-door convertible.

CONSTRUCTION Steel body and chassis.

ENGINES 292cid, 352cid, 390cid, 406cid V8s.

POWER OUTPUT 170–405 bhp.

TRANSMISSION Three-speed Cruise-O-Matic
automatic, optional four-speed manual.

SUSPENSION *Front*: coil springs;
Rear: leaf springs.

BRAKES Front and rear drums.

MAXIMUM SPEED 108–140 mph
(174–225 km/h)

0–60 MPH (0–96 km/h) 7.6–14.2 sec

A.F.C. 16–18 mpg (5.7–6.4 km/l)

Ford Galaxie 500XL Sunliner

291

IN '62 ALL FORDS HAD SELF-ADJUSTING BRAKES, 6,000-MILE (9,660-KM) LUBE INTERVALS, AND LIFE-OF-THE-CAR TRANSMISSION FLUID

SOUND-ABSORBENT MASTIC WAS APPLIED TO THE INSIDE SURFACES OF THE HOOD, DOORS, TRUNK LID, FENDERS, AND QUARTER PANELS

"The slab-sided Galaxie body was completely new for '62 and would set something of a styling trend for larger cars."

THE SPOTLIGHT MIRROR WAS A FACTORY OPTION; ON A CLEAR DAY, THE LIGHT COULD EMIT A BEAM ½ MILE (800 METERS) AHEAD

KANSAS 67
E L · 1175
MIDWAY USA

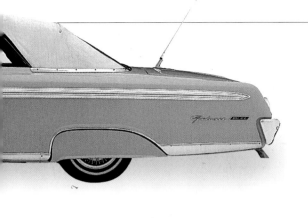

INTERIOR The interior was plush and palatial, with Mylar-trimmed, deep-pleated buckets flanking the center console. Seats could be adjusted four ways manually and six ways electronically. The dashboard was padded, and front seat belts were an option. Fiberglass "blankets" insulated the roof when it was up.

DETAIL The Galaxie's ornamentation was tasteful and stylish, a progression from the often garish and over-the-top decoration on models from just a few years earlier. The arrow-straight side flash, for example, was a far cry from the florid sweepspears that adorned most Fifties models.

Galaxie 500/XL sunliner *in Rangoon Red*

SALES BROCHURE

"This year, more than ever, Galaxie styling is the envy of the industry." Subjective sales literature maybe, but Ford's restyled Galaxies were a real success, and the new XL series offered peak performance in addition to the top trim level of the 500.

LARGE, ROUND, TAILLIGHT CLUSTER APED THE T-BIRD AND APPEARED ON THE FALCON AS WELL AS THE FAIRLANE, ALSO DEBUTING IN 1962

FORD Thunderbird (1963)

A car with a special place in the American psyche

IT WAS NO ACCIDENT that the third-generation T-Bird looked like it was fired from a rocket silo. Designer Bill Boyer wanted the new prodigy to have "an aircraft and missilelike shape," a subtext that wasn't lost on an American public vexed by the Cuban crisis and Khrushchev's declaration of an increase in Soviet military spending. The Sports Roadster model was the finest incarnation of the '61–'63 Thunderbird. With Kelsey-Hayes wire wheels and a two-seater fiberglass tonneau, it was one of the most glamorous cars on the block and one of the most exclusive. Virile, vast, and expensive, the Big Bird showed that Detroit still wasn't disposed to making smaller, cheaper cars. GM even impudently asserted that "a good used car is the only answer to America's need for cheap transportation." And anyway, building cars that looked and went like ballistic missiles was far more interesting and profitable.

THE ODD STYLING CREASE RAN FROM THE FENDER TO THE DOOR AND WAS THE MODEL'S LEAST BECOMING FEATURE

"With the top down, the Big Bird was one of the most attractive and stiffest convertibles Ford had ever made."

THREE SETS OF FIVE CAST-CHROME SLASH MARKS UNMISTAKABLY SUGGESTED TOTAL POWER

MODEL Ford Thunderbird Sports Roadster (1963)

PRODUCTION 455 (1963)

BODY STYLE Two-door, two/four-seater convertible.

CONSTRUCTION Steel body and chassis.

ENGINE 390cid V8.

POWER OUTPUT 330–340 bhp.

TRANSMISSION Three-speed Cruise-O-Matic automatic.

SUSPENSION *Front*: upper and lower A-arms and coil springs; *Rear*: leaf springs with live axle.

BRAKES Front and rear drums.

MAXIMUM SPEED 116–125 mph (187–201 km/h)

0–60 MPH (0–96 km/h) 9.7–12.4 sec

A.F.C. 11–20 mpg (3.9–7.1 km/l)

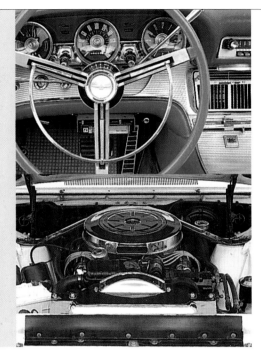

INTERIOR Aircraft imagery in the controls is obvious. The interior was designed around a prominent center console that split the cabin into two separate cockpits, delineating positions of driver and passenger. A Swing-Away steering wheel aided access for the more corpulent driver.

ENGINE The M-Series 390cid V8 was an option that could run all the way to 125 mph (201 km/h). It had three Holley two-barrels and five main bearings. The biggest unit on offer was the 427cid V8 which produced 425 bhp. The long-lived V8 gave 12 percent more torque than that on the previous model.

"Interior designer Art Querfield spent more time on the T-Bird's cabin than on any other car in his 40 years at Ford."

THE FRONT BORE AN UNCANNY RESEMBLANCE TO THE BRITISH FORD CORSAIR, WHICH IS NEITHER SURPRISING NOR COINCIDENTAL, SINCE THE CORSAIR WAS ALSO MADE BY UNCLE HENRY

TINTED GLASS, POWER SEATS AND WINDOWS, AND AM/FM RADIO WERE THE MOST POPULAR OPTIONS

19 SCENIC 68
2513
NEW HAMPSHIRE

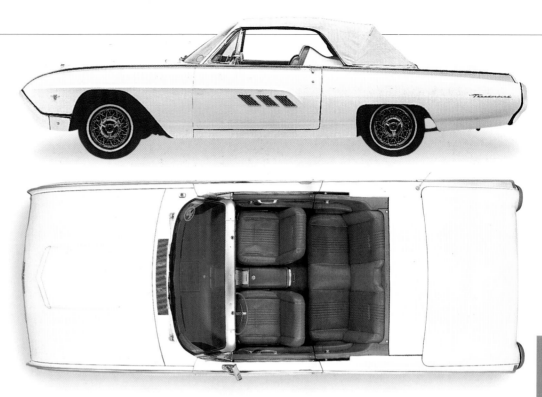

DIVINE DESIGN

Sales literature suggested that the T-Bird was the result of the combined efforts of Ford and God. *Motor Trend* said: "Ford's plush style-setter has plenty of faults... but it's still an example of a prestige car."

REAR OVERHANG WAS
PRODIGIOUS, BUT
PARKING COULD BE
MASTERED BY USING THE
REAR FIN AS A MARKER

THE LARGE TONNEAU
PANEL CAME OFF EASILY
BUT REQUIRED TWO
PEOPLE TO HANDLE IT

19 SCENIC 68
2513
NEW HAMPSHIRE

The original pony car that lived up to its hype

THIS ONE HIT THE ground running – galloping in fact, for the Mustang rewrote the sales record books soon after it burst on to the market in April 1964. It really broke the mold, for it was from the Mustang that the term "pony car" was derived to describe a new breed of sporty "compacts." The concept of an inexpensive sports car for the masses is credited to dynamic young Ford vice president, Lee Iacocca, who had been approached to bring back the two-seater Thunderbird. In realization, the Mustang was more than classless, almost universal in appeal. Its extensive options list meant there was a flavor to suit every taste. There was a Mustang for moms, sons, daughters, husbands, even young-at-heart grandparents. Celebrities who could afford a ranch full of thoroughbred race horses and a garage full of Italian exotics were also proud to tool around in Mustangs. Why, this car's truly democratic.

BOTH FRONT AND REAR SIDE WINDOWS WOUND COMPLETELY OUT OF SIGHT TO ENHANCE THE HARDTOP'S LOOKS AND KEEP THINGS COOL

"The Mustang II show car debuted at the US Grand Prix in 1963, and its success paved the way for the production Mustang, which to this day is still the fastest selling Ford ever."

HARDER SUSPENSION AND HANDLING SETS COULD BE ORDERED AS OPTIONAL EXTRAS

MODEL Ford Mustang (1964–68)

PRODUCTION 2,077,826

BODY STYLES Two-door, four-seat hardtop, fastback, convertible.

CONSTRUCTION Unitary chassis/body.

ENGINES Six-cylinder 170cid to 428cid V8.

POWER OUTPUT 195–250 bhp at 4000–4800 rpm or 271 bhp at 6000 rpm (289cid).

TRANSMISSION Three- or four-speed manual or three-speed automatic.

SUSPENSION *Front*: independent coil springs and wishbones; *Rear*: semielliptic leaf springs.

BRAKES Front and rear drums. Discs optional at front.

MAXIMUM SPEED 110–127 mph (177–204 km/h) (289cid)

0–60 MPH (0–96 km/h) 6.1 sec (289cid)

0–100 MPH (0–161 km/h) 19.7 sec

A.F.C. 13 mpg (4.6 km/l)

INTERIOR The first Mustangs shared their instrument layout with more mundane Ford Falcons *(see pages 286–89)*, but in a padded dash. The plastic interior was a little tacky, but at the price no one was going to complain. And anyway, customers could personalize their interiors with a myriad of decor option packages.

ENGINE Mustangs were offered with the option of V8 (289cid pictured) or six-cylinder engines; eights outsold sixes two-to-one in 1964–68. Customers could thus buy the car just for its good looks, and make do with 100 bhp, or order a highway-burner producing 400 bhp and enjoy real sports car performance.

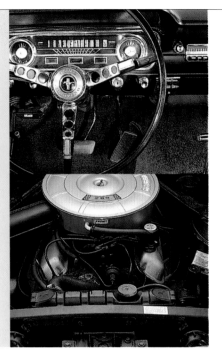

"In one stroke the Mustang revived the freedom of spirit of the early sporty Thunderbirds."

PUSH-BUTTON RADIO AND ANTENNA WERE ALL PART OF THE OPTIONS LIST

POWER FRONT DISC BRAKES WERE A NEW OPTION FOR 1965

LA JOLLA
SEP CALIFORNIA
588 FNM
HISTORICAL SOCIETY

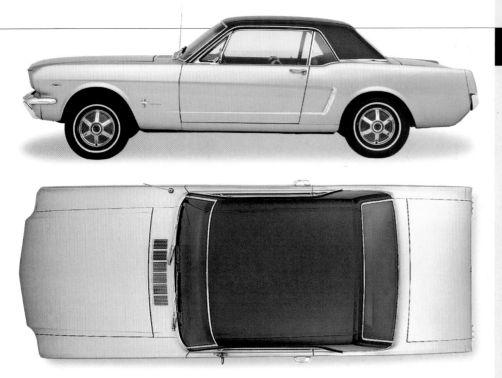

STEVE MCQUEEN

Steve McQueen, a skilful racer, insisted on doing as much driving as he could in the nine-minute chase sequence in *Bullitt*. But when filming was over, Solar Productions scrapped all but one of the remaining '68 Ford Mustang 390GTs. The surviving car, complete with camera mounts from filming, changed hands three times and was sold to its current owner in 1972. McQueen tried many times to buy the car, offering cash or a replacement Mustang, but the owner always refused to sell.

THE NOTCHBACK
REAR ASPECT HAD
CLASSICALLY PERFECT
PROPORTIONS

CALIFORNIA
588 FNM

The pony gets transformed into a stallion

LOOKING BACK FROM OUR era of environmental correctness, it's amazing to remember a time when you could buy this sort of stomach-churning horsepower straight from the showroom floor. What's more, if you couldn't afford to buy it, you could borrow it for the weekend from your local Hertz rent-a-car. The fact is that the American public loved the grunt, the image, and the Carroll Shelby Cobra connection. Ford's advertising slogan went straight to the point – Shelby Mustangs were "*The* Road Cars." With 289 and 428cid V8s, they were blisteringly quick and kings of both street and strip; the 428 pushed out a very respectable 360 bhp. By '67 they were civilized too, with options like factory air and power steering, as well as lots of gauges, a wood-rim Shelby wheel, and that all-important 140 mph (225 km/h) speedo. The little pony Mustang had grown into a thundering stallion.

> "There are tales of people renting 350s and 500s from Hertz and bringing them back with bald tires and evidence of racing numbers on the doors."

POWER-ASSISTED STEERING AND BRAKES ON THE '67 MODEL MEANT THAT THE ONCE ROUGH-RIDING SHELBY HAD TRANSFORMED INTO A LUXURY SLINGSHOT THAT WOULD SOON BECOME AN ICON

'67 SHELBYS HAD A LARGER HOOD SCOOP THAN PREVIOUS MODELS, PLUS A CUSTOM-BUILT FIBERGLASS FRONT TO COMPLEMENT THE STOCK MUSTANG'S NEW LONGER HOOD

MODEL Ford Shelby Cobra Mustang GT500 (1967)

PRODUCTION 2,048 (1967)

BODY STYLE Two-door, four-seater coupe.

CONSTRUCTION Steel unitary body.

ENGINE 428cid V8.

POWER OUTPUT 360 bhp.

TRANSMISSION Four-speed manual or three-speed automatic.

SUSPENSION *Front*: coil springs; *Rear*: leaf springs.

BRAKES Front discs, rear drums.

MAXIMUM SPEED 132 mph (212 km/h)

0–60 MPH (0–96 km/h) 6.8 sec

A.F.C. 13 mpg (4.6 km/l)

INTERIOR Stewart-Warner oil and amp gauges and a tachometer were standard equipment. Two interior colors were available – parchment and black. Interior decor was brushed aluminum with molded door panels and courtesy lamps. All GT350s and 500s boasted the standard and very practical fold-down rear seat.

ENGINE The GT500 came with the 428 Police Interceptor unit, which started life in the original AC Cobra *(see pages 24–27),* with two Holley four-barrel carbs. Oval, finned aluminum open-element air filter and cast-aluminum valve covers were unique to the big-block Shelby.

"Shelbys came in fastback only; there were no notchbacks, and convertibles were only available from '68."

RACING-STYLE LOCK PINS WERE STANDARD ON THE SHELBY'S HOOD

Lido Anthony Iacocca turned a half-formed thought into one of the most successful cars of all time. An engineering graduate, he become vice-president of Ford at the age of 35. Iacocca knew that the growing "baby boomer" market needed a low-cost, sporty compact, and by '61 he was leading the Mustang project. The Mustang made Iacocca a household name and helped propel him to become CEO of Chrysler.

GORDON KEEBLE GT

Designed by a legend, built like a tank

IN 1960, THIS WAS the most electrifying car the British magazine *Autocar & Motor* had ever tested. Designed by Giugiaro in Italy and built in Southampton, England, it boasted good looks, a fiberglass body, and a 5.4-liter, 300 bhp V8 Chevrolet Corvette engine. But, despite plenty of publicity, good looks, epic performance, and a glamorous clientele, the Gordon Keeble was a commercial disaster, with only 104 built. "The car built to aircraft standards," read the advertising copy. And time has proved the Keeble's integrity; a space-frame chassis, rustproof body, and that unburstable V8 has meant that over 90 Gordons have survived, with 60 still regularly used today. Born in an era where beauty mattered more than balance sheets, the Gordon Keeble failed for two reasons. First, the workers could not make enough of them, and second, the management forgot to put a profit margin in the price. How the car industry has changed...

THE ROOF WAS LENGTHENED AND THE SLANT OF THE C-PILLAR DECREASED TO GIVE WIDER GLASS AREAS AND MAXIMUM VISIBILITY

TWIN FUEL TANKS SAY MUCH ABOUT AN ERA WHEN GAS WAS CHEAP AND 14 MPG (5 KM/L) WAS CONSIDERED REASONABLE

THE KEEBLE'S DELICATE THREE-PIECE CHROME BUMPERS WERE SPECIALLY HANDMADE

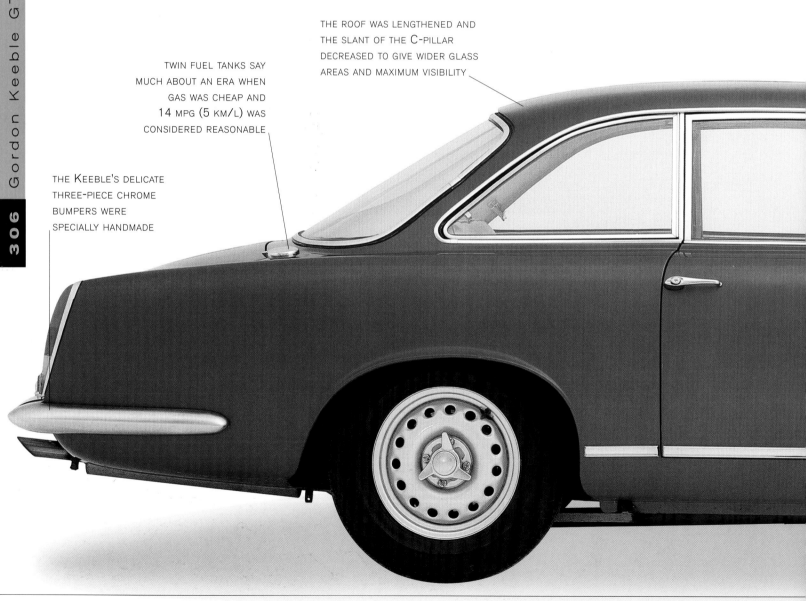

"For a '60s' design, the Gordon Keeble was a crisp, clean, and timeless car."

MODEL Gordon Keeble GT (1964–67)

PRODUCTION 104

BODY STYLE Four-seater fiberglass GT.

CONSTRUCTION Multitubular chassis frame, GRP body.

ENGINE 5.4-liter V8.

POWER OUTPUT 300 bhp at 5000 rpm.

TRANSMISSION Four-speed all-synchro.

SUSPENSION *Front*: independent; *Rear*: De Dion.

BRAKES Four-wheel discs.

MAXIMUM SPEED 141 mph (227 km/h)

0–60 MPH (0–96 km/h) 7.5 sec

0–100 MPH (0–161 km/h) 13.3 sec

A.F.C. 14 mpg (5 km/l)

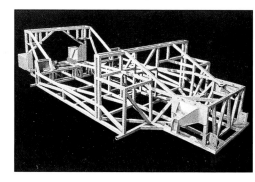

INTERIOR The interior is like the flight deck of an old Clipper flying boat – quilted aircraft PVC, black-on-white gauges, toggle switches, and that *de rigueur* accessory of all Sixties GT cars, a wood-rimmed steering wheel. The Keeble came equipped with a push-button radio, seat belts, and a fire extinguisher.

ENGINE The small block Sting Ray engine, supplied by General Motors, was an aristocrat among American V8s, delivering a massive 300 bhp of high-compression power. The engine's brutal performance meant 70 mph (113 km/h) in first gear and a mighty wall of torque that could destroy most other cars.

SPACE FRAME

The prototype space-frame chassis was finished in February 1960 and was made up of a composite skeleton of square tubes. It was flown to France, then went overland to Turin, where Giugiaro fitted a handsome grp body. In its day the Gordon Keeble's hand-finished, glass-reinforced plastic body was among the best.

GIUGIARO GAVE THE HOOD A DUMMY INTAKE SCOOP AND FASHIONABLY RAKED TWIN HEADLIGHTS

ELECTRIC WINDOWS USED THE SAME MOTORS AS THE ROLLS-ROYCE SILVER SHADOW

FEW 555D

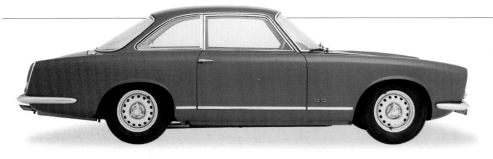

"The small block Sting Ray engine delivered a massive 300 bhp of high-compression power."

BUILT AT EASTLEIGH AIRPORT,
SOUTHAMPTON, ENGLAND,
MANY AIRCRAFT PARTS FOUND
THEIR WAY INTO THE KEEBLE

DESPITE RESTRAINED
ELEGANCE AND CONCEALED
TWIN EXHAUSTS, THE
KEEBLE COULD TOP
140 MPH (225 KM/H)

Born in Italy in 1938, Giorgio Guigiaro worked for renowned designer Bertone in the early Sixties, and the Gordon Keeble was one of his first confections. He moved over to the Ghia design house in 1966 and two years later set up his own studio, Italdesign. Since then the company has conceived over 100 production cars and branched out into designing other items, including cameras and watches.

FEW 555D

Gordon Keeble GT **309**

HOLDEN FX

Australia's finest automotive legend

At the end of World War II, Australia had a problem – an acute shortage of cars and a newly civilianized army with money to burn. Loaded with government handouts, General Motors-Holden came up with a four-door, six-cylinder, six-seater that would become an Australian legend on wheels. Launched in 1948, the 48-215, more generally known as the FX, was Australia's Morris Minor (*see pages* 426–29). Tubby, conventional, and as big as a Buick, it had a sweet, torquey engine, steel monocoque body, hydraulic brakes, and a three-speed column shift. Simple and unadorned, the FX had a plain shape that would not date. Light and functional, it so impressed Lord Nuffield (of Morris fame) with its simple efficiency that he had one shipped to England for his engineers to pull apart. The Australians did not care about the FX's humble underpinnings and bought 120,000 with grateful enthusiasm.

THE BODY WAS DUST-PROOF, WHICH HELPED IN THE HOT AUSTRALIAN CLIMATE. TAXI DRIVERS, THOUGH, COMPLAINED OF BODY FLEXING – DOORS COULD OPEN ON CORNERS

RECUMBENT LION HOOD ORNAMENT LENT THE FX AN ILLUSION OF PEDIGREE. IN REALITY, HOLDEN HAD NO BLOODLINE AT ALL

TK·377 NSW

ENGINE Power came from a sturdy 2170cc cast-iron straight-six, with an integral block and crankcase, push-rod overhead valves, and a single-barrel downdraft Stromberg carburetor. Though the unit only developed a modest 60 bhp, fuel consumption was a respectable 30 mpg (11 km/l).

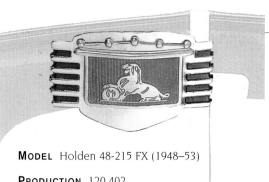

MODEL Holden 48-215 FX (1948–53)

PRODUCTION 120,402

BODY STYLE Six-seater, four-door family sedan.

CONSTRUCTION All-steel Aerobilt monocoque body.

ENGINE Six-cylinder cast-iron 2170cc.

POWER OUTPUT 60 bhp at 4500 rpm.

TRANSMISSION Three-speed manual.

SUSPENSION *Front*: coil and wishbone; *Rear*: leaf springs with live axle.

BRAKES Front and rear hydraulic drums.

MAXIMUM SPEED 73 mph (117 km/h)

0–60 MPH (0–96 km/h) 27.7 sec

A.F.C. 30 mpg (11 km/l)

Forerunner of a classic American racer

In 1948, Hudson's future could not have looked brighter. The feisty independent was one of the first with an all-new postwar design. Under the guidance of Frank Spring, the new Hudson Super Six not only looked stunning, it bristled with innovation. The key was its revolutionary "step-down" design, based on a unitary construction with the floor pan suspended from the bottom of the chassis frame. The Hudson was lower than its rivals, handled with ground-hugging confidence, and with its gutsy six-cylinder engine, outpaced virtually all competitors. In 1951, it evolved into the Hudson Hornet (*see pages 316–19*), dominating American stock car racing from 1951 to 1954. But the complex design could not adapt to the rampant demand for yearly revision, making it difficult to update; the 1953 car looked much like the 1948, and in 1954 Hudson merged with Nash, disappearing for good in 1957.

ONLY 60.4 IN (1.53 M) HIGH, THE SUPER SIX WAS LOWER THAN ITS CONTEMPORARIES

THE CHASSIS FRAME RAN OUTSIDE THE REAR WHEELS, SERVING AS "INVISIBLE SIDE BUMPERS"

"Along with Studebaker, the 1948 Hudson was one of the very first all-new post-war designs."

MODEL Hudson Super Six (1948–51)

PRODUCTION 180,499

BODY STYLES Four-door sedan, Brougham two-door sedan, Club coupe, hardtop coupe, two-door Brougham convertible.

CONSTRUCTION Unitary chassis/body.

ENGINE 262cid L-head straight-six.

POWER OUTPUT 121 bhp at 4000 rpm.

TRANSMISSION Three-speed manual, optional overdrive; semiautomatic.

SUSPENSION *Front*: independent, wishbones, coil springs, telescopic shocks, antiroll bar; *Rear*: live-axle, semielliptic leaf springs, telescopic shocks, antiroll bar.

BRAKES Hydraulic drums all around.

MAXIMUM SPEED 90 mph (145 km/h)

0–60 MPH (0–96 km/h) 14–18 sec

A.F.C. 12–18 mpg (4.2–6.4 km/l)

INTERIOR The dashboard was not wood but painted metal. Main instruments were a speedo and 30-hour windup clock, both of which were later moved ahead of the driver. "Idiot lights" rather than gauges were a traditional Hudson feature.

ENGINE The gutsy new 262cid six arrived the same year as the new-style Hudsons in 1948. It made the Hudson one of the swiftest cars on America's roads and, bored out to 308cid for the Hornet, it became a racing legend.

"The design team was led by Frank Spring, a long-time Hudson fixture, whose unusual blend of talents combined styling and engineering."

THE REAR OF THE HUDSON WAS ITS LEAST PLEASING FEATURE — A SLIGHTLY SAGGING LUMP

HUDSON

WYJ 969

HUDSON Hornet

One of the fastest cars of the Fifties

HUDSON DID ITS BEST in '54 to clean up the aged 1948 body. Smoother flanks and a lower, wider frontal aspect helped, along with a new dash and brighter fabrics and vinyls. And at long last the windshield was one piece. Mechanically it wasn't bad either. In fact, some say the last Step-Down was the best ever. With the straight-six came a Twin-H power option, a hot camshaft, and an alloy head that could crank out 170 bhp; it was promptly dubbed "The Fabulous Hornet." The problem was that everybody else had V8s, and by mid-'54 Hudson had hemorrhaged over $6 million. In April that year, Hudson was swallowed up by the Nash-Kelvinator Corporation. Yet the Hornet has been rightly recognized as a milestone car and one of the quickest sixes of the era. If Hudson is to be remembered for anything, it should be for its innovative engineers, who could wring the best from ancient designs and tiny budgets.

"These Hudsons were known as Step-Downs because you literally stepped down into the car."

HORNETS CAME IN ROMAN BRONZE, PASTURE GREEN, ALGERIAN BLUE, CORONATION CREAM, ST. CLAIR GRAY, OR LIPSTICK RED

AMAZINGLY, HUDSON NEVER OFFERED V8 POWER, WHICH WAS TO HASTEN ITS DOWNFALL

"Among the fastest cars of the Fifties, Hudsons boasted above-average power and crisp handling."

MODEL Hudson Hornet 7D (1954)

PRODUCTION 24,833 (1954 Hornets)

BODY STYLES Two-door coupe or convertible, four-door sedan.

CONSTRUCTION Steel body and chassis.

ENGINE 308cid straight-six.

POWER OUTPUT 160–170 bhp.

TRANSMISSION Three-speed manual, optional Hydra-Matic automatic.

SUSPENSION *Front:* coil springs; *Rear:* leaf springs.

BRAKES Front and rear drums.

MAXIMUM SPEED 110 mph (177 km/h)

0–60 MPH (0–96 km/h) 12 sec

A.F.C. 17 mpg (6 km/l)

DESPITE ITS LOW, GROUND-HUGGING STANCE, THE HORNET HAD PLENTY OF LEGROOM, AND FEW CARS BOASTED AS MUCH COMFORT IN '54

Hudson Hornet **317**

"NASCAR devotees watched many a Hudson trounce the competition, winning 22 out of 37 major races in '53 alone."

THE GRILLE AND FRONT FENDERS WERE NEW FOR 1954 AND COMMON TO ALL HORNET SHELLS

H U D S O N

JUL CALIFORNIA 18 54
LFO 227
1954 HUDSON HORNET

INTERIOR The dashboard was modern and glossy but still used Hudson's distinctive single-digit speedo. The Hornet's cabin was liberally laced with chrome, and trim was nylon worsted Bedford cloth and Plastihide in a choice of brown, blue, or green.

ENGINE The L-section 308cid straight-six developed 160 bhp and breathed through a Carter two-barrel. Compression was boosted for '54, with an $86 performance option on offer that bought you "the surging might of miracle H-Power" and squeezed an extra 10 bhp from the engine.

THE SLOPING BACK ON THE HUDSON FOUR-DOOR WAS VERY DIFFERENT FROM THE CONVENTIONALLY TRUNKED TWO-DOOR

HUDSON

HUDSON

JUL CALIFORNIA 19 54
LFO 227
1954 HUDSON HORNET

LFO 227
1954 HUDSON HORNET

JAGUAR XK120

A cat with a stunning profile and blistering speed

A CAR-STARVED BRITAIN glimpsed the future in October of 1948 at the Earl's Court Motor Show in London. The star of the show was the Jaguar Super Sports. It was sensational to look at from any angle, with a purity of line that did not need chrome embellishment. It was also sensationally fast; in production as the Jaguar XK120 it would soon be proven that 120 really did stand for 120 mph (193 km/h), making it the fastest standard production car in the world. The only trouble was that you could not actually buy one. The XK120 was originally planned as a short production-run, prestigious showstopper, but overwhelming interest at the 1948 show changed all that. Hand-built alloy-bodied cars dribbled out of the Jaguar factory in 1949, and you needed a name like Clark Gable to get your hands on one. Tooling was ready in 1950, and production really took off. Today the XK120 remains one of the most captivating cats ever.

"Many rate the fixed-head coupe as the most gorgeous of all XK120s, with a roof line and teardrop window reminiscent of the beautiful Bugatti Type 57SC Atlantic."

STANDARD WHEELS WERE THE SAME STEEL DISCS AS ON THE JAGUAR SEDANS. WIRE WHEELS WERE A POPULAR OPTION AND HELPED REDUCE THE BUILDUP OF HEAT IN THE DRUMS

MODEL Jaguar XK120 (1949–54)

PRODUCTION 12,055

BODY STYLES Two-seater roadster, fixed-head coupe, and drophead coupe.

CONSTRUCTION Separate chassis, aluminum/steel bodywork.

ENGINE 3442cc twin overhead cam six-cylinder, twin SU carburetors.

POWER OUTPUT 160 bhp at 5100 rpm.

TRANSMISSION Four-speed manual,

SUSPENSION *Front*: independent, wishbones and torsion bars; *Rear*: live axle, semielliptic.

BRAKES Hydraulically operated drums.

MAXIMUM SPEED 126 mph (203 km/h)

0–60 MPH (0–96 km/h) 10 sec

0–100 MPH (0–161 km/h) 35.3 sec

A.F.C. 17–22 mpg (6.1–7.8 km/l)

INTERIOR Surrounded by leather and thick-pile carpet, you feel good just sitting in an XK120. With its lush interior, purposeful instruments, and the bark of the exhaust from behind, you hardly notice that the cockpit is a little cozy – if not downright cramped. Walnut trim was a feature of fixed-head coupes and dropheads only.

ENGINE The famed XK six-cylinder engine was designed by Bill Heynes and Wally Hassan, and went on to power the E-Type *(see pages 330–33)* and other Jaguars up until 1986. Even this was "styled"; William Lyons insisted it had twin camshafts to make it resemble GP cars of the Thirties.

"With the XK120, once again Jaguar Boss William Lyons had pulled off his favorite trick: offering sensational value compared with anything else in its class."

XK SPOTTERS CAN TELL THIS IS A '53 XK120 BY THE BODY-COLORED SIDELIGHTS FAIRED INTO THE FENDER

SLIM SPLIT BUMPERS AND THIN GRILLE SLATS DISTINGUISH THE XK120 FROM THE THICKER-BUMPERED XK140 THAT SUPERSEDED IT

829 JGU

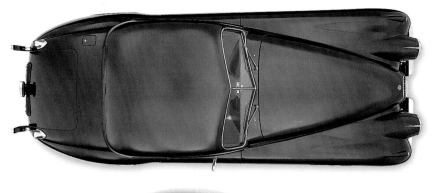

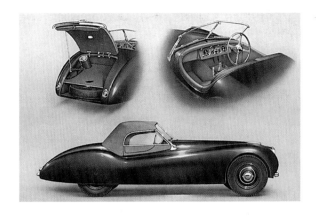

Selling the Dream

The original sales brochure for the XK120 used airbrushed photographs of the very first car built. Buyers didn't need much persuading, and over 12,000 XK120s were manufactured in the car's five-year production run.

FIXED-HEAD COUPES
HAD LIMITED VISION
THROUGH THE SMALL
REAR WINDOW

829·JGU

JAGUAR C-Type

Foundation stone of a proud sports tradition

THE C-TYPE IS THE CAR that launched the Jaguar racing legend and began a Le Mans love affair for the men from Coventry. In the 1950s, Jaguar boss Bill Lyons was intent on winning Le Mans laurels for Britain, just as Bentley had done a quarter of a century before. After testing mildly modified XK120s in 1950, Jaguar came up with a competition version, the XK120C (C-Type) in 1951. A C-Type won that year, failed in 1952, then won again in 1953. By then the C-Type's place in history

was assured, for it had laid the cornerstone of the Jaguar sports legend that blossomed through its successor, the D-Type, which bagged three Le Mans 24-hour wins in four years. C-Types were sold to private customers, most of whom used them for racing rather than road use. They were respectable road cars though, often driven to and from meetings; after their days as competitive racers were over, many were used as high-performance highway tourers.

"Designer Malcolm Sayer's aircraft industry background showed through in the smooth aerodynamic styling."

A CAR BUILT FOR RACING DOES NOT NEED TO CARRY BAGGAGE; REAR DECK COVERED THE MASSIVE FUEL TANK

QUICK-RELEASE GAS CAP WAS ANOTHER RACING FEATURE, AND COULD SAVE VALUABLE SECONDS IN A RACE

IT WAS EASIER TO STEP OVER THE DOOR THAN OPEN IT; THE PASSENGER DID NOT EVEN GET ONE

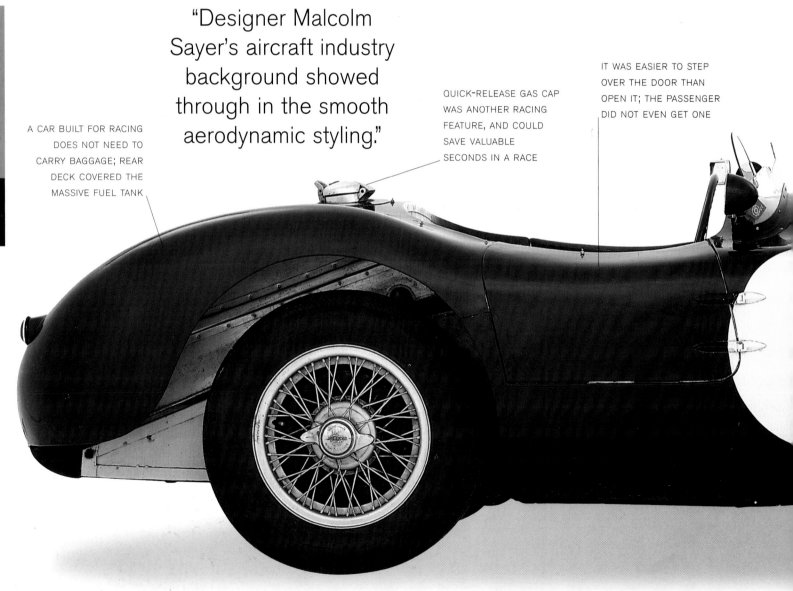

MODEL Jaguar C-Type (1951–53)

PRODUCTION 53

BODY STYLE Two-door, two-seater racer.

CONSTRUCTION Tubular chassis, aluminum body.

ENGINE Jaguar XK120 3442cc, six-cylinder, double overhead camshaft with twin SU carbs.

POWER OUTPUT 200–210 bhp at 5800 rpm.

TRANSMISSION Four-speed XK gearbox.

SUSPENSION Torsion-bars all around; wishbones at front, rigid axle at rear.

BRAKES Lockheed hydraulic drums; later cars used Dunlop discs all around.

MAXIMUM SPEED 144 mph (232 km/h)

0–60 MPH (0–96 km/h) 8.1 sec

0–100 MPH (0–161 km/h) 20.1 sec

A.F.C. 16 mpg (5.7 km/l)

INTERIOR The cockpit was designed for business, not comfort, but was roomy enough for two adults; passengers were provided with a grab handle in case the driver thought he was at Le Mans. The C-Type's snug-fitting seats supported the driver and passenger well during hard cornering.

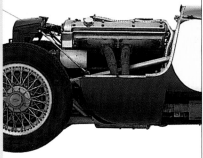

ENGINE The engine was taken from the XK120 and placed into the competition version. It snuggled neatly into its bay and was kept beneath a forward-hinged hood. Louvers on the hood allowed hot air to escape. Horsepower of the silky six was boosted each year until some 220 bhp was available.

"The clever blend of beauty and function retained the pouncing-cat Jaguar 'look,' while creating an efficient tool for the high-speed Le Mans circuit."

IN RACING TRIM, CARS RAN WITH A SINGLE AERODYNAMIC WINDSHIELD; THIS MODEL HAS AN ADDITIONAL FULL-WIDTH WINDSHIELD

COMPANY BOSS BILL LYONS HAD INSISTED ON FAMILY RESEMBLANCE TO THE XK120 PRODUCTION MODEL, RESULTING IN THE C-TYPE'S SIMILAR GRILLE

PUR 120

From Swallow sidecars and a credit limit of $1,500, Sir William Lyons built up one of the most powerful car brands in the world. No engineer, Lyons just knew instinctively when a car looked right. Father of the XKs, E-Type, and MkII sedans, no other motor mandarin did more to make high-performance cars affordable. In 1970 he watched a clumsy British Leyland rename the famous Coventry factory "The Large Car Division." He retired from the BL board in 1972.

PUR 120

JAGUAR XK150

Powered by one of the finest engines of all time

THE XK150 APPEARED in the Spring of 1957 and was the most refined of the XK trio. One of the last Jaguars to have a separate chassis, the 150 marked the beginning of the civilization of the Jaguar sports car. With its wider girth and creature comforts, it was to hold the market's interest until the then-secret E-Type project (*see pages 330–33*) was ready for unveiling in 1961. In the late 1950s, the XK150 was a seriously glamorous machine, almost as chic as an Aston Martin, but $4,200 cheaper. March 1958 saw more power with the "S" performance package, which brought the 3.4 up to 250 bhp; and in 1959 the 3.8's output soared to 265 bhp. Available as a roadster, drophead, or fixed-head coupe, the 150 sold a respectable 9,400 examples in its four-year run. Despite being eclipsed by the E-Type, the 150 was charismatic enough to be the personal transportation of racing ace Mike Hawthorn and starlet Anita Ekberg.

THE GORGEOUS CURVED BODY SAT ON A CONVENTIONAL CHASSIS. JOINTS AND CURVES WERE SMOOTHED OFF AT THE FACTORY USING LEAD

A TINY RED PEAK ON THE SIDELIGHT WAS TO REMIND THE DRIVER THAT THE LIGHTS WERE ON

VON 239

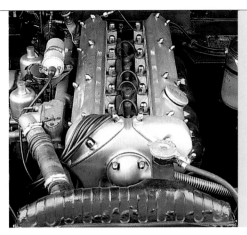

ENGINE The classic, twin overhead-cam design first saw the light of day in 1949 and was phased out as recently as 1986. Some say it is one of the finest production engines of all time. Sturdy, powerful, and handsome, the 3.8 powered the legendary D-Type Jaguars, which could top 197 mph (317 km/h).

JAGUAR WINNER LE MANS 1951 1953 1955 1958 1957 XK 150

MODEL Jaguar XK150 FHC (1957–61)

PRODUCTION 9,400

BODY STYLES Two-seater roadster, drophead, or fixed-head coupe.

CONSTRUCTION Separate pressed-steel chassis frame with box section side members.

ENGINES Straight-six, twin overhead-cam 3442cc or 3781cc.

POWER OUTPUT 190–265 bhp at 5500 rpm.

TRANSMISSION Four-speed manual, with optional overdrive, or three-speed Borg Warner Model 8 automatic.

SUSPENSION *Front:* independent; *Rear:* leaf springs with live rear axle.

BRAKES Dunlop front and rear discs.

MAXIMUM SPEED 135 mph (217 km/h)

0–60 MPH (0–96 km/h) 7.6 sec (3.8S)

0–100 MPH (0–161 km/h) 18 sec

A.F.C. 18 mpg (6.4 km/l)

VON 239

WIRE WHEELS WERE THE MOST COMMON CHOICE, THOUGH STEEL WHEELS WITH HUBCAPS WERE AVAILABLE. STANDARD TIRES WERE DUNLOP CROSSPLY RS5S

JAGUAR E-Type

A milestone in the history of the British sports car

WHEN JAGUAR BOSS William Lyons, by now Sir William, unveiled the E-Type Jaguar at the Geneva Motor Show in March 1961, its ecstatic reception rekindled memories of the 1948 British launch of the XK120 (*see pages* 320–23). The E-Type, or XKE as it is known in the US, created a sensation. British car magazines had produced road tests of pre-production models to coincide with the launch – and yes, the fixed-head coupe really could do 150 mph (242 km/h). OK, so the road-test cars were perhaps tweaked a little and early owners found 143 mph (230 km/h) a more realistic maximum, but the legend was born. It was not just a stunning, svelte sports car though; it was a trademark Jaguar sports package, once again marrying sensational performance with superb value. Astons and Ferraris, for example, were more than double the price.

THE THIN BUMPERS WITH LIGHTS ABOVE ARE AN EASY GIVEAWAY FOR E-TYPE SPOTTERS. FROM 1968, WITH THE INTRODUCTION OF THE SERIES 2, BULKIER LAMP CLUSTERS APPEARED BELOW THE BUMPERS

JAGUAR DESIGNED AN ALL-NEW INDEPENDENT SETUP AT THE REAR. HANDLING ON WET ROADS IS OFTEN CRITICIZED, BUT FOR ITS DAY THE E-TYPE WAS IMMENSELY CAPABLE

"The E-Type's amazing export success is summed up by the fact that, of every three built, two were exported."

MODEL E-Type Jaguar (1961–74)

PRODUCTION 72,520

BODY STYLES Two-seater roadster and fixed coupe, 2+2 fixed head coupe.

CONSTRUCTION Steel monocoque.

ENGINES 3781cc straight-six; 4235cc straight-six; 5343cc V12.

POWER OUTPUT 265–272 bhp.

TRANSMISSION Four-speed manual, optional automatic from 1966.

SUSPENSION *Front*: independent wishbones and torsion bar; *Rear*: independent coil and radius arm.

BRAKES Discs all around.

MAXIMUM SPEED 143–150 mph (230–242 km/h)

0–60 MPH (0–96 km/h) 7–7.2 sec

0–100 MPH (0–161 km/h) 16.2 sec (3.8)

A.F.C. 16–20 mpg (5.7–7 km/l)

INTERIOR The interior of this Series 1 4.2 is the epitome of sports car luxury, with leather seats, wood-rim wheel, and an array of instruments and toggle switches – later replaced by less sporty rocker and less injurious rocker switches. The 3.8s had an aluminum-finished center console panel.

ENGINE The twin-overhead cam six-cylinder was a development of the original 3.4-liter XK unit installed in the XK120 of 1949. First E-Types had a 3.8-liter unit, then a slightly more torquey 4.2 block was introduced from 1964. Configuration changed in 1971 to a wholly new V12 power plant.

"The impact the shape made at its launch on March 15, 1961, at the Geneva Motor Show is now the stuff of Jaguar lore."

THE STYLISH BUT INEFFICIENT LENS COVERS WERE REMOVED IN 1967. THIS VIEW OF THE E-TYPE'S BULGING, SCULPTURED HOOD IS STILL THE BEST OF ANY CAR

THIN-BACKED BUCKET SEATS OF THE 3.8S WERE CRITICIZED. IN THE 4.2, AS HERE, THEY WERE GREATLY IMPROVED

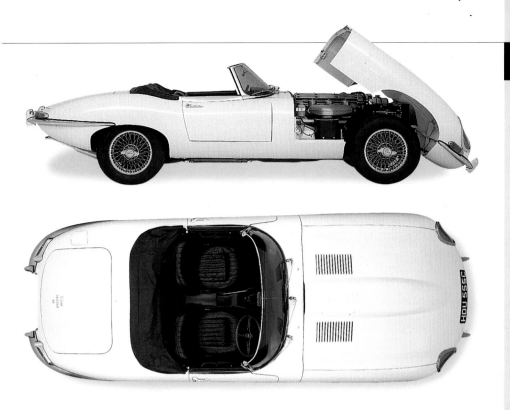

Sixties pop star Adam Faith was a household name in the UK and had money to burn. Seeing the new E-Type at the London Motor Show, he called William Lyons at Jaguar and begged him to sell him a 3.8 roadster. Lyons said that he had no RHD cars and that all vehicles were going to the US. Faith resigned himself to joining the two-year waiting list, but three days later Lyons called to say that Faith could have his personal car.

JENSEN Interceptor

A successful international project with British roots

THE JENSEN INTERCEPTOR was one of those great cars that comes along every decade or so. Built in a small Birmingham, Engand, factory, a triumph of tenacity over resources, the Interceptor's chiseled-jaw looks and tire-smoking power made the tiny Jensen company a household name. A glamorous cocktail of an Italian-styled body, American V8 engine, and genteel British craftsmanship, it became the car for successful swingers of the late 1960s and 1970s. The Interceptor was handsome, trendy, and formidably fast, with an interior made up of the finest leathers and plush Wilton carpets. But its tragic flaw was a big appetite for fuel – 10 mpg (3.5 km/l) if you enjoyed yourself. After driving straight into two oil crises and a worldwide recession, as well as suffering serious losses from the ill-fated Jensen-Healey project, Jensen filed for bankruptcy in 1975 and finally closed its doors in May 1976.

"The Interceptor's shape hardly changed over its 10-year life span and was widely acknowledged to be one of the most innovative designs of its decade."

BODIES WERE ALL-STEEL, WITH LITTLE ATTENTION PAID TO CORROSION-PROOFING. EARLY CARS WERE TRAGIC RUST BUCKETS

MODEL Jensen Interceptor (1966–76)

PRODUCTION 1,500

BODY STYLE All-steel occasional four-seater coupe.

CONSTRUCTION Separate tubular and platform-type pressed-steel frame.

ENGINE 6276cc V8.

POWER OUTPUT 325 bhp at 4600 rpm.

TRANSMISSION Three-speed Chrysler TorqueFlite automatic.

SUSPENSION *Front*: independent; *Rear*: live axle.

BRAKES Four-wheel Girling discs.

MAXIMUM SPEED 135 mph (217 km/h)

0–60 MPH (0–96 km/h) 7.3 sec

0–100 MPH (0–161 km/h) 19 sec

A.F.C. 13.6 mpg (4.9 km/l)

KAISER Darrin

An audacious, classically sculpted money-loser

"THE SPORTS CAR the world has been awaiting" was a monster flop. Designed by Howard "Dutch" Darrin, Kaiser's odd hybrid came about in 1953 as an accident. Henry J. Kaiser, the ill-mannered chairman of the Kaiser Corporation, had so riled Darrin that he disappeared into his California studio, spent his own money, and created a purse-lipped two-seater that looked like it wanted to give you a kiss. Its futuristic fiberglass body rode on a Henry J. chassis and was powered by a Willys six-pot mill. Alas, the body rippled and cracked, the sliding doors that disappeared into the front fenders wouldn't slide, and the weak 90 bhp single-carburetor flathead block was no match for Chevy's Corvette (*see pages* 122–25). At a costly $3,668, the Darrin was in Cadillac territory and only 435 found buyers. Late in '54, Kaiser-Willys went under, taking the Darrin with them. Few mourned either's demise.

"The Darrin was beautifully styled and, unlike most visions of the future, has hardly dated at all."

UNDENIABLY PRETTY, THE FENDER LINE SLOPED DOWN THROUGH THE DOOR AND MET A DRAMATIC KICK-UP OVER THE REAR WHEELARCH

Kaiser Darrin

MODEL Kaiser Darrin 161 (1954)

PRODUCTION 435 (total)

BODY STYLE Two-seater sports.

CONSTRUCTION Fiberglass body, steel frame.

ENGINE 161cid six.

POWER OUTPUT 90 bhp.

TRANSMISSION Three-speed manual with optional overdrive.

SUSPENSION *Front*: coil springs; *Rear*: leaf springs.

BRAKES Front and rear drums.

MAXIMUM SPEED 100 mph (161 km/h)

0–60 MPH (0–96 km/h) 15.1 sec

A.F.C. 27 mpg (9.6 km/l)

INTERIOR Standard equipment included electric wipers, tachometer, and a European-style dashboard, with leather trim an optional extra. The Darrin was remarkable for being only the third US production car to feature seat belts as standard.; the other two cars were a Muntz and a Nash.

ENGINE Kaiser opted for an F-head Willys version of the Henry J. six-pot engine *(see pages 340–43),* but with just one carb, it boasted only 10 more horses than standard. After the company folded, Darrin dropped 300 bhp supercharged Caddy V8s into the remaining cars, which went like wild.

STAR APPROVAL
The French singer Suzanne Bernard shows off the Darrin's dubious doors at the annual International Motor Sports Show in 1954. Modern restorations have since cured the door problem, but contemporary owners found them to be unreliable.

THE PROTOTYPE HEADLIGHT HEIGHT WAS TOO LOW FOR GOVERNMENT LIGHTING LAWS, SO KAISER STYLISTS HIKED UP THE FRONT FENDER LINE FOR THE REAL THING

SWIVELING PLEXIGLAS SIDESCREENS HELPED REDUCE COCKPIT BUFFETING

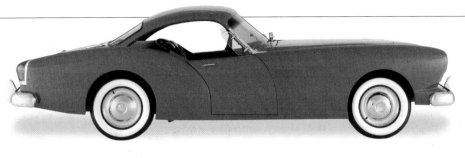

HARDTOP MADE THE
CABIN MUCH LESS
CLAUSTROPHOBIC AND
CRAMPED THAN THAT OF
THE SOFT-TOP MODEL

"The Darrin was first announced on September 26, 1952, but final production cars reached owners as late as January, 1954."

REAR FENDER AND
TAILLIGHT TREATMENT
WAS RESTRAINED
FOR THE YEAR AND
REDOLENT OF AN
XK JAGUAR

KAISER Henry J. Corsair

An overpriced compact that didn't live up to the hype

IN THE EARLY 1950s, the major car manufacturers figured that small cars meant small profits, so low-priced transportation was left to independent companies like Nash, Willys, and Kaiser-Frazer. In 1951, a streamlined, Frazerless Kaiser launched "America's Most Important New Car," the Henry J. An 80 bhp six-cylinder "Supersonic" engine gave the Corsair frugal fuel consumption, with Kaiser claiming that every third mile in a Henry J. was free. The market, however, was unconvinced. At $1,561, the Corsair cost more than the cheapest big Chevy, wasn't built as well, and depreciated rapidly. The "Smart Car for Smart People" soon earned itself a second-rate reputation. It's no wonder that only 107,000 were made. If America's first serious economy car been launched seven years later during the '58 recession, the Henry J. may well have been a best-seller.

"The stubborn head of Kaiser industries insisted that the Henry J., originally designed as a full-size car by designer Howard 'Dutch' Darrin, be scaled down."

BOLT-ON FRONT AND REAR FENDERS WERE PART OF THE HENRY J.'S MONEY-SAVING PHILOSOPHY

"Advertisers crowed that the Henry J. was 'the car that brings you luxurious performance for a penny a mile for gasoline.'"

MODEL Kaiser Henry J. Corsair Deluxe (1952)

PRODUCTION 12,900 (1952)

BODY STYLE Two-door, five-seater sedan.

CONSTRUCTION Steel body and chassis.

ENGINES 134cid four, 161cid six.

POWER OUTPUT 68–80 bhp.

TRANSMISSION Three-speed manual with optional overdrive, optional three-speed Hydra-Matic automatic.

SUSPENSION *Front*: coil springs; *Rear*: leaf springs with live axle.

BRAKES Front and rear drums.

MAXIMUM SPEED 87 mph (140 km/h)

0–60 MPH (0–96 km/h) 17 sec

A.F.C. 34 mpg (12 km/l)

INTERIOR Though sales literature described it as "the newest, smartest, most colorful interior on wheels," the cabin was very austere. Apart from overdrive and auto transmission, few factory options were available. The minimal controls included starter, light, and choke switches.

NAMEPLATE American Metal Products of Detroit created the Corsair's prototype, and the production model was built at the Willow Run factory in Michigan. "Greater today in every way" may have been the ad line, but the quality of the cars was generally poor.

RACING HENRY J.

In 1952, a Henry J. entered the Monte Carlo Rally. and to everybody's surprise, finished in a creditable 20th position. Pretty good, considering the production model could only hit 87 mph (140 km/h).

THE 100 IN (2.54 M) WHEELBASE WAS SHORT, BUT THE INTERIOR SPACE GENEROUS

Henry J. Kaiser was an entrepreneur who had earned millions mass-producing ships and houses. After WWII he joined up with Joe Frazer to make cars, but spiraling costs saw them post big losses by 1950. Five years later Kaiser sold his factory to GM and moved to Buenos Aires.

"The Henry J.'s high roof line owed its existence to the fact that Kaiser's chairman always wore a hat."

WITH THE REAR SEAT FOLDED DOWN, THE LUGGAGE SPACE WAS AMONG THE LARGEST OF ANY PASSENGER SEDAN

1953 PENNA
EXP. 3-31-54
4439S

LAMBORGHINI Miura

Genuine Italian supercar with serious cachet

THE LAUNCH OF THE Lamborghini Miura at the 1966 Geneva Motor Show was the decade's automotive sensation. Staggeringly beautiful, technically pre-eminent, and unbelievably quick, it was created by a triumvirate of engineering wizards all in their twenties. For the greater part of its production life the Miura was considered the most desirable car money could buy, combining drop-dead looks, awesome performance, and unerring stability, as well as a stunning V12 power plant that produced an emotive top speed of 175 mph (282 km/h). From its dramatic swooping lines – even Lamborghini thought it was too futuristic to sell – to its outrageously exotic colors, the Miura perfectly mirrored the middle Sixties. But, as the oil crisis of the Seventies took hold, the Miura slipped into obscurity, replaced in 1973 by the not so pretty, and some say inferior, Countach (*see pages 348–51*).

"Long, low, and delicate, the Miura is still considered one of the most handsome automotive sculptures ever."

IN AN ATTEMPT TO SILENCE A VIOLENTLY LOUD ENGINE, LAMBORGHINI PUT 4 IN (10 CM) OF POLYSTYRENE INSULATION BETWEEN ENGINE AND CABIN

BECAUSE THE MIURA SAT SO LOW, IT DISPLAYED VIRTUALLY ZERO BODY-ROLL; THEREFORE THERE WAS LITTLE WARNING BEFORE IT FISHTAILED

MODEL Lamborghini Miura (1966–72)

PRODUCTION Approximately 800.

BODY STYLE Two-seater roadster.

CONSTRUCTION Steel platform chassis, light alloy and steel bodywork.

ENGINE Transverse V12 4.0-liter.

POWER OUTPUT 350 bhp at 7000 rpm (P400), 370 bhp at 7700 rpm (P400S), 385 bhp at 7850 rpm (P400SV).

TRANSMISSION Five-speed with transaxle.

SUSPENSION Independent front and rear.

BRAKES Four-wheel ventilated disc.

MAXIMUM SPEED 175 mph (282 km/h) (P400SV)

0–60 MPH (0–96 km/h) 6.7 sec

0–100 MPH (0–161 km/h) 15.1 sec

A.F.C. 16 mpg (5.7 km/l)

INTERIOR The cockpit is basic but finely detailed, with a huge Jaeger speedo and tach. Six minor gauges on the left of the console tell the mechanical story. Only the gearbox is a disappointment, with a trucklike, sticky action that does not do the Miura's gorgeous engine any justice.

ENGINE The V12 4-liter engine was mid-mounted transversely to prevent the car's wheelbase from being too long. The gearbox, final drive, and crankcase were all cast in one piece to save space. Beneath the pipes slumber 12 pistons, four chain-driven camshafts, 24 valves, and four carburetors.

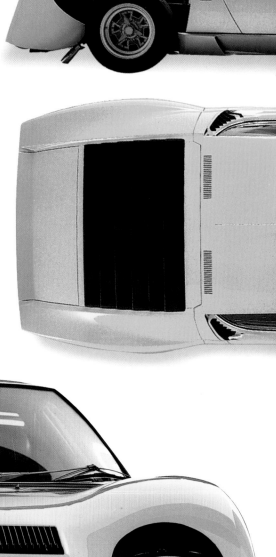

THE CAR WAS SO LOW THAT THE HEADLIGHTS HAD TO BE "POP-UP" TO RAISE THEM HIGH ENOUGH FOR ADEQUATE VISION

NEW JERSEY
FLA 352
GARDEN STATE

"In looks and layout the mid-engined Lambo owes much to the Ford GT40 but was engineered by Gianpaolo Dallara."

ONLY 150 SVs WERE BUILT. VERY FEW HAD A "SPLIT SUMP" THAT HAD SEPARATE OIL FOR THE ENGINE AND GEARBOX

The son of a farmer, Ferruccio Lamborghini started his engineering career as a tractor manufacturer. Bankrolled by his industrial fortune, he owned a series of Ferraris, which constantly broke down. A heated argument with Enzo Ferrari over a 250GT prompted Lamborghini to build his own supercar, the 350 GTV of 1963. His breathtaking Miura of 1966 attracted jet-setting buyers to Lamborghini and gained the company an enviable reputation. The Seventies' fuel crisis, financial problems, and labor unrest forced Ferruccio to sell 51 percent of the company in 1972.

NEW JERSEY
FLA · 352
GARDEN STATE

LAMBORGHINI Countach

Radical design married to phenomenal speed

THE COUNTACH WAS FIRST unveiled at the 1971 Geneva Motor Show as the Miura's replacement, engineered by Giampaolo Dallara and styled by Marcello Gandini of Bertone fame. For a complicated, hand-built car, the Countach delivered all the reliable high performance that its swooping looks promised. In 1982, a 4.75-liter 375 bhp V12 was shoehorned in to give the upcoming Ferrari Testarossa (*see pages* 266–69) something to reckon with. There is no mid-engined car like the Countach. The engine sits longitudinally in a multi-tubular space frame, with fuel and water carried by twin side-mounted tanks and radiators. On the down side, visibility is appalling, steering is heavy, and the cockpit is cramped. Yet such faults can only be considered as charming idiosyncrasies when set against the Countach's staggering performance – a howling 187 mph (301 km/h) top speed and a 0–60 mph (96 km/h) belt of 5 seconds.

"The shape of the Countach is a riot of creative genius that ignores all established rules of car design."

INCHES AWAY, ALL OCCUPANTS WERE ABLE TO HEAR EXACTLY WHAT THIS ENGINE HAD TO SAY

STEAMROLLERLIKE 12J FIVE-PORTHOLE ALLOY WHEELS SAT ON ULTRA-LOW PROFILE TIRES

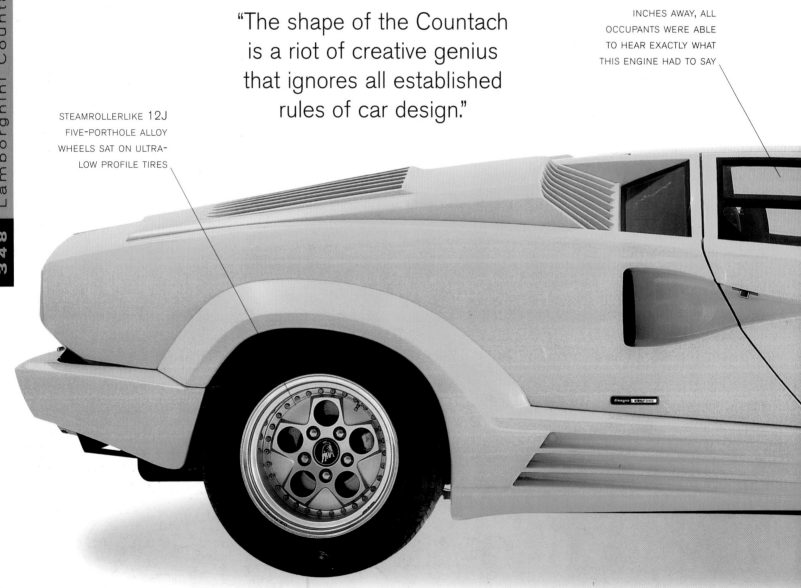

MODEL Lamborghini Countach (1973–90)

PRODUCTION Approximately 1,000

BODY STYLE Mid-engined, two-seater sports coupe.

CONSTRUCTION Alloy body, space-frame chassis.

ENGINE 4754cc four-cam V12.

POWER OUTPUT 375 bhp at 7000 rpm.

TRANSMISSION Five-speed manual.

SUSPENSION Independent front and rear with double wishbones and coil springs.

BRAKES Four-wheel vented discs.

MAXIMUM SPEED 187 mph (301 km/h)

0–60 MPH (0–96 km/h) 5.1 sec

0–100 MPH (0–161 km/h) 13.3 sec

A.F.C. 9 mpg (3.2 km/l)

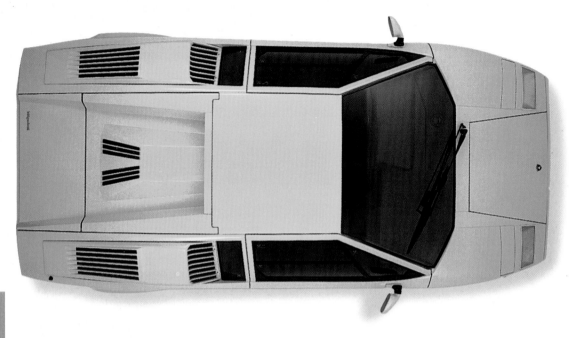

BADGING

The badge on the rear is to celebrate the 25-year anniversary of Lamborghini production in 1985, when the company released the 5000S pictured on these pages and the elite Quattrovalvole 5000S.

THE CABIN WAS CRUDE, WITH BRASH INTERIOR ARCHITECTURE. SWITCHES AND LEVERS WERE FIAT- AND LANCIA-SOURCED

THE COUNTACH WENT EXACTLY WHERE IT WAS POINTED THANKS TO ALMOST PERFECT WEIGHT DISTRIBUTION

SCANT BODY PROTECTION MEANT THAT MOST COUNTACHS ACQUIRED A TAPESTRY OF SCARS THAT REQUIRED THE COST OF A SMALL CAR TO REPAIR

"Everything on the Countach was built on a grand scale, with four exhausts, 12 cylinders, and six carbs."

LANCIA Aurelia B24 Spider

An Italian convertible that has become a style icon

BEAUTY IS MORE THAN just skin deep on this lovely little Lancia, for underneath those lean Pininfarina loins the Aurelia's innards bristle with innovative engineering. For a start, there is the compact alloy V6. Designed under Vittorio Jano, the man responsible for the great racing Alfas of the Twenties and Thirties, this free-revving, torquey little lump was the first mass-produced V6. At the back, the clutch and gearbox were housed in the transaxle to endow the

Aurelia with near-perfect weight distribution. These innovations were first matched with the Pininfarina body in 1951, producing the Aurelia B20 GT coupe, often credited as the first of the new breed of modern postwar GTs. And the point of it all becomes clear when you climb behind the wheel; for although the Aurelia was never the most accelerative machine, its handling was so impeccable that 40 years on it still impresses with its masterly cornering poise.

THE AURELIA SPIDER SCORED WELL IN LUGGAGE-CARRYING CAPABILITIES COMPARED WITH OTHER TWO-SEATERS OF THE TIME

"Today the rare and charismatic B24 Spider is the most prized of this illustrious family."

PILING ON THE REVS, THE THROBBING, GRUFF SOUND ROSE TO A RICH GURGLE THAT IS SINGULARLY TUNEFUL FROM THE TWIN EXHAUSTS

MODEL Lancia Aurelia B24 Spider (1954–56)

PRODUCTION 330

BODY STYLE Two-seater sports convertible.

CONSTRUCTION Monocoque with pressed steel and box-section chassis frame.

ENGINE Twin-overhead-valve aluminum alloy V6, 2451cc.

POWER OUTPUT 118 bhp at 5000 rpm.

TRANSMISSION Four-speed manual.

SUSPENSION Sliding pillar with beam axle and coil springs at front, De Dion rear axle on leaf springs.

BRAKES Hydraulic, finned alloy drums, inboard at rear.

MAXIMUM SPEED 112 mph (180 km/h)

0–60 MPH (0–96 km/h) 14.3 sec

A.F.C. 22 mpg (7.8 km/l)

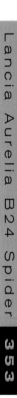

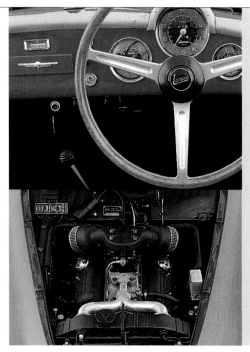

INTERIOR The panel has just three major dials and a clutch of switches on a painted metal dash. It was devoid of the walnut-leather trimmings that British carmakers of the time considered essential for a luxury sports car. The Nardi steering wheel was standard on the Spider.

ENGINE Aurelias featured the world's first mass-production V6, an all-alloy unit that progressively grew from 1754cc to 1991cc, to the 2451cc used in the B24 Spider. The flexible 60-degree V6 could pull the Spider from 20 mph (32 km/h) in top gear, yet ran to 5500 rpm.

CROSSED FLAGS

These are positioned in the middle of the Spider's trunk lid. They represent the joint input of Lancia, responsible for design and manufacture of the mechanical parts, and Pininfarina, which not only styled the body, but also built the cars.

FOR PERFECT BALANCE, THE WEIGHT OF THE ENGINE WAS OFFSET BY LOCATING CLUTCH AND GEARBOX IN A UNIT WITH DIFFERENTIAL AT THE REAR

THE SPIDER'S HOOD-TOP AIR-SCOOP WAS A UNIQUE FEATURE AMONG AURELIA MODELS

XSU 695

Pinin Farina joined his brother's carriage repair business at the age of 11. Father of the modern GT, he was the king of car design by 1953, working for Fiat, Austin, Peugeot, and Ferrari. Shortly before his death in '66, he changed his surname to Pininfarina, which has become the name of the company he founded, now run by his son Sergio.

LANCIA Stratos

A rally legend and a commercial disaster

THE LANCIA STRATOS WAS built as a rally winner first and a road car second. Fiat-owned Lancia took the bold step of designing an all-new car solely to win the World Rally Championship, and Lancia then commissioned Bertone to build the vehicle. The Stratos debuted at the 1971 Turin Show, and with a V6 Ferrari Dino engine (*see pages* 256–59) on board, it achieved notable success by winning three World Championships in 1974, '75, and '76. Rallying rules demanded that at least 500 cars be built, but Lancia needed only 40 for its rally program; the rest lay unsold in showrooms across Europe for years. Sales were so slow that they were still available new up until 1980 and were even given away as prizes to high-selling Lancia dealers. Never a genuine commercial proposition, the Stratos was an amazing mix of elegance, hard-charging performance, and thrill-a-minute handling.

"Shorter than a MkII Escort, and with the wheelbase of a Fiat 850, the stubby Stratos wedge looked almost as wide as it was long."

PLEXIGLAS SIDE WINDOWS WERE SO DEEPLY RECESSED WITHIN THE BODYWORK THAT THEY COULD BE FULLY OPENED WITHOUT CAUSING ANY WIND TURBULENCE

FLIMSY NOSE SECTION CONCEALED SPARE TIRE, RADIATOR, AND TWIN THERMOSTATICALLY CONTROLLED COOLING FANS

KCL 705N

KCL 705N

BERTONE

LANCIA

MODEL Lancia Stratos (1973–80)

PRODUCTION 492

BODY STYLE Two-seater mid-engined sports coupe.

CONSTRUCTION Fiberglass and steel unit construction body chassis tub.

ENGINE 2418cc mid-mounted transverse V6.

POWER OUTPUT 190 bhp at 7000 rpm.

TRANSMISSION Five-speed manual in unit with engine and transaxle.

SUSPENSION Independent front and rear with coil springs and wishbones.

BRAKES Four-wheel discs.

MAXIMUM SPEED 143 mph (230 km/h)

0–60 MPH (0–96 km/h) 6.0 sec

0–100 MPH (0–161 km/h) 16.7 sec

A.F.C. 18 mpg (6.4 km/l)

RALLY SUCCESS

Lancia commissioned Bertone to build a rally weapon, and the Stratos debuted at the 1971 Turin Show. The Stratos was homologated in 1974, and it won the World Championship that year as well as the next two years. The car's most successful year was 1976, when first and second places were secured in the Monte Carlo Rally, first in Sicily, Corsica, and Italy, and the top four places in the rally of Portugal.

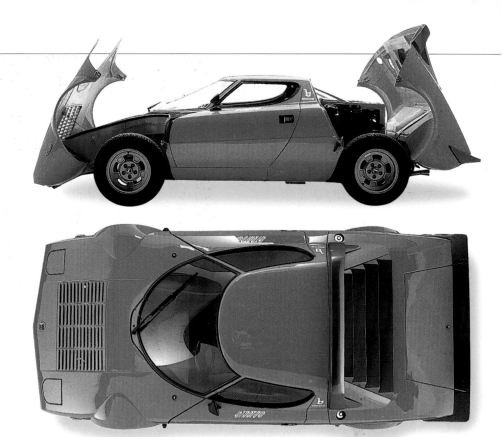

WINDSHIELD WAS CUT FROM THIN CYLINDRICAL GLASS TO AVOID DISTORTION

THE STRATOS WAS A TWO-THIRDS FIBERGLASS FEATHERWEIGHT, TIPPING THE SCALES AT A WHISKER OVER 2,000 LB (908 KG)

KCL 705N

> "Whatever the views on the Stratos' styling, there is no doubting the fact that the glorious metallic soundtrack is wonderful."

INTERIOR The Stratos was hopeless as a day-to-day machine, with a claustrophobic cockpit and woeful rear vision. The width of 67 in (1.72 m) and the narrow cabin meant that the steering wheel was virtually in the middle of the car. Quality control was dire, with huge panel gaps, mischievous wiring, and ventilation that did not work.

ENGINE Lifted straight out of the Dino 246, the 190 bhp transverse, mid-mounted V6 had four chain-driven camshafts spinning in alloy heads, which sat just 6 in (15 cm) from your ear. Clutch and throttle were incredibly stiff, which made smooth driving an art form. Factory rally versions had a four-valve V6 unit.

REAR SPRINGING WAS BY LANCIA BETA-STYLE STRUTS, WITH LOWER WISHBONES, AND HAD ANTIDIVE AND ANTI-SQUAT GEOMETRY

MOLDED FIBERGLASS REAR COWL LIFTED UP BY UNDOING TWO CLIPS, GIVING ACCESS TO MIDSHIPS-MOUNTED POWER PLANT

KCL 705N

LANCIA Delta HF Integrale

Probably the best car Lancia ever made

THIS NOT TERRIBLY well-built, boxy, turbocharged banshee is one of the finest cars Lancia ever made and the best joy ride since the prototype magic carpet. A change in the World Rally Championship rules in 1986 meant that Lancia's Delta HF 4WD became very competitive, winning the manufacturer's world championship in the first year of competition. Lancia's crew increased the Delta's power, flared the wheelarches, and dubbed the end result the Integrale.

The 185 bhp Integrale kicked out the sort of performance figures that could worry a Ferrari, but with awesome levels of grip. The ride is washboard hard, the interior trim flimsy, and the whole thing may rattle more than a bag of tools, but for sheer dollar-for-dollar driving enjoyment, nothing even comes close. The final run of 210 bhp and 215 bhp Evoluzione I and IIs were quicker still and have rightly been described as two of the greatest driver's cars of all time.

"Tiny, four-cylinder, double-overhead cam engine was a gem. Cylinder capacity may have been limited, but acceleration was as swift as a Ferrari 348."

THE CABIN WAS POORLY MADE WITH CHEAP, EIGHTIES ITALIAN SWITCHES AND GAUGES

BOXED ARCHES GAVE THE INTEGRALE A MUSCULAR STANCE AND COVERED WIDE SPEED-RATED RUBBER

"Along a winding road, very little could keep up with a well-driven 'Grale and its four-wheel drive system."

MODEL Lancia Delta HF Integrale (1992)

PRODUCTION Not available

BODY STYLE Four-seater, four-door sedan.

CONSTRUCTION Steel monocoque.

ENGINE 2000cc, four-cylinder, turbocharged.

POWER OUTPUT 185 bhp at 5300 rpm.

TRANSMISSION Five-speed manual, four-wheel drive.

SUSPENSION Independent front and rear.

BRAKES Four-wheel discs.

MAXIMUM SPEED 128 mph (206 km/h)

0-60 MPH (0–96 km/h) 6.6 sec

A.F.C. 28 mpg (9.9 km/l)

FOUR-WHEEL DRIVE
SYSTEM SPLIT
TORQUE 56/44,
FRONT-TO-REAR

GRILLE BADGE
WARNED OTHER
DRIVERS TO MOVE
OVER, FAST

"In the Eighties, no other car offered the same sort of balance, poise, brilliant steering, and fearsome acceleration at the same price as the Integrale."

V8 ENGINE WAS
DOCILE AND
TRACTABLE WITH
LITTLE TURBO LAG

ALL INTEGRALES
WERE MADE IN
LEFT-HAND DRIVE
FORM ONLY

AW·162 DG

LIKE ALL ITALIAN CARS
OF THE PERIOD,
INTEGRALES HAD SCANT
RUST PROTECTION

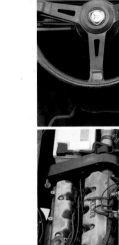

INTERIOR Contemporary road testers
complained bitterly about the Integrale's
mediocre fixtures and furnishings. Many test
cars would come with broken switches, non-
functioning gauges, and numerous different
electrical gremlins. The thing was that real
enthusiasts didn't care.

ENGINE The Integrale's sweet engine boasted
twin cams, counterrotating balancing shafts,
electronic ignition, turbocharger, overboost,
Nymonic valves, and intercooler. The Torsen
differential gave constant balance between the
rear wheels, while the Ferguson viscous coupling
split the power between front and rear axles.

PERPENDICULAR
AERODYNAMICS
SLOWED THE CAR DOWN
AT VERY HIGH SPEEDS

AW · 162 DG

LANCIA   DELTA HF integrale

LAND ROVER Series 1

The 4x4 that evolved into a suburban icon

IT'S HARD TO IMAGINE a world without Land Rovers; and if they didn't already exist, we'd have to invent them. Yet the original 4x4 legend was born accidentally, a child of postwar austerity. In 1946 the Rover Company badly needed export cash, steel was in short supply, and the market for new cars was limited. Rover wanted a model it could make out of aluminum without expensive tooling costs. Using as many existing Rover parts as possible, and literally welding the chassis together out of simple strips of steel, the first Land Rover was unveiled at the Amsterdam Motor Show of 1948. Within weeks, Rover were besieged by orders and had to limit sales to buyers who had a genuine need, like farmers and doctors. Developing countries clamored too; and impressed by the influx of export currency, the British government made sure that Rover got all the raw materials it needed. Before long, Rover was making more Land Rovers than cars.

REAR BENCH SEATS MAY HAVE BEEN UNYIELDING BUT MEANT THAT EVEN A SHORT WHEELBASE MODEL COULD CARRY SIX PEOPLE

ROVER ORIGINALLY WANTED A CENTER STEERING WHEEL TO OVERCOME THE EXTRA COSTS OF LHD/RHD TOOLING

"Simple, square-jawed, and devoid of any styling flourishes whatsoever, the original Land Rover was a triumph of function over form."

MODEL Land Rover Series 1 (1949)

PRODUCTION 3,000 (Series 1 models)

BODY STYLE Two-door utility vehicle.

CONSTRUCTION Aluminum body, steel chassis.

ENGINE 1595cc four-cylinder.

POWER OUTPUT 50 bhp at 4000 rpm.

TRANSMISSION Four-speed manual with permanent four-wheel drive.

SUSPENSION Front and rear leaf springs.

BRAKES Front and rear drums.

MAXIMUM SPEED 58 mph (93 km/h)

0–60 MPH (0–96 km/h) N/A

A.F.C. 18–23 mpg (6.4–8.1 km/l)

INTERIOR The stark interior had no creature comforts and a minimum of controls. Optional oil pressure and water temperature gauges were used to monitor vital fluids during stationary work using the power takeoff facility. Safety was nonexistent.

ENGINE The simple, four-cylinder 1595cc, inlet-over-exhaust powerplant was a slightly adapted version from the contemporary Rover P3 sedan, also launched in 1948. Performance was glacial with 40 mph (64 km/h) taking 18 seconds.

"Nearly all Series 1s had canvas tops. Station wagons with a hardtop are incredibly rare."

IT TOOK LAND ROVER OVER 30 YEARS TO OFFER A ONE-PIECE WINDSHIELD WITHOUT A CENTRAL PILLAR

SERIES 1 MODELS HAD PERMANENT FOUR-WHEEL DRIVE. LATER MODELS HAD A FLOOR-MOUNTED LEVER TO ENGAGE BOTH DIFFERENTIALS

MAURICE WILKS

Just after WWII Maurice Wilks bought an ex-army Willys Jeep to use on his farm. Then Managing Director of Rover, Wilks was impressed by the Jeep's abilities and knew that such a vehicle would be a big seller in Britain. He designed an all-terrain, four-wheel drive utility vehicle initially called the "Road Rover." Several months later the renamed Land Rover became so successful that there was a waiting list for the next five years.

TMY 157

LINCOLN Capri

A stylistically jumbled leviathan with a sting in its tail

IN POSSIBLY ONE OF THE most outrageous half-truths ever written, Lincoln copywriters insisted that the '58 Capri was "impressive without being ostentatious" and had a "tasteful, classic elegance." In reality, it was a stylistic nightmare, two-and-a-half tons of massive bumpers, sculpted wheelarches, and weirdly canted headlights. What's more, in the jumbo 430cid Continental V8 it had the largest engine available in a US production car at the time. This visual anarchy and the '58 recession meant that sales halved from the previous year, and Ford realized that the Capri was badly timed. However, the Lincoln had one solid advantage: it was quick *and* it handled. One magazine said, "it's doubtful if any big car could stick any tighter in the corners or handle any better at high speed," a homily helped by the unitary body, rear coil springs, and potent new brakes. The '58 Capri was one of the last driveaway dinosaurs. The door was closing on an era of kitsch.

"Ford's brief for the '58 Lincolns was to out-glitz Cadillac in every area, but somehow they didn't quite get it right."

AIR SUSPENSION WAS ON THE OPTION LIST, BUT ONLY TWO PERCENT OF LINCOLN BUYERS TOOK THE PLUNGE

THE UNITARY BODY ELIMINATED A CHASSIS FRAME FOR THE FIRST TIME IN 10 YEARS

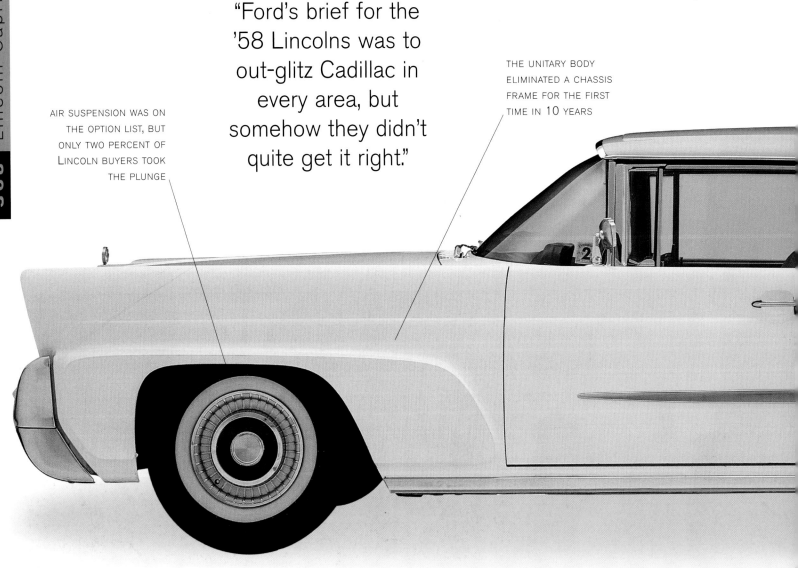

Lincoln

MODEL Lincoln Capri (1958)

PRODUCTION 6,859 (1958)

BODY STYLE Four-door, six-seater sedan.

CONSTRUCTION Steel unitary body.

ENGINE 430cid V8.

POWER OUTPUT 375 bhp.

TRANSMISSION Three-speed Turbo-Drive automatic.

SUSPENSION Front and rear coil springs.

BRAKES Front and rear drums.

MAXIMUM SPEED 115 mph (185 km/h)

0–60 MPH (0–96 km/h) 9 sec

A.F.C. 14 mpg (5 km/l)

INTERIOR For just under $5,000, standard features included electric windows with child-proof controls, a six-way Power Seat, a padded instrument panel, and five ashtrays, each with its own lighter. Seat belts and leather trim were also on the options list.

ENGINE The big, new 430cid engine walloped out 375 horses, giving a power output second only to the Chrysler 500D. Lowered final drive ratios failed even to pay lip service to fuel economy, with the Capri returning a groan-inspiring 10 mpg (3.5 km/l) around town.

THE LARGEST PASSENGER CAR OF THE YEAR, THE CAPRI COULD ACCOMMODATE SIX OR EVEN SEVEN PEOPLE, RIDING ON AN ENORMOUS, ELONGATED 131 IN (3.33 M) WHEELBASE

9x14 TIRES COULDN'T COPE WITH THE LINCOLN'S PRODIGIOUS WEIGHT — MOST CARS OF THE PERIOD WERE EQUIPPED WITH POTENTIALLY LETHAL UNDERSIZED RUBBER

TINTED GLASS WAS A $50 OPTION, ALONG WITH TRANSLUCENT SUN VISORS AT $27

"Prototypes of the unitary body flexed so badly that all kinds of stiffening reinforcements were added, negating any weight savings."

THE CAPRI USED EVERY STYLISTIC TRICK THAT MOTOWN HAD EVER LEARNED, BUT ONLY DESPERATE MEN WOULD PUT FINS ON THE REAR BUMPER

THIS WAS THE FIRST YEAR THAT LINCOLN HAD COIL SPRINGS FOR REAR SUSPENSION

LINCOLN Continental

One of Detroit's greatest achievements

THERE'S AN UNSETTLING IRONY in the fact that John F. Kennedy was shot in a '61 Lincoln Continental. Like him, the revamped '61 Continental had a new integrity. Substantial and innovative, it was bristling with new ideas and survived for nine years without major change. It was elegant, restrained, and classically sculptured, perfect for Camelot's new dynasty of liberalism. Ironic, too, that JFK liked the Lincoln – he often used a stock White House Continental for unofficial business. Nearly $7,000 bought one of the best-built American cars of the Sixties. It carried a two-year, 24,000-mile (39,000-km) warranty, every engine was bench-tested, and each car was given a 200-category shakedown. WASP America approved, and production doubled in the first year. Even the Industrial Design Institute was impressed, awarding its coveted bronze medal for "an outstanding contribution of simplicity and design elegance."

"Lincoln historian James Wagner described the '61 Continental as 'more like a Mercedes-Benz than a product of GM.'"

THE "SUICIDE" REAR-HINGED DOORS HARKED BACK TO CLASSIC PREWAR CAR-BUILDING. ON OLDER CONTINENTAL CONVERTIBLES, OPENING ALL FOUR DOORS AT ONCE COULD ACTUALLY FLEX THE FLOOR AND CHASSIS

THE CONTINENTAL'S SUSPENSION DAMPING WAS CONSIDERED THE BEST ON ANY CONTEMPORARY CAR

MODEL Lincoln Continental Convertible (1964)

PRODUCTION 3,328

BODY STYLE Four-door, five-seater convertible.

CONSTRUCTION Steel body and chassis.

ENGINE 430cid V8.

POWER OUTPUT 320 bhp.

TRANSMISSION Three-speed Turbo-Drive automatic.

SUSPENSION *Front:* control arms and coil springs; *Rear:* leaf springs with live axle.

BRAKES Front and rear drums.

MAXIMUM SPEED 115 mph (185 km/h)

0–60 MPH (0–96 km/h) 11 sec

A.F.C. 14 mpg (5 km/l)

"The seat covering on which JFK and Jackie Kennedy lay after the fatal shots were fired is preserved by Ford."

INTERIOR Every Continental had power steering and windows, walnut cappings, a padded dashboard, lush carpets, and vacuum-powered door locks as standard. Gauges showing fuel supply, oil pressure, water temperature, and battery charge were new for '64.

TOP ELECTRICS Eleven relays and a maze of linkages made the Continental's top disappear neatly into the trunk. The electrics were completely sealed and never needed maintenance. In another neat electrical touch, the locks operated automatically as soon as the car moved.

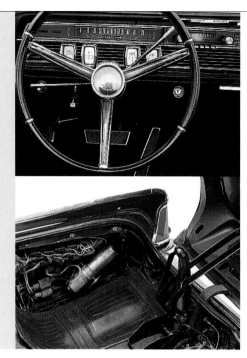

"Low, wide, and mighty, the '60s Continental was considered the epitome of good taste and discrimination."

HEADLIGHTS COULD SENSE ONCOMING TRAFFIC AND WOULD DIM AUTOMATICALLY

LEAST POPULAR OPTION IN '64 WAS THE ADJUSTABLE STEERING WHEEL

NEW YORK
KTS 340
LINCOLN

Probably the most famous car in the world, the 1961 Lincoln Continental in which JFK was assassinated still survives in the Henry Ford Museum. The navy blue elongated convertible was equipped with many special features designed by the secret service, and was leased from Ford to the White House for a nominal $500 a year. After the assassination, the Lincoln was sent back to Ford for an overhaul and was subsequently used by both Presidents Johnson and Nixon.

ALONG WITH THE TOP, THE SIDE GLASS AND WINDOW FRAMES ALSO DISAPPEARED FROM VIEW AT THE TOUCH OF A BUTTON

LINCOLN Continental Mk IV

A mammoth car with bags of attitude

IN 1972, $10,000 BOUGHT you TV detective Frank Cannon's corpulent Mark IV Continental, the luxury car fit to lock bumpers with Cadillac's finest. As big as they came and surprisingly fast, the all-new hunch-flanked body had a Rolls-Royce-esque grille and distinctive, fake spare-wheel cover. Road-testers were unanimous in their praise for its power, luxury, and size, remarking that the Mark IV's hood "looks like an aircraft carrier landing-deck on final approach." The list of luxury features was as long as a Chicago phonebook – air-conditioning, six-by-six-way power seats, power windows, antenna, and door locks. And all came as standard. The air-con was about as complex and powerful as a Saturn rocket and, to please the legislators, under a hood the size of a baseball field nestled a forest of emission pipes. America may have wanted to kick the smog habit, but trim its waistline? Never.

"Rolls-Royce was offended by the Continental's copy of its grille but didn't actually litigate. The management wished it had as the grille went on to become a Lincoln trademark."

77 PERCENT OF '72 CONTINENTALS CAME WITH OPTIONAL $70 TILTING STEERING WHEEL, TESTIMONY TO THE PROPORTIONS OF THE AVERAGE OWNER

SURE TRACK POWER BRAKE SYSTEM HAD TO WORK HARD TO HAUL TWO TONS TO A DEAD STOP

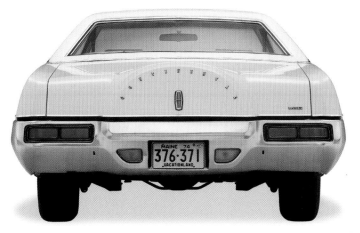

Continental MARK IV

MODEL Lincoln Continental Mark IV (1972)

PRODUCTION 48,591 (1972)

BODY STYLE Two-door, five seater hardtop.

CONSTRUCTION Steel body and chassis.

ENGINE 460cid V8.

POWER OUTPUT 224 bhp.

TRANSMISSION Three-speed Select-Shift automatic.

SUSPENSION Helical coil front and rear.

BRAKES Front power discs, rear drums.

MAXIMUM SPEED 122 mph (196 km/h)

0–60 MPH (0–96 km/h) 17.8 sec

A.F.C. 10 mpg (3.5 km/l)

INTERIOR Standard equipment on the Continental included a Cartier electric clock, wooden dashboard, and a six-way power Twin Comfort seat. Leather lounge seats could be ordered for an extra $179. Even so, the whole thing felt a bit tacky and didn't have the uptown cachet of European imports.

ENGINE At 460cid, the Continental's V8 may have been Olympian, but it was still eclipsed by Cadillac's contemporary 500cid powerplant. The Mark IV block's power output for '72 was 224 bhp, a stark contrast to the 365 horses pushed out only a year before. Federal restrictions on power were the reason.

SPACE AND COMFORT

A two-door in name, the Mark IV Continental had enough room for five, in part because it was longer and wider than the Mark III that preceded it. The baroque interior was typical of the period, and the tiny "opera" window in the huge rear pillar became a Lincoln styling metaphor.

SHUTTERED HEADLIGHTS AND HEAVYWEIGHT CHROME BUMPER ADDED TO THE CAR'S PRESENCE

THE VINYL, LEATHER-LOOK ROOF WAS STANDARD ON ALL MARK IVs

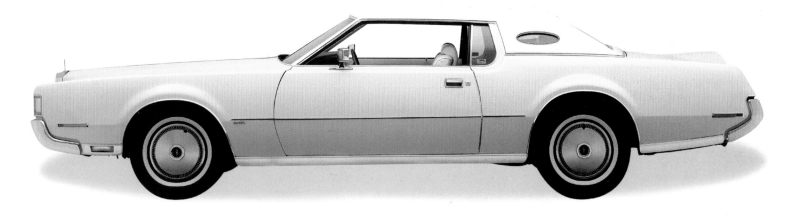

"The Continental wheel cover on the trunk had been a Lincoln styling trait since the early Mark Is."

THE GARISH YELLOW
COLOR SCHEME WAS
TYPICAL '70S, BUT ALL
MARK IVS COULD BE
PAINTED IN A METALLIC
HUE FOR $127

LOTUS Elite

One of the best-looking and best-handling GTs ever

IF EVER A CAR WAS A brand landmark, this is it. The Elite was the first Lotus designed for road use rather than out-and-out racing, paving the way for a string of stunning sports and GT cars that, at the least, were always innovative. The elegant coupe was a remarkable departure for the small company and a complete surprise when it appeared at the London Motor Show in October 1957. Its all-fiberglass construction – chassis as well as body – was a bold departure that, coupled with many other innovations, marked the Elite as truly exceptional, and all the more so considering the small-scale operation that created it. What's more, its built-in Lotus race-breeding gave it phenomenal handling, and this together with an unparalleled power-to-weight ratio brought an almost unbroken run of racing successes. It also happens to be one of the prettiest cars of its era; in short, a superb GT in miniature.

"The Elite's aerodynamic makeup was remarkable considering there were no full-scale wind-tunnel tests, only low-speed air-flow experiments."

MODEL Lotus Elite (1957–63)

PRODUCTION 988

BODY STYLE Two-door, two-seater sports coupe.

CONSTRUCTION Fiberglass monocoque.

ENGINE Four-cylinder single OHC Coventry Climax, 1216cc.

POWER OUTPUT 75–105 bhp.

TRANSMISSION Four-speed MG or ZF gearbox.

SUSPENSION Independent all around by wishbones and coil springs at front and MacPherson-type "Chapman strut" at rear.

BRAKES Discs all around (inboard at rear).

MAXIMUM SPEED 118 mph (190 km/h)

0–60 MPH (0–96 km/h) 11.1 sec

A.F.C. 35 mpg (12.5 km/l)

Lotus Elite **381**

INTERIOR Even tall people were universal in their praise for the Elite's driving comfort. The award-winning interior was crisp and neat, with light, modern materials. Main instruments were a speedo reading to 140 mph (225 km/h) and a 0–8000 rpm tachometer.

ENGINE The lightweight 1216cc four-cylinder engine was developed by Coventry Climax from its successful racing units. The unit's power rose from an initial 75 bhp to 83 bhp in the Elite's second series, but it was possible to extract over 100 bhp with options.

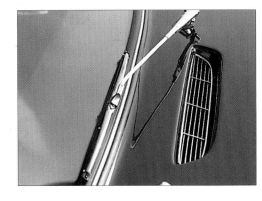

VENTILATION

The built-in cockpit ventilation system was fed by an intake on the scuttle; outlet vents were above the rear window. Inside the Elite there were cubby holes aplenty, especially inside the doors, to supplement trunk space.

LOW FRONTAL AREA, WITH AIR INTAKE BELOW THE BUMPER LIP, HELPED THE ELITE'S SPEED AND ECONOMY

THE ROOF WAS PART OF THE ELITE'S STRESSED STRUCTURE, WHICH MEANT THAT POPULAR CALLS FOR A CONVERTIBLE — ESPECIALLY FROM THE STATES — COULD NOT BE ANSWERED

LJC322

A race-car driver of considerable ability, Colin Chapman started Lotus Cars in 1955. His first significant success was the gorgeous Elite, quickly followed by the fine-handling and fast-selling Elan. In the Seventies he expanded his commercial empire, creating a complicated web of offshore tax havens. A hard taskmaster, Chapman was a brilliant engineer and ruthless businessman to whom nothing was impossible.

THE TINY DOOR
HANDLE WAS
LITTLE MORE
THAN A HOOK

Lotus Elite **383**

LJC 322

LOTUS Elan Sprint

Highly acclaimed beauty with solid racing roots

THE LOTUS ELAN RANKS as one of the best handling cars of its era. But not only was it among the most poised cars money could buy, it was also a thing of beauty. Conceived by engineering genius Colin Chapman to replace the race-bred Lotus 7, the Elan sat on a steel backbone chassis, clothed in a slippery fiberglass body, and was powered by a 1600cc Ford twin-overhead-cam engine. Despite a high price tag, critics and public raved, and the Elan became one of the most charismatic sports cars of its decade, selling over 12,000 examples. Over an 11-year production life, with five different model series, it evolved into a very desirable and accelerative machine, culminating in the Elan Sprint, a 121 mph (195 km/h) banshee with a sub-seven second 0–60 mph (96 km/h) time. As one auto magazine of the time remarked, "The Elan Sprint is one of the finest sports cars in the world." Praise indeed.

"Never slow to sing its own praises, Lotus equipped many Elans with a badge listing the company's string of Grand Prix victories."

THE DUO-TONE PAINTWORK WITH DIVIDING STRIP WAS A POPULAR FACTORY OPTION FOR THE SPRINT

MODEL Lotus Elan Sprint (1970–73)

PRODUCTION 1,353

BODY STYLE Two-seater drophead.

CONSTRUCTION Steel box section backbone chassis.

ENGINE Four-cylinder twin overhead cam, 1558cc.

POWER OUTPUT 126 bhp at 6500 rpm.

TRANSMISSION Four-speed manual.

SUSPENSION Independent front and rear.

BRAKES Discs all around.

MAXIMUM SPEED 121 mph (195 km/h)

0–60 MPH (0–96 km/h) 6.7 sec

0–100 MPH (0–161 km/h) 15 sec

A.F.C. 24 mpg (8.5 km/l)

INTERIOR The Sprint's interior accommodation was refined and upmarket, with all-black trim, wood veneer dashboard, and even electric windows. Safer recessed rocker switches were a legal requirement in most markets.

ENGINE The "Big Valve" engine in the Sprint pushed out 126 bhp and blessed it with truly staggering performance, but the twin 40 DCOE Weber carburetors were hard to keep in tune. The ribbed cam covers were especially designed to prevent oil leaks.

WHEEL RESPECT

Colin Chapman's signature was inscribed on the Elan's alloy steering wheel. The car's go-kart handling was down to Chapman's ability to adapt race-car engineering to a road car.

THE POP-UP HEADLIGHTS WORKED VIA A VACUUM SYSTEM, BUT OFTEN FAILED

THE ELAN WAS ONE OF THE FIRST CARS TO BE EQUIPPED WITH BUMPERS THAT FOLLOWED THE CAR'S CONTOURS

> "The red-and-gold combination had racing associations – the same look as the Gold Leaf racing team cars."

In the late Sixties, Diana Rigg drove a Lotus Elan convertible in the UK TV series, *The Avengers*. Next to the Jaguar E-Type, the Elan was one of the most fashionable cars of the time. The TV exposure boosted Elan sales and gave the car a sexy quality. Rigg's car is currently on exhibit at the Cars of the Stars Museum in Northumbria, England.

THE ELAN WAS POPULAR AS A TOURING CAR BECAUSE, DESPITE HOUSING THE BATTERY, ITS BOOT WAS LARGER THAN AVERAGE

MASERATI Ghibli

Possibly the best of the tridents

MANY BELIEVE THE GHIBLI is the greatest of all road-worthy Maseratis. It was the sensation of the 1966 Turin Show and 30 years later is widely regarded as Maserati's ultimate front-engined road car – a supercar blend of luxury, performance, and stunning good looks that never again quite came together so sublimely on anything with the trident. Pitched squarely against the Ferrari Daytona (*see page* 264) and Lamborghini Miura (*see page* 344–47), it outsold both. Its engineering may have been dated, but it had the perfect pedigree, with plenty of power from its throaty V8 engine and a flawless Ghia design. It is a true supercar, yet it is also a consummate continent-eating grand tourer. Muscular and perhaps even menacing, but not overbearingly macho, it is well mannered enough for the tastes of the superrich. There will only be one dilemma; do you take the winding back roads or blast along the highways? Why not a little of both.

"The Ghibli's dramatic styling is uncompromised. From its bladelike front to its short, bobbed tail, it looked fast even in static pose."

THE WIDE FRONT HAD A TENDENCY TO LIFT ABOVE 120 MPH (193 KM/H) AS THE STEERING COULD BECOME WORRYINGLY LIGHT

THE WINDSHIELD WAS HUGE, BUT THE MIGHTY HOOD COULD MAKE THE GHIBLI DIFFICULT TO MANEUVER

MODEL Maserati Ghibli (1967–73)

PRODUCTION 1,274

BODY STYLES Sports coupe or open Spider.

CONSTRUCTION Steel body and separate tubular chassis.

ENGINES V8, 4719cc or 4930cc (SS).

POWER OUTPUT 330–335 bhp.

TRANSMISSION ZF five-speed manual or three-speed Borg-Warner auto.

SUSPENSION *Front*: Wishbones and coil springs; *Rear*: rigid axle with radius arms/semielliptic leaf springs.

BRAKES Girling discs on all four wheels.

MAXIMUM SPEED 168 mph (270 km/h, SS)

0–60 MPH (0–96 km/h) 6.2 sec (SS)

0–100 MPH (0–161 km/h) 15.7 sec (SS)

A.F.C. 10 mpg (3.5 km/l)

INTERIOR A cliché certainly, but here you really feel you are on an aircraft flight-deck. The high center console houses air-conditioning, which was standard Ghibli equipment. The steering wheel is adjustable, and power steering was a later, desirable optional extra.

ENGINE The potent race-bred quad-cam V8 is even-tempered and undemanding, delivering loads of low-down torque and accelerating meaningfully from as little as 500 rpm in fifth gear. Pictured is the 4.9-liter engine of the featured 1971 Ghibli SS.

BODYWORK BY GHIA WAS ONE OF THE FINEST EARLY DESIGNS OF ITS BRILLIANT YOUNG ITALIAN EMPLOYEE, GIORGETTO GIUGIARO

MASERATI Kyalami

Dubious-looking supercar that won few friends

THE 1970s PRODUCED some true automotive lemons. It was a decade when barefaced badge engineering and gluttonous V8 engines were all the rage, and nobody cared that these big bruisers cost three arms and a leg to run. The Kyalami is one such monument to excess, a reworking of the De Tomaso Longchamp with Maserati's all-alloy V8 on board instead of Ford's 5.8-liter cast-iron lump. With a choice of five-speed manual or three-speed Borg Warner automatic, the Kyalami was meant to compete with the Jaguar XJS but failed hopelessly. Plagued with electrical gremlins, this was a noisy, bulky, and unrefined machine that was neither beautiful nor poised. Yet for all that, it still sports that emotive trident on its nose and emits a deep and strident V8 bark. The Kyalami might not be a great car, but most of us, at least while looking at it, find it hard to tell the difference.

"Maserati designer Petro Frua retouched the De Tomaso Longchamp design, turning it into the Kyalami."

"The front bumper looked cheap, while the grille and trident seem to have been bolted on as afterthoughts."

MODEL Maserati Kyalami 4.9 (1976–82)

PRODUCTION 250 approx.

BODY STYLE Two-door, 2+2 sports sedan.

CONSTRUCTION Steel monocoque body.

ENGINE 4930cc all-alloy V8.

POWER OUTPUT 265 bhp at 6000 rpm.

TRANSMISSION Five-speed ZF manual or three-speed Borg Warner automatic.

SUSPENSION *Front*: independent with coil springs and wishbones; *Rear*: independent with double coils, lower links, and radius arms.

BRAKES Four-wheel discs.

MAXIMUM SPEED 147 mph (237 km/h)

0–60 MPH (0–96 km/h) 7.6 sec

0–100 MPH (0–161 km/h) 19.4 sec

A.F.C. 14 mpg (3.6 km/l)

INTERIOR The cabin was a study of Seventies tastelessness, with leather seats and Alcantara dash top. Quality control in the Kyalami was poor, and many components, like the Ford steering column, were sourced from European manufacturers.

ENGINE The engine was a four-cam, five-bearing 4.9 V8, with four twin-choke Weber carbs, propelling the Kyalami to a touch under 150 mph (241 km/h). The vast air filter and cam covers were presented in crackle black as opposed to the usual polished Italian alloy.

MASERATI 300S

Maserati had an established racing bloodline that went back to 1930, when they won five Grand Prix events in a row. After World War II, Juan Fangio trounced the opposition in the legendary 250F, and the 300S sports-racing model went on to secure success at Le Mans.

POWER-ASSISTED STEERING ROBBED THE CAR OF MUCH NEEDED ACCURACY AND FEEL

THE KYALAMI GOBBLED LIQUID GOLD AT THE RATE OF 14 MPG (3.6 KM/L)

GVV 255X

"The Kyalami generated lots
of commotion from fat
205/70 Michelins."

DAINTY REAR LIGHT
CLUSTERS WERE
BORROWED FROM
THE CONTEMPORARY
FIAT 130 COUPE

THE REAR ASPECT
WAS TOO BOXY AND
ANGULAR FOR ITS
OWN GOOD

MAZDA RX7

The first successful rotary-powered sports car

THE RX7 ARRIVED IN American showrooms in 1978, and sales promptly went crazy. Even importing 4,000 a month, Mazda could not cope with demand and waiting lists were huge. For a while, RX7s changed hands on the black market for as much as $3,000 above the retail price. By the time production ceased in 1985, nearly 500,000 had found grateful owners, making the RX7 the best-selling rotary car of all time. The RX7 sold on its clean European looks and Swiss-watch smoothness. Inspired by the woefully unreliable NSU Ro80, Mazda's engineers were not worried about the NSU's ghost haunting the RX7. By 1978 they had completely mastered rotary-engine technology and sold almost a million rotary-engined cars and trucks. These days the RX7 is becoming an emergent classic – the first car to make Felix Wankel's rotary design actually work, and one of the more desirable and better made sports cars of the 1970s.

THE RX7'S SLIPPERY, WIND-EVADING SHAPE CLEAVED THE AIR WELL, WITH A DRAG COEFFICIENT OF ONLY 0.36 AND A TOP SPEED OF 125 MPH (210 KM/H). SMOOTH AERODYNAMICS HELPED THE RX7 FEEL STABLE AND COMPOSED WITH MINIMAL BODY ROLL

REAR SUSPENSION WAS IN THE BEST EUROPEAN SPORTS CAR TRADITION – WISHBONES AND A WATT'S LINKAGE

MAZDA

MODEL Maxda RX7 (1978–85)

PRODUCTION 474,565 (377,878 exported to US)

BODY STYLE All-steel coupe.

CONSTRUCTION One-piece monocoque bodyshell.

ENGINE Twin rotor, 1146cc.

POWER OUTPUT 135 bhp at 6000 rpm.

TRANSMISSION Five-speed all synchromesh/automatic option.

SUSPENSION *Front*: independent; *Rear*: live axle with trailing arms and Watt's linkage.

BRAKES Front ventilated discs, rear drums.

MAXIMUM SPEED 125 mph (210 km/h)

0–60 MPH (0–96 km/h) 8.9 sec

0–100 MPH (0–161 km/h) 24 sec

A.F.C. 21.3 mpg (7.5 km/l)

"The RX7 was originally planned as a two-seater, but Mazda was forced to include a small rear seat in the model."

POP-UP HEADLIGHTS HELPED REDUCE WIND RESISTANCE AND ADD GLAMOUR. BUT, UNLIKE THOSE ON THE LOTUS ESPRIT AND TRIUMPH TR7, THE MAZDA'S ALWAYS WORKED

THE RX7'S LOW HOOD LINE COULD NOT HAVE BEEN ACHIEVED WITH ANYTHING BUT THE COMPACT ROTARY ENGINE, WHICH WEIGHED ONLY 312 LB (142 KG)

INTERIOR Cockpit and dashboard are tastefully orthodox, with a handsome three-spoke wheel and five-gauge instrument housing. Five-speed manual transmission was standard, with automatic an extra. Quality suspension meant that the ride was comfortable.

ENGINE The twin-rotor Wankel engine gave 135 bhp in later models, although oil consumption was always quite high. Reliable, compact, and easy to tune, there was even a small electric winch on the bulkhead to reel in the choke if owners forgot to push it back in.

"The body design was perfect from the start, and in its seven-year production run few changes were made to the slim and balanced shape."

ORIGINAL DESIGN PLANS FOR THE RX7 FAVORED A ONE-PIECE REAR TAILGATE LIKE THE PORSCHE 944, BUT ECONOMICS DICTATED THAT AN ALL-GLASS HATCH WAS INCORPORATED INSTEAD

BOTH REAR AND FRONT BRAKES WERE WELL COOLED WITH VENTILATED DISCS AND FINNED REAR DRUMS

C418 DYV

A staggeringly beautiful German coupe

WITH ITS GORGEOUS gullwing doors raised, the 300SL looked like it could fly. And with them lowered shut it really could, rocketing beyond 140 mph (225 km/h) and making its contemporary supercar pretenders look ordinary. Derived from the 1952 Le Mans-winning racer, these mighty cars were early forebears of modern supercars like the Jaguar XJ220 and McLaren F1 in taking racetrack technology onto the streets. In fact, the 300SL can lay a plausible claim to being the first true postwar supercar. Awkward to enter, incorporating state-of-the-art aerodynamics, and with edgy high-speed handling, the Gullwing was sublimely impractical – it is a virtual supercar blueprint. It was a statement, too, that Mercedes had recovered from wartime devastation. Mercedes was back, and at the pinnacle of that three-pointed star was the fabulous 300SL, the company's first postwar sports car.

"The launch of the 300SL Gullwing prototype at the 1954 New York Motor Show announced to the world that Mercedes was back."

THE ENGINE BAY COULD GET VERY HOT SO GILLIKE SIDE VENTS WERE MORE THAN A MERE STYLING MOTIF

SOME SAY STEEL DISCS WERE USED TO KEEP COSTS DOWN, BUT THEY ALSO LOOKED MORE MUSCULAR THAN WIRES

MODEL Mercedes-Benz 300SL (1954–57)

PRODUCTION 1,400

BODY STYLE Two-door, two-seat coupe.

CONSTRUCTION Multitubular space-frame with steel and alloy body.

ENGINE Inline six-cylinder overhead camshaft, 2996cc.

POWER OUTPUT 240 bhp at 6100 rpm.

TRANSMISSION Four-speed all synchromesh gearbox.

SUSPENSION Coil springs all raound, with double wishbones at front, swinging half-axles at rear.

BRAKES Finned alloy drums.

MAXIMUM SPEED 135–165 mph (217–265 km/h)

0–60 MPH (0–96 km/h) 8.8 sec

0–100 MPH (0–161 km/h) 21.0 sec

A.F.C. 18 mpg (6.4 km/l)

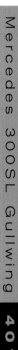

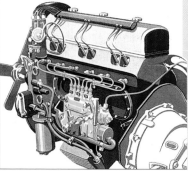

DASH In the Fifties, the bechromed dashboard was pure sci-fi. The large two-spoked wheel gave a good view of the dials, with the clock positioned in the center. On some cars, mostly for the US, the wheel tilted to ease access and became known as "the fat man's wheel."

ENGINE The engine was canted at 50 degrees to give a low hood-line and was the first application of fuel injection in a production car. The unit was from the 300-Series 3-liter sedans, then developed for the 1952 300SL racer, and two years later let loose in the road-going Gullwing.

"The 300SL reestablished Mercedes' position at the pinnacle of sports car excellence."

ONE HOOD BULGE WAS FOR AIR INTAKES, THE OTHER FOR AESTHETIC BALANCE

THE BIG THREE-POINTED STAR DOMINATED THE FRONTAL ASPECT AND WAS REPEATED IN ENAMEL ON THE HOOD EDGE

HD·WD 34

The Gullwing exists because of the 300SLR, a hugely successful race car driven by Stirling Moss at Le Mans, the Targo Florio, and the Mille Miglia in 1955. Moss helped establish both the SLR and the SL as automotive legends. When asked what his favorite car of all time was, Moss has consistently answered the Mercedes SLR. Both of Moss' silver competition steeds survive.

THE GULLWING'S SMOOTH STYLING EXTENDED TO THE SIMPLE REAR; THE TRUNK LOOKS SPACIOUS, BUT THIS WAS NOT THE CASE

MERCEDES 280SL

A gem of a sports car that was built to last

THE MERCEDES 280SL has mellowed magnificently. In 1963 the new SLs took over the sports mantle of the aging 190SL. Named W113 in Mercedes parlance, they evolved from the original 230SL, through the 250SL, and on to the 280SL. The most remarkable thing is how modern they look, for with their simple, clean-shaven good looks, it is hard to believe that the last one was made in 1971. Underneath the timelessly elegant sheet metal, they were based closely on the earlier Fintail sedans, sharing even the decidedly unsporty recirculating-ball steering. Yet it is the looks that mark this car as something special; and the enduring design, with its distinctive so-called pagoda roof, is down to Frenchman Paul Bracq. While it might not be the most masculine of models, this well-manicured car is a beautifully built boulevardier that will induce a sense of supreme self satisfaction on any journey.

"The public perception of the SL was as more of a grand tourer than a genuine sports car."

THE MOST DISTINCTIVE FEATURE OF THE 280SL WAS THE SO-CALLED PAGODA-ROOF REMOVABLE HARDTOP

SWING-AXLE REAR SUSPENSION WAS TAMED TO PROVIDE NATURAL UNDERSTEER

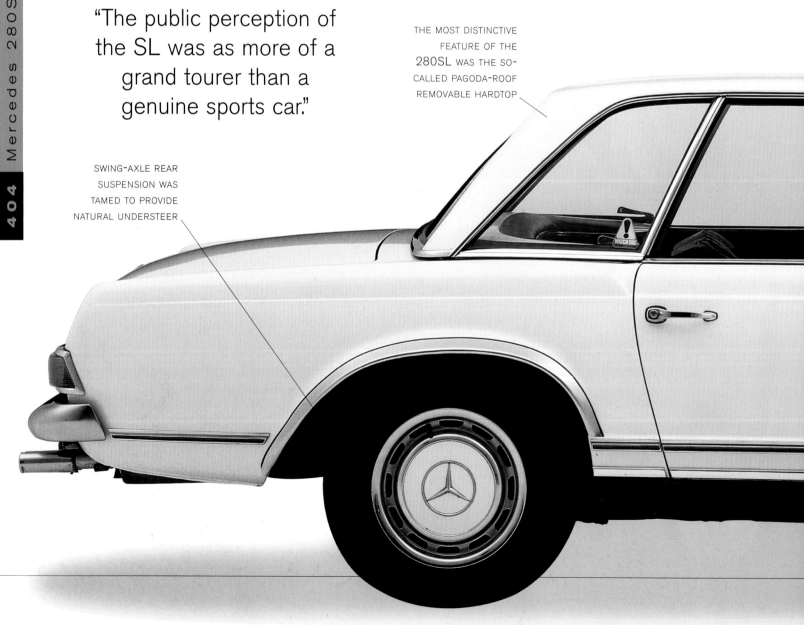

MODEL Mercedes-Benz 280SL (1968–71)

PRODUCTION 23,885

BODY STYLE Two-door, two-seater convertible.

CONSTRUCTION Pressed-steel monocoque.

ENGINE 2778cc inline six; two valves per cylinder; single overhead camshaft.

POWER OUTPUT 170 bhp at 5750 rpm.

TRANSMISSION Four- or five-speed manual, optional four-speed auto.

SUSPENSION *Front*: independent, wishbones, coil springs, telescopic shocks; *Rear*: swing axle, coil springs, telescopic shocks.

BRAKES Front discs, rear drums.

MAXIMUM SPEED 121 mph (195 km/h, auto)

0–60 MPH (0–96 km/h) 9.3 sec

0–100 MPH (0–161 km/h) 30.6 sec

A.F.C. 19 mpg (6.7 km/l)

"The pagoda roof is said to have evolved from the need to provide deep windows for a more balanced side-view of the car, without making it look top-heavy."

INTERIOR With the huge steering wheel (albeit attached to an energy-absorbing column), the painted dash, and the abundance of chrome, the interior is one area where the 280SL shows its age. It is still elegant, though. The D-shaped horn ring allowed a clear view of the dials.

ENGINE The six-cylinder ohc engine saw a process of steady development, starting in July 1963 with the 2281cc, 150 bhp 230SL. In December 1966 came the 2496cc 250SL, and the final 2778cc, 170 bhp 280SL shown here was available from 1968 to 1971.

SO-CALLED "STACKED" HEADLIGHTS ARE UNMISTAKEABLE MERCEDES TRADEMARKS. EACH OUTER LENS CONCEALED ONE HEADLAMP, INDICATOR, AND SIDELIGHT

THE FULL-WIDTH FRONT BUMPER FEATURED A CENTRAL RECESS JUST BIG ENOUGH FOR A STANDARD BRITISH LICENSE PLATE

JBW 620

"With standard power-assisted steering and a small turning circle, the SL handled city streets with aplomb."

WINDSHIELD WIPERS WERE OF THE CHARACTERISTIC "CLAP HANDS" PATTERN BELOVED OF MERCEDES

THE SL WAS ESSENTIALLY A TWO-SEATER, ALTHOUGH A THIRD, SIDEWAYS-FACING REAR SEAT WAS AVAILABLE AS A (RARE) OPTIONAL EXTRA

280 SL
AUTOMATIC

JBW 620

MERCURY Monterey

A powerful line with Hollywood connections

FORD'S UPMARKET MERCURY division was on a roll in 1954. Out went its ancient flathead V8, and in came a new 161 bhp Y-block mill. *Motor Trend* magazine said: "That power will slam you back into the seat when you stomp the throttle." Buyers loved the idea of so much heave and drove away Montereys by the thousands, sending Mercury to an impressive seventh slot in the sales league. Chic, suave, and still glowing from the James Dean association,

Montereys were perfect cruisers for these confident, fat years. Unemployment was low, wages were high, and the economy was thumping. Everyone wanted a Merc – "The car that makes any driving easy" – and the company's output for 1954 was a whopping 259,300 units. The following year would be the automobile industry's best ever as customers thronged to showrooms, packing them tighter than Jane Russell's famous brassiere.

VIEWERS VIED TO WIN THEIR OWN DREAM MERCURY IN 1956 WHEN TV HOST ED SULLIVAN GAVE AWAY 80 MERCURY PHAETONS

THE NEW V8 WAS ROAD-TESTED OVER 4 MILLION MILES (6.44 MILLION KILOMETERS), AND PROVED HIGHLY COMPETITIVE ON THE STOCK-CAR CIRCUIT

THE FOUR-DOOR SEDAN WAS THE SECOND-MOST POPULAR MONTEREY OF '54, WITH 64,995 MADE

MODEL Mercury Monterey (1954)

PRODUCTION 174,238 (1954)

BODY STYLES Two- or four-door hardtop, station wagon, and convertible.

CONSTRUCTION Steel body and chassis.

ENGINE 256cid V8.

POWER OUTPUT 161 bhp.

TRANSMISSION Three-speed manual with optional overdrive, optional Merc-O-Matic Drive automatic.

SUSPENSION *Front:* independent coil springs; *Rear:* leaf springs.

BRAKES Front and rear drums.

MAXIMUM SPEED 100 mph (161 km/h)

0–60 MPH (0–96 km/h) 14 sec

A.F.C. 20 mpg (7 km/l)

INTERIOR Montereys came in a variety of interiors, and options included $140 Bendix power steering, which the industry had only just refined. Road testers of the day believed it to be the best setup around. Bendix also supplied the Monterey's power brakes.

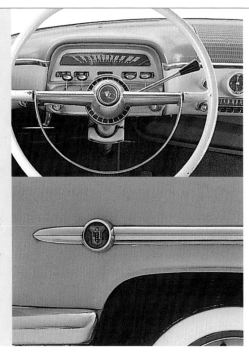

CHROME Montereys were the fanciest Mercurys and said as much on their front fenders, which sported a medallion along with distinctive chrome side trim. All body types in this series, except the station wagons, were called Monterey Customs and had special chrome on the windows.

CONVERTIBLE OPTIONS

This 1954 ad shows the comely Convertible, priced at $2,554. For another $28, you could own America's first transparent-roofed car, the Monterey Sun Valley, painted in either pale yellow or mint green. The front half of the roof incorporated a tinted Plexiglas section.

THE HEAVY GRILLE, CHUNKY HOOD MOTIF, AND SLIGHT SCOWL MADE THE MONTEREY'S FRONT END LOOK MORE THAN A LITTLE MEAN

NEW BALL-STUD FRONT SUSPENSION WAS THE SAME AS '53 LINCOLNS

SAFETY PAYS
5960M4
—IND - 62—

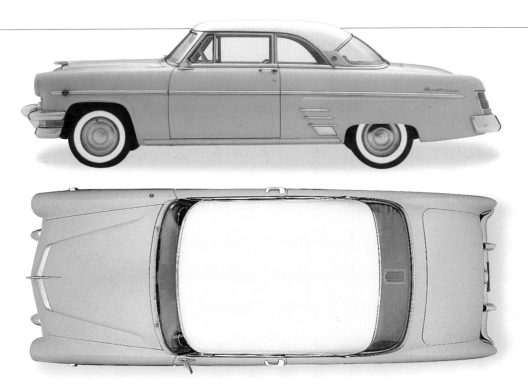

"The rear view evokes earlier Mercurys, as loved by roof-chopping hot-rodders and famously driven over the edge by James Dean in *Rebel Without a Cause*."

THE CAR'S UPTOWN IMAGE WAS REFLECTED IN COLOR NAMES SUCH AS PARK LANE GREEN, YOSEMITE YELLOW, AND COUNTRY CLUB TAN

INTERIORS CAME IN A WIDE VARIETY OF SOLID AND TWO-TONE CLOTH, VINYL, AND LEATHER TRIM COMBINATIONS

MERCURY Cougar

A watershed car that revived the company

THAT THE COUGAR was such a runaway success is empirical proof that the mid-Sixties "pony car" market really was turbocharged. After all, this was just an upscale, stretched Mustang, and nobody thought that the small Lincoln-Mercury dealer base could cope anyway. But cope they did, selling 150,000 Cougars in its debut year of '67 and 110,000 in '68, as a performance-hungry America rushed to get a slice of Mercury's "untamed luxury." Mercury fielded three Cougar models for '67: the base, the GT, and the XR-7. GTs had the bad-boy 390cid V8, and XR-7s the 289cid V8 with plush hide trim. The Cougar scooped *Motor Trend's* Car of the Year award for '67, and Lincoln-Mercury boasted that it was "the best-equipped luxury sports car money can buy." Admirably plugging the gap between the Mustang and the T-Bird, the Cougar had European styling, American power, and a luxury options list as long as a Sears catalog.

"With their Remington shaver grilles, concealed headlights, and faired-in bumpers, Cougars were good-looking cars."

ALL COUGARS FEATURED PONY-CAR ESSENTIALS LIKE WALNUT-GRAIN STEERING WHEEL, STANDARD BUCKET SEATS, CENTER CONSOLE, AND FLOOR SHIFT

SIDE LIGHTS DIFFERENTIATED BETWEEN '67 AND '68 MODELS

MODEL Mercury Cougar (1968)

PRODUCTION 113,726 (1968)

BODY STYLE Two-door, four-seater coupe.

CONSTRUCTION Steel unitary body.

ENGINES 289cid, 302cid, 390cid, 428cid V8s.

POWER OUTPUT 210–335 bhp.

TRANSMISSION Three-speed manual,
optional four-speed manual, or three-speed
Merc-O-Matic automatic.

SUSPENSION *Front*: coil springs;
Rear: leaf springs.

BRAKES Front and rear drums; optional
front discs.

MAXIMUM SPEED 105–130 mph
(169–209 km/h)

0–60 MPH (0–96 km/h) 7.3–10.2 sec

A.F.C. 16 mpg (5.7 km/l)

MALE MERCURY

"The relationship between a man and his car is a very special thing" opined the '67 Mercury sales brochure. No real surprise from a company that prided itself on making "the man's car."

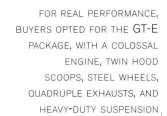

FOR REAL PERFORMANCE, BUYERS OPTED FOR THE GT-E PACKAGE, WITH A COLOSSAL ENGINE, TWIN HOOD SCOOPS, STEEL WHEELS, QUADRUPLE EXHAUSTS, AND HEAVY-DUTY SUSPENSION

THE DUAL HYDRAULIC BRAKE SYSTEM ALLOWED SEPARATE OPERATION OF FRONT AND REAR BRAKES

LIKE THE MUSTANG, THE COUGAR FEATURED A LITANY OF OPTIONS, THE WACKIEST OF WHICH WAS A "PAISLEY" VINYL ROOF

HEADLIGHT The Cougar's disappearing headlights were hidden behind vacuum-powered slatted covers that opened automatically when the lights were turned on. It made for a very mean-looking front aspect to the car.

ENGINE Standard fare for the '68 was the 210 bhp 302cid V8. Power could be gently upped by specifying a 230 brake version, or boosted with a variety of blocks up to the massive 335 bhp 428cid GT-E V8. Three-speed manual was the standard transmission.

SEQUENTIAL TAILLIGHTS À LA T-BIRD WERE NOW A STANDARD FORD TRADEMARK

Mercury Cougar **415**

MG TC Midget

The MG that started it all

EVEN WHEN IT WAS new, the MG TC was not new. Introduced in September 1945, it displayed a direct lineage back to its prewar forbears. If you were a little short on soul, you might even have called it old-fashioned. Yet it was a trailblazer, not in terms of performance, but in opening up new export markets. Popular myth has it that American GIs stationed in England latched on to these quaint sporting devices, and when they went home were eager to take a little piece of England with them. Whatever the reality, it was the first in a long line of MG export successes. There was simply nothing remotely like this TC coming out of Detroit. It had a cramped cockpit, harsh ride, and lacked creature comforts; but when the road got twisty the TC could show you its tail and leave soft-sprung sofa-cars lumbering in its wake. It was challenging to drive, and all the more rewarding when you got it right.

TOP UP OR DOWN, THE TC LOOKED SPORTIER THAN ITS PERFORMANCE FIGURES PROVED IT TO BE

ROWDY EXHAUST NOTE WAS MUSIC TO THE EARS

FBT 112

FBT 112

"The export trend begun so successfully by the TC really took off with the TD, which sold three times the number."

MODEL MG TC Midget (1947–49)

PRODUCTION 10,000

BODY STYLE Two-door, two-seater sports.

CONSTRUCTION Channel-section ladder-type chassis; ash-framed steel body.

ENGINE Four-cylinder overhead valve 1250cc, with twin SU carburetors.

POWER OUTPUT 54 bhp at 5200 rpm.

TRANSMISSION Four-speed gearbox with synchromesh on top three.

SUSPENSION Rigid front and rear axles on semielliptic springs, lever-type shock absorbers.

BRAKES Lockheed hydraulic drums.

MAXIMUM SPEED 73 mph (117 km/h)

0–60 MPH (0–96 km/h) 22.7 sec

A.F.C. 28 mpg (9.9 km/l)

INTERIOR Big Jaeger dials were in true British sports-car tradition; the driver got the tach, while the speedo was in front of the passenger. A warning light on the dash – to the left of the speedo – illuminated if you exceeded Britain's 30 mph (48 km/h) urban speed limit.

ENGINE The center-hinged hood meant that ease of accessibility and maintenance was another of the TC's attractions. The XPAG engine was first used on some TB Midgets in 1939, then became standard MG wear until replaced by a 1500cc version in 1955.

"The TC was a popular race car, especially in the US where it launched many careers and one world champion, Phil Hill."

THOUGH NOT A FACTORY OPTION, SHORROCK SUPERCHARGERS WERE OFTEN USED

WITH ITS SQUARE FRONT AND SEPARATE HEADLIGHTS, SWEEPING FRONT FENDERS, AND CUT-AWAY DOORS, IT IS A TRUE SPORTS CLASSIC

THE TC WAS REPLACED BY THE TD, WITH SMALLER DISC WHEELS AND CHROME HUBCAPS

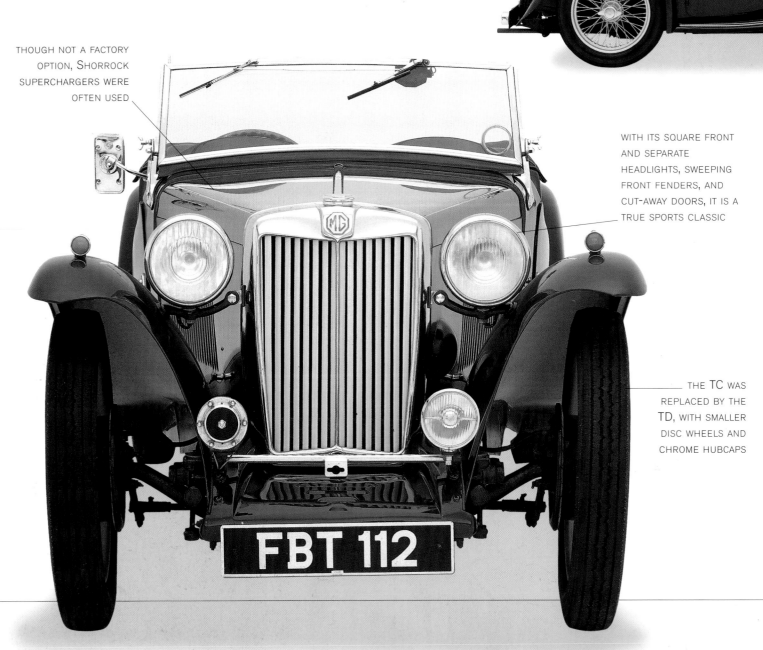

FBT 112

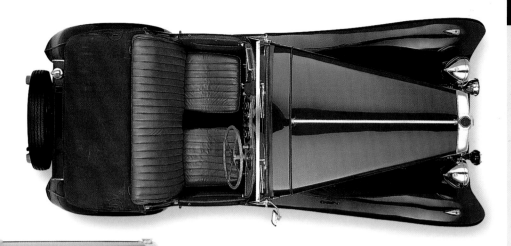

Creator of the MG line, Kimber started as general manager of Morris Garages of Oxford in 1922. Tuning a Morris Oxford won him a gold medal in the London to Land's End Trial of '23, and the firm's sports credentials were born. Obsessed with breaking records, Kimber continued to make MG synonymous with performance but died in a freak train crash in 1945. The same year saw the launch of one of the most charismatic MGs ever, the TC.

ALTHOUGH OVER 2,000 WERE SOLD IN THE US, ALL TCs WERE RIGHT-HAND DRIVE

ROOMIER THAN EARLIER MIDGETS, THE TC COCKPIT WAS STILL CRAMPED BY COMPARISON WITH LESS SPORTY CONTEMPORARIES

LOCKHEED DRUM BRAKES BALANCED THE LIMITED POWER OUTPUT

FBT 112

MG A

The car that earned MG a million dollars

LAUNCHED IN SEPTEMBER 1955, the MGA was the first of the modern sports MGs. The chassis, engine, and gearbox were all new, as was the smooth, Le Mans-inspired bodywork – the steel panels were hand-pressed and the bodies were finished by hand, which means that no two are exactly the same. Compared to its predecessor – the TF, which still sported old-fashioned running boards – the MGA was positively futuristic. Buyers thought so, too; and

being cheaper than its nearest rivals, the Triumph TR3 and Austin Healey 100, helped MG sell 13,000 cars in the first year of the MGA's production. The company's small factory at Abingdon, near Oxford, managed to export a staggering 81,000 MGAs to the United States. The car also earned an enviable reputation in competition, with an early prototype reaching 116 mph (187 km/h). The Twin Cam was the most powerful of the MGA engines.

THE TOUGH B-SERIES, PUSH-ROD ENGINE WENT WELL AND LASTED FOREVER. A HEATER UNIT IN FRONT OF THE BULKHEAD WAS AN OPTIONAL EXTRA.

THE 1600 MODEL FEATURED FRONT DISC BRAKES AND PUSHED OUT 80 BHP

BSK 215

MG B

The best-selling single model sports car ever

WIDELY ADMIRED FOR its simple nature, timeless good looks, and brisk performance, the MGB caused a sensation back in 1962. The now famous advertising slogan "Your mother wouldn't like it" was quite wrong. She would have wholeheartedly approved of the MGB's reliability, practicality, and good sense. In 1965 came the even more practical tin-top MGB GT. These were the halcyon days of the MGB – chrome bumpers, leather seats, and wire wheels.

In 1974, in pursuit of modernity and American safety regulations (the US was the MGB's main market), the factory burdened the B with ungainly rubber bumpers, a higher ride height, and garish striped nylon seats, making the car slow, ugly, and unpredictable at the limit. Yet despite this, the B went on to become the best-selling single model sports car ever, finding 512,000 grateful owners throughout the world.

THE MGB'S SHAPE WAS A MIRACLE OF COMPACT PACKAGING. THE ONE-PIECE STEEL MONOCOQUE BODYSHELL WAS STRONG AND ROOMY

EBW 45B

MORGAN Plus Four

An English sports car unspoilt by progress

IT IS REMARKABLE THAT they still make them, but there are many gents with cloth caps and corduroys who are grateful that they do. Derived from the first four-wheeled Morgans of 1936, this is the car that buoyed Morgan after the war while many of the old mainstays of the British car industry wilted around it. Tweedier than a Scottish moor on the first day of the grouse shooting season, it is as quintessentially English as a car can be. It was a hit in the US and other markets, and it has also remained the backbone of the idiosyncratic Malvern-based company, which refuses to move with the times. Outdated and outmoded it may be, but there is still a very long waiting list to purchase a Morgan. First introduced in 1951, the Plus Four, with a series of Standard Vanguard and Triumph TR engines, laid the foundations for the modern miracle of the very old-fashioned Morgan Motor Company.

THE EARLIER TWO-SEAT DROPHEAD COUPE RETAINED REAR-HINGED "SUICIDE" DOORS; SPORTS MODELS HAD FRONT-HINGED DOORS

UNLIKE MOST CONVERTIBLES, THE PLUS FOUR HAS A TOP WHICH CAN BE PARTIALLY FOLDED BACK

MORGANS HAVE LIMITED LUGGAGE CAPACITY, SO MANY OWNERS ATTACHED EXTERNAL RACKS

MODEL Morgan Plus Four (1951–69)

PRODUCTION 3,737

BODY STYLES Two- and four-seater sports convertible.

CONSTRUCTION Steel chassis, ash frame, steel and alloy outer panels.

ENGINES 2088cc OHV inline four (Vanguard); 1991 or 2138cc overhead-valve inline four (TR).

POWER OUTPUT 105 bhp at 4700 rpm (2138cc).

TRANSMISSION Four-speed manual.

SUSPENSION *Front*: sliding stub axles, coil springs, and shock absorbers; *Rear*: live axle, semielliptic leaf springs, and lever-arm shock absorbers.

BRAKES Front and rear drums; front discs standard from 1960.

MAXIMUM SPEED 100 mph (161 km/h)

0–60 MPH (0–96 km/h) 12 sec

A.F.C. 20–22 mpg (7–7.8 km/l)

"The second-generation Plus Four was the first of what are generally considered the 'modern-looking' Morgans."

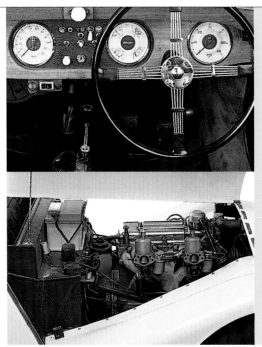

INTERIOR From 1958, Plus Fours had a slightly wider cockpit with a new dash, identifiable by the cubbyhole on the passenger's side. The speedometer, switches, warning lights, and minor gauges were grouped in a central panel on the dashboard.

ENGINE The later Triumph TR3A 2138cc engine, as here, provided increased torque. The 2138cc engine was available in the TR3A from summer 1957. The earlier Triumph 1991cc engine was still available for those wanting to compete in sub-two-liter racing classes.

MAJOR DISTINGUISHING FEATURES ON THE SECOND-GENERATION MORGAN INCLUDE THE COWLED RADIATOR GRILLE

HEADLIGHTS ARE BIG, BOLD AFFAIRS SET IN PODS ON THE FRONT FENDERS, BUT SIDELIGHTS ARE ABOUT AS VISIBLE AS A PAIR OF GLOWWORMS

326 EPW

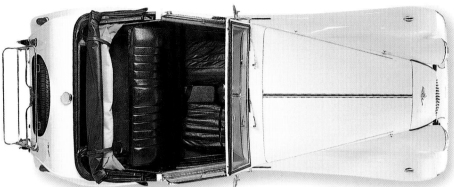

Influenced by a descendent of the famous locomotive engineer, George Stephenson, Henry Morgan built his first three-wheeler in 1910 and appointed the London department store Harrods to sell it. By 1920 the Malvern company was building 30 cars a week. A fanatical engineer, Morgan died in 1959 at the age of 77.

326 EPW

MORRIS Minor MM Convertible

"The best little car in the world"

THE MORRIS MINOR IS an automotive milestone. As Britain's first million seller it became a "people's car," staple transportation for everyone from nurses to building contractors. Designed by Alec Issigonis, the genius who later went on to pen the Austin Mini (*see pages* 50–53), the new Series MM Morris Minor of 1948 featured the then novel unitary chassis-body construction. The 918cc side-valve engine of the MM was rather more antique, a carryover from the prewar Morris 8. Its handling and ride comfort more than made up for the lack of power. With independent front suspension and crisp rack-and-pinion steering, it embarrassed its rivals and even tempted the young Stirling Moss into high-speed cornering antics that lost him his license for a month. Of all the 1.5 million Minors, the most prized are the now rare Series MM convertibles. Ragtops remained part of the Minor lineup until 1969.

"Sales literature described the Minor as 'The Best Little Car in the World.'"

THE ORIGINAL MM TOURER HAD SIDE CURTAINS, REPLACED BY GLASS REAR WINDOWS IN 1952

"Most Minor engines are willing starters, but all models to the end of production came with a starter handle in the toolkit."

MODEL Morris Minor (1948–71)

PRODUCTION 1,620,000

BODY STYLES Two- and four-door sedan, two-door convertible (Tourer), station wagon (Traveller), van, and pickup.

CONSTRUCTION Unitary body/chassis; steel.

ENGINES Straight-four, 918cc, 803cc, 948cc, and 1098cc.

POWER OUTPUT 28–48 bhp.

TRANSMISSION Four-speed manual.

SUSPENSION *Front*: torsion bar independent; *Rear*: live-axle leaf-spring.

BRAKES Front and rear drums.

MAXIMUM SPEED 62–75 mph (100–121 km/h)

0-60 MPH (0–96 km/h) 50+ sec for 918cc, 24 sec for 1098cc

A.F.C. 36–43 mpg (12.7–15.2 km/l)

INTERIOR This simple early dashboard was never really updated, but the speedometer was later moved to the center of the dash. The sprung-spoke steering wheel was a traditional touch, but rack-and-pinion steering produced a crisp, light feel.

ENGINE The original 918cc side-valve engine was replaced progressively in 1952 and 1953 by the Austin A-series 803cc overhead valve engine, then by the A-series 948cc, and finally the 1098cc. Power outputs rose from 28 bhp on the 918 to 48 bhp on the 1098.

INDICATORS

With no door pillars above waist height, semaphore indicators were mounted lower down on the tourers. Flashers eventually replaced semaphores in 1961. Another design change saw the split windshield substituted with a curved one in 1956.

UNDER-HOOD SPACE AND EASY ENGINE ACCESS MAKE THE MINOR A TINKERER'S FAVORITE

IN 1950, THE HEADLIGHTS ON ALL MINORS WERE MOVED TO THE TOP OF THE FENDERS. EARLIER MODELS SUCH AS THIS ARE NOW DUBBED "LOW LIGHTS"

LGO 786

Son of a Greek marine engineer, Issigonis ranks as one of the most influential car designers in the world. He designed the million-selling Minor and, by 1959, was able to put his revolutionary engineering into practice with the now-legendary transverse-engined Mini. Every single modern front-wheel drive car owes its existence to the brilliant Sir Alec Issigonis.

AT 61 IN (155 CM) THE PRODUCTION CAR WAS 4 IN (10 CM) WIDER THAN THE PROTOTYPE

LGO 786

NSU Sport Prinz

A pocket dynamo incorporating Teutonic efficiency

WE SHOULDN'T DISMISS the tiny Sport Prinz as just another nameless, pseudo GT. Apart from those handsome Bertone lines, NSU's charming coupe was a delight to drive, well-assembled, and endearingly frugal. A product of German postwar austerity, the Sport Prinz was that rare thing – a miniature car that delivered miracles of economy, along with a large helping of style. Compared to contemporary "bubble cars," this was a mini-Mercedes. And, like a Mercedes, it was technically audacious, with an overhead camshaft, hemispherical combustion chambers, common gearbox, and final drive, plus all-around independent suspension. The end result was a disarmingly fun driving experience, with a rifle-bolt gear change, sweet spinning engine, near-neutral handling, and pencil-sharp steering. Deservedly popular, the Sport Prinz found over 20,000 grateful owners between 1959 and 1967.

"Bertone styling was clean, austere, and almost Bauhaus. Sales brochures made a virtue of 'no silly fins and frills.'"

THE REAR ENGINE CONFIGURATION MEANT THAT LUGGAGE LIVED UNDER THE HOOD

"The rear engine gave near perfect weight distribution and extremely poised handling balance."

NSU Sport PRINZ

MODEL NSU Sport Prinz (1967)

PRODUCTION 20,831 (1959–67)

BODY STYLE Two-seater coupe.

CONSTRUCTION All steel monocoque.

ENGINE 583cc, two-cylinder, air-cooled.

POWER OUTPUT 36 bhp at 5500 rpm.

TRANSMISSION Four speed, all-syncromesh manual.

SUSPENSION Independent all around.

BRAKES Front discs, rear drums.

MAXIMUM SPEED 81 mph (130 km/h)

0–60 MPH (0–96 km/h) 27.7 sec

A.F.C. 42 mpg (14.9 km/l)

"The Prinz's build quality was high, with chrome plating underlaid by copper plate for longevity."

THE LOW HOOD LINE MEANT THAT THE WHOLE CAR MEASURED ONLY 49 IN (124 CM) FROM GROUND TO ROOF, YET THE CABIN WAS DECEPTIVELY ROOMY

INTERIOR The interior was spartan but well finished, with painted tin dash, heavy chrome door fixtures and horn ring, stylish clock, and map pockets on the doors. Really just a two-seater, most owners piled luggage on the very occasional rear seat. Despite a low stance, interior headroom was surprisingly good.

LIGHTS Front light treatment shows the success of Bertone's economical styling, with good relationships between lights, hood, and bumpers, plus flourishes like decorative air vents and broad headlight bezels. Bumper-mounted fog and driving lights were a period accessory, but spoil the otherwise uncluttered lines.

THE TWO-CYLINDER, FOUR-STROKE, 583CC ENGINE DEVELOPED ONLY 36 BHP BUT COULD PROPEL THE PRINZ TO A DIZZY 81 MPH (130 KM/H)

YRD 28F

OLDSMOBILE Starfire

Suburban cruiser with impressive powerplant

IN 1964, LYNDON B. JOHNSON signed a tax-cut bill, *Peyton Place* was a TV hit, and Coca-Cola launched a new single-calorie soda called Tab. While America was on a roll, the auto industry was busy telling customers that bucket seats and center consoles would enrich their lives. Oldsmobile trumpeted that their sporty Starfire Coupe offered "high adventure that starts right here!". Lame copy aside, the original 1961 Starfire was quick with Olds' most powerful lump, a 394cid V8 that could knock on the door of 120 mph (193 km/h). A terrifying thirst for gas didn't deter buyers for the first few years of its life, especially since these were big, softly sprung mile-eaters, groaning with convenience options. Elegant and unadorned, the Starfire was one of a new breed of suburban starlets designed to make the WASP middle classes look as confident as they felt. And it worked.

Oldsmobile Starfire

434

"The Starfire's simple, extruded look was typical of the period and very few traces of jukebox styling remained by the mid-Sixties."

THE $43 TILT-AWAY STEERING WHEEL COULD BE MOVED INTO SEVEN POSITIONS

THE STARFIRE SHARED THE DYNAMIC 88'S 123 IN (312 CM) WHEELBASE

MODEL Oldsmobile Starfire (1964)

PRODUCTION 25,890 (1964)

BODY STYLES Two-door, five-seater coupe and convertible.

CONSTRUCTION Steel body and chassis.

ENGINE 394cid V8.

POWER OUTPUT 345 bhp.

TRANSMISSION Three-speed Hydra-Matic automatic.

SUSPENSION Front and rear coil springs.

BRAKES Front and rear drums.

MAXIMUM SPEED 120 mph (193 km/h)

0–60 MPH (0–96 km/h) 9 sec

A.F.C. 12 mpg (4.2 km/l)

Oldsmobile Starfire **435**

CONVERTIBLE OPTION

The Starfire was easy on the hands, with power everything. Detroit knew that the "little woman" was becoming increasingly important in buying decisions and started to pitch their products at the shopping mall.

"The original '61 Starfire was positively exhilarating, but three years down the line the extra weight and creature comforts meant it wasn't that quick."

GUIDE-MATIC
HEADLIGHTS
AUTOMATICALLY DIMMED
WHEN ONCOMING
CARS APPROACHED

"The Starfire's lines were clean and assertive, appealing to the affluent society's newfound sophistication."

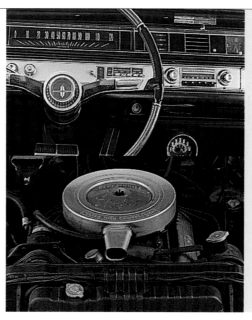

INTERIOR Oldsmobile gave the Starfire plenty of standard gear, including Hydra-Matic automatic transmission, bucket seats, safety padded dash, center console, tachometer, leather trim, as well as power steering, brakes, and windows.

ENGINE Standard on the Starfire Coupe and Convertible was the mighty cast-iron block 394cid V8 with Rochester four-barrel carb, which churned out a hefty 345 bhp. Compared to original '61 models, though, performance was ordinary.

POSITIVE-TRACTION REAR AXLE WAS A FACTORY-EQUIPPED OPTION

THE STARFIRE WAS NO FEATHERWEIGHT; ALL THOSE LUXURY ADD-ONS PUSHED THE CURB WEIGHT TO NEARLY TWO TONS

BY '64 FINS WERE GETTING MORE TRUNCATED BY THE DAY. THEY HAD ALMOST COMPLETELY DISAPPEARED BY '65

OLDSMOBILE 4-4-2

A performance option turned into a separate series

1971 WAS THE LAST of the 4-4-2's glory years. A performance package par excellence, it was GM's longest-lived muscle car, tracing its roots all the way back to the heady days of '64 when a 4-4-2 combo was made available for the Oldsmobile Cutlass F-85. Possibly some of the most refined slingshots ever to come from any GM division, 4-4-2s had looks, charisma, and brawn to spare. The 4-4-2 nomenclature stood for a four-barrel carb, four-speed manual transmission, and two exhausts. Olds cleverly raided the storeroom, using hotshot parts previously only available to police departments. At $3,551, the super-swift Hardtop Coupe came with a 455cid V8, Rallye suspension, Strato bucket seats, and a top speed of 125 mph (201 km/h). The 4-4-2 package might have run and run had it not hit the '71 fuel crisis head on. Which proved a shame, because it was to be a long time before power like this would be seen again.

OLDSMOBILE NEVER TIRED OF PROCLAIMING THAT ITS 455CID MILL WAS THE LARGEST V8 EVER PLACED IN A PRODUCTION CAR

"Despite legislation that curbed the 4-4-2's power output and led to the series being deleted after '71, the 4-4-2 had made its mark and put Oldsmobile on the muscle-car map."

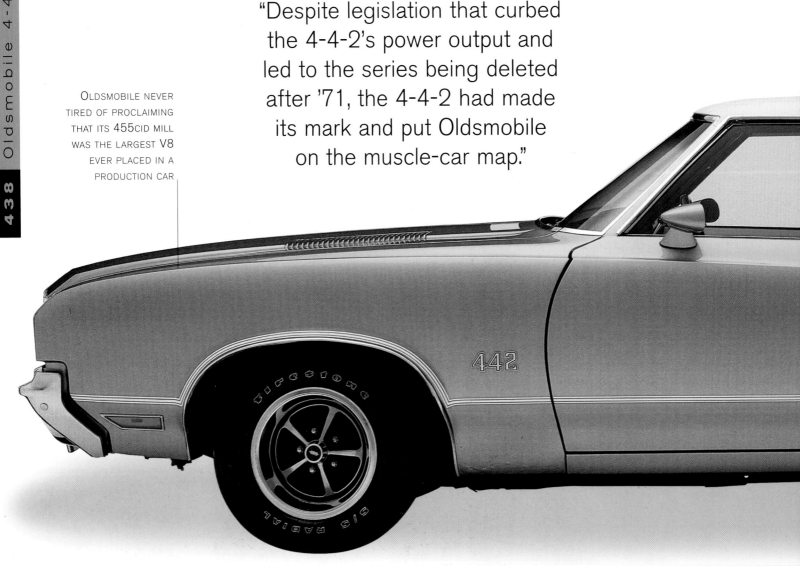

MODEL Oldsmobile 4-4-2 (1971)

PRODUCTION 7,589 (1971)

BODY STYLES Two-door coupe and convertible.

CONSTRUCTION Steel body and chassis.

ENGINE 455cid V8.

POWER OUTPUT 340–350 bhp.

TRANSMISSION Three-speed manual, optional four-speed manual, or three-speed Turbo Hydra-Matic automatic.

SUSPENSION *Front*: coil springs; *Rear*: leaf springs.

BRAKES Front discs, rear drums.

MAXIMUM SPEED 125 mph (201 km/h)

0–60 MPH (0–96 km/h) 6.4 sec

A.F.C. 10–14 mpg (3.5–5 km/l)

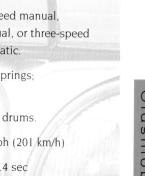

INTERIOR Despite the cheap-looking, wood-grain vinyl dash, the 4-4-2's cabin had a real race car feel. Bucket seats, custom steering wheel, and Hurst Competition gear shift came as standard. The sports console and Rallye pack with clock and tacho were $84 extras.

ENGINE "Factory blueprinted to save you money," screamed the ads. The monster 455cid V8 was stock for 4-4-2s in '71, but it was its swansong year and power output would soon dwindle. By the late Seventies, the 4-4-2 performance pack had been seriously emasculated.

"Advertising literature espoused the 4-4-2's torquey credentials: 'A hot new number. Police needed it, Olds built it, pursuit proved it.'"

IN ADDITION TO THIS VIKING BLUE, OLDS ADDED BITTERSWEET, LIME GREEN, AND SATURN GOLD TO THEIR '71 COLOR RANGE

APART FROM THE BADGE, THE TWIN DRAINPIPE EXHAUSTS WERE THE ONLY CLUE THAT YOU WERE TRAILING A WILD MAN

442

Y·8828
SEE VERMONT 71

PACKARD Hawk

The European-styled US coupe that bombed

DISTINCTIVE, BIZARRE, and very un-American, the '58 Hawk was a pastiche of European styling cues. It boasted tan pleated-leather upholstery, white-on-black instruments, Jaguaresque fender vents, a gulping hood air-scoop, and a broad fiberglass shovel-nostril that could have been lifted off a Maserati. And it was supercharged. But Packard's attempt to distance themselves from traditional Detroit iron failed. At $4,000, the Hawk was overpriced, under-refined, and overdecorated. Packard had merged with Studebaker back in 1954, and although it was initially a successful alliance, problems with suppliers and another buyout in 1956 sealed the company's fate. Only 588 Hawks were built, with the last Packard rolling off the line on July 13, 1958. Today the Hawk stands as a quaint curiosity, a last-ditch attempt to preserve the Packard pedigree. It remains one of the most fiercely desired of the final Packards.

"Even for the '50s, most buyers found the Hawk's frontal aspect a little too much, preferring instead the more traditional Detroit 'million dollar chromium grin.'"

UNIQUELY, THE HAWK HAD EXTERIOR VINYL ARMRESTS RUNNING ALONG THE SIDE WINDOWS AND A REFRESHING LACK OF CHROME GAUDINESS ON THE FLANKS

FRONT FENDER VENTS WERE SHAMELESSLY CULLED FROM BRITISH MK IX AND XK JAGUARS

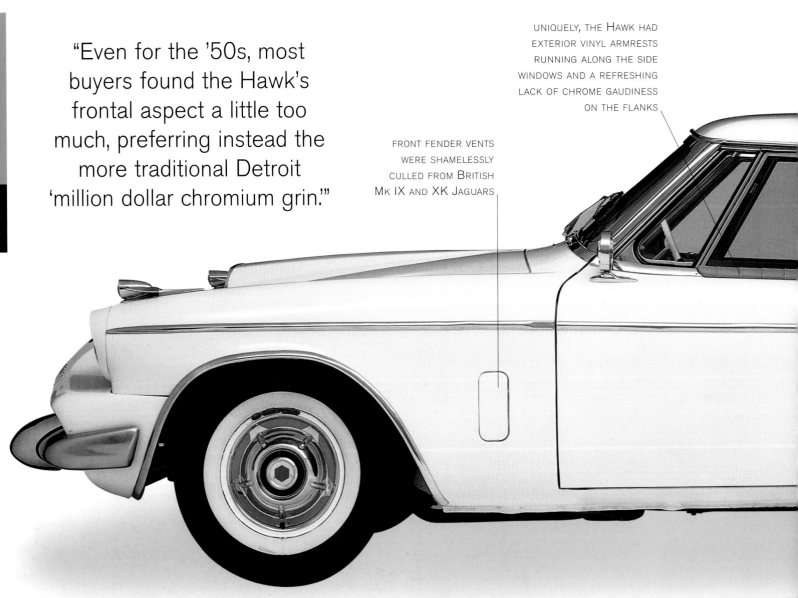

MODEL Packard Hawk (1958)

PRODUCTION 588

BODY STYLE Two-door, four-seater coupe.

CONSTRUCTION Steel body and chassis.

ENGINE 289cid V8.

POWER OUTPUT 275 bhp.

TRANSMISSION Three-speed Flight-O-Matic automatic, optional overdrive.

SUSPENSION *Front:* independent coil springs; *Rear:* leaf springs.

BRAKES Front and rear drums.

MAXIMUM SPEED 125 mph (201 km/h)

0–60 MPH (0–96 km/h) 8 sec

A.F.C. 15 mpg (5.3 km/l)

INTERIOR To stress the Hawk's supposed sporty bloodline, the interior was clad in soft leather with sports instrumentation. In addition you could specify a pile of convenience options that included power steering.

ENGINE Flight-O-Matic automatic transmission and a hefty, supercharged 289cid V8 came as standard, hurtling out 275 horses; 0–60 mph (96 km/h) took just under eight seconds. The Hawk's blower was a McCulloch supercharger.

"Sales literature for the Hawk heralded the arrival of 'a distinctive, new, full-powered sports-styled car.'"

POWER STEERING WAS A $70 FACTORY OPTION

THE MAILBOX AIR INTAKE AND SOFTLY SHAPED FRONT BUMPER MADE THE HAWK LOOK NOTHING LIKE CONTEMPORARY AMERICANA

THE HAWK WAS ONE OF THE FEW PACKARDS THAT DARED TO SPORT SINGLE HEADLIGHTS

"The Hawk's roof line and halo roof band are aeronautical, and the belt line is tense."

NOBODY WAS TOO SURE ABOUT THE SPARE WHEEL IMPRESSION ON THE TRUNK

DESPITE ITS EUROPEAN AIRS, NO AMERICAN CAR COULD ESCAPE THE VOGUE FOR FINS, AND THE HAWK HAS TWO BEAUTIES

PANHARD PL17 Tigre

Quirky Gallic design married to a frugal engine

PANHARD WAS ONE OF the world's oldest names in car manufacturing, dating back to 1872. But by 1955 it had lost its upmarket image and had to be rescued by Citroën, who eventually bought the company out completely in 1965. The Dyna, produced after the war in response to a need for a small, practical, and economical machine, had an aluminum alloy frame and bulkhead, and horizontally opposed, air-cooled, twin-cylinder engine. In 1954, the Dyna was transformed into a front-wheel drive model, with a bulbous but streamlined new body. The 848cc flat-twin engine was a gem, and in post-1961 Tigre guise pushed out 60 bhp; this gave 90 mph (145 km/h), enough to win a Monte Carlo Rally. Eclipsed by the innovative Citroën DS (*see pages* 192–95), the Panhard PL17 was meant to be a vision of the future. Sold as "the car that makes sense," the PL17 was light, quick, miserly on fuel, and years ahead of its time.

"With its aerodynamically shaped body, Panhard claimed the lowest drag coefficient of any production car in 1956."

THE PL17 WAS A STANDOUT FOR SAFETY AND SPORTED A HUGE, FULL-WIDTH POP-OUT WINDSHIELD – RARE FOR 1961

"The Tigre had drum brakes on all four wheels, but with a top speed of only 90 mph (145 km/h), there was no real need for much else."

MODEL Panhard PL17 Tigre (1961–64)

PRODUCTION 130,000 (all models)

BODY STYLE Four-door, four-seater sports sedan.

CONSTRUCTION Separate chassis with steel and aluminum body.

ENGINE 848cc twin horizontally-opposed air-cooled.

POWER OUTPUT 60 bhp at 5800 rpm.

TRANSMISSION Front-wheel drive four-speed manual.

SUSPENSION *Front*: independent with twin transverse leaf; *Rear*: torsion bar.

BRAKES Front and rear drums.

MAXIMUM SPEED 90 mph (145 km/h)

0–60 MPH (0–96 km/h) 23.1 sec

A.F.C. 38 mpg (13.5 km/l)

FRONT-WHEEL DRIVE
ENSURED STABILITY AND
SAFETY, WITH CLASS-LEADING
SPACE FOR AN 848CC CAR

INSIDE, THE LACK OF A
TRANSMISSION TUNNEL
MEANT A FLAT FLOOR AND
INCREASED LEGROOM

THE STEERING WAS OF
THE TECHNICALLY
ADVANCED RACK-AND-
PINION VARIETY

DESPITE ITS QUIRKY GALLIC LOOKS, THE PL17 WAS A TRIUMPH OF OUTSTANDING EFFICIENCY

INTERIOR The Tigre's unusual interior included bizarre oval-shaped pedals, column shift, and a generally unsuccessful pastiche of American styling themes. The steering only required two turns lock-to-lock.

ENGINE The engine design dated back to 1940. Cylinders were cast integral with their heads in light alloy, cooling fins, and cast-iron liners. Heads had hemispherical combustion chambers and valve-gearing incorporating torsion bars.

SIMPLE DESIGN MEANT FEWER MOVING PARTS, MORE POWER, AND MORE MILES TO THE GALLON

EMPHASIS WAS ON SAVING WEIGHT, WITH INDEPENDENT SUSPENSION AND AN ALUMINUM FRAME AND BULKHEAD

VCH 615

B.H.V. - ACCESSOIRES AUTO - 42.74.96.72 - B.H.V.

PEUGEOT 203

A French best-seller with advanced mechanics

COMPARED TO THE scores of upright postwar sedans that looked like church pews, Peugeot's 203 was a breath of fresh air. As well as being one of the French carmaker's most successful products, the 203's monocoque body and revolutionary engine set it apart. In its day, the 1290cc OHV powerplant was state-of-the-art, with an aluminum cylinder head and hemispherical combustion chambers, said to be the inspiration for the famous Chrysler "Hemi" unit. In the Fifties there were many companies that could give the 203 more urge, and many of the cars were souped up and campaigned in rallies like the Monte Carlo. With a line that included two- and four-door cabriolets, a family station wagon, and a two-door coupe, the French really took to the 203, loving its tough mechanics, willing progress, and supple ride. By its demise in 1960, the 203 had broken records for Peugeot, with nearly 700,000 sold.

QUALITY TOUCHES ABOUND, SUCH AS THE EXTERIOR BRIGHTWORK IN STAINLESS STEEL

THE FUEL FILLER-CAP WAS CONCEALED UNDER A FLUSH-FITTING FLAP – UNHEARD OF IN 1948

"The 203's stylish, sweeping curves were influenced by the 1946 Chevrolet."

MODEL Peugeot 203 (1948–60)

PRODUCTION 685,828

BODY STYLES Two-door coupe, two- or four-door convertible, family station wagon.

CONSTRUCTION All-steel monocoque rigid one-piece body shell.

ENGINE Four-cylinder OHV 1290cc.

POWER OUTPUT 42–49 bhp at 3500 rpm.

TRANSMISSION Four-speed column shift with surmultiplié overdrive.

SUSPENSION *Front:* transverse leaf independent; *Rear:* coil spring with Panhard rod.

BRAKES Front and rear drums.

MAXIMUM SPEED 73 mph (117 km/h)

0–60 MPH (0–96 km/h) 20 sec

A.F.C. 20–35 mpg (7–12.4 km/l)

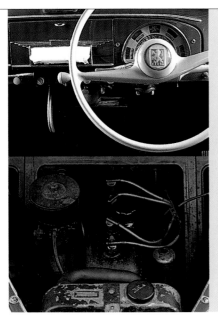

INTERIOR With postwar steel in short supply, aluminum was put to good use in the underdash handbrake and column gear shift. The handsome fastback body gave plenty of room for passengers inside the cabin.

ENGINE The 49 bhp OHV push-rod engine was the 203's most advanced feature. With wet liners, low compression ratio, and alloy head, it was smooth, free-revving, and long-lasting. The basic design was used in Peugeot's 505 in the 1980s.

QUALITY WIPERS

"Clap hand" windshield wipers may look like a period piece, but the motor was so robust that it was still in use 43 years later on the tailgate wiper of the 504 model. Other elements of the 203 were less impressive – the rubber mats, metal dashboard, and cloth seat facings all indicated that the interior was built to a budget.

WIDELY ACCLAIMED AT THE 1948 PARIS MOTOR SHOW, THE 203'S SLIPPERY SHAPE WAS WINDTUNNEL TESTED IN MODEL FORM AND CLAIMED TO HAVE A RATHER OPTIMISTIC DRAG COEFFICIENT OF JUST 0.36

THE 203 WAS MODIFIED IN 1953 WITH A CURVED WINDSHIELD, REVISED DASHBOARD, AND FRONT QUARTER LIGHTS. THIS MODEL WAS REGISTERED IN 1955

THE FOUR-SPEED GEARBOX WAS REALLY A THREE WITH OVERDRIVE

OAA 950

"The hood swung up on counterbalanced springs and the grille came away by undoing a butterfly nut."

A VAST TRUNK WITH A
LOW-LOADING SILL
MADE THE 203 IDEAL
FAMILY TRANSPORTATION

INTEGRAL MOUNTING
POINTS FOR A ROOF
RACK WERE A NICE
STYLING TOUCH

OAA
950

PEUGEOT 504

Stylish convertible courtesy of Italian design input

THIRTY YEARS AGO Peugeot built plodding, dreary cars. Trusty hacks like the 504 were dependable, practical, and tough, but utterly devoid of charisma. In 1969, stung by criticisms of worthiness, the French firm called in stylist Pininfarina, who worked his magic on the 504 sedan, creating a fetching coupe and convertible. In 1974, a rather good 2.6-liter V6 engine was added. Suddenly Peugeot had a very desirable commodity on its hands. Brisk, pretty, and very upmarket, the 504 V6 Cabriolet may not have been as good as the contemporary Mercedes 350SL, but it was half the price, had four seats, and looked like a million dollars. Bodies were made at Pininfarina's Turin factory and then shipped overland to Peugeot, which added the drivetrain. Hardly a runaway success, fewer than 1,000 V6 Cabriolets found buyers, but the project was successful enough to teach Peugeot important lessons about image, branding, and style.

"Convertibles lacked the torsional rigidity of the tin-top Coupes and displayed pronounced scuttle-shake over rough roads."

V6 504 CABRIOLETS WERE ONLY EVER AVAILABLE IN LEFT-HAND DRIVE FORM

BODIES WERE MADE FROM SEVENTIES' ITALIAN STEEL, WHICH HAD A HIGH RECYCLED CONTENT AND RUSTED ALARMINGLY QUICKLY

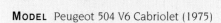

MODEL Peugeot 504 V6 Cabriolet (1975)

PRODUCTION 977 (total)

BODY STYLE Two-door, four-seater convertible.

CONSTRUCTION Steel monocoque.

ENGINE 2664cc V6.

POWER OUTPUT 136 bhp at 5750 rpm.

TRANSMISSION Four-speed manual.

SUSPENSION Independent front and rear.

BRAKES Four-wheel discs.

MAXIMUM SPEED 115 mph (185 km/h)

0–60 MPH (0–96 km/h) 11 sec

A.F.C. 24 mpg (8.5 km/l)

INTERIOR Later cars had much plusher cabins with leather trim, tachometer, and power windows, although the expensive Nardi wood-rim steering wheel is an after-market accessory. The four-seater 504 Cabriolet was very practical and was pitched against the Triumph Stag, Reliant Scimitar GTC, and BMW 2002 Cabriolet.

ENGINE The V6 engine offered a decent turn of speed and had an alloy block and twin carburetors, although later units were equipped with fuel injection. Known as the PRV unit (Peugeot/Renault/Volvo), this engine also saw service in the Peugeot 604, 505, and 605, the Renault 30, Volvo 264, Citroën XM, Renault-Alpine, and even the ill-fated DeLorean DMC 12.

WITH SUCH LOW PRODUCTION NUMBERS AND A PROPENSITY TO RUST, V6 CABRIOLETS ARE BECOMING INCREASINGLY RARE

THE ALL-ALLOY V6 ENGINE DEVELOPED AN IMPRESSIVE 136 BHP AND WAS A JOINT COLLABORATION BETWEEN PEUGEOT, RENAULT, AND VOLVO

"Even with the top up, the ragtop 504 looked disarmingly handsome, betraying no trace of its ordinary sedan origins."

SUPPLY OF NEW REPLACEMENT BODY PANELS IS RAPIDLY DRYING UP, MAKING RESTORATION EXPENSIVE AND DIFFICULT

FABRIC TOP NOT ONLY LOOKED GOOD, BUT WAS SURPRISINGLY EASY TO ERECT, TAKING ONLY A FEW SECONDS

5493 TT 75

PLYMOUTH Fury

One of the meanest cars on the block

AMAZINGLY, THE '59 FURY was aimed squarely at middle-class, middle-income America. Amazingly, because it was as loud as Little Richard and as sexy as Jayne Mansfield. One of the most stylistically adventurous cars on the road, the futuristic Fury was pure "Forward Look" and the '59 model was the most strident of the group. That razor-edged profile made Plymouth a name to kill for, especially if it was the top-of-the-line Sport Fury, which came with a personalized aluminum plaque that read "Made Expressly For...". Sales of Plymouth's suburban trinket boomed in '59, with 89,114 Furys helping Plymouth rank third in the industry and celebrate the company's 11-millionth vehicle. With serious power and looks to stop a speeding train, the Fury wowed God-fearing America. But that rakish impudence couldn't last, and by '61 the Fury's fins were tragically trimmed. In the annals of kitsch, this one goes down as a real honey.

"Along with a number of stylish models from the Chrysler line, the '59 Fury is rightly regarded as one of Virgil Exner's all-time masterpieces."

OPTIONAL EXTRAS RANGED FROM TWO-TONE PAINT AND THE GOLDEN COMMANDO V8 TO POWER BRAKES

SPORT FURYS DEVELOPED 260 BRAKE WITH SOLID LIFTERS AND A CARTER AFB FOUR-BARREL CARB

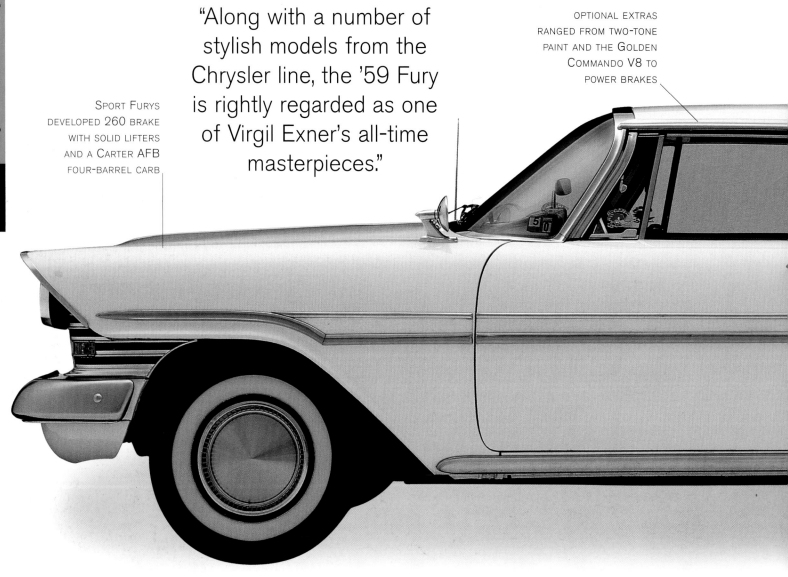

Fury

MODEL Plymouth Fury (1959)

PRODUCTION 105,887 (1959, all body styles, including Sport Furys)

BODY STYLE Two-door hardtop.

CONSTRUCTION Steel body and chassis.

ENGINES 318cid V8 (360cid V8 optional for Sport Fury).

POWER OUTPUT 230 bhp (Sport Fury 260 bhp, or 305 bhp with 360cid V8).

TRANSMISSION Three-speed manual with optional overdrive, optional three-speed TorqueFlite auto, and PowerFlite auto.

SUSPENSION *Front*: torsion bars; *Rear*: leaf springs.

BRAKES Front and rear drums, optional power assistance.

MAXIMUM SPEED 105–110 mph (169–177 km/h)

0–60 MPH (0–96 km/h) 11 sec

A.F.C. 17 mpg (6 km/l)

INTERIOR Inside was comic-book spaceship, with push buttons galore. Swiveling front and rear seats on Sport Furys were aimed at portlier buyers. Contoured floormats could be specified as an option, as could the padded steering wheel at $12.

ENGINE The 318cid V8 pushed out just 230 bhp, but Chrysler was starting to beat the performance drum as hard as it could. With a three-figure top speed and brisk acceleration, the sheer bulk of the car on those skinny tires must have made things scary at high speed.

GOOD TASTE IS NEVER EXTREME

TASTEFUL FLAIR

Is that slogan tongue-in-cheek? Plymouth sold the Fury's bold lines as the perfect example of taste and discrimination. To be fair, while almost every car had fins back in '59, the Fury's showed real class.

CROSS-SLATTED GRILLE WAS ALL-NEW FOR '59 AND MADE THE FRONT END LOOK LIKE IT COULD BITE

HAWAII 1961
89 · 851
ALOHA STATE

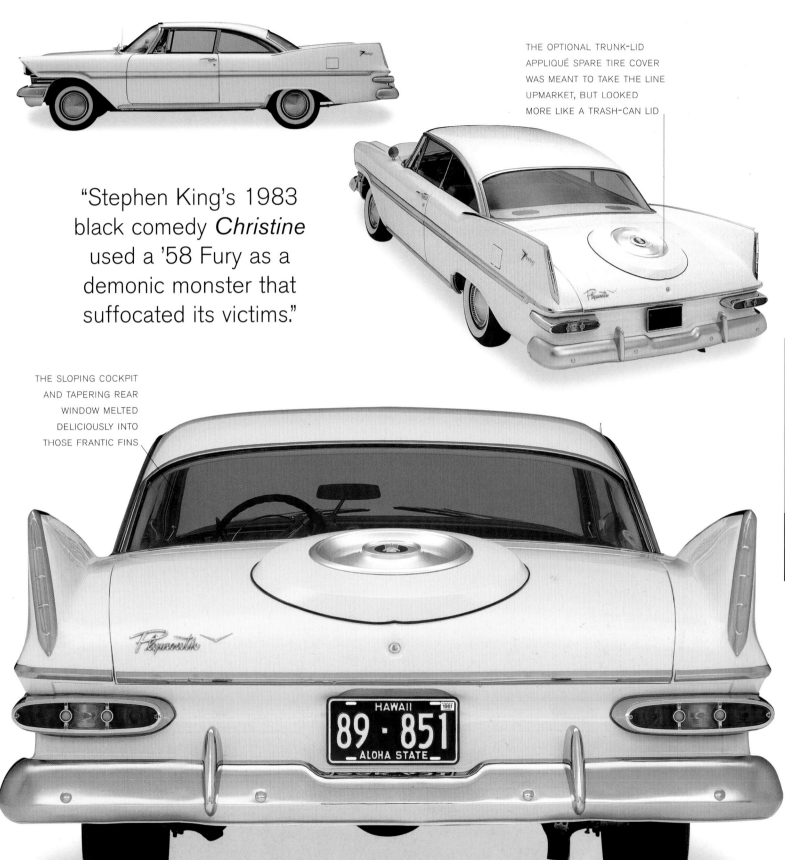

THE OPTIONAL TRUNK-LID
APPLIQUÉ SPARE TIRE COVER
WAS MEANT TO TAKE THE LINE
UPMARKET, BUT LOOKED
MORE LIKE A TRASH-CAN LID

"Stephen King's 1983 black comedy *Christine* used a '58 Fury as a demonic monster that suffocated its victims."

THE SLOPING COCKPIT
AND TAPERING REAR
WINDOW MELTED
DELICIOUSLY INTO
THOSE FRANTIC FINS

HAWAII 1961
89 · 851
ALOHA STATE

PLYMOUTH Barracuda (1964)

A valiant attempt to beat the original pony car

THE BIG THREE WEREN'T slow to cash in on the Sixties' youth boom. Ford couldn't keep its Mustang project secret, and the Chrysler Corporation desperately wanted a piece of the action. Chrysler took its existing compact, the Plymouth Valiant, prettied up the front, added a wraparound rear window, and called it the Barracuda. It hit the showroom floors in April 1964, two weeks before the Mustang. A disarming amalgam of performance, poise, and refinement, Plymouth had achieved a miracle on the scale of loaves and fishes – they made the Barracuda fast, yet it handled crisply and gave a smooth ride. The 273cid V8 made the car quicker than a Mustang, but that bizarre rear window aged badly and Mustangs outsold Barracudas 10-to-one. Plymouth believed the long-hood-short-trunk "pony" formula wouldn't captivate consumers like a swooping, sporty fastback. Half a million Mustang buyers told them they'd backed the wrong horse.

"*Road and Track*
magazine said, 'for sports
car performance and
practicality, the
Barracuda is perfect.'"

POWER BRAKES WERE
STANDARD ON THE
BARRACUDA, WITH BIG
DRUMS FRONT AND REAR

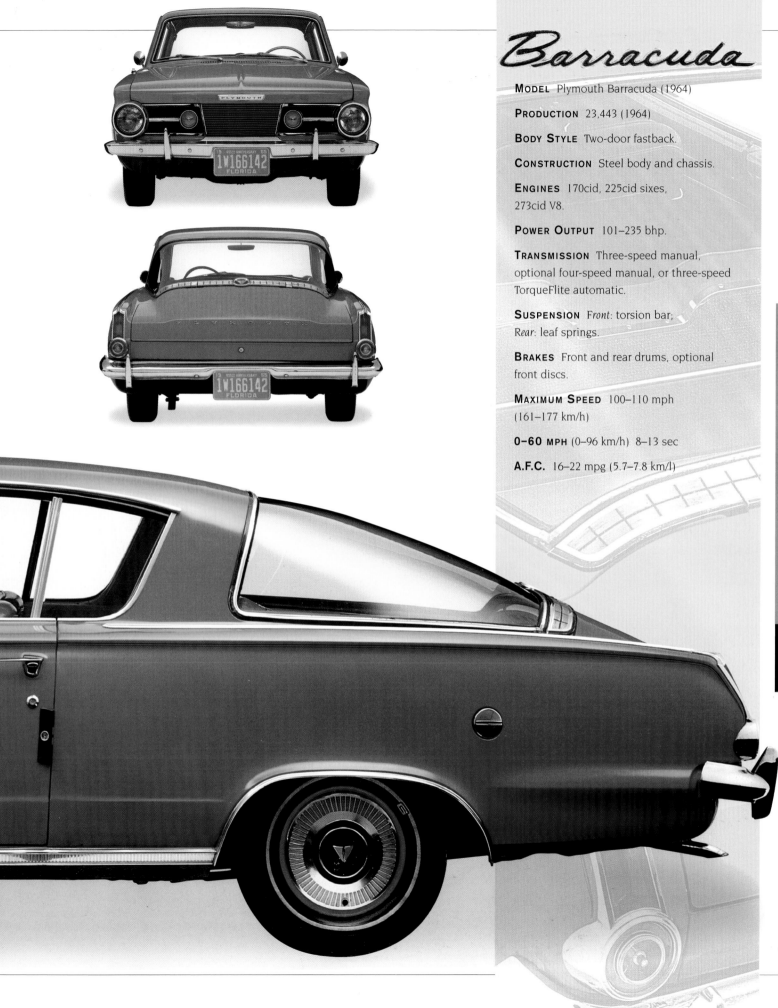

Barracuda

MODEL Plymouth Barracuda (1964)

PRODUCTION 23,443 (1964)

BODY STYLE Two-door fastback.

CONSTRUCTION Steel body and chassis.

ENGINES 170cid, 225cid sixes, 273cid V8.

POWER OUTPUT 101–235 bhp.

TRANSMISSION Three-speed manual, optional four-speed manual, or three-speed TorqueFlite automatic.

SUSPENSION *Front*: torsion bar; *Rear*: leaf springs.

BRAKES Front and rear drums, optional front discs.

MAXIMUM SPEED 100–110 mph (161–177 km/h)

0–60 MPH (0–96 km/h) 8–13 sec

A.F.C. 16–22 mpg (5.7–7.8 km/l)

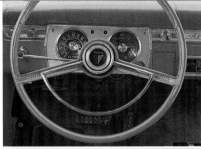

INTERIOR Instruments were matte silver with circular chrome bezels. The padded dash was a $16.35 extra, as was a wood-grain steering wheel that the brochure insisted "gave you the feel of a racing car." TorqueFlite automatic transmission could be ordered as an extra.

ENGINE The 'Cuda's base engine was a 170cid slant six. Other mills were the 225cid straight-six, producing 145 bhp, and a two-barrel 273cid V8. Optional was Chrysler's new Hurst-linkage manual transmission along with new Sure-Grip differential.

HOT INSIDE

The greenhouse interior got hot on sunny days but was well detailed and enormously practical. Standard fare was bucket seats and bucket-shaped rear bench seat.

THE PRISMATIC DAY-AND-NIGHT MIRROR COULD BE ADJUSTED TO DEFLECT ANNOYING HEADLIGHT GLARE AT NIGHT

COMPARED WITH THE MUSTANG, THE BARRACUDA'S FRONT WAS BUSY, CLUTTERED, AND LACKED SYMMETRY, BUT IT WAS A BRAVE AND BOLD DESIGN

PLYMOUTH

19 400TH ANNIVERSARY 65
1W166142
FLORIDA

Did you know

that the 1965 Plymouth Barracuda has an optional Formula 'S' sports package that includes a Commando 273-cu.-in. V-8 engine*; heavy-duty shocks, springs, and sway bar; a tachometer; wide-rim (14-in.) wheels, special Blue Streak tires, and simulated bolt-on wheel covers?

You do now.

THE ROARING 65s
FURY
BELVEDERE
VALIANT
BARRACUDA

Formula S Option

Despite the fact that the Formula S offered a V8 block plus race trimmings, this was still rather tame by Plymouth standards. The '61 Fury, for example, had a 318cid unit that pushed out 230 bhp.

THE FASTBACK GLASS WRAPPED DOWN TO THE REAR FENDER LINE AND WAS WAS THE LARGEST USE OF GLASS IN ANY PRODUCTION CAR TO DATE

POWER BRAKES WERE STANDARD, WITH BIG DRUMS ON ALL FOUR WHEELS

THE REAR SEATS FOLDED FORWARD TO PRODUCE AN ASTRONOMICAL CARGO AREA THAT MEASURED 7 FT (2.14 M) LONG

PLYMOUTH 'Cuda (1970)

Performance offspring of a classy classic

THE TOUGH-SOUNDING '70s 'Cuda was one of the last flowerings of America's performance binge. Furiously fast, it was a totally new incarnation of the first '64 Barracuda and unashamedly aimed at committed street-racers. Cynically, Plymouth even dubbed its belligerent model lineup "The Rapid Transit System." '70 Barracudas came in three styles – the 'Cuda was the performance model – and nine engine choices, topped by the outrageous 440cid Magnum. Chrysler's advertising men bellowed that the Hemi was "our angriest body wrapped around ol' King Kong hisself." But rising insurance rates and new emission standards meant that the muscle car was an endangered species. By 1973 Plymouth brochures showed a 'Cuda with a young married couple, complete with a baby in the smiling woman's arms. The party was well and truly over, and the Barracuda was axed before the '75 model year.

UNSILENCED AIR FILTERS SUCH AS THIS WEREN'T ALLOWED IN CALIFORNIA BECAUSE OF NOISE REGULATIONS

"With the energy crisis just around the corner, the Barracuda's days were numbered."

THE '70 'CUDA'S CRISP, TAUT STYLING IS SHARED WITH THE DODGE CHALLENGER, AND THE CLASSIC LONG-HOOD-SHORT-TRUNK DESIGN LEAVES YOU IN NO DOUBT THAT THIS IS A PONY CAR

'cuda 440-6

MODEL Plymouth 'Cuda (1970)

PRODUCTION 30,267 (1970)

BODY STYLES Two-door, four-seater coupe and convertible.

CONSTRUCTION Steel unitary body.

ENGINES 383cid, 426cid, 440cid V8s.

POWER OUTPUT 335–425 bhp.

TRANSMISSION Three-speed manual, optional four-speed manual, or three-speed TorqueFlite automatic.

SUSPENSION *Front*: torsion bars; *Rear*: leaf springs with live axle.

BRAKES Front discs, rear drums.

MAXIMUM SPEED 137–150 mph (220–241 km/h)

0–60 MPH (0–96 km/h) 5.9–6.9 sec

A.F.C. 12–17 mpg (4.2–6 km/l)

Plymouth 'Cuda (1970)

INTERIOR 'Cuda interiors were flamboyant, with body-hugging bucket seats, Hurst pistol-grip shifter, and wood-grain steering wheel. This model has the Rallye instrument cluster, with tachometer, oil pressure gauge, and 150 mph (241 km/h) speedometer.

ENGINE The 440cid "six-pack" Magnum engine cranked out 385 bhp and drank through three two-barrel Holley carbs, explaining the six-pack label. Base engine was a 335 bhp 383cid V8. Government legislation ensured that '71 was the last year of the big-engined Barracudas.

"The 'Cuda had ballooned in proportions since the first Barracuda models of the mid-Sixties, and along with the Mustang, now started to lose its *raison d'être*."

THE DISTINCTIVE SHAKER TOP, ALLOWING THE AIR FILTER SPACE TO VIBRATE THROUGH THE TOP OF THE HOOD, WAS A STANDARD 'CUDA FEATURE

WINDSHIELD WIPERS WERE NEATLY CONCEALED BEHIND THE REAR LIP OF THE HOOD

DEC CALIFORNIA
595 VNP

"Plymouth stylists kept the shape uncluttered, with tapered-in bumpers, concealed wipers, flush door handles, smooth overhangs, and subtly flared wheelarches."

'CUDAS CAME IN 18 STRIDENT COLORS, WITH FUNKY NAMES LIKE IN VIOLET, LEMON TWIST, AND VITAMIN C

PONTIAC Chieftain

Classy postwar convertible with limited power plant

UP UNTIL '49, PONTIACS LOOKED and felt like prewar leftovers. Sure, they were reliable and solid, but they had a reputation as middle-of-the-road cars for middle-aged, middle-class buyers. Pontiac was out of kilter with the glamour boom of postwar America. 1949 was a watershed for Pontiac – the first postwar restyles were unveiled, with the new Harley Earl-designed envelope bodies trumpeted as "the smartest of all new cars." Ads promised that "Dollar for Dollar, You Can't Beat a Pontiac," and the Chieftain was proof that Pontiac wasn't bluffing. In reality, its Silver Streak styling was old hat, tracing its origins back to the Thirties. But although mechanically tame – with aged flathead sixes and eights – the '49 Chieftain Convertibles mark the transition from upright prewar designs to postwar glitz. These were the days when the modern convertible really came into its own.

"The rear seat was positioned ahead of the rear axle and fender to give what Pontiac dubbed a 'cradle ride.'"

THE WINDSHIELD WAS CALLED THE SAFE-T-VIEW AND WAS ONE OF A SERIES OF GIMMICKY PONTIAC NAMES THAT ALSO INCLUDED THE CARRY-MORE TRUNK, TRU-ARC SAFETY STEERING, AND EASY-ACCESS DOORS

MODEL Pontiac Chieftain Convertible (1949)

PRODUCTION Not available

BODY STYLE Two-door convertible.

CONSTRUCTION Steel body and chassis.

ENGINES 239cid straight six, 249cid straight eight.

POWER OUTPUT 90–103 bhp.

TRANSMISSION Three-speed manual, optional four-speed Hydra-Matic automatic.

SUSPENSION *Front:* coil springs; *Rear:* leaf springs.

BRAKES Front and rear drums.

MAXIMUM SPEED 80–95 mph (129–153 km/h)

0–60 MPH (0–96 km/h) 13–15 sec

A.F.C. 15 mpg (5.3 km/l)

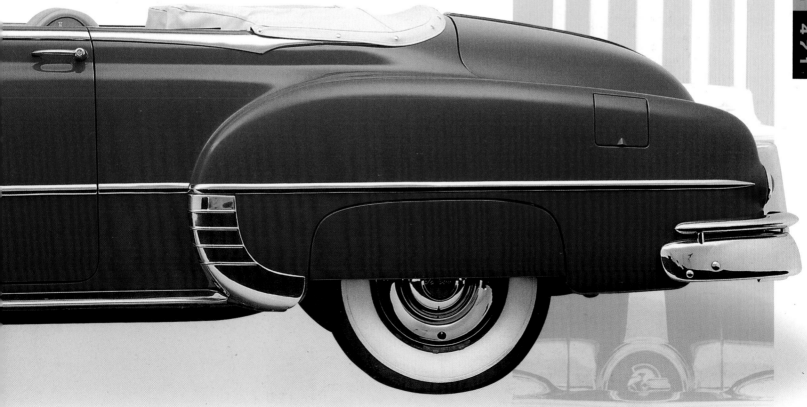

INTERIOR The interior could seat five, and a three-speed synchromesh gearbox with column shift was standard. '49 was only the second year for the newfangled Hydra-Matic four-speed automatic option at an extra cost of $159. There was no power steering or power brakes.

ENGINE Six-pot engines were cast-iron with four main bearings, solid valve lifters, and a puny Carter one-barrel carb. Choosing the straight-eight gave you a measly extra 13 bhp, but cost only $23 more. Pontiac did not offer a V8 unit in any of its models until 1955.

"The five parallel chrome bars were a Silver Streak hallmark and were copied by the British Austin Atlantic."

VANITY OPTIONS INCLUDED TISSUE DISPENSER, COMPASS, DE LUXE ELECTRIC CLOCK, GLOVE COMPARTMENT LIGHT, AND EVEN VENETIAN BLINDS

THE ENGINE WAS SET WELL FORWARD IN A VERY RIGID CANTILEVER BOX GIRDER FRAME

1949 PENNA
ED637

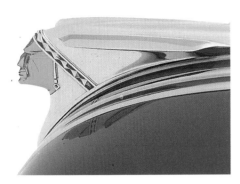

CHIEFTAIN ORNAMENT

The Indian chief hood ornament was a stylish piece, and, though it never smiled, the head was illuminated at night by a 2-watt bulb that gave a warm, yellow glow. Another Chieftain logo, this time in chrome, was to be found on the center of the grille.

THE INTRICATE BUMPER WAS DESIGNED TO PREVENT YOUNG WOMEN IN HOOPED SKIRTS FROM GETTING THEM CAUGHT IN THE BUMPER WHEN OPENING THE TRUNK

DUAL SIDE-MOUNTED SPOTLIGHTS WERE TRIGGER-OPERATED

Pontiac

1949 PENNA
ED637

PONTIAC Bonneville

A giant of a coupe with a certain appeal

IN THE LATE '50s, Detroit was worried. Desperately trying to offer something fresh, manufacturers decided to hit the aspirational thirtysomethings with a new package of performance, substance, and style. Pontiac's "Wide Track" Bonneville of '59 was a sensation. General Manager Bunkie Knudsen gave the line an image of youth and power, and Wide Track became all the rage. *Car Life* picked the Bonneville as its "Best Buy," and so did consumers. By 1960, soaring sales had made Pontiac the third most successful company in the industry. The prestigious Bonneville was also a dream to drive. The 389cid V8 pushed out up to 345 horses. and when the Tri-Power mill was employed, top speeds hit 125 mph (201 km/h). In 1959, Americans spent $300 million on chewing gum, the supermarket was the temple, and the jingling ad the national anthem. A self-obsessed utopia of comfort and convenience was about to go horribly wrong.

"Flushed with success, Pontiac claimed that it was the maker of 'America's Number One Road Car.'"

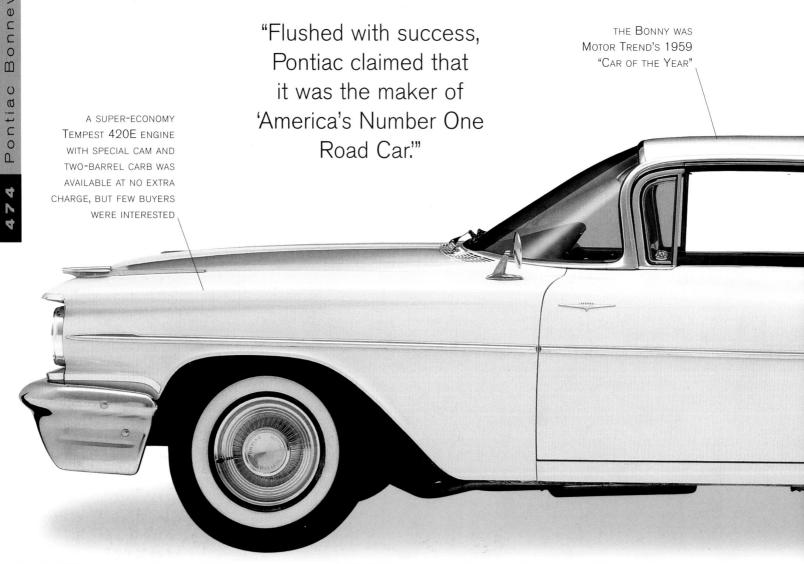

THE BONNY WAS MOTOR TREND'S 1959 "CAR OF THE YEAR"

A SUPER-ECONOMY TEMPEST 420E ENGINE WITH SPECIAL CAM AND TWO-BARREL CARB WAS AVAILABLE AT NO EXTRA CHARGE, BUT FEW BUYERS WERE INTERESTED

MODEL Pontiac Bonneville Sport Coupe (1959)

PRODUCTION 27,769 (1959)

BODY STYLE Two-door, six-seater coupe.

CONSTRUCTION Steel body and chassis.

ENGINE 389cid V8.

POWER OUTPUT 260–345 bhp.

TRANSMISSION Three-speed manual, optional four-speed Super Hydra-Matic automatic.

SUSPENSION Front and rear coil springs.

BRAKES Front and rear drums.

MAXIMUM SPEED 110–125 mph (177–201 km/h)

0-60 MPH (0–96 km/h) 9–11.5 sec

A.F.C. 15 mpg (5.3 km/l)

INTERIOR The riotous interior had as much chrome as the exterior, and buyers could specify Wonderbar radio, electric antenna, tinted glass, and padded dash. The under-dash air-conditioning unit is a later, aftermarket accessory.

UPHOLSTERY The garish three-color striped upholstery was meant to give the Bonneville a careless jauntiness and appeal to the young at heart. The warehouselike interior dimensions made it a true six-seater.

WITH CONSUMERS CRYING OUT FOR INDIVIDUALITY, PONTIAC GAVE THE BONNEVILLE NOT TWO FINS, BUT FOUR

DESPITE THEIR SAFETY SIGNIFICANCE, DIRECTION INDICATORS WERE A HASTILY APPLIED AFTERTHOUGHT TUCKED AWAY IN THE FRONT BUMPER

THE SPLIT GRILLE WAS NEW FOR '59. AFTER REVERTING BACK TO A FULL-LENGTH GRILLE FOR JUST ONE YEAR, IT BECAME A PONTIAC TRADEMARK IN THE EARLY '60S

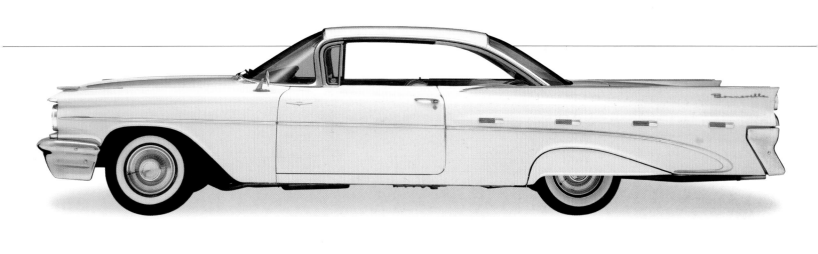

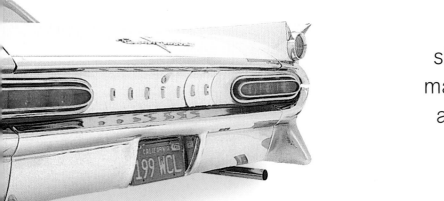

"The Bonneville's broad-shouldered appearance was macho, tough, and suggestive, and appealed to the public."

THE CHASSIS WAS KNOWN AS SPREAD-TREAD AND GAVE MUCH CRISPER CORNERING THAN IN PREVIOUS MODELS

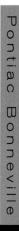

PONTIAC GTO

The first true muscle car and a real contender

"THE GREAT ONE" WAS Pontiac's answer to a youth market with attitude and disposable cash. In 1964, John DeLorean, Pontiac's chief engineer, shoe-horned the division's biggest V8 into the timid little Tempest compact with electrifying results. He then beefed up the brakes and suspension, threw in three two-barrel carbs, and garnished the result with a name that belonged to a Ferrari. In 1966 it became a model in its own right, and Detroit's first "muscle car" had been born. Pundits think the flowing lines of these second-generation GTOs make them the best-looking of all. Engines were energetic performers too, with a standard 335 bhp 389cid V8 that could be specified in 360 bhp high-output form. But by '67 GTO sales had tailed off by 15 percent, depressed by a burgeoning social conscience and federal meddling. The performance era was about to be legislated into the history books.

"John DeLorean's idea of placing a high-spec engine in the standard Tempest body paved the way for a whole new genre."

PONTIAC WAS THE FIRST MAINSTREAM MANUFACTURER TO COMBINE BIG-CUBE POWER WITH A LIGHT BODY

GTOS COULD BE ORDERED WITH RALLY CLUSTER GAUGES, CLOSE-RATIO FOUR-ON-THE-FLOOR, CENTER CONSOLE, AND WALNUT GRAIN DASH INSERT

MODEL Pontiac GTO Convertible (1966)

PRODUCTION 96,946 (1966, all body styles)

BODY STYLES Two-door, five-seater hardtop, coupe, and convertible.

CONSTRUCTION Steel unitary body.

ENGINE 389cid V8s.

POWER OUTPUT 335–360 bhp.

TRANSMISSION Three-speed manual, optional four-speed manual, or three-speed Hydra-Matic automatic.

SUSPENSION Front and rear coil springs.

BRAKES Front and rear drums, optional discs.

MAXIMUM SPEED 125 mph (201 km/h)

0–60 MPH (0–96 km/h) 6.8–9.5 sec

A.F.C. 15 mpg (5.3 km/l)

INTERIOR GTOs were equipped to the same high standard as the Pontiac Tempest Le Mans. Items included ashtray lights, cigarette lighter, carpeting, and a power top for convertibles. Air-conditioning and power steering could be ordered at $343 and $95 respectively.

ENGINE The base 335 bhp 389cid block had a high-output Tri-Power big brother that pushed out 360 bhp for an extra $116. The range was expanded in '67 to include an economy 255 bhp 400cid V8 and a Ram-Air 400cid mill that also developed 360 bhp but at higher rpm.

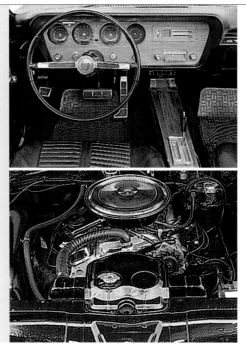

Speak softly and carry a GTO

APPEALING TO THE YOUNG

Effective advertising helped sales to peak in 1966, with over 95,000 GTOs going to power-hungry young drivers whose average age was 25.

TURN SIGNALS IN THE GRILLE WERE MEANT TO MIMIC EUROPEAN-STYLE DRIVING LIGHTS

THE STACKED HEADLIGHTS WERE NEW FOR PONTIACS IN '65 AND WERE RETAINED ON GTOS UNTIL THE END OF THE DECADE

62663
VERMONT 67

"*Road & Track* magazine said the theft of the GTO name from Ferrari was 'an act of unforgivable dishonesty.'"

THE GTO CAME WITH HEAVY-DUTY SHOCKS AND SPRINGS AS STANDARD, ALONG WITH A STABILIZER BAR

IT MIGHT LOOK LONG, BUT THE GTO WAS ACTUALLY 15 IN (38 CM) SHORTER THAN PONTIAC'S LARGEST MODELS

PONTIAC

62663
6 8
VERMONT 67

PONTIAC Trans Am

A hard-muscled commando of a car

IN THE SEVENTIES, for the first time in American history, the government intervened in the auto industry. With the 1973 oil crisis, the Big Three were ordered to tighten their belts, and the big-block Trans Am became the last of the really fast cars. The muscular Firebird had been around since 1969, and gas shortage or not, the public liked the '73 Trans Am. The 455 Super Duty V8 put out 310 horsepower, and while Pontiac bravely tried to ignore the killjoy legislation, someone remarked that their High Output 455 was the largest engine ever offered in a pony car. The game was up, and within months modifications to comply with emission regulations had brought power down to 290 bhp. The hell-raising 455 soldiered on until 1976, and that athletic fastback body until '82. But the frenetic muscle years of 1967–73 had irretrievably passed, and those wonderful big-block banshees would never be seen again.

"The 'screaming chicken' graphics gracing the hood were new for 1973. They were a modern rendition of the Native American phoenix symbol."

DUAL BODY-COLORED MIRRORS WERE STANDARD, WITH REMOTE CONTROL ON THE DRIVER'S SIDE

HONEYCOMBED WHEELS, COLORED SILVER, WERE A $36 OPTION

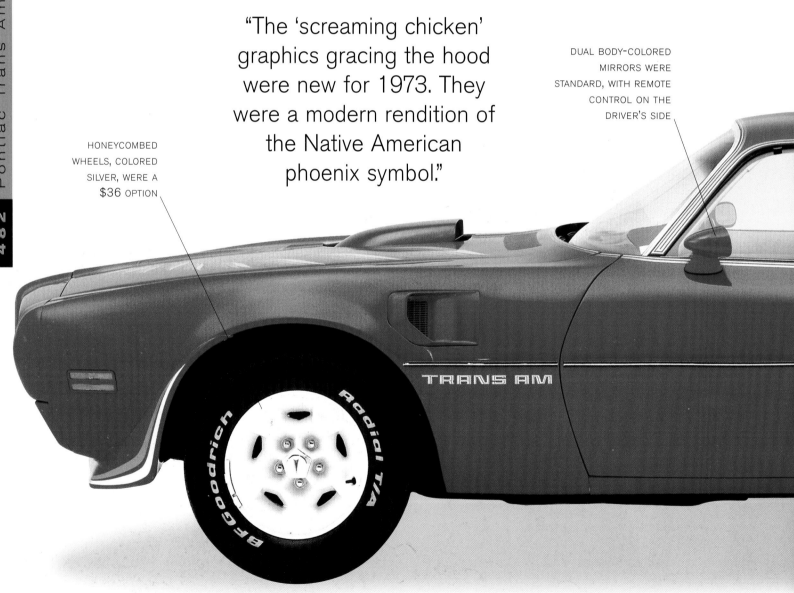

TRANS AM

MODEL Pontiac Firebird Trans Am (1973)

PRODUCTION 4,802 (1973)

BODY STYLE Two-door, four-seater fastback.

CONSTRUCTION Steel unitary body.

ENGINE 455cid V8.

POWER OUTPUT 250–310 bhp.

TRANSMISSION Four-speed manual or three-speed Turbo Hydra-Matic automatic.

SUSPENSION *Front*: coil springs; *Rear*: leaf springs with live axle.

BRAKES Front discs, rear drums.

MAXIMUM SPEED 135 mph (217 km/h)

0–60 MPH (0–96 km/h) 5.4 sec

A.F.C. 17 mpg (6 km/l)

PONTIAC

INTERIOR The second-edition Trans Ams had a standard engine-turned dash insert, Rally gauges, bucket seats, and a Formula steering wheel. The tach was calibrated to an optimistic 8000 rpm. The speedo was just as untruthful, with a maximum of 160 mph (257 km/h).

ENGINE The big-block Trans Ams were Detroit's final salute to performance. The 455 Super Duty gave "the sort of acceleration that hasn't been seen in years" – it could reach 60 mph (96 km/h) in under six seconds, and run all the way to 135 mph (217 km/h).

NEW FRONT VALANCE PANEL WITH SMALL AIR DAM APPEARED IN 1973

THE REAR-FACING "SHAKER" HOOD SCOOP WAS AN INDICATION OF THE TRANS AM'S IMMENSE POWER

DLR 3055 D
MASSACHUSETTS

PORSCHE 356

The car that converted James Dean to car racing

ONE OF ONLY ABOUT 50 surviving pre-A 356s, this gorgeous model shows us just how much of a Volkswagen the early 356 really was. Engines were the 1086cc unit taken from the contemporary Beetle, gearboxes had KdF ("Strength Through Joy") stamped on their casings, suspension was Beetle lever-arm shocks, and even the brakes were taken straight out of the VW parts bin. Yet despite the prosaic engineering origins, the original 356 still possessed an exotic aura.

Maybe it was the smooth teardrop shape, the white steering wheel, or the minimalist, Bauhaus chrome detailing, but from the moment the first 356 clattered into life, everyone knew that this was a very special little car – special enough for 356s to be sold to fashionable New Yorkers as early as 1951. This beautifully chaste, pure and simple gem of a car is the foundation stone of every single modern Porsche and a wonderfully authentic piece of automotive history.

"In 1951 *Autocar* said that the 356 offered 'unique comfort, performance, and economy for which people will pay a high price.'"

EARLY CARS STILL HAD A TWO-PIECE WINDSHIELD WITH CENTRAL DIVIDE, JUST LIKE THE BEETLE

PORSCHE COULDN'T COPE WITH THE HUGE DEMAND FOR 356S, SO REUTTER MADE THE BODIES

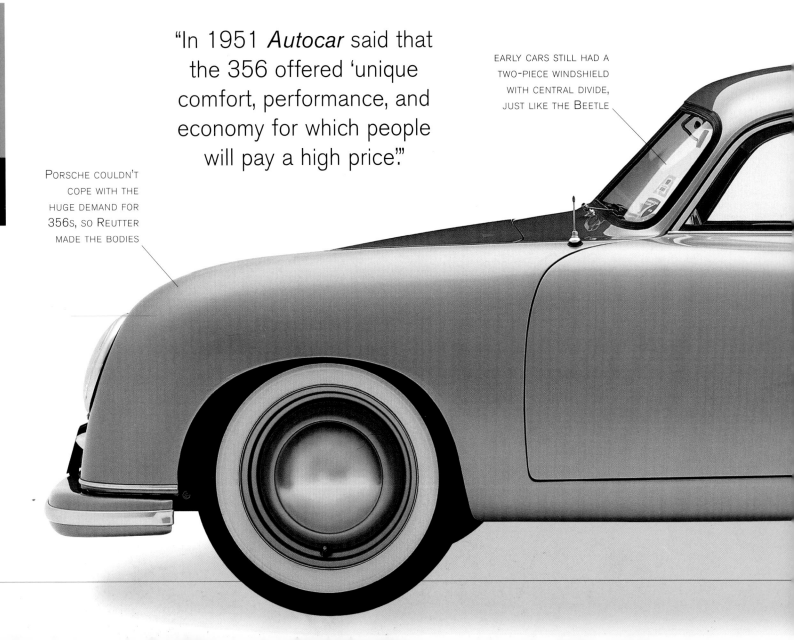

"The 356 was marketed in a logical and intellectual way, a Porsche tradition that continues to this day."

MODEL Porsche Pre-A 356 (1950)

PRODUCTION 298 (1950 only)

BODY STYLE Two-door, two-seater coupe.

CONSTRUCTION Steel body, steel platform chassis.

ENGINE Air-cooled, 1086cc, flat-four.

POWER OUTPUT 40 bhp at 4000 rpm.

TRANSMISSION Four-speed non-syncromesh.

SUSPENSION *Front:* independent trailing arms; *Rear:* swing axle with lever shock absorbers.

BRAKES Hydraulic drums all around.

MAXIMUM SPEED 85 mph (137 km/h)

0-60 MPH (0–96 km/h) 15 sec

A.F.C. 35 mpg (12.4 km/l)

Porsche 356 | 487

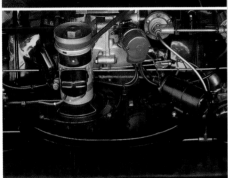

INTERIOR Despite a high scuttle and tiny windows, the cabin is roomy with lots of head and leg room, plus plenty of luggage space on the rear seats. The white plastic wheel is a wonderful period piece, but controls are stuck all over the dash like hard candy. Correct Fifties radio unit looks very space age.

ENGINE Engine is a 40 bhp, Type 369, VW-based, air-cooled flat-four with special cylinder heads and twin Solex carburetors. The standard VW unit developed just 25 horses, but modified heads with larger inlet valves and ports boosted power output and raised the compression ratio from 5.8:1 to 7.0:1.

SALES BROCHURE

Period brochure sold the 356 on its absolute engineering excellence. With typical German efficiency, the copy boasts "unexcelled road-holding qualities," "faultless steering," and "absolute control and safety."

BODIES WERE HAND-BUILT BY REUTTER BUT PROVED VERY RUST-PRONE, WHICH IS WHY SO FEW EARLY CARS SURVIVE

356S WEREN'T CHEAP AND ACTUALLY COST MORE THAN JAGUAR'S MUCH FASTER AND MORE GLAMOROUS XK120 (SEE PAGES 320–23)

"Distinctive humpbacked silhouette was penned by Erwin Komenda and had an amazingly low aerodynamic resistance of just 0.29Cd."

James Dean, the world's most famous Porsche aficionado, may have died at the wheel of a silver 550 Spyder, but prior to that he owned a white 356 1500 Speedster, that got him into car racing. One of a pilot-run of 200 cars sold in the US, Dean raced the Speedster in weekend Sports Car Club of America events.

REAR ENGINE CONFIGURATION HAS BEEN A PORSCHE FEATURE FOR 50 YEARS, BUT INEXPERIENCED DRIVERS ALWAYS FOUND HANDLING TRICKY AT THE LIMIT

PORSCHE

UXB 12

PORSCHE 356B

A triumph of creative expediency

BY THE TIME THE 356 reached the early '60s, it had evolved from a VW special into a refined, sophisticated, and elegant GT. The 356B of '63 was faster, quieter, prettier, and much more comfortable than its basic predecessor. The body was given a subtle facelift, there was more rear headroom, better syncromesh on the gearbox, and finned aluminum brake drums to improve the 356's previously diffident retardation. But the most significant improvement was the addition of the high-revving Super 90 engine that pushed out 90 horses and took the top speed to 110 mph (117 km/h). The motoring press were unanimous in their praise for the now urbane and civilized 356, with *The Motor* remarking that "It is amazing that it still has so few competitors or imitators." The much-admired 356 was unique – an obtuse-looking sports car that baffled its critics and beguiled its adherents.

"The busy air-cooled 'thrum' is an unmistakeable trademark sound that was appreciated by thousands of buyers."

WITH LIMITED LUGGAGE ACCOMMODATION IN THE FRONT, THE REAR RACK PROVIDED USEFUL EXTRA LUGGAGE SPACE

THIS WAS NOT A COVERED JACKING POINT BUT AN ACCESS COVER TO ALLOW YOU TO RETRIEVE THE TORSION BAR

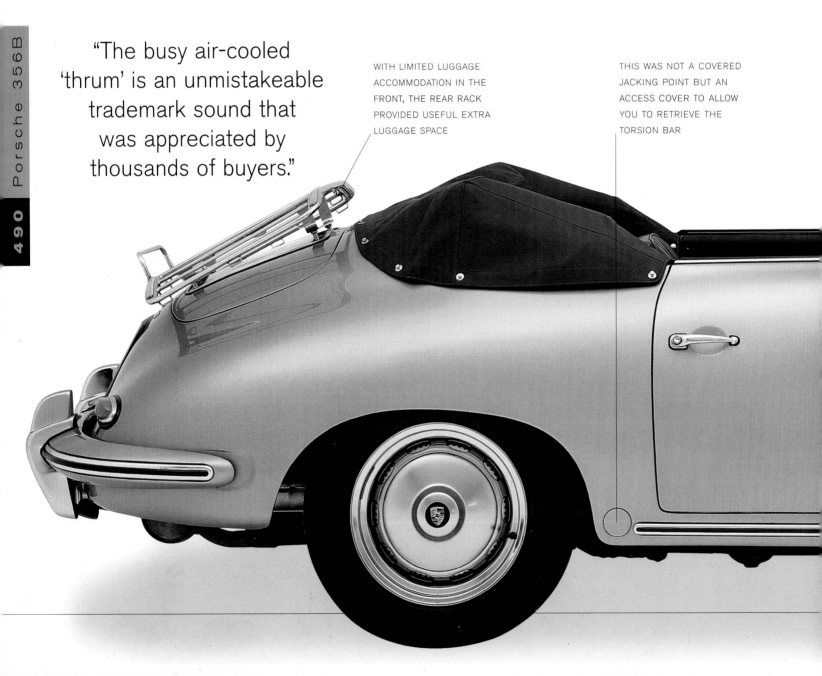

PORSCHE

MODEL Porsche 356B (1959–63)

PRODUCTION 30,963

BODY STYLES Two-plus-two fixed-head coupe, convertible, and Speedster.

CONSTRUCTION Unitary steel body with integral pressed-steel platform chassis.

ENGINE Air-cooled, horizontally opposed flat-four 1582cc with twin carbs.

POWER OUTPUT 90 bhp at 5500 rpm (Super 90).

TRANSMISSION Four-speed manual, all synchromesh, rear-wheel drive.

SUSPENSION *Front:* independent, trailing arms with transverse torsion bars and anti-roll bar; *Rear:* independent, swing half-axles, radius arms, and transverse torsion bars. Telescopic shocks.

BRAKES Hydraulic drums all around.

MAXIMUM SPEED 110 mph (177 km/h)

0–60 MPH (0–96 km/h) 10 sec

A.F.C. 10.6–12.5 km/l (30–35 mpg)

INTERIOR The interior is delightfully functional, simple, fad-free, and, because of that, enduringly fashionable. Below the padded dash are the classic green-on-black instruments. Seats are wide and flat, and the large, almost vertical steering wheel has a light feel. The passenger gets a grab handle.

ENGINE The rear-engined layout was determined by reliance on VW Beetle mechanics and running gear. The flat-four engine, with its so-called "boxer" layout of horizontally opposed cylinders, is not pure Beetle, but a progressive development. Engines grew from 1086cc to 1996cc.

TRACK RECORD

Here Porsches are seen retro racing at Palm Springs, Florida. The first 356s distinguished themselves almost immediately with a 1951 Le Mans class win and a placing of 20th overall. Since then, Porsche has always been associated with performance.

ON THE 356B, HEADLIGHTS AND BUMPERS MOVED HIGHER UP THE FENDER

ON CONVERTIBLES, THE REARVIEW MIRROR WAS ATTACHED TO A SLIM CHROME BAR THAT GAVE A DECEPTIVE SPLIT-WINDOW APPEARANCE FROM THE FRONT

DYU 40C

"This 1962 356B Super 90 was produced just two years before the birth of the 911, which although a very different beast, is still an evolution of the original shape."

ANOTHER DIFFERENCE ON THE 356B WAS THAT TWIN EXHAUSTS EXITED ON EACH SIDE THROUGH BUMPER OVER-RIDERS

For six decades Ferdinand Porsche was involved in cars as diverse as the Mercedes SSK, the mighty Auto Union racers, and the world's numerically most successful car, the VW Beetle. An undisputed engineering genius, he got on well with Hitler and was close friends with Henry Ford. After WWII, he went on to found Porsche, financed by a 5DM royalty he received on every VW built.

Porsche 356B 493

PORSCHE Carrera 911 RS

One of the ultimate road cars of all time

AN INSTANT LEGEND, the Carrera RS became the classic 911. With lighter body panels and stripped out interior trim, the RS is simply a featherweight racer. The classic, flat-six engine was bored out to 2.7 liters and boasted uprated fuel injection and forged flat-top pistons – modifications that helped to push out a sparkling 210 bhp. Porsche had no problem selling all the RSs it could make, and a total of 1,580 were built and sold in just 12 months. Standard 911s were often criticized for tail-happy handling, but the Carrera RS is a supremely balanced machine. Its race-bred responses offer the last word in sensory gratification. With one of the best engines ever made, an outstanding chassis, and 150 mph (243 km/h) top speed, the RS can rub bumpers with the world's finest. Collectors and Porsche buffs consider this the preeminent 911, with prices reflecting its cultlike status. The RS is the original air-cooled screamer.

THE POLYESTER BUMPERS, THIN STEEL BODYWORK, AND LIGHTWEIGHT "GLAVERBELL" GLASS HELP THE RS TO WEIGH IN AT JUST OVER 1,984 LB (900 KG); STANDARD PORSCHES TIP THE SCALES AT 2,194 LB (995 KG)

"The bored-out, air-cooled 2.7-liter 'Boxermotor' produces huge reserves of power. Externally, it is identifiable only by extra cylinder cooling fins."

THE STEEPLY RAKED WINDSHIELD HELPED THE 911'S WIND-EVADING SHAPE

MODEL Porsche Carrera 911 RS (1972–73)

PRODUCTION 1,580

BODY STYLE Two door, two seater coupe.

CONSTRUCTION Thin-gauge steel panels.

ENGINE Flat-six, 2687cc.

POWER OUTPUT 210 bhp at 5100 rpm.

TRANSMISSION Close-ratio, five-speed manual.

SUSPENSION Front and rear torsion bar.

BRAKES Ventilated discs front and rear, with aluminum calipers.

MAXIMUM SPEED 150 mph (243 km/h)

0–60 MPH (0–96 km/h) 5.6 sec

0–100 MPH (0–161 km/h) 12.8 sec

A.F.C. 23 mpg (8.1 km/l)

RAMBLER Ambassador

Dour offering that promised more than it delivered

WHILE THE GOVERNMENT was telling consumers "You auto buy now," American Motors boss George Romney was telling the president that "Consumers are rebelling against the size, horsepower, and excessive styling of the American automobile." Romney's Ramblers were the only industry success story for a recession-racked '58, when for the first time ever, more cars were imported than exported. The Ambassador was Rambler's economy flagship, and road testers liked its speed, room, luxury, thrift, and high resale value. Also, it was reasonably priced, had a safety package option, "deep-dip" rustproofing, and a thoroughly modern monocoque shell with chassisless body construction. But buyers weren't buying. Drivers may have wanted economy and engineering integrity, but cars still had to be cool. The sensible Ambassador was an ugly, slab-sided machine for middle-aged squares.

"With modest tailfins and a plain rump, the Ambassador was no movie idol and looked more like a taxi than an upmarket sedan."

SWEEPSPEAR WAS ONE OF FEW CONCESSIONS TO ORNAMENTATION BUT HELPED BREAK UP AN OTHERWISE SOLID FLANK

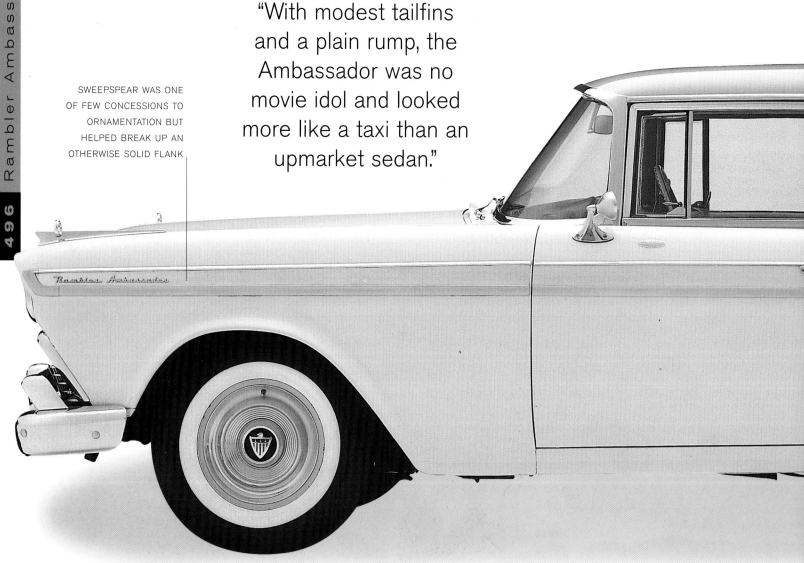

"AMC stylist Ed Anderson did a good job with the '58 models, cleverly reskinning '56 and '57 models with longer hoods and different grilles."

AMERICAN MOTORS CORP.
DETROIT   MICHIGAN

MODEL Rambler Ambassador (1958)

PRODUCTION 14,570 (1958, all body styles)

BODY STYLE Four-door, six-seater sedan.

CONSTRUCTION Steel monocoque body.

ENGINE 327cid V8.

POWER OUTPUT 270 bhp.

TRANSMISSION Three-speed manual with optional overdrive, optional three-speed Flash-O-Matic automatic.

SUSPENSION *Front:* independent coil springs; *Rear:* coil with optional air springs.

BRAKES Front and rear drums.

MAXIMUM SPEED 105 mph (169 km/h)

0–60 MPH (0–96 km/h) 10 sec

A.F.C. 18 mpg (6.4 km/l)

INTERIOR The custom steering wheel was an optional extra, along with power steering. Flash-O-Matic three-speed auto transmission could be column-operated or controlled by push buttons on the dash.

ENGINE The cast-iron 327cid V8 engine gave 270 bhp and, despite a one-barrel carburetor, could hit 60 mph (96 km/h) in 10 seconds. The same engine had powered the '57 Rambler Rebel.

WHAT, NO CHASSIS?

The chassisless body was a Nash/AMC tradition also used by many European companies, namely Jaguar. Few American manufacturers, however, were interested in following suit. Despite modest dimensions, the Ambassador was accommodating and could just about seat six.

COFFIN ROOF AND SQUARE-SIDE WINDOWS DIDN'T DO MUCH FOR THE AMBASSADOR'S LOOKS

Y·580
NY EMPIRE STATE 58

THIS IS A
DOUBLE—SAFE
**SINGLE UNIT
BODY**

BUILT WITH AN ADVANCED
METHOD OF BODY CON-
STRUCTION IN WHICH THE
BODY AND FRAME ARE
COMBINED INTO A SINGLE
ALL-WELDED STRUCTURAL
UNIT

PIONEERED AND BUILT
EXCLUSIVELY BY

AMERICAN MOTORS CORP.
DETROIT   MICHIGAN

SQUEAK REDUCTION

The single-unit body meant
that 9,000 electric welds
replaced conventional bolts,
thereby reducing in-car
rattles and squeaks.

SALES LITERATURE
CHAMPIONED THE
"SENSIBLE FIN HEIGHT" AS
AN AID TO SAFER DRIVING
BY NOT OBSTRUCTING
REAR VISION

LARGE REAR WINDOW
MEANT VISIBILITY FOR
THE DRIVER WAS GOOD

Rambler Ambassador **499**

RENAULT 4CV

A sedan that beat the odds to achieve success

THE RENAULT 4CV WAS a war baby. Conceived in the middle of hostilities, by 1946 it emerged into a post-war world that was desperate for hope, optimism, and mobility. A little jewel of modernity, the 4CV had a water-cooled, rear-mounted engine, unitary construction, all-independent suspension, hydraulic brakes, and a surprisingly pretty body. Yet one of Renault's most successful cars had a rocky start in life. Senior management at the French company didn't approve of the new small car, and the few prototypes that existed during the war were almost destroyed by Allied bombs. At its Paris Salon launch in '46 it was painted sand yellow, the only color available from stocks of camouflage paint. But for all its difficulties, the 4CV was an immediate success and demand was so high that Renault had to introduce the first automated lines to speed production. By the end of production in 1961 over a million 4CVs had been built.

"In 1956 a 4CV averaged 68.75 mph (110.69 km/h) over 15 hours on the rugged 1000-mile (1610-km) Mille Miglia; 50 percent of the other entrants dropped out."

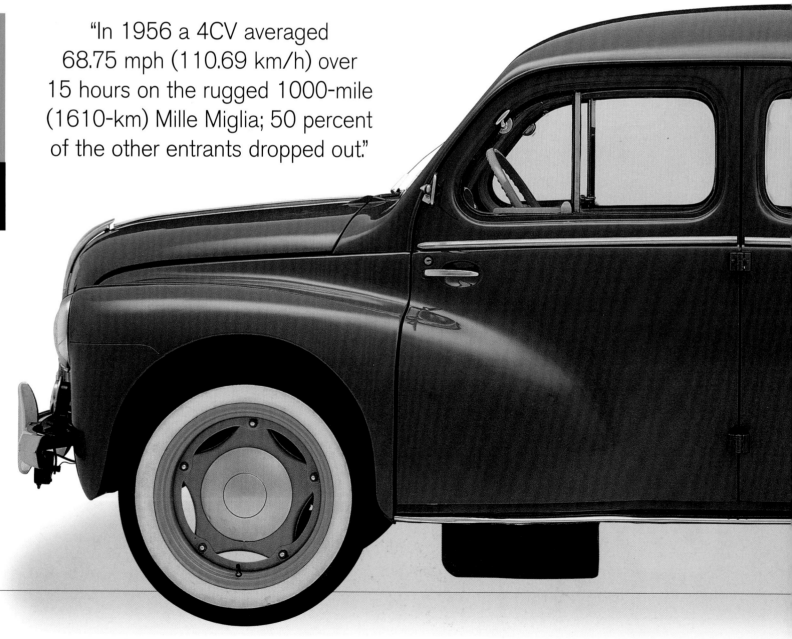

TINY LIGHT ON THE
REAR PANEL WAS FOR
NIGHT PARKING,
ALTHOUGH SOME WERE
CONVERTED TO BECOME
TURN INDICATORS

MODEL Renault 4CV (1956)

PRODUCTION 1,105,543 (total)

BODY STYLE Four-door, four-seater sedan.

CONSTRUCTION All steel unitary body.

ENGINE 747cc, rear-mounted, four-cylinder.

POWER OUTPUT 21 bhp at 5000 rpm.

TRANSMISSION Three-speed syncromesh.

SUSPENSION All independent, front and rear
coil springs.

BRAKES Hydraulic drums front and rear.

MAXIMUM SPEED 59 mph (95 km/h)

0-60 MPH (0–96 km/h) N/A

A.F.C. 35 mpg (12.4 km/l)

Renault 4CV **501**

INTERIOR The 4CV's interior was fairly well appointed, with a heater/demister, map and courtesy lights, sun visors, "stain resistant" upholstery, glove compartment, self-starter, automatic thermo choke, and even a sliding sunroof and automatic clutch option.

ENGINE The 747cc overhead valve, rear engine was mounted longitudinally and produced just 21 bhp. Performance was hardly sensational, with 50 mph (80.5 km/h) taking nearly 30 seconds and a top speed of only 59 mph (95 km/h).

"Dummy front grille concealed the fact that the 4CV's engine lived not at the front but at the back."

THE 4CV'S FRONT DOORS WERE OF THE "SUICIDE" VARIETY, HINGED TO THE CENTRAL PILLAR AND OPENING AGAINST THE TRAFFIC FLOW

UNITARY CONSTRUCTION HAD NO SEPARATE CHASSIS AND USED 0.028 IN SHEET STEEL FOR PANEL WORK AND 0.38 IN FOR THE FLOOR SECTIONS

"In 1950 *Autocar* magazine raved, saying, 'to many people, the Renault may represent motoring at its most practical.'"

FLAMBOYANTLY
STYLED ALUMINUM
WATER FILLER-CAP
FED A PRESSURIZED
RADIATOR LOCATED
BEHIND THE ENGINE

REAR FENDERS WERE
DETACHABLE AND
DESIGNED TO BE
REPLACED QUICKLY
AND CHEAPLY IN THE
EVENT OF AN ACCIDENT

RENAULT - Alpine A110

One of the world's most successful rally cars

THE RENAULT-ALPINE A110 may be diminutive in its proportions, but it has a massive and deserved reputation, particularly in its native France. Although wearing the Renault badge, this pocket rocket is testimony to the focused dedication of one man – Jean Redélé, a passionate motor sport enthusiast and son of a Renault dealer. As he took over his father's garage he began to modify Renault products for competition, then develop his own machines based on Renault engines and mechanics. The A110, with its fiberglass body and backbone chassis, was the culmination of his effort, and from its launch in 1963 it went on to rack up a massive list of victories in the world's toughest rallies. On the public roads, it had all the appeal of a thinly disguised racer, as nimble as a mountain goat, with sparkling performance, and just about the most fun you could have this side of a Lancia Stratos (*see pages 356–59*).

"Squat, nimble, and slightly splay-footed on its wide tires, the Alpine looked purposeful from any angle."

THE STEERING WAS LIGHT AND THE GRIP LIMPET-LIKE, BUT WHEN IT DID LET GO THAT TAIL WAGGED THE DOG IN A BIG WAY

EVEN THOUGH ONLY A LITTLE OVER 8,000 A110S WERE BUILT, THEY WERE ASSEMBLED IN SPAIN, MEXICO, BRAZIL, AND BULGARIA, AS WELL AS FRANCE

Richard Tyzack
Mick Briggs

MILLERS
RAC International Hist
of Great Bri

10

MODEL Renault-Alpine A110 Berlinette (1963–77)

PRODUCTION 8,203

BODY STYLE Two-seater sports coupe.

CONSTRUCTION Fiberglass body integral with tubular steel backbone chassis.

ENGINES Various four-cylinders of 956–1796cc.

POWER OUTPUT 51–66 bhp (956cc) to 170 bhp (1796cc)

TRANSMISSION Four- and five-speed manual, rear-wheel drive.

SUSPENSION Coil springs all around. *Front:* upper/lower control arms; *Rear:* trailing radius arms & swing-axles.

BRAKES Front and rear discs.

MAXIMUM SPEED 132 mph (212 km/h) (1595cc)

0–60 MPH (0–96 km/h) 8.7–10 sec

A.F.C. 27 mpg (7.6 km/l) (1296cc)

INTERIOR The instrument layout was typical of sports cars of the period, and the stubby gearstick was handily placed for ease of operation. Getting in and out was not easy though because of the low roof line and high sills. Examples built for road rather than race use lacked racing seats but were better trimmed.

ENGINE Myriad engine options mirrored Renault's offerings, but in Alpine form – by Gordini or Mignotet – it really flew. First models used Dauphine engines, progressing through R8 and R16 to R12. This 1967 car sports the 1442cc unit. Engines were slung behind the rear axle.

ALPINE ACTION
The Alpine was most at home in rally conditions and won everything on the world stage, including a staggering 1, 2, 3 in the 1971 Monte Carlo Rally. The picture shows our featured car on the way to winning the Millers Oils RAC Rally Britannia in 1994.

THE COCKPIT WAS TIGHT, WHICH MADE THE DRIVER FEEL PART OF THE CAR, ESPECIALLY WITH THE DELICIOUS BARRAGE OF NOISE

SADLY FOR BRITISH ENTHUSIASTS, THE ALPINE A110 WAS ONLY AVAILABLE IN LEFT-HAND DRIVE

RIA 64

THE ALPINE WAS A COMPACT LITTLE PACKAGE JUST 44.5 IN (1.16 M) HIGH, 60 IN (1.5 M) WIDE, AND 151.5 IN (3.85 M) IN LENGTH

"On the move, the sting in the Alpine's tail is exhilarating as it buzzes behind you like an angry insect."

SAFETY CUTOUT

External cutout switches are a competition requirement, allowing outsiders to switch off the engine to prevent fire in an accident. The Alpine's are on the rear fender next to the engine cover, which was attached slightly open to aid cooling.

CARS WERE KNOWN AT FIRST AS ALPINE-RENAULTS, THEN BECAME RENAULT-ALPINES AS RENAULT INFLUENCE GREW

DRIVE WAS TAKEN TO THE GEARBOX IN FRONT OF THE REAR AXLE

ROLLS-ROYCE Silver Cloud

A grand old English institution

In 1965, $15,300 BOUGHT a seven-bedroom house, 11 Austin Minis, or a Rolls-Royce Silver Cloud. The Rolls that everybody remembers was the ultimate conveyance of landed gentry and captains of industry. But, by the early Sixties, Britain's social fabric was shifting. Princess Margaret announced she was to marry a divorcee, and aristocrats were so short of old money that they had to sell their mansions to celebrities and entrepreneurs. Against such social revolution the Cloud was a resplendent anachronism. Each took three months to build, weighed two tons, and had 12 coats of paint. The body sat on a mighty chassis and drum brakes were preferred because discs made a vulgar squealing noise. Beneath the hood slumbered straight-six or V8 engines, whose power output was never declared, but merely described as "sufficient." The Silver Cloud stands as a splendid monument to an old order of breeding and privilege.

"When the Cloud II was unveiled in 1962, one magazine saw the changes as 'more power, more passenger space, better lighting, and easier steering.'"

THE ROOF LINE WAS HIGH IN THE BEST LIMOUSINE TRADITION — PASSENGERS HAD ENOUGH ROOM TO WEAR TOP HATS

ROLLS CLAIMED ITS CHROME PLATING WAS THICKER THAN ON ANY OTHER CAR IN THE WORLD

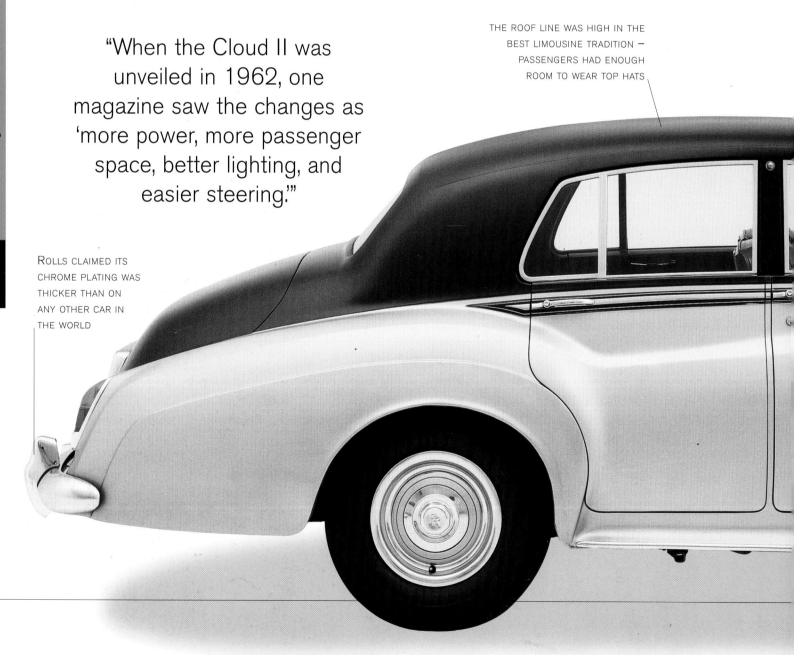

"By the late Sixties the Cloud, looking like a prodigious antique, fell rapidly from grace and could be bought from dealers for a few thousand dollars."

ROLLS
RR
ROYCE

MODEL Rolls-Royce Silver Cloud III (1962–65)

PRODUCTION 2,044 Standard Steel

BODY STYLE Five-seater, four-door sedan.

CONSTRUCTION Girder chassis with pressed-steel body.

ENGINE 6230cc five-bearing V8.

POWER OUTPUT 220 bhp (estimate).

TRANSMISSION Four-speed automatic.

SUSPENSION *Front*: independent with coils and wishbones; *Rear*: leaf springs and hydraulic dampers.

BRAKES Front and rear drums with mechanical servo.

MAXIMUM SPEED 116 mph (187 km/h)

0–60 MPH (0–96 km/h) 10.8 sec

0–100 MPH (0–161 km/h) 34.2 sec

A.F.C. 12.3 mpg (4.4 km/l)

Rolls-Royce Silver Cloud

INTERIOR A haven of peace in a troubled world, the Silver Cloud's magnificent interior was a veritable throne room, with only the finest walnut, leather, and Wilton carpeting. All Clouds were automatic, using a four-speed GM Hydra-Matic box, and the gear shift sat behind the steering wheel.

ENGINE Cloud IIs and IIIs – aimed at the American market – had a 6230cc five-bearing V8 power unit, squeezed into a cramped engine bay. The engine was accessed by a traditional side-opening hood. Cloud Is had a straight-six, 4.9-liter power plant that could trace its origins back to before World War II.

LEATHER COMFORT

The rear compartment might have looked accommodating, but Austin's little 1100 actually had more legroom. Standard walnut picnic tables were ideal for champagne and caviar picnics. Rear leaf springs and hydraulic shocks kept the ride smooth for passengers.

THE 150-WATT 5¾-IN (14-CM) LUCAS DOUBLE HEADLIGHTS WERE NECESSITATED BY ONEROUS NORTH AMERICAN SAFETY REQUIREMENTS

EVERYTHING ABOUT THE CLOUD'S STYLING WAS ANTIQUE, LOOKING MORE LIKE A PIECE OF ARCHITECTURE THAN A CAR

EEL 800C

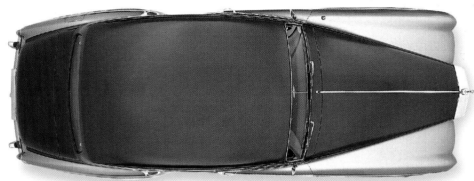

Charles Stewart Rolls was an aristocratic adventurer who raced cars, cycles, balloons, and planes. In 1903 he started a business dealing cars in Conduit Street, London, which later became the offices of Rolls-Royce Ltd. Sir Henry Royce made electrical fittings in Manchester. In 1903 he bought his first car, but thought it so unreliable he built one of his own, the 10 bhp Royce. A partnership with C.S. Rolls followed.

DOORS WERE
SECURED BY THE
HIGHEST QUALITY
YALE LOCKS

EEL 800C

GB

Silver Cloud
III

SAAB Sonett

The sporty Saab that failed miserably

TO BE HONEST, the Saab Sonett was a bit of a lemon. The Swedish firm had been tinkering with the idea of a sports car since the Fifties and, after various false starts, launched the three-cylinder, two-stroke Sonett II in 1966. The US market, for which it was aimed, was singularly unimpressed, and sales were virtually nonexistent. Things got better with a V4 engine in '68, but by then most buyers had heard that Saab's GT was underpowered, expensive, and ugly. Which is why just 899 Sonett IIs found buyers in '68 and only 639 in '69. Generally considered to be one of Saab's few serious mistakes, the Sonett had a dumpy fiberglass body that lacked quality, the column gear shift was notchy, the 100 mph (161 km/h) top speed too low, and for a GT it looked as sexy as a bus. The Sonett III of 1970 carried on until '74, when it was killed off by American emission regulations. Few people mourned its passing.

"*Sports Car Graphic* magazine called the Sonett 'grotesque, noisy, and uncomfortable,' adding: 'Take a look at one. Would you want to own that for $3,695?'"

UGLY PLASTIC BODY HAD A STRONG STEEL MONOCOQUE BENEATH AND INTEGRAL ROLLOVER BAR

FIBERGLASS BODY WAS FAIRLY CRUDE WITH LOTS OF PRODUCTION PROBLEMS. EARLY CARS HAD TO HAVE THEIR PLASTIC PANELS REINFORCED

"In 1968 *Road & Track* said of the V4 model: 'The styling is inept, luggage inaccessible, gearshift clumsy, and the seats tight.'"

MODEL Saab Sonett V4 (1968)

PRODUCTION 10,249 (all models)

BODY STYLE Two-door, two-seater sports.

CONSTRUCTION Fiberglass on steel platform.

ENGINE 1498cc four-cylinder V4.

POWER OUTPUT 65 bhp.

TRANSMISSION Four-speed manual, column shift.

SUSPENSION *Front*: independent; *Rear*: coil springs.

BRAKES Front discs, rear drums.

MAXIMUM SPEED 100 mph (161 km/h)

0–60 MPH (0–96 km/h) 12 sec

A.F.C. 35 mpg (12.4 km/l)

Saab Sonett **513**

INTERIOR The interior was typically Saab, with a utilitarian feel and precious little ambiance. Baulky column shift was a major turn-off for most buyers, along with narrow seats and a dash that reflected badly in the windshield at night. For a GT, the cabin was neither comfortable nor elegant.

ENGINE The simple engine had some clever design touches, like the horizontal galvanized steel pipe, which braced the front suspension and doubled up as a radiator header tank. Prominent air filter was the highest point of the engine and meant that the hood needed a large bulge for clearance.

HOOD BULGE DENOTES COLOGNE-BUILT FORD TAUNUS 1498CC V4 ENGINE, WHICH ONLY MANAGED A WEAK 65 BHP

THE ENTIRE HOOD AND FRONT SECTION SWUNG FORWARD TO GIVE MAXIMUM ACCESS TO THE ENGINE, TRANSMISSION, AND FRONT SUSPENSION

SONETT V4

SAAB

NAV II5F

Sonett III

The Sonett III of 1970 was slightly more successful, with shaplier styling, an opening rear hatch, and floor-mounted gearshift. Power was increased to 1.7 liters and 75 bhp, but top speed remained the same, and a 0–60 time of 14.4 seconds was actually slower than the previous model. Sales didn't improve much either.

REAR THREE-QUARTER
VENTS DUCTED STALE
AIR FROM PASSENGER
COMPARTMENT, BUT
LOOKED AWFUL

THE REAR END WAS
NOT THE SONETT'S
BEST VIEW AND MADE
IT LOOK TOO MUCH
LIKE A CHEAP KIT-CAR

NAV 115F

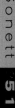

SAAB 99 Turbo

Family sedan with a little extra under the hood

EVERY DECADE OR SO, one car comes along that overhauls accepted wisdom. In 1978, the British car magazine *Autocar* wrote, "this car was so unpredictably thrilling that the adrenalin started to course again, even in our hardened arteries." They had just road-tested a Saab 99 Turbo. Saab took all other car manufacturers by surprise when it announced the world's first turbocharged family car, which promptly went on to be the first "blown" car to win a world championship rally. Developed from the fuel-injected EMS model, the Turbo had Bosch K-Jectronic fuel injection, a strengthened gearbox, and a Garrett turbocharger. A hundred prototypes were built, and between them they covered 2.9 million miles (4.8 million kilometers) before Saab was happy with its prodigy. Rare, esoteric, and historically significant, the mold-breaking 99 Turbo is an undisputed card-carrying classic.

HATCHBACK THREE-DOOR VERSIONS ARE THE MOST COMMON 99 TURBO INCARNATION. THE TRUNKED, FASTER, AND LIGHTER TWO-DOOR CARS ARE MUCH RARER, WITH ONLY 1,000 MADE

A SLIDING STEEL SUNROOF CAME AS STANDARD, AS DID A FRONT SPOILER

THE SHELL WAS STIFF AND LIGHT, AND A FULL FOUR-SEATER. IT WAS REMARKABLY DURABLE TOO, WITH FACTORY UNDERSEAL AND CAVITY WAX INJECTION

"The turbo was reliable, but its Achilles' heel was a couple of seconds lag on hard acceleration."

SAAB

MODEL Saab 99 Turbo (1978–80)

PRODUCTION 10,607

BODY STYLES Two/three/five-door, four-seater sports sedan.

CONSTRUCTION Monocoque steel bodyshell.

ENGINE 1985cc four-cylinder turbo.

POWER OUTPUT 145 bhp at 5000 rpm.

TRANSMISSION Front-wheel drive four/five-speed manual with auto option.

SUSPENSION *Front*: independent double wishbone and coil springs; *Rear*: beam axle, coil springs, and Bilstein shock absorbers.

BRAKES Four-wheel servo discs.

MAXIMUM SPEED 122 mph (196 km/h)

0–60 MPH (0–96 km/h) 8.2 sec

0–100 MPH (0–161 km/h) 19.8 sec

A.F.C. 26 mpg (9.3 km/l)

INTERIOR The Seventies interior looks a little tacky now, with red velour seats and imitation wood. Buyers did get a leather steering wheel and heated driver's seat. One of the dials on the dash was a turbo boost gauge; when the needle swept up its arc, acceleration was phenomenal.

ENGINE The five-bearing, chain-driven single overhead cam engine was an 1985cc eight-valve, water-cooled, four cylinder unit, with low-compression pistons and altered cam timing. The result was an output of 145 bhp and top speed of 122 mph (196 km/h).

RALLY BREAKTHROUGH

Stig Blomqvist won the 1977 Swedish Rally and the next year gave the 99 Turbo some serious exposure. He made a thunderous run on the first televised rally sprint – with a punctured front tire.

SAAB   99 turbo

DAN 982V

SIMCA Aronde Plein Ciel

Stylish million-selling French fancy

By copying Fifties' America styling trends and giving its cars regular face-lifts, Simca metamorphosed from a company building Fiats under license into France's top privately owned carmaker. And the Aronde was the car that turned the tide. Brainchild of Henri-Théodore Pigozzi, the comely Aronde was the first popular French car to have postwar transatlantic lines. Over a 12-year lifespan, 1.3 million Arondes were sold, and by 1955 Simca had overtaken both Peugeot and Citroën in terms of the amount of cars produced. With bodywork by Facel of Facel Vega fame (*see pages 244–47*), the Aronde was an affordable *haute couture* confection based on run-of-the-mill mechanics. 1958 saw a complete American-influenced restyle, with engine names such as "Flash Special." Even so, the Aronde is a quaint hybrid that stands as a testament to the penetrating influence of Fifties' Detroit design.

"The Aronde handled as well as it looked, but because it did not have the soft ride synonymous with traditional Gallic motors, the French automotive press disapproved."

PLEIN CIEL ("OPEN AIR") MOTIF ACCORDS WITH THE AIRY COCKPIT AND GENEROUS GLASS AREA

DESPITE CONVENTIONAL UNDERPINNINGS, THE ARONDE FELT SPORTY WITH POSITIVE, IF SERVOLESS, BRAKES AND A FIRMLY TIED-DOWN CHASSIS

"The Aronde's full-width, polished hubcaps and wheel trims were an American fad, embraced by European imitators."

MODEL Simca Aronde Plein Ciel (1957–62)

PRODUCTION 170,070 (Facel-bodied Arondes)

BODY STYLES Cabriolet or fixed-head sports coupe.

CONSTRUCTION Steel body over separate steel chassis frame.

ENGINE 1288cc four-cylinder push-rod.

POWER OUTPUT 57 bhp at 4800 rpm ("Flash Special").

TRANSMISSION Four-speed manual.

SUSPENSION *Front*: independent by coil springs and wishbones; *Rear*: half-elliptic leaf springs.

BRAKES Four-wheel drums.

MAXIMUM SPEED 87 mph (140 km/h)

0–60 MPH (0–96 km/h) 15.6 sec

A.F.C. 28 mpg (9.9 km/l)

INTERIOR The Aronde's interior is pure Pontiac pastiche, with six different types of plastic used – the cabin is nothing less than a riot of two-tone synthetic. The single dial on the dashboard is a speedometer that reads to a maximum of 160 km/h (99 mph).

ENGINE The "Flash Special" had a four-cylinder, 57 bhp push-rod engine bored out to 1288cc, and breathing through a single Solex carburetor. The four-speed manual gearbox was operated by an obligatory American-style column shift.

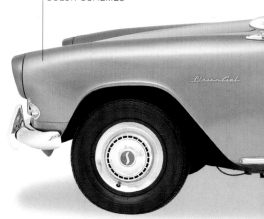

THE ARONDE WAS AVAILABLE IN 22 DIFFERENT DUOTONE COLOR SCHEMES

THE "FLASH SPECIAL" ENGINE HAD PUNCHIER LOW-RANGE TORQUE, STRONGER CRANKSHAFT, AND BIG-END JOURNALS

THE MOUSTACHELIKE GRILLE AND RECESSED SIDELIGHTS LENT THE ARONDE AN AIR OF CLASS AND QUALITY

7162 PF 59

SIMCA OCEAN

The 1957 Ocean was one of Simca's other contemporary models and bore a deliberate resemblance to the Ford Thunderbird *(see pages 278–81)*. The Ocean Convertible was a rebodied Aronde available up until 1963, when the line disappeared in favor of the 1300 and 1500 models.

DESPITE ITS SLOPING
REAR ROOF LINE, THE
ARONDE WAS JUST
ABOUT A FOUR-SEATER

THE ELONGATED
FINNED REAR
MEANT THAT THE
TRUNK COULD BE
SURPRISINGLY AMPLE

ARONDE

7162 PF 59

SKODA Felicia

A pretty convertible from a surprising source

IN THE SIXTIES, the only time Westerners ever saw a Skoda was in a Len Deighton movie. But in Communist Czechoslovakia the Felicia convertible was the equivalent of a Jaguar E-Type. Buyers lined up for years to own one, and waiting lists stretched into the horizon. Based on the Octavia sedan, the four-seater drophead wasn't that sporty, producing only 53 bhp, and the handling wasn't much to shout about either. The separate chassis, swing axle rear suspension, and tall skinny tires could catch the unwary on wet roads. But it was hardy, tough, and very cheap. Imports into the UK began in 1961, but few British drivers took up the challenge and only a handful of Felicias found buyers. However, to today's Volkswagen-owned Skoda, a company with global ambitions, this cute Sixties throwback is its heritage. The Felicia may not have been a great car, but it was the start of something that would eventually surprise us all.

"*Motorsport* magazine's praise was genuine, if modest: 'For those seeking something different at a modest price, the Felicia convertible cannot fail to be of interest.'"

TINY DORSAL FINS PAID HOMAGE TO THE MUCH MORE GLAMOROUS AMERICAN CARS OF THE PERIOD

A GENUINE FOUR-SEATER, THE FELICIA COULD BE SUPPLIED WITH AN OPTIONAL HARDTOP FOR $182

"Two factory-prepared Skoda Octavias finished first and second in their class in the 1961 Monte Carlo Rally."

MODEL Skoda Felicia Convertible (1963)

PRODUCTION 15,864 (total)

BODY STYLE Two-door, four-seater convertible.

CONSTRUCTION Separate steel chassis, steel body.

ENGINE 1221cc, four-cylinder.

POWER OUTPUT 53 bhp at 5000 rpm

TRANSMISSION Four-speed manual.

SUSPENSION Independent all around.

BRAKES Front and rear drums.

MAXIMUM SPEED 84 mph (135 km/h)

0–60 MPH (0–96 km/h) 27.5 sec

A.F.C. 30 mpg (10.6 km/l)

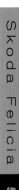

SALES BROCHURE

Contemporary literature began with the words "Do You Know The Felicia?" and emphasized how the car was designed for "the individual." It went on to list Skoda's racetrack successes and then espoused the Felicia's comfort, saying it was like that of a limousine.

"More tourer than sports car, flat-out the Felicia could manage only 84 mph (135 km/h)."

SINGLE HEADLIGHTS AND GRATED GRILLE ARE A CONFUSED MIX OF '50S AND '60S DETROIT STYLING THEMES

THE MODEST 1221CC, FOUR-CYLINDER ENGINE COULD RUN ON LOW-GRADE GAS AND RETURN OVER 30 MPG (10.6 KM/L)

DMD 192 A

INTERIOR The interior was fairly utilitarian, with rubber mats and plastic upholstery. Standard equipment included heater, radiator blind, and sun visors. Fuel gauge was wildly inaccurate and measured more with the engine off than on.

BADGING The Felicia name is Latin-derived and means happiness. Previously known as the 450 Convertible, Skoda decided to drop numerical model designations in 1959 and switch to names instead, which the public preferred.

CONTEMPORARY TESTERS PRAISED THE WIDE TRUNK, WHICH COULD TAKE THREE SUITCASES AND THE SPARE WHEEL

THE FLUSH CANVAS TONNEAU COVERED THE CAR'S INTERIOR WHEN PARKED WITH THE TOP DOWN

DMD 192 A

STUDEBAKER Avanti

A thoroughly modern classic from a design guru

THE AVANTI WAS A BIG DEAL for Studebaker and the first all-new body style since 1953. The last car design of the legendary Raymond Loewy, it rode on a shortened Lark chassis with a stock Studey 289cid V8. The Avanti was one of Loewy's instant classics, and its striking simplicity of shape meant it was a real humdinger. Studebaker's prodigy was fairly audacious too, with a fiberglass body, antisway bars, and wind-evading aerodynamics. Dealers, however, could not meet the huge wave of orders and this, combined with other niggles like flexing of the fiberglass shell, resulted in impatient buyers defecting to the Corvette camp instead. Fewer than 4,650 Avantis were made, and production ceased in December 1963, the Avanti concept being sold to a couple of Studebaker dealers. They went on to form the Avanti Motor Corporation, which successfully churned out Avantis well into the Eighties.

"More European than American, the Avanti had a long neck, razor-edged front fenders, and no grille."

THE 289CID WAS THE BEST STUDEBAKER V8 EVER MADE, DEVELOPING 240 BHP IN STANDARD R1 FORM. SUPERCHARGED R2 AND R3 BOASTED 290 AND 335 BHP RESPECTIVELY

IN 1962 AN AVANTI R3 BROKE 29 BONNEVILLE SPEED RECORDS, TRAVELING FASTER THAN A STANDARD AMERICAN CAR HAD EVER DONE BEFORE

THE SLIPPERY SHAPE WAS NOT WIND-TUNNEL TESTED, BUT A PIECE OF GUESSWORK BY LOEWY

Avanti

MODEL Studebaker Avanti (1963)

PRODUCTION 3,834 (1963)

BODY STYLE Two-door, four-seater coupe.

CONSTRUCTION Fiberglass body, steel chassis.

ENGINES 289cid, 304cid V8s.

POWER OUTPUT 240–575 bhp (304cid R5 V8 fuel-injected).

TRANSMISSION Three-speed manual, optional Power-Shift automatic.

SUSPENSION *Front*: upper and lower A-arms, coil springs; *Rear*: leaf springs.

BRAKES Front discs, rear drums.

MAXIMUM SPEED 120 mph (193 km/h)

0–60 MPH (0–96 km/h) 7.5 sec

A.F.C. 17 mpg (6 km/l)

Studebaker Avanti **529**

INTERIOR The Avanti's dashboard is a study in simplicity, with Mercedes-type gauges and very little in the way of chrome extravagance. The center console would look more at home in a light aircraft. Standard equipment included internal trunk and hood releases and vinyl bucket seats.

STYLING Unmistakable from any angle, early '63 Avantis had round headlights, but most later '64 models sported square ones. The Avanti Motor Corporation decided to build a new Avanti in 2000 and the new model contains much of the front styling cues of the round-lights original.

"Early sketches show Loewy's inspiration, with telltale annotations scribbled on the paper that read 'like Jaguar, Ferrari, Aston Martin, Mercedes.'"

THE AVANTI WAS THE FIRST FOUR-DOOR US PRODUCTION CAR TO HAVE FRONT DISC BRAKES AS STANDARD

TINTED WINDSHIELD CAME AS STANDARD, BUT YOU HAD TO PAY EXTRA FOR TINTED SIDE WINDOWS

Loewy went from France to the US in 1922, and by the end of the Forties was running one of the largest design agencies in New York. Many of his designs have since become classics and include the Lucky Strike cigarette packet, Coca-Cola dispensers, and Coldspot refrigerators. His influence on US design was far-reaching.

SUNBEAM Tiger

V8 power clothed in a British design

THERE WAS NOTHING new about putting an American V8 into a pert English chassis. After all, that is exactly what Carroll Shelby did with the AC Ace to create the awesome Cobra (*see pages* 24–27). When Rootes in Britain decided to do the same with its Sunbeam Alpine, it also commissioned Shelby to produce a prototype; and although Rootes already had close links with Chrysler, the American once again opted for a Ford V8. To cope with the 4.2-liter V8, the

Alpine's chassis and suspension were beefed up to create the fearsome Tiger late in 1964. In 1967, the Tiger II arrived with an even bigger 4.7-liter Ford V8 – the famous 289, but not in the same state of tune as those used in Shelby Cobras. However, this was a brief swansong as Chrysler took control of Rootes and was not going to sanction a car powered by rivals Ford. Often dubbed "the poor man's Cobra," the Tiger is still a lot of fun to grab by the tail.

ADAPTED ALPINE

The Alpine's chassis and suspension had to be beefed up to cope with the weight and power of the V8. Resulting modifications included a heavy-duty back axle, sturdier suspension, and chassis stiffening.

THE MkII TIGER HAD AN EGG-CRATE GRILLE TO DISTINGUISH IT FROM THE ALPINE

OPC 53E

TOYOTA 2000GT

A Japanese sports coupe with unfulfilled potential

TOYOTA'S 2000GT IS MORE than a "might have been" – it's a "should have been." A pretty coupe with performance and equipment to match its good looks, it predated the rival Datsun 240Z (*see pages* 212–15), which was a worldwide sales success. The design of the 2000GT is based on an earlier prototype penned by Albrecht Goertz, creator of the BMW 507 (*see pages* 72–75) and Datsun 240Z. The Toyota failed to reach much more than 300 sales partly because of low capacity, but even more because the car was launched before Japan was geared to export. That left only a domestic market, largely uneducated in the finer qualities of sports cars, to make what they could of the offering. As a design exercise, the 2000GT proved that the Japanese auto industry had reached the stage where its products rivaled the best in the world. It is just a pity not more people were able to appreciate this fine car firsthand.

THE ENGINE WAS A TRIPLE-CARB SIX-CYLINDER YAMAHA, WHICH PROVIDED 150 BHP. A COMPETITION VERSION BOOSTED OUTPUT TO 200 BHP

TRIUMPH TR2

Foundation stone of a proud sports tradition

IF EVER THERE WAS A sports car that epitomized the British bulldog spirit it must be the Triumph TR2. It is as true Brit as a car can be, born in the golden age of British sports cars, but aimed at the lucrative American market, where the Jaguar XK120 (*see pages 320–23*) had already scored a hit. At the 1952 Earl's Court Motor Show in London, the new Austin-Healey stole the show, and the "Triumph Sports" prototype's debut at the same show was less auspicious. It was a brave attempt to create an inexpensive sports car from a company with no recent track record in this market segment. With its dumpy derriere, the prototype was no oil painting; as for handling, chief tester Ken Richardson described it as a "bloody deathtrap." No conventional beauty certainly, but a bluff-fronted car that was a worthy best-of-breed contender in the budget sports car arena, and the cornerstone of a stout sports car tradition.

"The design, by Walter Belgrove, was a far cry from the razor-edged Triumph Renown and Mayflower sedans that he had previously styled."

THE FIRST TR2S CAME WITH PRESSED-STEEL DISC WHEELS, BUT MOST CUSTOMERS PREFERRED THE OPTION OF WIRE WHEELS

THE TR2 HAD A FOLDAWAY TOP; THE LATER TR3 HAD THE OPTION OF A LIFT-OFF HARDTOP

MODEL Triumph TR2 (1953–55)

PRODUCTION 8,628

BODY STYLE Two-door, two-seater sports car.

CONSTRUCTION Pressed-steel chassis with separate steel body.

ENGINE Four-cylinder, overhead valve, 1991cc, twin SU carburetors.

POWER OUTPUT 90 bhp at 4800 rpm.

TRANSMISSION Four-speed manual with Laycock overdrive option, initially on top gear only, then on top three (1955).

SUSPENSION *Front*: coil springs and wishbone; *Rear*: live axle with semielliptic leaf springs.

BRAKES Lockheed hydraulic drums.

MAXIMUM SPEED 105 mph (169 km/h)

0–60 MPH (0–96 km/h) 12 sec

A.F.C. 30+ mpg (10.6+ km/l)

INTERIOR The stubby gear stick and full instrumentation gave the TR a true sports car feel; the steering wheel was large, but the low door accommodated an "elbows out" driving style. The seating position was so low that you could reach over the doors and touch the road.

ENGINE Legend says that the TR2 engine came from a Ferguson tractor – in fact it was developed from a Standard Vanguard engine, as was the tractor's. The twin-carb TR2 version was reduced to just under two liters, giving a top speed of 105 mph (169 km/h).

SPORTING PROWESS
The car on these pages was a "factory" competition car, pictured here with its driver Ken Richardson. The TR2 began a fine tradition of sporty TRs that was only let down by the controversially styled, wedge-shaped TR7 of the 1970s.

THE UNUSUAL RECESSED GRILLE PRESENTS A SLIGHTLY GRUMPY DISPOSITION

THE WINDSHIELD HAD A SLIGHT CURVE TO PREVENT IT FROM BOWING AT HIGH SPEED, WHICH IS WHAT THE PROTOTYPE'S FLAT WINDSHIELD DID

OVC 276

STOCK DESIGN

The orthodox design of the pressed-steel chassis was a simple ladder with X-shaped bracing.

A REVISED REAR, ALL-NEW CHASSIS, AND OTHER MODIFICATIONS, SAW STANDARD-TRIUMPH'S NEW TR2 EMERGE INTO A WINNER AT THE GENEVA MOTOR SHOW IN MARCH 1953

WHILE THE PROTOTYPE HAD A STUBBY TAIL, THE PRODUCTION MODEL HAD A REAL OPENING TRUNK

OVC 276

TRIUMPH TR6

The best-selling model of all the TR series

To most TR traditionalists this is where the TR tale ended, the final flourishing of the theme before the TR7 betrayed an outstanding tradition. In the mid-Sixties, the TR line was on a roll and the TR6 continued the upward momentum, outselling all earlier offerings. It was a natural progression from the original TR2; the body evolved from the TR4 of 1961, which was the first TR to carry all-new Michelotti-styled bodywork, and was updated by Karmann into the TR6. The 2.5-liter power unit came from the TR5, which became the first of the six-cylinder TRs in 1967. Crisply styled, with square-jawed good looks, the TR6 in early fuel-injected form heaved you along with 152 galloping horses. This was as hairy chested as the TR got, and a handful too, with some critics saying that, like the big Healeys, its power outstripped its poise. But that just made it more fun to drive.

"Big, wide-opening doors gave easy access to the TR6, a long cry from the tiny doors of the TR2 and 3."

WIDER WHEELS WERE A TR6 FEATURE, AS WAS THE ANTIROLL BAR AT THE FRONT

A ONE-PIECE HARDTOP WAS AVAILABLE AS AN OPTION, AND MORE PRACTICAL THAN THE TWO-PIECE JOB SEEN ON EARLIER MODELS

TR6

MODEL Triumph TR6 (1969–76)

PRODUCTION 94,619

BODY STYLE Two-seater convertible.

CONSTRUCTION Ladder-type chassis with integral steel body.

ENGINE Inline six-cylinder, 2498cc, fuel-injection (carburetors in US).

POWER OUTPUT 152 bhp at 5500 rpm (1969–1973), 125 bhp at 5250 rpm (1973–1975), 104 bhp at 4500 rpm (US).

TRANSMISSION Manual four-speed with optional overdrive on third and top.

SUSPENSION Independent by coil springs all around; wishbones at front, swing-axles and semitrailing arms at rear.

BRAKES Front discs, rear drums.

MAXIMUM SPEED 150 bhp: 119 mph (191 km/h); US: 107 mph (172 km/h)

0–60 MPH (0–96 km/h)   8.2 sec (150 bhp); 9.0 sec (125 bhp), 10.6 sec (104 bhp)

0–100 MPH (0–161 km/h)   29 sec

A.F.C. 25 mpg (8.8 km/l)

"The TR6's good looks, and a long production run, made this model the biggest selling of all TR models."

LEYLAND LINKS
The TR6 was launched just after the 1968 merger of Leyland and BMC. British Leyland would send out technical service bulletins to Triumph dealerships, offering advice on how to deal with various problems.

THE STEERING-WHEEL SIZE WAS REDUCED AT THE TIME OF OTHER MID-MODEL CHANGES IN 1973

VIRTUALLY ALL BULGES, LIKE THE TR5'S HOOD "POWER BULGE" AND COWLED HEADLIGHTS, HAD BEEN IRONED OUT ON THE TR6

YHR 687K

"The TR6's squared-off tail was longer than earlier TRs. Even so, there was only space in the trunk for a set of golf clubs and an overnight bag."

INTERIOR The interior is still traditional but more refined than earlier TRs. Yet with its big dials, wooden dash, and short-throw gear knob, its character is still truly sporty. The cockpit was more spacious than earlier TRs, providing an excellent driving position.

ENGINE The first engines, as on this 1972 car, produced 152 bhp, but public pressure for something more well-mannered resulted in a 125 bhp version in 1973. Americans had to make do with just over 100 bhp and carburetors instead of fuel injection.

THE DEEP-THROATED BURBLE FROM THE EXHAUSTS IS STILL A TR6 TURN-ON

THE TR6'S CHOPPED-OFF TAIL WAS CONSIDERED TO BE AN AERODYNAMIC AID

YHR 687K

TRIUMPH
INJECTION

TUCKER Torpedo

The car of the future held back in the past

THERE'S NO OTHER POSTWAR car that's as dramatic or advanced as Preston Tucker's futuristic '48 Torpedo. With four-wheel independent suspension, rear-mounted Bell helicopter engine, pop-out safety windshield, and uncrushable passenger compartment, it was 20 years ahead of its time. "You'll step into a new automotive age when you drive your Tucker '48," bragged the ads. It was a promise that convinced an astonishing 300,000 people to place orders, but their dreams were never to be realized. Major problems with the engine and Tuckermatic transmission, plus a serious cash-flow crisis, meant that only 51 Torpedos left the Chicago manufacturing plant. Worse still, Tucker and five of his associates were indicted for fraud by the Securities Exchange Commission. Their acquittal came too late to save America's most eccentric car from an undignified end.

"The public loved the Tucker not only for its comfort, power, and safety, but also because the styling was completely free from the usual prewar clichés."

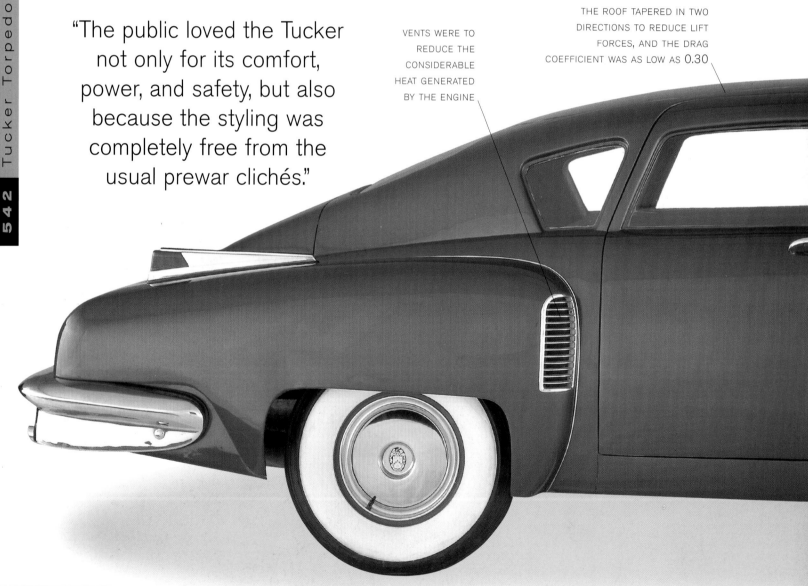

VENTS WERE TO REDUCE THE CONSIDERABLE HEAT GENERATED BY THE ENGINE

THE ROOF TAPERED IN TWO DIRECTIONS TO REDUCE LIFT FORCES, AND THE DRAG COEFFICIENT WAS AS LOW AS 0.30

MODEL Tucker Torpedo (1948)

PRODUCTION 51 (total)

BODY STYLE Four-door sedan.

CONSTRUCTION Steel body and chassis.

ENGINE 335cid flat-six.

POWER OUTPUT 166 bhp.

TRANSMISSION Three-speed Tuckermatic automatic or four-speed manual.

SUSPENSION Four-wheel independent.

BRAKES Front and rear drums.

MAXIMUM SPEED 120 mph (193 km/h)

0-60 MPH (0–96 km/h) 10.1 sec

A.F.C. 30 mpg (10.6 km/l)

INTERIOR Some say that Detroit conspired to destroy Tucker, but steering wheels on Torpedos were from the Lincoln Zephyr, given freely by Ford as a gesture of assistance. Although the interior was groaning with safety features, the Tucker sales team felt it was too austere. The horn on the steering wheel was adorned with the Tucker family crest.

ENGINE The first of the Tucker engines was a monster modified helicopter unit, but the 589cid aluminum flat-six was a bit of a disaster that proved difficult to start and ran too hot. It was replaced by a 6ALV 335cid flat-six block, developed by Air-Cooled Motors of Syracuse. Perversely, Tucker later converted this unit to a water-cooled system.

"The interior was designed by Audrey Moore, who had worked with Raymond Loewy on Studebakers."

A REAR WINDOW DEFROSTER WAS ONE OF ONLY FOUR OPTIONS AVAILABLE

THE FRONT WAS LIKE NO OTHER AMERICAN CAR, WITH A FIXED CIRCULAR HEADLIGHT LENS THAT PIVOTED WITH THE STEERING

PRESTON TUCKER

Preston Tucker took on the established US auto giants, and lost. A flamboyant visionary, he talked the US government into leasing him a huge old aero-engine plant in Chicago, and raised $8 million from prospective Tucker dealers before he even had a working prototype. Sadly, he was tried and acquitted for fraud in 1949 because the car described in his stock-market prospectus didn't match up to the production reality. His trial, widely seen as a sinister auto industry conspiracy, meant that the Tucker Corporation went into liquidation.

THE NOVEL ENGINE WAS POSITIONED LOWER THAN THE REAR PASSENGER SEAT TO DIMINISH NOISE, HEAT, AND FUMES

VOLKSWAGEN Beetle Karmann

A card-carrying classic from Volkswagen

BEETLE PURISTS MAY wax lyrical about the first-of-breed purity of the original split-rear-window Bugs and the oval window versions of 1953 to 1957, but there is one Beetle that everybody wants – the Karmann-built Cabriolet. Its development followed that of the sedans through a bewildering series of modifications, but it always stood apart. With its top retracted into a bulging bustle, this Beetle was not only cheerful, but chic too, a classless cruiser at home equally on Beverly Hills boulevards, the streets in Cannes, and the Kings Road, London. The final incarnation of the Karmann convertible represents the ultimate development of the Beetle theme, with the peppiest engine and improved handling. It's strange to think that the disarming, unburstable Bug was once branded with the slogan of the Hitler Youth, "Strength through Joy." Today, its strength has given joy to millions of drivers as the undisputed people's car.

ORIGINAL 16-IN (40-CM) WHEELS WERE REDUCED TO 15 IN (38 CM) IN 1952. FRONT DISC BRAKES WERE INTRODUCED IN 1966

THE FIRST BEETLES HAD SEMAPHORES; THEN INDICATORS WERE FENDER-MOUNTED

"Produced continuously since 1945, every Beetle that rolls off the remaining Mexican and Brazilian production lines sets a new production record."

MODEL VW Beetle Karmann Cabriolet (1972–1980)

PRODUCTION 331,847 (Karmann Cabriolets from 1949 to 1980)

BODY STYLE Four-seater convertible.

CONSTRUCTION Steel-bodied, separate chassis/body.

ENGINE Rear-mounted, air-cooled flat-four, 1584cc.

POWER OUTPUT 50 bhp at 4000 rpm.

TRANSMISSION Four-speed manual.

SUSPENSION *Front*: independent MacPherson strut; *Rear*: independent trailing arm and twin torsion bars.

BRAKES Front discs, rear drums.

MAXIMUM SPEED 82.4 mph (133 km/h)

0–60 MPH (0–96 km/h) 18 sec

A.F.C. 24–30 mpg (8.5–10.6 km/l)

INTERIOR The Beetle is still bare, its dash dominated by the one minimal instrument; on this model the speedo incorporates a fuel gauge. It also has a padded dash, replacing the original metal one. The four-spoke steering wheel is not as classic as earlier thin-rimmed two- and three-spoked wheels.

ENGINE You can always tell that a Beetle is on its way before it comes into sight thanks to the distinctive buzzing of the air-cooled, horizontally opposed four-cylinder engine. The Beetle's capacity grew from 1131cc to 1584cc, and the engines have a deserved reputation as robust, rev-happy units.

HITLER AND FERDINAND PORSCHE

Adolf Hitler's vision for mass motoring began when he entrusted Dr. Ferdinand Porsche with the Beetle project. Both Hitler and Porsche were influenced by the fabulous streamlined Czechoslovakian Tatras, and the Beetle bore a resemblance to early Tatras.

CURVED "PANORAMIC" WINDSHIELD REPLACED THE FLAT WINDOW IN 1972

REAR VISION WITH THE HOOD RAISED WAS NOT MUCH BETTER THAN ON EARLY SPLIT-WINDOW AND OVAL-WINDOWED MODELS

"With the top raised, the Karmann Cabriolet was a little claustrophobic, but it came into its own as a timeless top-down cruiser."

MANY LATER DESIGN CHANGES LIKE THESE "ELEPHANT FOOTPRINT" TAILLIGHT CLUSTERS WERE DRIVEN BY US REGULATIONS

Without Heinz Nordhoff, the VW Beetle wouldn't exist. Yet he once described the world's best-selling car as "an ugly thing with more defects than a dog has fleas." An engineer and salesman, Nordhoff was chosen by the British to run the VW factory in 1948. He transformed the company into a global sensation and can genuinely claim to be the spiritual father of the Beetle.

VOLKSWAGEN Golf GTi

The hot-shoe hatch that began the GTi genre

EVERY DECADE OR SO a really great car comes along. In the Seventies it was the Golf. Like the Beetle before it, the Golf was designed to make inroads into world markets; yet while the Beetle evolved into the perfect consumer product, the Golf was planned that way. The idea of a "hot" Golf was not part of the grand plan. It was the brainchild of a group of enthusiastic Volkswagen engineers who worked evenings and weekends, impressing VW's board so much that the

GTi became an official project in May 1975. Despite its youth, the GTi is as much of a classic as any Ferrari. Its claim to fame is that it spawned a traffic jam of imitators and brought an affordable cocktail of performance, handling, and reliability to the mass-market buyer. Few other cars have penetrated the suburban psyche as deeply as the original Golf GTi, and fewer still have had greatness thrust upon them at such an early age.

MUCH ADMIRED CROSS-SPOKE BBS ALLOY WHEELS WERE BOTH A FACTORY-EQUIPPED AND AFTERMARKET OPTION

FL-65-JH

FL-65-JH

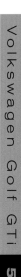

MODEL Volkswagen Golf GTi Mk 1 (1976–83)

PRODUCTION 400,000

BODY STYLE Three-door five-seater hatchback.

CONSTRUCTION All steel/monocoque body.

ENGINES Four-cylinder 1588cc/1781cc.

POWER OUTPUT 110–112 bhp at 6100 rpm.

TRANSMISSION Four- or five-speed manual.

SUSPENSION *Front*: independent; *Rear*: semi-independent trailing arm.

BRAKES Front discs, rear drums.

MAXIMUM SPEED 111 mph (179 km/h)

0–60 MPH (0–96 km/h) 8.7 sec

0–100 MPH (0–161 km/h) 18.2 sec

A.F.C. 29 mpg (10.3 km/l)

THE DRIVER'S WINDSHIELD WIPER HAD A SMALL AERODYNAMIC WING – THE FASTER YOU WENT, THE MORE WIND PRESSURE PUSHED THE WIPER ONTO THE GLASS

FACTORY SPEC GOLFS WERE UNDERSTATED, WITH JUST A GTI BADGE AND A THIN RED STRIPE AROUND THE GRILLE

FL·65·JH

INTERIOR With its dark headlining trim, the cockpit may be Teutonically austere, but features like the golfball-shaped gear stick knob add a touch of humor. Inside, the Mark I Golf was neat, roomy, and compact. The two main dials on the dashboard were a speedometer and a tachometer.

ENGINE Capable of 150,000 miles (240,000 km) in its stride, the 1588cc four-cylinder power unit breathed through Bosch K-Jetronic fuel injection, pushing out 110 bhp. Later cars were blessed with a five-speed gearbox and even more willing 1781cc engines.

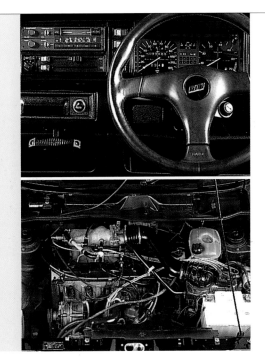

"Initially only 5,000 GTis were to be built for racing homologation, but the silky smooth engine and poised handling meant sales went berserk."

GTi SUSPENSION WAS LOWER AND FIRMER THAN THE STANDARD GOLF, WITH WIDER TIRES AND WHEELS

VOLVO P544

A Stateside success for the conservative Swedes

MAYBE THE VOLVO P544 sold so well in America because it looked so much like a Forties Ford. A direct descendant of the P444, the 544 became one of Gothenburg's most profitable cars and helped Volvo carve a deep and profitable market in the US. Lively, well built, and with surprisingly poised handling, the 544 had five seats, a four-speed gearbox, and the option of a twin-carb Sport engine. From '61, a new five-bearing engine raised the top speed to 100 mph (161 km/h). Americans, disenchanted with Detroit dinosaurs, took to the upright Swede like they did VW's Beetle, and the car soon enjoyed cult status in California. By 1959, 30,000 544s had been imported into the US, and it was even the subject of a song by the Medallions, called '59 *Volvo*. All of which is quite remarkable since Volvo's crusty old warhorse didn't incorporate a single technical advance that wasn't present in virtually every other car of the period.

"Until '58 the special Sport engine was only available in America. Swedes bought crated engines from the US and installed them quietly to avoid extra customs duty."

FAMOUS BODY LONGEVITY WAS DUE TO SIX COATS OF PAINT, RUST INHIBITOR, UNDERSEAL, AND ANTICORROSIVE OIL

"Bizarrely, window washer jets came as standard on the P544, but the pump was an optional extra."

MODEL Volvo P544 (1961)

PRODUCTION 243,995 (total)

BODY STYLE Two-door, five-seater sedan.

CONSTRUCTION All steel monocoque.

ENGINE 1778cc four-cylinder.

POWER OUTPUT 90 bhp at 5000 rpm.

TRANSMISSION Four-speed manual.

SUSPENSION *Front*: independent; *Rear*: live axle.

BRAKES Hydraulic, duo-servo drums.

MAXIMUM SPEED 100 mph (161 km/h)

0–60 MPH (0–96 km/h) 14.2 sec

A.F.C. 28 mpg (9.9 km/l)

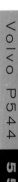

INTERIOR The dash was American in style and unlike the rest of the 544's traditionalism. The trendy horizontal speedo was calibrated to 112 mph (180 km/h), and the steering wheel had a chrome horn ring. Standard luxuries included a two-speed fan.

SAFETY FIRST Volvo was offering front and rear seat belts years before anyone else, along with padded sun visors and instrument panel, servo-brakes, and safety steering wheel. An antidazzle rearview mirror was another standard safety feature.

BADGE

The B18 badge denotes the most significant modification in the 544's life, with the use of the B18 engine in 1961. The single carb B18A was rated at 75 bhp, while the B18D with twin SU carbs managed 90 bhp.

NEW CURVED WINDSHIELD WAS 22 PERCENT BIGGER THAN ON THE P444

90 HORSEPOWER B18 ENGINE HAD FULL-FLOW OIL FILTER, FIVE BEARING CRANKSHAFT, HIGH-COMPRESSION CYLINDER HEAD, AND TWIN CARBURETORS

"Swedish newspapers heralded the 544's arrival with the headline, 'A new beauty is coming to town.'"

SLATE BLUE WAS A NEW COLOR FOR 1960. 544S WERE ONLY AVAILABLE IN FIVE HUES, WITH RUBY RED THE MOST POPULAR

THE REAR VIEW MAY NOT HAVE BEEN THE 544'S BEST, BUT THE HIGH TRUNK WAS TRULY CAPACIOUS WITH ROOM FOR THREE SUITCASES

DXM 9 945

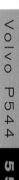

VOLVO P1800

The first Volvo with real attitude

THERE HAS NEVER BEEN a Volvo like the P1800, for this was a one-time flight of fancy by the sober Swedes, who already had a reputation for building sensible sedans. As a sports car, the P1800 certainly looked stunning; every sensuous curve and lean line suggesting athletic prowess. But under that sharp exterior were most of the mechanics of the Volvo Amazon, a worthy workhorse sedan. Consequently, the P1800 was no road-burner; it just about had the edge on the MGB (*see page* 421), but only in a straight line. Another competitor, the E-Type Jag (*see pages* 330–33), was launched in 1961, the same year as the P1800, and at almost the same price, but there the comparison ends. The P1800 did have style, though, and its other virtues were pure Volvo – strength, durability, and reliability. These combined to create something quite singular in the sporting idiom – a practical sports car.

THERE WAS SPACE FOR TWO TODDLERS IN THE BACK, OR ONE ADULT SITTING SIDEWAYS; REAR SEAT FOLDED DOWN FLAT TO INCREASE LOAD CAPACITY

AS YOU WOULD EXPECT, THE SENSIBLE SPORTS CAR HAD A DECENT-SIZED TRUNK

MODEL Volvo P1800 (1961–73)

PRODUCTION 47,707 (all models)

BODY STYLES Two-plus-two fixed-head coupe; sports wagon (P1800ES).

CONSTRUCTION Unitary steel body/chassis.

ENGINES 1778cc straight-four, overhead valves; 1985cc from 1968–73.

POWER OUTPUT 100–124 bhp.

TRANSMISSION Four-speed manual with overdrive/optional automatic.

SUSPENSION *Front*: independent coil-sprung with wishbones; *Rear*: rigid axle, coil-sprung, Panhard rod.

BRAKES Front discs, rear drums.

MAXIMUM SPEED 115 mph (185 km/h) (E/ES)

0-60 MPH (0–96 km/h) 9.7–13.2 sec

A.F.C. 20–25 mpg (7–10 km/l)

WILLYS Jeep MB

The original off-roader with a great sense of history

AS ONE WAR CORRESPONDENT said, "It's as faithful as a dog, as strong as a mule, and as agile as a mountain goat." The flat-fendered Willys Jeep is one of the most instantly recognizable vehicles ever made. Even General Eisenhower was impressed, saying "the three tools that won us the war in Europe were the Dakota and the landing craft and the Jeep." In 1940, the American Defense Department sent out a tough spec for a military workhorse. Many companies took one look at the seemingly impossible specification and 49-day deadline and turned it down flat. The design that won the tender and made it into production and the history books was a mixture of the ideas and abilities of Ford, Bantam, and Willys-Overland. A stunning triumph of function over form, the Jeep not only won the war, but went on to become a cult off-roader that's still with us now. The Willys Jeep is surely the most original 4x4 by far.

LEFT-HAND SUSPENSION SPRINGS HAD A STIFFER RATING TO COPE WITH THE WEIGHT OF THE ENGINE

THE BOX-SECTION CHASSIS WAS TOUGH, YET FLEXIBLE ENOUGH TO ALLOW THE FRAME TO TWIST FOR MAXIMUM WHEEL ARTICULATION

"The Jeep's claim to fame is that it spawned utility vehicles from Nissans and Isuzus to Discoverys and Range Rovers."

MODEL Willys Jeep MB (1943)

PRODUCTION 586,000 (during World War II)

BODY STYLE Open utility vehicle.

CONSTRUCTION Steel body and chassis.

ENGINE 134cid straight-four.

POWER OUTPUT 60 bhp.

TRANSMISSION Three-speed manual, four-wheel drive.

SUSPENSION Leaf springs front and rear.

BRAKES Front and rear drums.

MAXIMUM SPEED 105 km/h (65 mph)

0–60 MPH (0–96 km/h) 22 sec

A.F.C. 16 mpg (5.7 km/l)

DOORS WOULD HAVE
ADDED WEIGHT, SO SIDE
STRAPS WERE A TOKEN
GESTURE TOWARD
DRIVER SAFETY

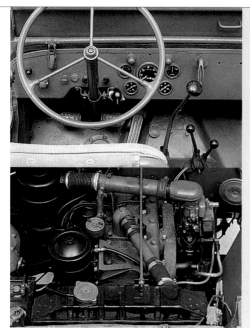

INTERIOR Driver safety wasn't a Jeep strong point – many GIs ended up impaled on the steering column even after low-speed impacts. Only the generals fought the war in comfort, and Jeep accommodation was strictly no frills. Very early Jeeps have no glove compartment.

ENGINE Power was from a Ford straight-four, which took the Jeep to about 65 mph (105 km/h), actually exceeding US Army driving regulations. The Warner three-speed manual box was supplemented by controls allowing the driver to select two- or four-wheel drive.

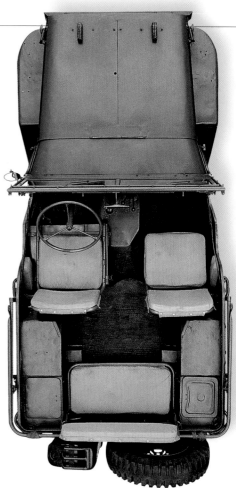

EARLIER JEEPS HAD A SLATTED RADIATOR GRILLE INSTEAD OF THE LATER PRESSED-STEEL BARS, AS HERE

Despite being the Supreme Commander of Allied Forces in Europe, General Dwight D. Eisenhower always took the opportunity to drive a Jeep himself. When Eisenhower became President in 1953, he asked to have a Jeep in the White House garage for sentimental reasons, but the secret service refused on the grounds of personal safety.

"Some say that the Jeep was named after Eugene the Jeep, a character in a 1936 Popeye cartoon."

READY-FOR-ANYTHING
JEEPS CAME WITH GAS CAN,
SHOVEL, LONG-HANDLED
AX, AND GRAB BARS

Willys Jeep MB **563**

INDEX

569

571

TU

V

W

XYZ

ACKNOWLEDGMENTS

Dorling Kindersley would like to thank the following:

Georgina Lowin and Richard Dabb for picture research; John Dinsdale for the jacket design; and Margaret McCormack for compiling the index; Acorn Studios PLC; Action Vehicles of Shepperton Film Studios; Sarah Ashun; Philip Blythe for supplying number plates; Bob and Ricky from D.J. Motors; Andy Brown; Geoff Browne at Classic Car Weekly; Silvia Bucher; Phillip Bush at Readers Digest, Australia for supervising the supply of the Holden; Paul Charlton; Terry Clarke; Classic American magazine; Cobra Studios, Manchester; Coulsdon Mark; Cricket; Barry Cunlisse of the AAC (NW); Al Deane; Michael Farrington; Derek Fisher; Jenny Glanville and Kirstie Ashton Bell at Plough Studios; Rosie Good of the TR Owners Club; Andy Greenfield of the Classic Corvette Club (UK); Peter Grist of the Chrysler Corp. Club (UK); William (Bill) Greenwood of the Cadillac Owners Club of Great Britain; Rockin' Roy Hunt; Louie Joseph; Kilian and Alistair Konig of Konig Car Transport for vehicle transportation and invaluable help in sourcing cars; Dave King; Michel Labat; Bill McGarth; Ken McMahon at Pelican Graphics; Bill Medcalf; Ben, Dan, and Rob Milton; Geoff Mitchell; Mr DeVoe Moore, Jeff Moyes of AFN Ltd; Colin Murphy; Terry Newbury; Colin Nolson; Garry Ombler; John Orsler; Paul Osborn; Ben Pardon; Tony Paton; Derek Pearson; Pooks motor bookshop and Cars and Stripes for original advertising material and brochures; Tony Powell at Powell Performance Cars; Antony Pozner at Hendon Way Motors for helpful advice and supply of nine cars; Kevin O' Rourke of Moto-technique; Dave Rushby; Peter Rutt; Ian Shipp; David and Christine Smith; Ian Smith; George Solomonides for help with sourcing images; John Stark; Richard Stephenson; Steve at Trident Recovery; Straight Eight Ltd; Ashley Straw; Dave and Rita Sword of the AAC; Tallahasee Car Museum, Tallahasee, Florida; Gary Townsend; Marc Tulpin (Belgian representative of the AAC); John Weeks of Europlate for number plate assistance; Rob Wells.

Dorling Kindersley would like to thank the following for allowing their cars to be photographed:

Page 20 courtesy of Anthony Morpeth; p. 24 A.J. Pozner (Hendon Way Motors); p. 28 Louis Davidson; p. 32 Richard Norris; p. 34 Valerie Pratt; p. 38 Brian Smail; p. 42 Desmond J. Smail; p. 46 David and Jon Maughan; p. 50 Tom Turkington (Hendon Way Motors); p. 54 restored and owned by Julian Aubanel; p. 58 courtesy of Austin-Healey Associates Ltd, Beech Cottage, North Looe, Reigate Road, Ewell, Surrey, KT17 3DH; p. 62 courtesy of Mr. Willem van Aalst; p. 66 A.J. Pozner (Hendon Way Motors); p. 68 1959 Isetta (Plus model) owned and restored by Dave Watson; p. 76 Terence P.J. Halliday; p. 80 L & C BMW Tunbridge Wells; p. 82 The Rt. Hon. Greg Knight; p. 86 "57th Heaven" Steve West's 1957 Buick Roadmaster; p. 90 Geoff Cook;

p. 94 Tony Powell of Powell Performance Cars; p. 99 Tony Powell; p. 102 Liam Kavanagh; p. 106 Stewart Homan, Dream Cars; p. 110 Garry Darby, American 50's Car Hire; p. 114 Tim Buller; p. 118 William (Bill) Greenwood (COC of GB); p. 122 Alfie Orkin; p. 126 Dream Cars; p. 130 Mike and Margaret Collins; p. 134 Phil Townend; p. 136 Mark Surman; p. 140 Benjamin Pollard of the Classic Corvette Club UK (vehicle preparation courtesy of Corvette specialists D.A.R.T. Services, Kent, UK); p. 144 Colin Nolson; p. 148 car owned and restored by Bill Leonard; p. 152 Rick and Rachel Bufton; p. 156 Alex Gunn; p. 160 Tallahassee Car Museum; p. 164 Mike Webb; p. 168 Colin Nolson; p. 172 Geoff Mitchell; p. 176 Alex Greatwood; p. 180 Geoff Mitchell; p. 184 Classic Restorations; p. 188 on loan from Le Tout Petit Musée/Nick Thompson, director Sussex 2CV Ltd; p. 192 Classic Restorations; p. 196 Derek E.J. Fisher; p. 200 Steve Rogers; p. 204 Daimler SP 250 owned by Claude Kearley; p. 208 Steve Gamage; p. 212 Kevin Kay; p. 216 D. Howarth; p. 220 Nando Rossi; p. 224 Lewis Strong; p. 228 David Gough; p. 232 Neil Crozier; p. 236 Gavin and Robert Garrow; p. 240 Charles Booth; p. 244 owned and supplied by Straight Eight Ltd (London); p. 256 A.J. Pozner (Hendon Way Motors); p. 260 A.J. Pozner (Hendon Way Motors); p. 264 A.J. Pozner (Hendon Way Motors); p. 265 Dr. Ismond Rosen; p. 266 by kind permission of J.A.M. Meyer; p. 270 Janet & Roger Westcott; p. 274 Bell & Colvill PLC, Epsom Road, West Horsley, Surrey KT24 6DG, UK; p. 278 Dream Cars; p. 282 Rockin' Roy Hunt – '50s aficionado; p. 286 David Stone; p. 290 M. Fenwick; p. 294 Teddy Turner Collection; p. 298 Max & Beverly Floyd; p. 302 Roy Hamilton; p. 306 Gordon Keeble by kind permission of Charles Giles; p. 312 David Selby; p. 316 Mike and Margaret Collins; p. 320 Jeff Hine; p. 328 c/o Hendon Way Motors; p. 330 owner Phil Hester; p. 334 John F. Edwins; p. 336 Tallahassee Car Museum; p. 340 John Skelton; p. 344 privately owned; p. 348 A.R.J. Dyas; p. 352 courtesy of Ian Fraser, restoration Omicron Engineering, Norwich; p. 356 courtesy of Martin Cliff; p. 360 Rickie Short, for use of Lancia Delta HF Integrale 8V; p. 364 Andrew Stevens (co-founder and Chairman of the Land Rover Series One Club); p. 368 John Gardner; p. 372 Michael Farrington; p. 376 Ian Hebditch and Jane Shepherd; p. 380 Geoff Tompkins; p. 384 owner Phillip Collier, rebuild by Daytune; p. 388 Alexander Fyshe; p. 392 Edwin J. Faulkner; p. 396 Irene Turner; p. 404 Mrs. Joan Williams; p. 408 Dream Cars; p. 412 Lee Birmingham (dedicated to Bob Richards of Newport Pagnell); p. 416 courtesy of Chris Alderson; p. 420 John Venables; p. 421 John Watson, Abingdon-on-Thames; p. 422 Martin Garvey; p. 426 E.J. Warrilow saved this car from the scrapyard in 1974; restored by the owner in 1990, maintaining all original panels and mechanics; winner of many concourse trophies; p. 430 Peggie Pollard; p. 434 A & M Motors; p. 438 Cared for and cruised in by Mark Phillips; p. 442 Peter

Morey; p. 446 Panhard PL17 owned by Anthony T.C. Bond, Oxfordshire, editor of "Panoramique" (Panhard Club newsletter); p. 450 Nick O'Hara; p. 454 Peter Vaughan (Chairman, Club Peugeot, UK); p. 458 Steve Friend; p. 462 Maurice Harvey; p. 466 Alan Tansley; p. 470 Tony Paton; p. 474 Rockin' Roy Hunt – '50s aficionado; p. 478 courtesy of Peter Rutt; p. 482 Roger Wait; p. 486 Simon Bowrey; p. 490 Owner Mr P.G.K. Lloyd; p. 494 c/o Hendon Way Motors; p. 496 Bob and Kath Silver; p. 500 John E. Pigeon; p. 504 Richard Tyzack's historic rally Alpine; p. 508 owned by Ian Shanks of Northamptonshire; p. 512 Chris Day; p. 516 David C. Baughan; p. 520 Julie A. Lambert (formerly Julie A. Goldbert); p. 524 Skoda UK; p. 528 Dream Cars; p. 532 Peter Matthews; p. 533 Lord Raynham of Norfolk; p. 534 E.A.W. Holden; p. 538 Brian Burgess; p. 542 Mr. DeVoe Moore, Tallahassee Car Museum, Tallahassee, Florida; p. 546 Nick Hughes & Tim Smith; p. 550 Roy E. Craig; p. 554 Tony Miles; p. 558 Kevin Price, Volvo Enthusiasts' Club; p. 560 Peter Barber-Lomax.

PICTURE CREDITS

The publisher would like to thank the following for their kind permission to reproduce their photographs:
(Abbreviations key: t=top, b=bottom, r=right, l=left, c=centre)

Midsummer Books Ltd/Aerospace Images: 72b, 73tc, 73tr, 73c, 74tc, 74c, 74b, 75tr, 75cr, 75b, 196b, 197tc, 197c, 198tc, 198c, 198b, 199tl, 199cl, 199b, 224tc, 224c, 224b, 225tr, 226tc, 226c, 226b, 227tc, 227c, 227b, 244b, 245tc, 245tr, 245c, 246tc, 246c, 246b, 246b, 247tc, 247c, 247b, 252cr, 252bcr, 253tl, 253tr, 253cl, 254cl, 254bcr, 255tc, 255tr, 255c, 324b, 325tl, 325tr, 326tc, 326c, 326b, 327tc, 327c, 327b, 348b, 349tc, 349tr, 349c, 350tc, 350tr, 350b, 351c, 401tc, 401tr, 401c, 402b, 403tc, 403c, 403b. 533tr, 533b, 568bl, 568-569tc, 569tr.

AKG London: 493tr.

Auto Express: 15br.

Bell & Colville: 276tr.

British Motor Industry Heritage Trust: 367tr.

Neill Bruce Motoring Photolibrary: 262tr, 263c, 268tr.

Peter Roberts Collection: 60tl.

Bruce Coleman Ltd: 154tr.

Corbis: 8tr, 9tl, 9br, 563tr, 219tr, 227tr, 247tr, 259tr, 281tr, 305tr, 309tr, 338tr, 355tr, 375tr.

Corbis-Bettmann/UPI: 545tr.

Fiat: 273tr.

Ford Motor Company Ltd: 293cr.

Fraser Photos: 288tr.

Ronald Grant Archive: 41tr, 301tr.

Hulton Getty: 147tr, 195tr, 251tr, 285tr, 333tr, 387tr, 511tr, 511trc.

Kobal Collection: 235c (1968 Warner Brothers).

Lamborghini: 347tr.

Lexus: 15tr.

Ludvigsen Library: 143tr.

Magnum Photos Ltd: 549tr (Heinz Norhoff).

Mercedes Benz: 10t, 16tl.

Morgan Motor Company: 425tr.

Motoring Picture Library/National Motor Museum: 8b, 27tr, 53tr, 57tr, 191tr, 207tr, 327tr, 342tr, 358tl, 400b, 401tr, 419tr, 429tr.

Peter Newark's American Pictures: 297tr.

Poole Collection: 26tr.

Quadrant Picture Library: 198tl, 226tr, 383tr.

Reader's Digest: 310b, 311tl, 311tr, 311cl, 311b.

Science Photo Library: 11cr (Martin Bond).

All other images © Dorling Kindersley.

For further information see:
www.dkimages.com

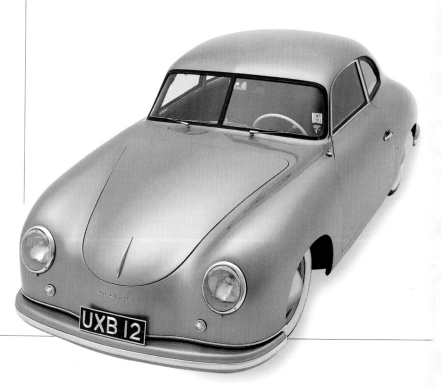